MATH
Connections®

A Secondary Mathematics Core Curriculum

William P. Berlinghoff
Clifford Sloyer
Robert W. Hayden

Published by IT'S ABOUT TIME, Inc. © 2000 MATHconx, LLC

Published in 2000 by
It's About Time, Inc.
84 Business Park Drive
Armonk, NY 10504
Phone (914)273-2233
Fax (914)273-2227
www.ITS-ABOUT-TIME.com
www.mathconnections.com

Publisher
Laurie Kreindler

Design
John Nordland

Production Manager
Barbara Zahm

Studio Manager
Leslie Jander

Copyright ©2000 by MATHconx, LLC. All rights reserved. Printed and bound in the United States of America.
First Printing ©1998, Second Printing ©1999 Field-test printing ©1992, 1996

MATH *Connections®: A Secondary Mathematics Core Curriculum* was developed under the National Science Foundation Grant
No. ESI-9255251 awarded to the Connecticut Business and Industry Association.

ISBN 1-891629-84-0   MATH *Connections* Teacher Edition   Book   2a   (Soft Cover)
ISBN 1-891629-89-1   MATH *Connections* Teacher Edition   Books 2a, 2b Set   (Soft Cover)

ISBN 1-891629-20-4   MATH *Connections* Teacher Edition   Book   2a   (3-Ring Binder)
ISBN 1-891629-79-4   MATH *Connections* Teacher Edition   Books 2a, 2b Set   (3-Ring Binder)

2 3 4 5 D 02 01 00 99

This project was supported, in part,
by the
National Science Foundation
Opinions expressed are those of the authors
and not necessarily those of the Foundation.

MATH *Connections*: A Secondary Mathematics Core Curriculum

Table of Contents

Chapter 1 The Building Blocks of Geometry: Making and Measuring Polygons

Chapter 2 Similarity and Scaling: Growing and Shrinking Carefully

Chapter 3 Introduction to Trigonometry: Tangles With Angles

MATH *Connections*® *Team*

PRINCIPAL INVESTIGATORS

June G. Ellis, Director

Robert A. Rosenbaum
Wesleyan University

Robert J. Decker
University of Hartford

ADVISORY COUNCIL

James Aiello
Oakton Consulting Group, VA

Laurie Boswell
Profile High School, NH

Glenn Cassis
Connecticut Pre-Engineering Program

Daniel Dolan
Project to Improve Mastery in
Mathematics & Science

John Georges
Trinity College, CT

Renee Henry (retired)
Florida State Department of
Education

James Hogan Jr.
Connecticut Chapter of the National
Technology Association

Lauren Weisberg Kaufman
CBIA Education Foundation

James Landwehr
AT&T Bell Laboratories, NJ

Donald LaSalle
Talcott Mountain Science Center

Daniel Lawler (retired)
Hartford Public Schools

Steven Leinwand
Connecticut Department of Education

Valerie Lewis
Connecticut Department of Higher
Education

William Masalski
ex officio
University of Massachusetts

Gail Nordmoe
Cambridge Public Schools, MA

Thomas Romberg
Wisconsin Center for Educational
Research

Kenneth Sherrick
Berlin High School

Albert Shulte
Oakland Public Schools, MI

Irvin Vance
Michigan State University

Cecilia Welna
University of Hartford

SENIOR WRITERS

William P. Berlinghoff
Colby College, Maine

Clifford Sloyer
University of Delaware

Robert W. Hayden
Plymouth State College,
New Hampshire

STAFF

Robert Gregorski
Associate Director

Lorna Rojan
Program Manager

Carolyn Mitchell
Administrative Assistant

CONTRIBUTORS

Don Hastings (retired)
Stratford Public Schools

Kathleen Bavelas
Manchester Community-
Technical College

George Parker
E. O. Smith High School, Storrs

Linda Raffles
Glastonbury High School

Joanna Shrader Panning
Middletown High School

Frank Corbo
Staples High School, Westport

Thomas Alena
Talcott Mountain Science Center,
Avon

William Casey
Bulkeley High School, Hartford

Sharon Heyman
Bulkeley High School, Hartford

Helen Knudson
Choate Rosemary Hall,
Wallingford

Mary Jo Lane (retired)
Granby Memorial High School

Lori White Moroso
Beth Chana Academy for Girls,
Orange

John Pellino
Talcott Mountain Science Center,
Avon

Pedro Vasquez, Jr.
Multicultural Magnet School,
Bridgeport

Thomas Willmitch
Talcott Mountain Science Center,
Avon

Leslie Paoletti
Greenwich Public Schools

Robert Fallon (retired)
Bristol Eastern High School

ASSESSMENT SPECIALIST

Don Hastings (retired)
Stratford Public Schools

Published by IT'S ABOUT TIME, Inc. © 2000 MATHconx, LLC

NSF ADVISORY BOARD

Margaret Cozzens
J. "Spud" Bradley
Eric Robinson
Emma Owens

FIELD-TEST SITES

**Hill Career Magnet
High School,** *New Haven*:
John Crotty
Martin Hartog, SCSU
Harry Payne II
Angel Tangney

Cheshire High School:
Andrew Abate
Pauline Alim
Marcia Arneson
Diane Bergan
Christopher Fletcher
John Kosloski
Christina Lepi
Michael Lougee
Ann Marie Mahanna
Carol Marino
Nancy Massey
Denise Miller
John Redford
Cynthia Sarlo

**Coginchaug Regional
High School,** *Durham*:
Theresa Balletto
Anne Coffey
John DeMeo
Jake Fowler
Ben Kupcho
Stephen Lecky
Philip Martel

Crosby High School, *Waterbury*:
Janice Farrelly
Rosalie Griffin

Danbury High School:
Adrienne Coppola
Lois Schwaller

Dodd Middle School,
Cheshire:
William Grimm
Lara Kelly

Gay Sonn
Alexander Yawin

Manchester High School:
Pamela Brooks
Carl Bujaucius
Marilyn Cavanna
Paul DesRosiers
Mariamma Devassy-Schwob
Frank Kinel
Larry Olsen
Julie Thompson
Matthew Walsh

Montville High School:
Lynn Grills
Janice Hardink
Diane Hupfer
Ronald Moore
Mark Popeleski
Henry Kopij
Walter Sherwin
Shari Zagarenski

**Oxford Hills
Comprehensive
High School,**
South Paris, ME:
Mary Bickford
Peter Bickford
Allen Gerry
Errol Libby
Bryan Morgan
Lisa Whitman

**Parish Hill Regional
High School**:
Peter Andersen
Gary Hoyt
Vincent Sirignano
Deborah Whipple

Southington High School:
Eleanor Aleksinas
Susan Chandler
Helen Crowley
Nancy Garry
John Klopp
Elaine Mulhall
Stephen Victor
Bernadette Waite

Stonington High School:
Joyce Birtcher
Jill Hamel
Glenn Reid

TECHNOLOGY SUPPORT

Texas Instruments:
Graphing Calculators and
View Screens

Presto Press:
Desktop Publishing

Key Curriculum Press:
Geometer's Sketchpad

PROFILES

Barbara Zahm
David Bornstein
Alex Straus
Mimi Valiulis

EXTERNAL EVALUATORS

Donald Cichon Associates:
Donald Cichon
Nancy Johnson
Kevin Sullivan and
Sharon Soucy McCrone

Connecticut State Department
of Education:
Michelle Staffaroni
Graduate Intern

EQUITY AND ACCESS REVIEWERS

Leo Edwards, Director
Mathematics and Science
Education Center
Fayetteville State University,
NC

Ray Shiflett
California Polytechnic
University, Pomona

READABILITY STUDY

Elaine Eadler Associates:
Elaine Eadler, University
of Maine at Farmington

Welcome to MATH *Connections*®
A Secondary Mathematics Core Curriculum

MATH *Connections* is an exciting, challenging, three-year core curriculum for secondary mathematics! True to its name, this curriculum is built around connections of all sorts:

- between different mathematical areas;
- between mathematics and science;
- between mathematics and other subjects (history, literature, art, etc.);
- between mathematics and the real world of commerce, law, and people.

The following few pages tell you where this program came from, what it is designed to accomplish, and how it is constructed. We hope that reading this will help you, the teacher, become partners with us in making this curriculum come to life for your students.

The History

MATH *Connections* began in 1992 when a team of educators associated with the Connecticut Business and Industry Association (CBIA), Wesleyan University, and the University of Hartford collaborated on the development of a new secondary mathematics core curriculum based on the *NCTM Standards*. Funded by a $4.9 million grant from the National Science Foundation awarded to the CBIA Education Foundation, the principal investigators assembled a team of people, including:

1. Senior writers: university mathematics professors with considerable teaching and writing experience who developed and wrote drafts and final copy of all the books.

2. Contributing writers: sixteen high school and community college mathematics teachers and two science specialists who reviewed the chapter drafts and wrote additional problems, projects, and ancillary materials.

3. Advisory Council: twenty respected professionals from the fields of mathematics, science, education and business, who met annually to review the overall direction of the project and to provide advice about various aspects of the emerging materials.

4. Classroom teachers and students: more than 100 field-test teachers and approximately 2500 students from seventeen different inner city, urban, suburban and rural high schools who used preliminary versions of these materials and provided feedback from their classroom experiences.

A many-faceted external evaluation of the MATH *Connections* program was an integral part of the project. External evaluators provided comprehensive reports on student achievement on standardized tests and how well MATH *Connections* met its objectives. Consultants reviewed the materials for gender equity, multicultural equity, and readability.

The Vision and The Mission

The Vision: *All students can learn mathematics, be critical thinkers and be problem solvers.*

The Mission: *The conceptual understanding of the learner.*

The MATH *Connections* team designed the program to meet the following objectives:

MATH *Connections* is for *all* students. It is relevant to students as future citizens, parents, voters, consumers, researchers, employers and employees — people with a healthy curiosity about ideas. It serves well the needs and interests of all high school students, those who will go on to further math-intensive studies and science-related careers, as well as those who choose to pursue other fields of study. In fact, it enchances students' understanding of the interrelatedness of all fields and increases the attractiveness of mathematics and science as it is applied in the real world.

MATH *Connections* is flexible, allowing students with different learning styles equal opportunity to master the ideas and skills presented. This means providing both interactive group work and individual learning experiences, encouraging frequent student-teacher and student-student interaction, in finding answers and in discussing mathematics, relevant student experiences, opinions, and judgments.

The main technological tools of the world of work are an integral part of the material. Students learn to be comfortable with graphing calulators and computers, in order to cope with and profit from the opportunities of our increasingly technological world.

It is reality based. All the mathematical ideas in the curriculum are drawn from and connected to real world situations. Students can immediately see how the mathematics they are learning relates to their own lives and the world around them.

MATH *Connections* focuses on the conceptual aspects of mathematics — reasoning, pattern seeking, problem solving, questioning, and communicating with precision — because those are the features of a mathematical education that are important to lawyers, doctors, business leaders, teachers, politicians, social workers, military officers, entrepreneurs, artists, or writers as they are to scientists or engineers.

Each of the three years of MATH *Connections* is built around a general theme which serves as a unifying thread for the topics covered. Each year is divided into two half-year books consisting of three or four large chapters. Every chapter has a unifying conceptual theme that connects to the general theme of the year.

Year 1 — Data, Numbers, and Patterns

Book 1a begins and ends with data analysis. It starts with hands-on data gathering, presentation, and analysis, then poses questions about correlating two sets of data. This establishes the goal of the term — that students be able to use the linear regression capabilities of a graphing calculator to do defensible forecasting in real world settings. Students reach this goal by mastering the algebra of first degree equations and the coordinate geometry of straight lines, gaining familiarity with graphing calculators.

    Chapter 1. Turning Facts into Ideas
    Chapter 2. Welcome to Algebra
    Chapter 3. The Algebra of Straight Lines
    Chapter 4. Graphical Estimation

Book 1b generalizes and expands the ideas of *Book 1a*. It begins with techniques for solving two linear equations in two unknowns and interpreting such solutions in real world contexts. Functional relationships in everyday life are identified, generalized, brought into mathematical focus, and linked with the algebra and coordinate geometry already developed. These ideas are then linked to an examination of the fundamental counting principle of discrete mathematics and to the basic ideas of probability. Along the way, *Book 1b* poses questions about correlating two sets of data.

    Chapter 5. Using Lines and Equations
    Chapter 6. How Functions Function
    Chapter 7. Counting Beyond 1, 2, 3
    Chapter 8. Introduction to Probability: What Are the Chances?

Year 2 — Shapes in Space

Book 2a starts with the most basic ways of measuring length and area. It uses symmetries of planar shapes to ask and answer questions about polygonal figures. Algebraic ideas from Year 1 are elaborated by providing them with geometric interpretations. Scaling opens the door to similarity and then to angular measure, which builds on the concept of slope from Year 1. Extensive work with angles and triangles, of interest in its own right, also lays the groundwork for right angle trigonometry, the last main topic of this book. Standard principles of congruence and triangulation of polygons are developed and employed in innovative ways to make clear their applicability to real world problems.

Chapter 1. The Building Blocks of Geometry: Making and
Measuring Polygons
Chapter 2. Similarity and Scaling: Growing and Shrinking Carefully
Chapter 3. Introduction to Trigonometry: Tangles with Angles

Book 2b begins by exploring the role of circles in the world of spatial relationships. It then generalizes the two dimensional ideas and thought patterns of *Book 2a* to three dimensions, starting with foldup patterns and contour lines on topographical maps. This leads to some fundamental properties of three dimensional shapes. Coordinate geometry connects this spatial world of three dimensions to the powerful tools of algebra. That two way connection is then used to explore systems of equations in three variables, extending the treatment of two variable equations in Year 1. In addition, matrices are shown to be a convenient way to organize, store, and manipulate information.

Chapter 4. Circles and Disks
Chapter 5. Shapes in Space
Chapter 6. Linear Algebra and Matrices

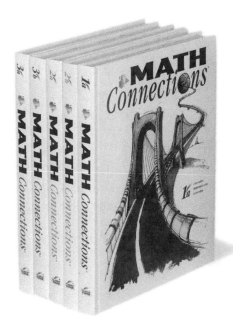
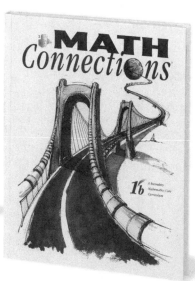

Year 3 — Mathematical Modeling

Book 3a examines mathematical models of real world situations from several viewpoints, providing innovative settings and a unifying theme for the discussion of algebraic, periodic, exponential, and logarithmic functions. These chapters develop many ideas whose seeds were planted in Years 1 and 2. The emphasis throughout this material is the utility of mathematical tools for describing and clarifying what we observe. The modeling theme is then used to revisit and extend the ideas of discrete mathematics and probability that were introduced in Year 1.

Chapter 1. Algebraic Functions
Chapter 2. Exponential Functions and Logarithms
Chapter 3. The Trigonometric Functions
Chapter 4. Counting, Probability, and Statistics

Book 3b begins by extending the modeling theme to Linear Programming, optimization, and topics from graph theory. Then the idea of modeling itself is examined in some depth by considering the purpose of axioms and axiomatic systems, logic, and mathematical proof. Various forms of logical arguments, already used informally throughout Years 1 and 2, are explained and used to explore small axiomatic systems, including the group axioms. These logical tools then provide guidance for a mathematical exploration of infinity, an area in which commonsense intuition is often unreliable. The final chapter explores Euclid's plane geometry, connecting his system with many geometric concepts from Year 2. It culminates in a brief historical explanation of Euclidean and non-Euclidean geometries as alternative models for the spatial structure of our universe.

Chapter 5. Optimization: Math Does It Better
Chapter 6. Playing By the Rules: Logic and Axiomatic Systems
Chapter 7. Infinity — The Final Frontier?
Chapter 8. Axioms, Geometry, and Choice

Appendices

Appendix A. Using a TI-82 (TI-83) Graphing Calculator. This appendix appears in all the books because graphing calculators are important tools for virtually every chapter. It provides a gentle introduction to these machines, and also serves as a convenient student reference for the commonly used elementary procedures.

Appendix B. Using a Spreadsheet. This appendix also appears in all the books. Although a spreadsheet is not explicitly required anywhere in these books, it is very handy for doing many problems or Explorations. It should be considered as a legitimate, optional tool for anyone with access to one.

Appendix C. Programming the TI-82 (TI-83). This appendix also appears in all the books. Students can use it to learn useful general principles of programming, as well as techniques specific to the TI-82 (TI-83).

Appendix D. Linear Programming with Excel. This appendix, which appears in Years 2 and 3, is not primarily a tool for doing problems within the chapters. Rather, it describes a technological approach to ideas that come up from time to time in various chapters. Linear Programming itself is discussed in detail in Chapter 5 of *Book 3b*. This appendix can be used either as a precursor to that discussion, or as an extension of it.

The Features

Here is an overview of the distinctive features that combine to make MATH *Connections* unique.

Standards-based — The NCTM Standards were guiding principles in the development of MATH *Connections*. In particular, various creative devices were employed to implement the four process standards:

- **Problem Solving** — MATH *Connections* demonstrates how mathematics is primarily about asking your own questions and looking for patterns, rather than finding someone else's answers and calculating with numbers. Marginal notes called *Thinking Tips* guide students in specific problem solving strategies. Within sections, many of the *Discuss this* questions and *Explorations* focus students' attention on the problem solving process, while the Problem Sets that conclude virtually all sections further challenge and extend their problem solving skills.

- **Communication** — MATH *Connections*' reading level has been carefully tailored to be, on average, at least one year below grade level. In addition, definitions of all mathematical terms used are clearly identified in the text. The most important ones are displayed as *Words (or Phrases) to Know*. The marginal devices *About Words* and

About Symbols explain fundamental mathematical language and notation. The *Discuss this* and *Write this* questions expect students to talk and write about mathematics in every chapter. The Problem Sets offer many open-ended questions that are suitable for group discussions, or homework writing assignments.

- **Reasoning** — The habit of logical justification is begun in Chapter 1 of *Book 1a* and carried through the entire series. Evaluation of suppositions and arguments occurs throughout all chapters of all books. In Year 1, the reasoning required is largely informal, progressing in Year 2 to more formal justifications. The idea of a counterexample is introduced formally at the beginning of the year and used routinely after that. Expectations of logical justification become more rigorous in Year 3. Also, formal proofs within axiomatic systems (not just in geometry), including mathematical induction, are examined and required.

- **Connections** — This is the defining theme of the entire MATH *Connections* program. The mathematical ideas are connected to the real world by different real life applications — more than 50 professions, 20 job fields and most academic disciplines — within the problems, Explorations and situations of the texts. The most common applications are to science (physics, chemistry, astronomy, biology, archaeology), but there are also applications to theater, music, business and the social sciences, as well as to daily life.

Blended — MATH *Connections* provides a proven approach in which students learn the underlying structure and the skills of mathematics. By presenting mathematics as the subject is used and by blending ideas from traditionally separate fields, students learn not only the topics but also the connections between algebra, geometry, probability, statistics, discrete mathematics, Dynamic and Linear Programming and optimization. By bringing ideas from a wide range of areas to bear on a question, MATH *Connections* presents mathematics as a seamless fabric perhaps with different patterns and colors in different areas, but with no clear boundary lines. Here are some typical examples of the blending of mathematics in MATH *Connections*, one from each year.

- In *Book 1a*, the discussion of carbon dating in Section 4.4 uses first degree equations (algebra), straight line graphs (geometry), least-squares differences (algebra and statistics), and a graphing calculator (technology) to solve a problem in archaeology (natural science). All these tools come together naturally in this context.

- At the end of Section 5.4 in *Book 2b*, algebra, geometry (the volume of a cone) and Cavalieri's Principle (usually in precalculus) are combined to calculate the volume of a sphere.

- In Chapter 6 of *Book 3b*, properties of axiomatic systems (logic) are introduced by examining the rules of a simple card game and the probabilities of certain kinds of outcomes. In Section 6.5 axiomatic systems are related to physics via the Law of the Lever and also to the arithmetic properties of the number systems. The Problem Set for this section includes ideas about population growth, physics, and integer arithmetic.

Accessible — Every major idea in MATH *Connections* is introduced from a commonsense viewpoint using ordinary, nonmathematical examples. For instance, coordinate geometry starts with reading map coordinates, slope follows from building a wheelchair ramp, the concept of function begins with fingerprint files, etc. This helps students see that a mathematical view of the world is not so very different from their view of the world.

Real — This curriculum is firmly grounded in the real world of the students' present and future. The scenarios are realistic, the data sets are drawn from real world sources, the applications are real. Even the whimsical settings use realistic measurements and conditions. Students see for themselves how mathematics is actually used.

Flexible — MATH *Connections* provides for a wide variety of student backgrounds and learning styles. There is plenty of opportunity for student-teacher and student-student interaction in discussing mathematics, students' experiences, opinions, and judgments. Two types of materials are available for each chapter which enhance a teacher's ability to meet the individual needs of all students.

- Supplemental materials for students whose understanding would be strengthened by additional problems or for those who are absent or enter the MATH *Connections* program in midstream

- Extension units for students who want to investigate in greater depth the concepts introduced in a particular section, either individually or in groups

Technological — Your students' future success is likely to depend, at least in part, on their ability to cope with and use the fast-changing tools of electronic technology. We treat the basic technological tools available in the world of work, particularly graphing calculators, as an integral part of the course material. Students are encouraged to use these tools whenever they are appropriate to the work at hand. Students are introduced to the graphing calculator early and are expected to use it routinely as they go along.

The Appendices of every book are filled with simple, illustrative examples of the calculator's basic tasks and functions. In addition, this Teacher Commentary contains many suggestions of where and how you can incorporate other technological tools — spreadsheets, Geometer's Sketchpad, or other geometry software — into your teaching.

Organized — The organization of these books is student friendly:

• Every chapter starts from a point of view that makes sense in the students' world. The expected Learning Outcomes are explicitly stated at the beginning of each section.

• The definitions of all technical terms and the statements of all important facts (theorems) are typographically distinctive, making them easy to find when reviewing.

• Each chapter ends with a retrospective paragraph to help students reflect on their learning.

• Each book contains a glossary, an index, and appendices.

Cooperative Learning

Classes designed around small group and whole class interaction fit the MATH *Connections* curriculum very well. Many of the *Do this now* and *Discuss this* activities are best done in groups. They are particularly useful in traditional and block scheduling situations where there is time for both group work and for direct teacher instruction or discussions involving the entire class. When students work in cooperative settings, they benefit from the interaction and insights of classmates. Student discussions on specific textbook questions often yield surprising and unexpected results. Moreover, working with graphing calculators is greatly enhanced by the group process, as students reinforce their understanding.

MATH *Connection's* classroom experiences reinforce the understanding that learning is a social process and that cooperative learning activities are essential if students are to be able to construct their own knowledge.

Suggested Reading
How to Use Cooperative Learning in the Mathematics Class, Second Edition
By Alice F. Artzt and Claire M. Newman
From the NCTM Educational Materials and Products Catalog
ISBN 0-87353-437-9 #650E1
1-800-235-7566

Elements

About Words are margin paragraphs that explain technical terms and other words that are not part of everyday language, showing how the mathematical use of a word is related to its usage outside of mathematics. This feature facilitates the integration of mathematics with English, especially with English as a second language.

About Symbols are margin paragraphs that point out how specific symbolic conventions are reasonable shorthand ways of writing and communicating the ideas they represent.

Thinking Tips are margin paragraphs that highlight the use of specific problem solving techniques.

A Word to Know and **A Phrase to Know** signal particularly important definitions. Some words appear in boldface where they are defined or first described.

A Fact to Know signals an important mathematical result. In mathematicians' terms, they are significant theorems.

 Do this now identifies questions that students should deal with before moving ahead. Often, these questions are answered within the few pages that follow. If the students don't wrestle with the question when it appears, its value as a learning experience may be lost.

 Discuss this identifies questions intended to provoke interchange among students, open-ended Explorations, and/or a variety of opinions. They can be done as soon as they appear in the text, but you might want to delay some and omit others, depending on your sense of how they might work best with your students.

 Write this identifies student writing exercises and requires students to gather information or reflect upon a topic. These exercises are suitable for group work and reporting, and can be assigned individually as homework or completed in class.

Pacing

Each school district will need to evaluate the pacing of the curriculum according to the needs of their students and schedule it has adopted. The two models shown here are examples of how school systems have adapted MATH *Connections* to fit their needs. Each semester assumes 16 weeks of class time, allowing two weeks per semester for other activities such as projects, statewide testing, etc.

3-YEAR PACING MODEL

Year 1:

Book 1a	Chapter 1	4 weeks including assessments
	Chapter 2	5 weeks including assessments
	Chapter 3	4 weeks including assessments
	Chapter 4	3 weeks including assessments
Book 1b	Chapter 5	4 weeks including assessments
	Chapter 6	6 weeks including assessments
	Chapter 7	3 weeks including assessments
	Chapter 8	3 weeks including assessments

Year 2:

Book 2a	Chapter 1	5 weeks including assessments
	Chapter 2	6 weeks including assessments
	Chapter 3	5 weeks including assessments
Book 2b	Chapter 4	5 weeks including assessments
	Chapter 5	6 weeks including assessments
	Chapter 6	5 weeks including assessments

Year 3:

Book 3a	Chapter 1	6 weeks including assessments
	Chapter 2	5 weeks including assessments
	Chapter 3	4 weeks including assessments
	Chapter 4	3 weeks including assessments
Book 3b	Chapter 5	3 weeks including assessments
	Chapter 6	3 weeks including assessments
	Chapter 7	4 weeks including assessments
	Chapter 8	4 weeks including assessments

(Teachers sometimes assign Chapter 8 as independent study resulting in student projects and research papers.)

The sections within each chapter vary in length and each is built around a major idea. Several sections might take only one class period; others may take two, three or four class periods. MATH *Connections* gives you the flexibility to successfully match the capabilities of your students with the program. Higher level classes complete the *a* and *b* books in one year, making this a 3-year program. In other situations, however, MATH *Connections* can be taught over $3^1/_2$ to 4 years.

3 $^1/_2$ - YEAR PACING MODEL

Year 1:

Book 1a	Chapter 1	5 weeks including assessments
	Chapter 2	6 weeks including assessments
	Chapter 3	6 weeks including assessments
	Chapter 4	4 weeks including assessments
Book 1b	Chapter 5	5 weeks including assessments
	Chapter 6	6 weeks including assessments

Year 2:

Book 1b	Chapter 7	3 weeks including assessments
	Chapter 8	2 weeks including assessments
Book 2a	Chapter 1	9 weeks including assessments
	Chapter 2	8 weeks including assessments
	Chapter 3	3 weeks including assessments
Book 2b	Chapter 4	4 weeks including assessments
	Chapter 5	3 weeks including assessments (up to section 5.5)

Year 3:

Book 2b	Chapter 5	3 weeks including assessments (start at section 5.6)
	Chapter 6	4 weeks including assessments
Book 3a	Chapter 1	7 weeks including assessments
	Chapter 2	6 weeks including assessments
	Chapter 3	5 weeks including assessments
	Chapter 4	7 weeks including assessments

Year 4:

Book 3b	Chapter 5	4 weeks including assessments
	Chapter 6	4 weeks including assessments
	Chapter 7	5 weeks including assessments
	Chapter 8	5 weeks including assessments

Published by IT'S ABOUT TIME, Inc. © 2000 MATHconx, LLC

Materials Included With Teacher Edition

MATH *Connections* provides a full range of support materials. In addition to the Teacher Edition, each year includes:

Assessments Form A — Allows students to use a variety of formats to demonstrate their knowledge of mathematical concepts and skills. Assessments are tied to specific mathematics objectives and are linked to the Learning Outcomes for each section of the chapter. Form A was developed for each quiz and chapter test.

The Solution Key and Scoring Guide for each quiz and chapter test contains solutions to all questions as well as suggestions for scoring based on a 100 point scale.

Blackline Masters — Contain spreadsheets, graphs, tables and forms which can be copied and distributed to students in the class or used as transparencies.

Ancillary Materials

Assessments Form B — Provides teachers with an alternative but equivalent assessment for each quiz and chapter test along with corresponding Solution Keys. They can be used as alternate assessments or makeup tests, etc.

Supplements — Complement the MATH *Connections* curriculum for students whose understanding of mathematics would be strengthened by additional work or for those who have been absent or enter the MATH *Connections* program in midstream.

Extensions — Enable students to investigate in greater depth the concepts and activities introduced in a particular section.

Test Banks — Allow teachers to prepare tests such as Midterms and Final Exams that are specifically tailored to the particular needs of their students. They include sample formats and test questions, along with the corresponding Solution Keys.

Professional Development Videos — It is always preferable to attend Professional Development Workshops. But sometimes schedules and budgets make attendance difficult. We developed these videos to support the professional development of teachers as they implement MATH *Connections* in their classrooms.

NCTM 9-12 Standards Correlation

Integrated into all three years of **MATH** *Connections*
are the four process standards:

1. **Mathematics as Problem Solving:** **Explorations, Projects, Simulations and Problem Solving**

2. **Mathematics as Communication:** *Do this now, Discuss this, Write this, About Words, About Symbols, Justify Opinions*

3. **Mathematics as Reasoning:** **A thematic thread in all three years**

4. **Mathematics as Connections:** **Connections with more than 50 professions, 20 job fields and all academic disciplines**

	Year 1	Year 2	Year 3
5. Algebra	Chap. 2, 3, 4, 5	Chap. 1, 2, 6	Chap. 1, 5
6. Functions	Chap. 5, 6	Chap. 1	Chap. 1, 2, 3
7. Geometry from a Synthetic Perspective	Chap. 5, 6	Chap. 1, 2, 4, 5	Chap. 1, 5, 6, 8
8. Geometry from an Algebraic Perspective	Chap. 3	Chap. 1, 4, 5	Chap. 1
9. Trigonometry		Chap. 3, 4, 5	Chap. 3
10. Statistics	Chap. 1, 4, 5, 8		Chap. 4
11. Probability	Chap. 7, 8		Chap. 4
12. Discrete Mathematics	Chap. 1, 2, 4, 5, 7, 8	Chap. 2, 5, 6	Chap. 4, 5, 6
13. Conceptual Underpinnings of the Calculus	Chap. 2, 5, 6	Chap. 2, 5, 6	Chap. 1, 7
14. Mathematical Structure	Chap. 2, 4	Chap. 2	Chap. 6, 7, 8

Planning Guide Book 2a

This book starts with the most basic concepts of choosing ways to measure length and area. It uses symmetries of planar shapes to ask and answer questions about polygonal figures. Algebraic ideas from *Year 1* are elaborated by using geometric interpretations. Scaling opens the door to similarity and then to angular measure, which builds on the concept of slope from *Year 1*. Extensive work with angles and triangles, of interest in its own right, also lays the groundwork for right angle trigonometry, the last main topic of this book. Standard principles of congruence and triangulation of polygonal figures are developed and employed in innovative ways to make clear their applicability to real world problems.

Chapter Objectives	*Pacing Range	Assessments Form A (A)	Blackline Masters
Chapter 1 The Building Blocks of Geometry: Making and Measuring Polygons Starting with the primitive idea of a unit of length, this chapter builds up many fundamental geometric concepts, including symmetries and triangulation of polygons, the Pythagorean Theorem, area, and volume. It provides geometric interpretations of some algebraic relationships, and introduces direct and inverse variation.	5-9 weeks including Assessments	Quiz 1.1-1.2(A) Quiz 1.3-1.4(A) Quiz 1.5-1.7(A) Quiz 1.8-1.10(A) Chapter Test(A)	Student pp. 46, 53, 73-74, 87-88, 89-90
Chapter 2 Similarity and Scaling: Growing and Shrinking Carefully This chapter is long and rich. It uses similarity and scaling factors to explain and unify a wide range of important topics, including angle measurement, the relationships among angles formed by cutting parallels, congruence of triangles, the effect of scaling on areas and volumes, and the utility of rotations and reflections. It interweaves geometry and algebra via proportionality. By using the calculator's TAN function keys to convert between slope and degree measure of angles, it illustrates the idea of inverse functions and foreshadows the next chapter.	6-8 weeks including Assessments	Quiz 2.1-2.2(A) Quiz 2.3-2.4(A) Quiz 2.5-2.6(A) Quiz 2.7-2.8(A) Quiz 2.9-2.10(A) Chapter Test(A)	Student pp. 128-129, 139, 186
Chapter 3 Introduction to Trigonometry: Tangles With Angles Chapter 3 introduces the three basic functions of right angle trigonometry – sine, cosine, and tangent – and discusses the inverses of these functions in relation to the calculator. The Law of Sines and the Law of Cosines are explained and applied, and the graphs of the sine and cosine functions are connected with circular motion via the unit circle, setting the stage for parametric representation of circles in Chapter 4.	3-5 weeks including Assessments	Quiz 3.1-3.2(A) Quiz 3.3(A) Quiz 3.4-3.6(A) Chapter Test(A)	No Blackline Masters for this chapter

*Pacing Range Teachers will need to adjust this guide to suit the needs of their own students. Not all classes will complete each chapter at the same pace. Flexibility — which accommodates different teaching styles, school schedules and school standards — is built into the curriculum.

Ancillary Materials

Assessments Form B (B)	Supplements for Chapter Sections	Extensions	Test Banks
Quiz 1.1-1.2(B) Quiz 1.3-1.4(B) Quiz 1.5-1.7(B) Quiz 1.8-1.10(B) Chapter Test(B)	1.1 Measuring Lengths — 3 Supplements 1.2 Paths, Polygons, and Perimeter — 3 Supplements 1.3 Symmetry — 4 Supplements 1.4 Regular Polygons — 1 Supplement 1.5 Areas of Right-Angled Figures — 4 Supplements 1.6 Area and Algebra — 2 Supplements 1.7 Triangles and Triangulation — 2 Supplements 1.8 The Pythagorean Theorem — 6 Supplements 1.9 It Varies With The Square — 4 Supplements 1.10 Volume — 4 Supplements	1.5 An Optimal Rectangle	To be released
Quiz 2.1-2.2(B) Quiz 2.3-2.4(B) Quiz 2.5-2.6(B) Quiz 2.7-2.8(B) Quiz 2.9-2.10(B) Chapter Test(B)	2.1 The Same Shape — 5 Supplements 2.2 Similar Triangles and Rectangles — 4 Supplements 2.3 How to Measure Angles — 3 Supplements 2.4 Finding Angle Size Efficiently — 3 Supplements 2.5 Parallel Lines and the Angle Sum of a Triangle — 3 Supplements 2.6 Parallelograms and Congruent Triangles — 4 Supplements 2.7 Other Tests for Congruent Triangles — 1 Supplement 2.8 Other Polygons — 1 Supplement 2.9 Stretching and Shrinking Angles and Areas — 3 Supplements 2.10 Stretching and Shrinking Volumes — 1 Supplement	Following 2.10 Build It Up & Tear It Down: A Problem Solving Strategy	To be released
Quiz 3.1-3.2(B) Quiz 3.3(B) Quiz 3.4-3.6(B)) Chapter Test(B)	3.1 The Sine of an Acute Angle — 4 Supplements 3.2 The Cosine of an Acute Angle — 2 Supplements 3.3 The Tangent of an Acute Angle — 3 Supplements 3.4 What Do These SIN^{-1}, COS^{-1}, and TAN^{-1} Keys Do? — 3 Supplements 3.5 The Law of Sines - The Law of Cosines — 2 Supplements 3.6 Sine and Cosine Curves: Going Around in Circles — 1 Supplement	3.4 Vectors in a Plane "Favorite" Triangles	To be released

Chapter 1 Planning Guide

Chapter 1 The Building Blocks of Geometry: Making and Measuring Polygons

Starting with the primitive idea of a unit of length, this chapter builds up many fundamental geometric concepts, including symmetries and triangulation of polygons, the Pythagorean Theorem, area, and volume. It provides geometric interpretations of some algebraic relationships, and introduces direct and inverse variation.

Assessments Form A (A)	Assessments Form B (B)	Blackline Masters
Quiz 1.1-1.2(A) Quiz 1.3-1.4(A) Quiz 1.5-1.7(A) Quiz 1.8-1.10(A) Chapter Test (A)	Quiz 1.1-1.2(B) Quiz 1.3-1.4(B) Quiz 1.5-1.7(B) Quiz 1.8-1.10(B) Chapter Test (B)	Student pp. 46, 53, 73-74, 87-88, 89-90

Extensions	Supplements for Chapter Sections	Test Banks
1.5 An Optimal Rectangle	1.1 Measuring Lengths — 3 Supplements 1.2 Paths, Polygons, and Perimeter — 3 Supplements 1.3 Symmetry —4 Supplements 1.4 Regular Polygons — 1 Supplement 1.5 Areas of Right-Angled Figures — 4 Supplements 1.6 Area and Algebra — 2 Supplements 1.7 Triangles and Triangulation — 2 Supplements 1.8 The Pythagorean Theorem — 6 Supplements 1.9 It Varies With The Square — 4 Supplements 1.10 Volume — 4 Supplements	To be released

Pacing Range 5-9 weeks including Assessments
Teachers will need to adjust this guide to suit the needs of their own students. Not all classes will complete each chapter at the same pace. Flexibility — which accommodates different teaching styles, school schedules and school standards — is built into the curriculum.

Teacher Commentary is indexed to the student text by the numbers in the margins (under the icons or in circles). The first digit indicates the chapter — the numbers after the decimal indicate the sequential numbering of the comments within that unit. Example:

1.9   (1.37)

Student Pages in Teacher Edition

1.9   (1.37)

Teacher Commentary Page

Observations

Helen Crowley
Southington High School, CT

"The focus in Chapter 1 is polygons, although it may be a very different approach to the subject from how you taught it in the past. It's not just looking at triangles, quadrilaterals, and pentagons; the program's approach is to look at a variety of things at the same time. For example, we look at area and some algebra concepts also in the same section. I think it's so important to make algebra and geometry partners, rather than isolated subjects."

Errol Libby
Oxford Hills Comprehensive
High School, ME

"The nicest thing about Chapter 1 — in fact the entire series but most especially here in the geometry chapters — is the way the material is presented based on meaningful real world situations. The students really relate to these problems. They build their mathematical understanding from the ground up. In the more traditional approach, it was the other way around. First we taught them the abstract concepts and only later gave them a few real world applications. I find that the students learn best and retain more when they can hang what they're learning on something that they can relate to in the real world.

"Also in this chapter they have a nice beginning to precalculus concepts which will be revisited in later chapters. This program does a great job of developing important ideas very carefully and then revisiting them. I think it's pretty unusual to introduce the beginning elements of calculus in the beginning of geometry, but it really makes sense."

John Hoffman
Mapping the Surface of the Earth

John Hoffman's firm, Aerial Images, takes photos of Earth from outer space. Cameras mounted on satellites send back digitized pictures. These shots are used to make maps or just to see what's happening anywhere on Earth. "The new digital image technologies along with aerial photography are rapidly changing the way maps of the Earth's surface are made," he exclaims.

John became an expert in this field while in the military. He studied to be a pilot and later he learned aerial photography. He explains that while using aerial images to make maps was at first a big step forward, "You can't get high enough to get a broad picture of Earth. So you end up with a perspective problem. The outer edges of the image lean and you have diverging scales from the center to its edges. To solve this curvature problem we take many overlapping images. Then we piece them together using basic geometric theorems. Without geometry, we can't do our work.

"Satellite photography has revolutionized the whole field," John continues. "We've changed the altitude, getting the camera way up. Now the delta — the change in the angle from the center of the image to the outer — becomes much smaller.

"Future technologies will be amazing," John exults. "They'll give us much greater control over many large-scale planetary issues. Using this system, we can now even count trees. So if you're concerned about the deforestation of the rain forest in Brazil, we can actually inventory those trees."

2

Published by IT'S ABOUT TIME, Inc. © 2000 MATHconx, LLC

Chapter 1 The Building Blocks of Geometry: Making and Measuring Polygons

The main theme of **MATH** *Connections* Year 2 is shapes in space. While the emphasis is decidedly geometric, this is far more than a traditional course in plane geometry. Instead, this course extends students' prior experiences and visual intuition by organizing many things that they have already seen around a few basic principles and methods.

The topics of geometry can be presented in many ways. We believe that the approach we have chosen maximizes understanding while minimizing rote memory tasks. Moreover, our organizing themes make it easy to connect geometric ideas with real world applications and with other parts of mathematics. Chapter 1 plays a key role in this development, both by what it contains and by what it does *not* contain.

- It shows how the construction and measurement of polygons depends on straight line segments and their lengths.

- It shows how a unit of length is a *choice* which determines the units of area and volume measure.

- It uses symmetry to describe and classify polygons and other shapes.

- It *deliberately* sidesteps angle measure, in order to avoid confusion with linear measure. *Please* do not introduce this idea early; doing so will undercut a main theme of Chapter 2!

- It explains triangulation as a way to reduce questions about polygons to questions about triangles.

The Building Blocks of Geometry: Making and Measuring Polygons

CHAPTER 1

1.1 Measuring Lengths

Learning Outcomes

After studying this section, you will be able to:

Explain how mathematics can be used to model real situations;

Describe differences between a globe and a flat map as models of the world;

Tell the difference between discrete and continuous quantities;

Describe what a unit of measure is and explain why it must be constant;

Measure a given length with a given unit.

You can think of geometry as the visual side of mathematics. It deals with shape, form, and size. We begin this book by looking carefully at some of the surprisingly simple, fundamental ideas on which all of geometry rests. *Really* understanding these few simple ideas is the key to this powerful part of mathematics.

Earlier in **MATH** *Connections* you used geometry to visualize some of the other things you were doing. For example, you learned to use coordinate geometry to create graphs of functions and equations. You also used tree diagrams to visualize counting processes. One role of geometry is to provide pictures that help us to understand some other part of mathematics. A picture often gives a quick, intuitive grasp of a situation, which then can be made more precise by a symbolic expression or an exact computation. The connection between geometric figures and algebra or arithmetic is measurement. When we measure a geometric shape, we get numbers. We can do arithmetic with the numbers, or plug them into an algebraic equation. For this reason, we will start with measurement.

3

1.1 Measuring Lengths

This section opens with a sequence of activities involving maps. You may wish to do this cooperatively with a geography or social studies teacher, who may wish to enrich the activity with additional material from that other subject area. You will need at least one map of the world, a globe, and various measuring devices. All the measurements can be made with an ordinary cloth measuring tape.

The point of these Explorations is to get students thinking about such basic ideas as *straightness* and *distance*. You should encourage lots of discussion but not attempt to lead the class to any particular answers. For the rest of this chapter, we will stay in the plane where these concepts will be reviewed and developed. The realization that things could be different on the sphere may help motivate students to examine these basic ideas. Without the counterexample of the sphere, they might seem too simple and obvious to bother with.

The key idea of this section is that lengths are measured by the repeated application of a chosen unit. Students should experience this idea physically, by actually laying off a unit over and over again. For that reason, it is good to use some made up units and some units that do not have subdivisions marked on them. If your students have done quite a bit of this in elementary and middle school, you won't need to spend a lot of time on such activities, but you should spend some time on them.

Additional Support Materials:

Assessments	Qty
Form (A)	1
Form (B)	1

Blackline Masters	Qty

Extensions	Qty

Supplements	Qty
Measuring Lengths	3

1.1 Measuring Lengths

About Words

The word *geometry* comes from Greek roots that mean earth measurement. One of the earliest uses of geometry was to measure the boundaries of farmland.

Probably the most basic thing we can measure is length. Our units for area and volume measurements are based on length units. In addition, many measuring devices express their results as length along a scale rather than in terms of the thing measured. For example, in a traditional thermometer we do not see the heat directly. Instead, we see how far the column of mercury has risen. The speedometers of some cars are read on a similar scale turned sideways. We judge speed by how *far* the indicator has moved clockwise, not by how fast it moves. Studying how length is measured will help us to understand other kinds of measurements, so this is where we begin.

What other things in your everyday life are measured or sized in terms of length? Can you think of half a dozen? A dozen? More?

1.1

The tenth grade mathematics class at Euclid School has been studying China. Two of the students found a pen pal in Beijing! The class reads their letters. The students are curious to know where Beijing is, how far away it is, and how long it would take to get there. They know that there are planes to China leaving from Philadelphia, and they know where Philadelphia is. They decide to make plans for an imaginary trip to Beijing. They are looking at maps to see how to get there. They also want to know how far they would have to travel and how long it would take. Look at a flat map of the world (in an atlas or on a wall chart) and help them out by answering these questions.

1.2

1. **What route would the class fly? Do you think they would fly over Denver? Hudson Bay? California? Japan? Siberia?**

2. **About how far would they travel? To figure this out from the map, you need a scale for judging distances. It is approximately 25,000 miles around the Earth at the equator. Measure the width of your map and figure out the scale of the map at the equator. Then measure how far it is from Philadelphia to Beijing on the map. If the scale at the equator works for this route, how far is it from Philadelphia to Beijing?**

4

1.1

This need not take much time. Its purpose is to focus students' attention on the variety of forms of length measurements all around them. Besides the obvious things (thread, shoelaces, lumber, shoes, etc.) try to get students to suggest some cases in which length is used as a proxy for something else that is being measured, as in the thermometer and speedometer examples. Here are a few more suggestions.

- TV screens and video monitors are sized by the length of their diagonals.

- The output volume of a stereo system is sometimes registered by a light along a horizontal scale.

- A popular carnival concession measures strength by how high (along a vertical scale with a bell at the top) a weight goes when the base is hit by a large hammer.

- The amount of coffee left in a large restaurant coffee urn is measured by the height of a column of coffee in a transparent tube.

There are many others.

1.2

These questions lend themselves to hands-on, group work in class. Their point, in conjunction with the questions that follow, is that even useful, common models of reality—in this case, the world—are imperfect. Moreover, sometimes their distortions may not be obvious.

The flat, rectangular map you use should be a Mercator projection or some similar kind of cylindrical projection. The Mercator map is a very old, common type—the classic schoolroom map. Here are some hallmarks of the Mercator projection map.

- There is a grid of vertical and horizontal parallel straight lines representing longitude and latitude.

- The North and South Poles do not appear on the map.

- The map is perfectly rectangular, with no curved or irregular boundaries.

- Greenland looks almost bigger than South America, and it is much taller than it is wide.

Cylindrical projections share the first three of these properties, but there is a little less relative distortion between Greenland and South America.

1. On such a map, the obvious path from Philadelphia to Beijing runs along the 40th parallel. This path runs very close to Denver, but nowhere near Hudson Bay. It crosses northern California and Japan, but does not come anywhere near Siberia.

2. Be careful in defining the width of your map. Some maps are more than a world wide, with overlap between the outside edges. In that case,

Unfortunately, the world is not flat like a map. The students decide that they also want to look at their trip on a globe. That's a good idea for us, too.

1. Use a flexible ruler or cloth tape to measure on a globe the route you chose from Philadelphia to Beijing. Be sure that the tape follows the route accurately! (Check some places along the way to make sure.) Then measure around the globe at the equator. The Earth is about 25,000 miles around. Find the scale for your globe and use it to find the length of your path.

1.3

2. How great is the east-west distance around the world at the latitude of Philadelphia?

3. Use your answer to part 2 and the measurements you made on your flat map to recalculate the distance from Philadelphia to Beijing. Compare this result with your result for part 1.

The Earth is a three dimensional object, and we live on or near its surface. A flat map is an attempt to represent this surface. Because the Earth is not flat, any flat map is an approximation. There are different ways of making flat maps. Each has its advantages and disadvantages. The classic flat map of the world is called a **Mercator map**.

The Mercator map was designed for planning long trips for ships on the ocean. It represents directions very well. If *A* is northwest of *B* on a Mercator map, then sailing northwest from *A* will eventually get you to *B*. However, the farther you move away from the equator, the more a Mercator map distorts size. Other types of flat maps of the world preserve size, but they distort other things, such as shape or direction. It is not possible to make a flat map of the world that preserves both size and direction at the same time. (The fact that this cannot be done was actually proved by Leonhard Euler, an 18th century Swiss mathematician.)

About Words

The *Mercator map* was devised by Gerhardus Mercator, a Flemish mapmaker who lived from 1512 to 1594. He named North and South America and was the first person to call a collection of maps an atlas.

Published by IT'S ABOUT TIME, Inc. © 2000 MATHconx, LLC

5

measure the distance between the appearances of any feature that appears twice. Using this scale, your students should get some number between 11,000 and 12,000 miles as the approximate distance between Philadelphia and Beijing. This turns out to be much larger than the real distance because, in fact, the scale based on the equator *doesn't* work. The next set of questions brings this out.

1.3

Answers to these questions will necessarily be very rough approximations, of course.

1. This should come out to be about 9000 miles.

2. About 19,000 miles.

3. By basing their scale on 19,000 miles as the width of the world at the Philadelphia–Beijing level, students should get an answer close to that of part 1, about 9000 miles.

NOTES

1.4

1. How big is Greenland compared with South America on a Mercator map? Now compare them on the globe. How accurate is the map, compared to the globe?

2. Besides distorting distance, a flat map can mislead us about the shortest route from one place to another. To find the shortest route from Philadelphia to Beijing on a globe, put one end of a string at Philadelphia, pull the string taut, then mark the point where the string reaches Beijing. Measure that length and then calculate the distance between Philadelphia and Beijing by that route. How does this distance compare with the east-west distance (along the 40th parallel) that you found before?

3. Would the class fly over Denver if they took the route you found in part 2? Over Hudson Bay? California? Japan? Siberia?

The flat map and the globe are **models** of the surface of our planet. Each one represents some features of our world that are considered important for a particular purpose and leaves out many others that are not. Neither model is perfect. The globe is a better model for charting paths of long air flights. The flat map is more useful if you just want to find your way around a small region, like Minneapolis. It's also a lot easier to fold up and put in your pocket!

Maps and globes are models made of paper, metal, or plastic. We can also make models with mathematics. When a mathematical object such as an equation or a function is used to describe a situation outside of mathematics, that object is a *mathematical model*. For example, if a record club sells CDs at $10.99 each and charges $3 per order for shipping, then the total amount billed, b (in dollars), is a function of the number n of CDs ordered. That is, the function

$$b(n) = 3 + 10.99n$$

is a mathematical model of the billing process. You saw many similar mathematical models of real situations earlier in **MATH** *Connections*.

6

Published by IT'S ABOUT TIME, Inc. © 2000 MATHconx, LLC

1.4

1. On a Mercator map, Greenland appears larger than South America. On a cylindrical flat projection map, it appears about the same size. On a globe Greenland appears much, much smaller than South America. The relative sizes of Greenland and South America are represented correctly on the globe.

2. If you let the string follow its own inclination, it will settle on a route from Philadelphia to Beijing that passes very close to the North Pole. This path, called a *great circle route*, is only about 7000 miles long. That's about 2000 miles shorter than the east-west distance.

3. They would fly over Hudson Bay and Siberia, but nowhere near Denver or California or Japan.

NOTES

George Box, a well-known statistician, once said, "All models are wrong; some models are useful."[1] What do you think he meant by this?

1.5

For many years, the traditional subject of *plane geometry* was a mathematical model of how flat maps work. Plane geometry began with the surveying of land in ancient Egypt. This mathematical model does not describe the entire surface of the earth accurately, because that surface is not flat. However, it is accurate enough for surveying fields or for taking short trips. This book begins with a long, close look at the plane geometry model and its power to describe many things well.

One reason why plane geometry is such a powerful tool is that it is built on a small number of very simple, basic ideas. But be careful! Their simplicity can be deceiving. You must think hard about these basic ideas until you really understand why they are important. Otherwise, like a house of cards with one or two bottom cards just a little out of place, your understanding of geometry may fall apart without warning.

Measurement is one of those basic ideas. Like the ancient Egyptians, this is where we begin our study of geometry. Measurement is one of two main ways of relating numbers to the world around us. The other way is by counting. You have had lots of practice with counting things—pennies, dollars, candy bars, cars, tickets, pages, people, and so on. Any time we want to know *how many* of some object, we count. The objects have to be separate, distinct things; they are said to be *discrete*. The branch of mathematics that deals with processes related to counting such things is called **discrete mathematics**. The counting principles and probability laws that you studied before are part of discrete mathematics. The rest of this section, like most of this book, is *not* about discrete mathematics.

About Words

A Spanish word for *flat* is *plano*.

---

[1]Box, George, *"Robustness in the Strategy of Scientific Model Building,"* in Lanner and Wilkerson, eds., *Robustness in Statistics* (New York: Academic Press, 1979), pp. 201–236.

Published by IT'S ABOUT TIME, Inc. © 2000 MATHconx, LLC

7

1.5

This question should generate a brief discussion focusing students on the fact that models are necessarily imperfect representations. The main idea is that a model usually agrees with reality in some respects but not in others. As long as it agrees in all respects in which you are interested, it can be useful. If you wish, you might ask students to come up with specific examples of models from any source and point out where they are wrong and how they are useful. However, such an extended discussion is not necessary for the work that follows.

Chapter 1

NOTES

The other main way in which we connect numbers to things is by measuring properties of a single object, such as its weight, length, or temperature. Any time we want to know *how much* of something, we measure. These measurements are not restricted to the counting numbers; they may take on any values, including negative values, fractions, and others. The branch of mathematics that deals with this kind of situation is called *continuous mathematics*. The most famous branch of continuous mathematics is calculus, but the part of geometry that deals with measuring lengths, areas, and volumes is continuous mathematics, too.

1.6

Which of the following questions refer to counting, and which refer to measuring? (You don't have to answer the questions.)

1. **What is the population of your state?**

2. **What is the average annual rainfall in your state?**

3. **What is the record high temperature for your state?**

4. **How many people in your class are left-handed?**

5. **How many people in your class are over six feet tall?**

6. **What quantity of hot dogs was sold at yesterday's ball game?**

7. **What quantity of popcorn was sold at yesterday's ball game?**

Measuring continuous quantities starts with choosing a unit. The key word here is "choosing." Any measurement system is based on a small number of independent units of measure, sometimes called **base units**. These base units are *chosen* for their *convenience*. All other units of measure within the system are then defined in terms of the base units. For instance, the base unit of length measure in the metric system is the *meter*; in the English system, it is the *foot*.

1.6

The ideas of measurement data and counting data represent endpoints on a spectrum. There are many in between and borderline cases. Even so, the distinction is useful.

1. Counting

2. Measurement

3. Measurement

4. Counting

5. Both. You must count the people in a category that is defined by a measurement.

6. Either. If the answer is the number of hot dogs, it's counting. If the answer is the pounds of hot dogs, it's measurement.

7. Measurement. Popcorn is sold in bulk, in various sizes of containers, so this question must be answered with either bulk measure or weight measure.

Note that there is a grammatical distinction in English, all too often overlooked in the everyday vernacular of TV announcing, between *number* and *amount*. Number refers to discrete quantities; amount refers to continuous quantities. For example, we might say that the *number* of teenagers at a party was 50 people, but the *amount* of ice cream they consumed was 7 gallons. We can talk about paying for the ice cream with a *number* of dollars or with an *amount* of money. You might want to alert your students to this distinction.

NOTES

Many older units of length, such as the *foot,* were based (**1.7**) on parts of the body of a "typical" person. Others that were used include:

- the *span:* the distance from the tip of the thumb to the tip of the little finger with the fingers spread out;

- the *palm:* the width of the palm of a hand or of the four fingers held close together;

- the *digit:* the width of the first finger.

Here are some lesser known units of length based originally on objects from everyday life.

cable   chain   fathom   furlong   hand

Write a sentence or two about each, describing
- the object on which it is based,

1.8

- how it compares with inches, feet, or miles, and

- the occupation, activity, or situation in which it is used.

Look up the ones you don't know.

The problem with units of length such as *span, palm, digit,* and *foot* is obvious: the sizes of hands and feet vary from person to person. Having a unit of measure that is different for each person would be like each person speaking a different language. Nobody would know what anyone else was talking about! One way around this problem is to pick some special person, such as a king, to define a unit. In England, King Henry I (1068–1135) declared a yard to be the distance from the tip of his nose to the tip of his right thumb with his arm outstretched. That became the basis for the English system of measurement, the system still used today in the United States.

How long would a "yard" be if *you* were the monarch on which it was based? Collect data from each member of your class on the distance from the tip of the nose to the tip of the right thumb with the arm outstretched. Make a boxplot of all the data, and find the mean and median. Is either one close to the standard 36 inch yard?

1.9

1.7 Here's a story about an unusual unit length that might interest your students.

Many years ago, one of the fraternities at MIT decided to initiate a freshman by measuring the length of the Harvard Bridge, using the initiate as a unit of length. Mr. Smoot was laid out on the bridge the appropriate number of times, and the length was duly marked off and recorded. These markings were renewed each year by the fraternity. When the Metropolitan District Commission wanted to redo the bridge, the markings were given protection as historical landmarks! Eventually Smoot's son attended MIT, and the markings were redone. It was found that not all Smoots are created equal.

1.8 This can be used in class discussion, if you prefer. Some of your students may know some of these terms, depending on their extra curricular interests. A couple of them are very obscure. The point here is that our usual ways of measuring lengths, based on feet or meters, are merely two among many choices that have been used throughout history. As the text points out soon after these questions, the emergence of the English system and the metric system as "standards" is based on more widespread acceptance than on any intrinsic superiority of their unit lengths.

cable—a nautical unit of measure. It is based on the length of a long rope or chain used to moor or anchor a ship. Its length depends on where you are: 608 feet ($\frac{1}{10}$ of a nautical mile, or about 100 fathoms) in England, 720 feet (120 fathoms) in the U.S.

chain—based on the length of a standard 100 link chain used in surveying. It is equivalent to 66 feet.

fathom—another nautical unit, used primarily to measure the depth of water. It is equivalent to 6 feet. Its origin is not obvious from the word itself, but it is related to an Old English word meaning arms outstretched.

furlong—used in horse racing (to measure the length of a racetrack) and in surveying. It is based on the length of a plowed furrow in a farmer's field. One mile is 8 furlongs. That is, a furlong is 660 feet.

hand—a common unit of measuring the height of a horse. It is the breadth of the palm of a hand. In modern times, this has been standardized to 4 inches.

1.9 This is a hands-on activity in the most literal sense! It is not essential to the chapter, but it reinforces the idea of variability of person based units of length. It also reviews some of the basic data analysis skills from **MATH** *Connections* Year 1. You may want to pair students off for this activity and have them measure one another. The pooling of results can be done in larger groups or as an all class activity. The results will vary, of course. It is helpful to have a measuring device that is longer than the longest yard, such as a meter stick or a tape measure.

In order for any system of measurement to work well, the base unit must be constant; it cannot change from time to time or from place to place. To make sure this happens, person-based units of length have been replaced with units defined by metal bars kept in scientific laboratories. These bars stay the same size year after year. In the United States, the National Bureau of Standards oversees these official units of measure (and many others).

Once a unit of length is chosen, we measure something by applying the unit over and over, counting how many units it takes to make up the whole. Unlike your feet, rulers usually are marked in a variety of units and subdivisions. For example, a ruler may be marked in centimeters and millimeters on one side, and inches on the other. The inches may be divided into tenths, or eighths, or sixteenths. In a sense, these subdivisions are just a way of choosing smaller, related units when they are needed for more exact measurement. We can measure the lengths of many different things, but most of them have the same mathematical model: the measurement of a line segment.

1.10

Display 1.1 shows four line segments. Measure each segment with a ruler, using these three different base units of length: inches, centimeters, millimeters. In each case, which base length did you think was easiest to use? Why?

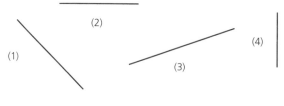

Display 1.1

1.10

This emphasizes the idea of choosing base units for convenience. If the figure is not distorted by the printing process, the answers are as follows.

(1) $1\frac{3}{16}$ inches; 3 cm; 30 mm

(2) 1 inch; 2.5 cm; 25 mm

(3) $1\frac{3}{8}$ inches; 3.5 cm; 35 mm

(4) $\frac{11}{16}$ inches; 1.7 cm; 17 mm

There may be some slight variation due to ruler markings, student visual accuracy, etc. The answers to "easiest to use" may vary, but probably most students will identify centimeters as the easiest for (1), inches for (2), and millimeters for (4). None of the units is really good for (3).

Chapter 1

NOTES

In geometry, we distinguish between a *line,* which goes on forever in both directions, and a **line segment,** a piece of a line which does *not* go on forever in either direction. A segment consists of two endpoints and all the points on that straight line that are between those endpoints. It is common to label interesting points with capital letters, and we usually label the end points of a line segment. Display 1.2 shows a line segment with its endpoints labeled *A* and *B.* We can refer to this segment simply as *AB.* (Notice that point *C* is not part of the line segment because it is not on the line through *A* and *B.*)

A ————————————————— B

•C

Display 1.2

Whenever you measure a length, you can think of it as the length of a line segment. For example, if you measure the width of your classroom, you have to pick some (imaginary) line along the floor or wall on which you can make your measurement. (Note: In measuring length, we assume that all the lines and line segments are straight. As you saw earlier in this section, straightness is not always as obvious or as simple as it seems. This assumption simplifies our work, but we have to be careful not to apply the results to situations where "straightness" doesn't hold.)

Published by IT'S ABOUT TIME, Inc. © 2000 MATHconx, LLC

NOTES

One way to work with basic measurements is to use a compass. If you have a segment to measure and a base unit of length, set the distance between the two points to match the unit. Then use the compass to mark off copies of the base length on the segment. Display 1.3 illustrates this method with a compass of the type drafters use. First the compass is set to match the unit. Then we put the point at *A* and use the pen to mark off one unit, at *B*. We repeat the process, starting at *B*, and keep on going until we run out of segment. This shows that it is somewhat more than four units from *A* to *C*.

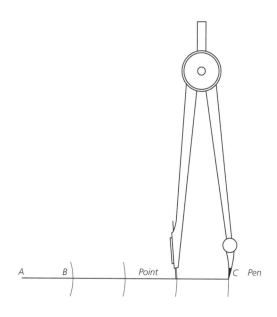

A　　B　　　　　　　Point　　　　　C　Pen

Display 1.3

1.11

Trace or copy the longer of the line segments in Display 1.4. Then measure it with a compass, using the shorter segment, the wobbit, as your unit length.

─────── The Wobbit, a Unit of Length

Display 1.4

12

Published by IT'S ABOUT TIME, Inc. © 2000 MATHconx, LLC

1.11

You may have to instruct some students about using a compass, if the type available in your school differs from the one described in the text. They should find that the longer segment is about 4.3 wobbits long.

Note that you should not skip this exercise. The wobbit unit is used again in these exercises and also later in the text.

NOTES

Chapter 1

Problem Set: 1.1

1. Find what looks like the shortest route from Miami, Florida to Oslo, Norway, on a flat map and also on a globe. Which of these routes passes closest to Nova Scotia? Which route is shorter?

2. In which ways is a globe *not* an accurate model of the Earth? Make a list. Which things on your list are also inaccuracies of flat maps?

3. Two campers get up in the morning and find that a bear has raided the food supply at their camp. They set out after the bear. They walk one mile south, then one mile east, then one mile north. At this point they find themselves right back at camp, where the bear is having lunch! What color is the bear?

4. (a) Measure the width and the height of a page from your notebook in wobbits. (Use a compass set to one wobbit.)
   (b) In centimeters, how long is a wobbit?
   (c) In wobbits, how long is a foot? (Measure a ruler using a compass set to one wobbit.)
   (d) In centimeters, how long is a foot? (Answer this by any method you choose.)
   (e) Which is longer, a 15 centimeter stick or a 15 inch stick?
   (f) If a stick is 10 wobbits long, is it more or less than 10 inches long? Is it more or less than 10 centimeters long?

Published by IT'S ABOUT TIME, Inc. © 2000 MATHconx, LLC

13

Problem Set: 1.1

1. On the map, a straight line route stays far to the southeast of Nova Scotia. On a globe, the shortest route gets very close to Nova Scotia.

2. You may need to prime the class on this one. Here are probably more leading questions than you will need.

   Is the water on the globe wet?
   Can you feel the Alps? Are they cold?
   Is the globe the same size as the Earth?
   Is there really a sign saying "Chicago" that is more than 200 miles long?

3. The bear is white; it's a polar bear. On a globe, there is exactly one point for which this south, then east, then north path takes you back to your starting point: the North Pole. The trap here, of course, is that we tend to think of the situation in terms of a flat map; that is, we think that making two right angle turns should put the campers a mile east of where they started.

4. The purpose of these questions is to improve students' intuitive sense of relative length and their ability to switch from thinking in terms of one unit length to thinking in terms of another without formal calculations.

   (a) Answers will vary, depending on the size of the notebooks.
   (b) Assuming no unexpected alteration when this book was printed, a wobbit is $2\frac{1}{4}$ cm long.
   (c) about $13\frac{1}{2}$ wobbits
   (d) about 30.5 cm
   (e) a 15 inch stick
   (f) It's less than 10 inches long, but more than 10 cm long.

NOTES

_____

_____

_____

_____

_____

_____

5. Time is a little harder to define and measure than length. You can't see a second.

   (a) List as many different units of time as you can. Relate each unit in your list to another one in your list. Example: 14 days = 1 fortnight.

   (b) Units of time are usually based on some repeated event, such as the motions of the Earth or Moon. A globe is usually built so that it can turn like the Earth.

      (i) How long does it take the Earth to rotate once on its axis?

      (ii) How long does it take the Earth to go around the Sun?

   (c) On Mars, the day length is very similar to that on Earth. It takes Mars 24.6 hours to rotate once on its axis. However, it takes Mars 687 days to go around the Sun. Calculate your age, to the nearest year, if you lived on Mars. Would you have more or fewer birthday parties on Mars than on Earth? Explain.

6. Sometimes people misuse the words *discrete* and *discreet*. When one of the authors told his mother he was teaching discrete mathematics, she thought that was very funny. Why was she laughing? A dictionary might help you.

7. Who was Euclid? Read about him in an encyclopedia or history book. Write a paragraph summarizing what you find out. Please be sure to write it in your own words. Using someone else's writing as if it were your own is *plagiarism*, a form of stealing.

Published by IT'S ABOUT TIME, Inc. © 2000 MATHconx, LLC

14

5. Time units are messier than length units.

   (a) Units of time include the second, minute, hour, day, week, fortnight, month, year, decade, century, and millennium. The month is unusual in being of varying length, and of course leap years are longer than regular years. The light-year is not a unit of time, but rather of distance; it is how far light travels in a year.

   (b) The Earth rotates on its axis once a day and goes around the Sun about once a year. These units are based on this motion. Unfortunately, the time to go around the Sun is not an integral number of days.

   (c) There are several ways to calculate a student's age on Mars. One way is illustrated by the following example. Say that a student was born on March 1, 1983 and today's date is October 1, 1997. The student is 14 years and 7 months old. Ignoring leap years and assuming 30 days per month we can calculate that the student has been alive for approximately

   $$14 \cdot 365 + 7 \cdot 30 = 5320 \text{ Earth days}$$

   Since Earth days are about the same length as Mars days, divide by 687 to get the student's age on Mars.

   $$\frac{5320}{687} = 7.7 \text{ Mars years}$$

   Thus, the student will have had only 7 birthday parties on Mars, compared with 14 birthday parties on Earth.

6. The word *discrete* is defined in the text; *discreet* suggests caution and prudence, especially as regards things that might be private, embarrassing, or even scandalous.

7. This writing exercise refers to the name of the school at the beginning of the section. Some students might know of a town called Euclid (there's one in Ohio), but not connect the name with a mathematician.

NOTES

1.2 Paths, Polygons, and Perimeter

Suppose you want to get to the principal's office. Chances are you cannot go there in a straight line because there are walls and furniture in the way. A single line segment is not a good model of your route. But you could probably chart a route made up of several line segments, as in Display 1.5.

Display 1.5

Display 1.5 shows a path that starts in a classroom at *A*, goes out into the hallway at *B*, down that hallway to *C*, where it turns left and goes to the entrance to the principal's office at *D*, and finally into that office at *E*. This is an example of a **polygonal path**, a sequence of line segments in which each is connected to the next by having an endpoint in common. The first segment (for example, *AB* in Display 1.5) has an endpoint (*B*) in common with the second segment (*BC*); the second segment has an endpoint (*C*) in common with the third segment (*CD*); and so on.

Some more examples of polygonal paths appear in Display 1.6. Notice that some segments may cross others, and that the last segment may connect to the first.

Do you think *all* the paths in Display 1.6 should be called *polygonal*? Why or why not?

1.12

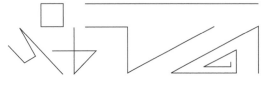

Display 1.6

Learning Outcomes

After studying this section, you will be able to:

Describe situations that can be modeled by polygonal paths;

Distinguish polygons from other planar shapes;

Use the standard names for polygons with 3 to 10 sides;

Write and use algebraic formulas for finding the perimeters of some polygons.

About Words

A *polygonal* path is a path with many knees. In ancient Greek, the prefix *poly-* means many, and the root *-gon* comes from the word for knee (or corner).

Published by IT'S ABOUT TIME, Inc. © 2000 MATHconx, LLC

15

1.2 Paths, Polygons, and Perimeter

This section reviews some ideas about polygons that most students probably saw in middle school, but may have forgotten. In addition, it shows how these basic geometric objects are used to model everyday situations. The latter part of the section contains some connections with algebraic formulas and functions.

1.12

This question is not profound, but there is a general point to be made about the way in which mathematical terms are defined. If polygonal means *many* corners, should it apply to a path with only two corners? Or only one? Or none? To avoid having to fuss about special cases, mathematicians refer to all of these cases as polygonal paths. It's a matter of convenient definition, rather than necessity. Just as collections containing no elements or only one are defined to be sets, so paths with only one or two corners or none at all are defined as polygonal paths. Thus, a segment is a polygonal path.

Chapter 1

Additional Support Materials:

Assessments	Qty
Form (A)	1
Form (B)	1

Blackline Masters	Qty

Extensions	Qty

Supplements	Qty
Paths, Polygons, and Perimeter	3

To find the length of a polygonal path, just measure each segment and add up the lengths. Polygonal paths are often used to model such things as driving distances between cities, railroad or airline routes, and many other time or distance relationships between things. For example, on the map of Display 1.7, the mileages and driving times between the cities are represented by polygonal paths. In such cases, the actual length of a segment on the map or diagram may not be directly related to the "length" it represents. In Display 1.7, the length in miles that a segment represents is the whole number (above it). Its length in driving time is the number below it, with hours and minutes separated by a colon. (The length of the segment between Des Moines, Iowa, and Hannibal, Missouri, is 271 miles, or 5 hours and 8 minutes.)

These questions refer to Display 1.7.

1.13

1. Find the shortest polygonal path between Kansas City and Texarkana. Calculate its length in distance and in time. What is unusual about two of the segments on this path?

2. If you want to go from Kansas City to Texarkana, but want to avoid Ft. Smith (for personal reasons), is it shorter to go by way of Springfield, Missouri, and Little Rock, Arkansas, or by way of Fort Scott, Tulsa and Atoka, Oklahoma? Is the shorter route in miles also the shorter route in time? Justify your answers.

3. Using the map as is, measure (in millimeters) the segments that make up the two polygonal paths of part 2. Which is the shorter path? How does this answer compare with your answers to part 2?

You can think of a polygonal path as a trip with some turns along the way. Often, when we travel, we want to make a round trip, to come back to where we started. If the polygonal path describes a round trip that doesn't visit any place twice along the way, then it is a *polygon*. In other words, a **polygon** is a polygonal path that starts and ends at the same place and doesn't cross over itself anywhere in between. In Display 1.7, for instance, the polygonal path that describes the trip from Lincoln to Sioux City to Dubuque to Des Moines to Omaha to Lincoln is a polygon.

Published by IT'S ABOUT TIME, Inc. © 2000 MATHconx, LLC

1.13

These questions reinforce some routine map reading skills while also implicitly making the point that a good geometric model does not have to be an accurate scale drawing of a situation.

1. This path, which goes through Ft. Scott and Ft. Smith, is 501 miles long. Its total driving time is 10 hours and 28 minutes. The segment between Ft. Scott and Ft. Smith is 50 miles longer than the segment between Ft. Smith and Texarkana, but they both show exactly the same driving time!

2. Let *KSLX* represent the route through Springfield and Little Rock, and let *KFTAX* represent the route through Ft. Scott, Tulsa, and Atoka. *KSLX* is 21 miles shorter than *KFTAX* (532 vs. 553). Its driving time is 7 minutes shorter (10:53 vs. 11:00).

3. We specify millimeters because that is the most accurate of the standard ruler subdivisions. The sum for *KSLX* is about 4 mm shorter than the sum for *KFTAX*. Thus, the actual lengths of the segments match the mileage data fairly well, but don't match the time data well at all. If you want to push your students for a more refined answer, look at the percentage of difference, relative to the length of route *KSLX*. The real mileage difference is only about 4%, but the difference in the sums of the segments is about 6%.

NOTES

Chapter I

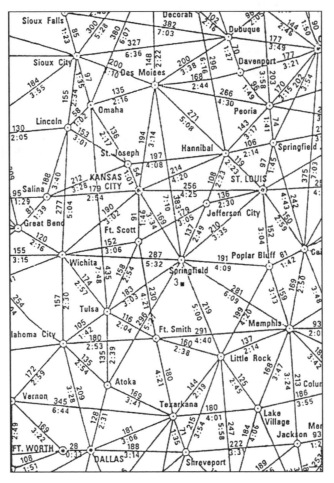

Display 1.7

17

Chapter 1

NOTES

1.14

Which of the figures in Display 1.8 are polygons? Justify your answers.

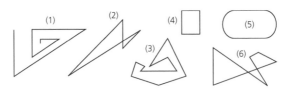

Display 1.8

The segments that make up a polygon are usually called its *sides*. It is hard to tell from a picture of a polygon which is the beginning side (segment) and which is the ending one. The good news is that it doesn't usually matter.

Mathematicians and scientists (and other people, too) like to *classify* things. That is, they like to separate things into groups whose members share some common property. This often makes it easier to deal with a whole collection of things all at once. Polygons are classified in a variety of ways. One way is to classify them by the number of sides they have. Display 1.9 lists the standard names of polygons of three to ten sides.

No. of Sides	Name of Figure	Root of Name
3	triangle	Greek: *tria* = three
4	quadrilateral	Latin: *quattuor* = four
5	pentagon	Greek: *pente* = five
6	hexagon	Greek: *hex* = six
7	heptagon	Greek: *hepta* = seven
8	octagon	Greek: *okto* = eight
9	nonagon	Latin: *nonus* = nine
10	decagon	Greek: *deka* = ten

Display 1.9

The table in Display 1.9 explains only the first part of each word. As for the second part.
* tri*angle*: three *corners*
* quadri*lateral*: four *sides* (In football, a *lateral* is a "sideways" pass.)
* penta*gon*: five *corners* (literally, five *knees*)

Published by IT'S ABOUT TIME, Inc. © 2000 MATHconx, LLC

1.2 Paths, Polygons, and Perimeter

Only (3) and (4) are polygons. Path (1) doesn't begin and end in the same place, (2) and (6) cross over themselves, and (5) is not a polygonal path at all.

1.14

NOTES

Label each of the polygons in Display 1.10 with one of the names in the table of Display 1.9.

a
1.15

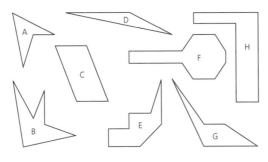

Display 1.10

The distance around a polygon—its length as a polygonal path—is called its **perimeter**. The perimeter of a polygon is the sum of its sides.

In some cases, this tedious addition process can be replaced by multiplication. For instance, if all the sides of a polygon are the same length, its perimeter is just the product of the length of any one side times the number of sides. Such polygons are called *equilateral*. In symbols, the perimeter, *P*, of an equilateral polygon with *n* sides, each of length *s*, is

$$P = n \cdot s$$

1. An equilateral decagon has a side 7 cm long. How long is its perimeter?

b
1.16

2. What is a simpler name for an equilateral quadrilateral? Write a formula using multiplication to find the perimeter of such a figure. Be sure to state the meaning of any letter you use.

3. Rectangles are quadrilaterals that have two pairs of equal sides. Write an efficient formula for finding the perimeter of such a figure. (Be sure to state the meanings of the letters.) Use your formula to find the perimeter of a 12 foot by 17 foot rectangle.

4. Some hexagons have three pairs of equal opposite sides. Write a formula for finding the perimeter of such a figure. (State the meanings of any letters you use.)

About Words

The Greek prefix *peri-* means around. A *periscope* is a tool for looking around. The *perimeter* of a figure is the measurement around it.

Published by IT'S ABOUT TIME, Inc. © 2000 MATHconx, LLC

1.2 Paths, Polygons, and Perimeter

19

1.15

This exercise is completely straightforward. Its purpose is to get students to focus on the polygon names in Display 1.9 and also on the fact that these names depend solely on the number of sides. We tend to think of pentagons, hexagons, etc., as nicely shaped figures, but that's by no means always the case. A—quadrilateral; B—hexagon; C—quadrilateral; D—triangle; E—octagon; F—decagon; G—pentagon; H—hexagon.

1.16

These questions combine finding perimeters of equilateral polygons with some exercises in writing (and hence understanding) simple algebra. Although the ideas are quite easy, some students may have trouble expressing them with formulas. Make sure that your students state clearly the meanings of any symbols in the formulas they write. We use P for perimeter in all these answers.

1. $7 \cdot 10 = 70$ cm

2. A square. If s is the length of one side of a square, then $P = 4s$.

3. It is customary (but not essential) to represent the two side lengths as l (length) and w (width). Then $P = 2l + 2w$ or $P = 2(l + w)$.
   The perimeter of the given rectangle is $2 \cdot 12 + 2 \cdot 17 = 2 \cdot 29 = 58$.

4. This is analogous to part 3. If the three side lengths are denoted by a, b, and c, then $P = 2a + 2b + 2c$ or $P = 2(a + b + c)$.

5. Yes, this house really exists; it's on the corner of High and Perham Sts. The perimeter is $8 \cdot 25 = 200$ bricks $= 1600$ inches $= 133\frac{1}{3}$ feet.

NOTES

....

....

....

....

....

....

....

....

5. The "footprint" (the shape of the base) of an historic brick house in Farmington, Maine, is an equilateral octagon. Each side is 25 bricks long. A standard brick is 8 inches long. In feet, what is the perimeter of the footprint of this house?

Here are some customs that make writing and speaking about polygonal paths more efficient.

- The endpoints of the segments in a polygonal path are called its **vertices**. (A single one is called a **vertex**.) If you are walking along a polygonal path, a vertex is a point where you change direction. We usually label vertices with capital letters—*A*, *B*, *C*, etc.—in order along the path. (See Display 1.11.)

- With the possible exception of the endpoints of the path, a vertex is also a place where the endpoints of two segments are joined together. Any time two segments have an endpoint in common, they form an **angle**. The angle is named by the three endpoints of the segments, with the letter of the common endpoint in the middle. For instance, in Display 1.11, the angle at *B* can be called either ∠*ABC* (angle *ABC*) or ∠*CBA* (angle *CBA*).

1.17

1. Sketch a copy of the path in Display 1.11 and finish labeling its vertices in order.

2. List all the angles along this path, using the three-letter notation just described.

3. Which of the following are not angles of this path? Justify your answers.

  ∠*DCB*   ∠*BDC*   ∠*DEF*   ∠*DFE*   ∠*GFE*

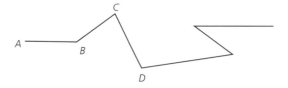

Display 1.11

1.17

1. The only thing to watch for here is that students label the remaining three vertices in the order *of the path*, not in left to right reading order. That is, the final segment of this path should be *FG*, not *EG*. Correct ordering here determines some of the answers to parts 2 and 3.

2. ∠*ABC*, ∠*BCD*, ∠*CDE*, ∠*DEF*, ∠*EFG*. These triples of letters in reverse order are also correct.

3. ∠*BDC* is not an angle of this path because *D* is not between *B* and *C* along the path. *BD* is not a segment of the path. Similarly, ∠*DFE* is not an angle of this path. The other three are.

Chapter 1

NOTES

Problem Set: 1.2

1. This problem refers to the driving map of Display 1.7. You are planning a trip from your home in St. Louis to see the Dallas Cowboys play a home football game.

   (a) Find the shortest route in miles from St. Louis to Dallas. (List the cities at the vertices of your path.) How long is it?

   (b) Find the shortest route in hours and minutes from St. Louis to Dallas. Does your answer agree with part (a)? How long is it?

   (c) On your way home from Dallas, you want to visit a friend in Wichita, Kansas. Plan the most efficient way to make this return trip. (List the cities at the vertices of your path.) How long is it in miles and in driving time?

   (d) Your round trip is represented on the map by a polygon. What type of polygon is it? (See the list of Display 1.9.) Is the real driving route a polygon? Why or why not?

   (e) According to the map, what should be your average driving speed (in mph) for the trip down to Dallas? For the return trip to St. Louis? For the round trip? Round your answers to one decimal place. Be prepared to justify your answers.

   (f) On which half of the trip do you think there are more Interstate highways? Why? (See part (e).)

2. One of the polygon types listed in Display 1.9 has the same name as a famous building.

   (a) Which one is it?
   (b) Who works in the famous building?
   (c) Where is the famous building located?
   (d) How did it get its name?

3. Label each polygon in Display 1.12 with an appropriate name from the list in Display 1.9.

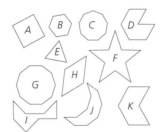

Display 1.12

Published by IT'S ABOUT TIME, Inc. © 2000 MATHconx, LLC

21

Chapter I

Problem Set: 1.2

1. (a) St. Louis to Springfield (MO) to Atoka (OK) to Dallas 634 miles.
   (b) The same route; 11 hours, 33 minutes.
   (c) Dallas to Oklahoma City to Wichita to Kansas City to St. Louis; 812 miles; 13 hours, 25 minutes.
   (d) It is a heptagon (a 7-sided polygon). The real route is not a polygon because the roads between the cities are not straight line segments.
   (e) This part will require students to convert minutes into fractions of an hour, a likely source of error. Down: 54.9 mph; back: 60.52 mph; round trip: 57.92 mph.
   (f) There must be more Interstate highways on the return trip because the expected average speed is almost 61 mph, much higher than the average speed for the way down.

2. (a) The Pentagon.
   (b) The Joint Chiefs of Staff and other high ranking military people. The Department of Defense is headquartered here.
   (c) This particular pentagon is in Arlington, VA, near Washington, DC.
   (d) The building is shaped like a geometric pentagon.

3. Triangle: E; quadrilaterals: A, H; hexagons: B, K; heptagon: D; octagon: I; nonagon: C; decagons F, G, J.

NOTES

4. Four of the names in Display 1.9 are related to the names of months.

   (a) Which polygons go with which months?
   (b) Do the names make sense in terms of the numerical meanings of the root words? Explain.

5. Amanda Leport, an architect, is making designs for windows above doorways. She is considering two different designs, shown as polygons (1) and (2) in Display 1.13. In both designs, the base segment must be 34 inches, which is the width of the doorway.

   (a) In design (1), she is experimenting with the length of the short sides, all of which are equal in length. If each short side is 12 inches, what is the perimeter of the window?
   (b) Write a formula for the perimeter in inches of design (1) if each short side is s inches.
   (c) For design (2), she tries to get a sense of balance by choosing the perimeter first and then calculating the lengths of the short sides, all of which are equal in length. If the perimeter is to be $2\frac{1}{2}$ times the length of the base, what is the length of each short side?

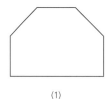

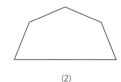

(1) (2)

Display 1.13

Published by IT'S ABOUT TIME, Inc. © 2000 MATHconx, LLC

4. This problem can be used as a link to an ancient history course. If you are at a school where Latin is taught, you can connect it with that subject, too.

   (a) The easy ones are October, November and December. Once you notice those, September seems to fit in, even though the first letter does not match with heptagon.

   (b) The names make sense in that they come in the correct numerical order, but it seems strange that the ninth, tenth, eleventh, and twelfth months should have names related to the numbers seven, eight, nine, and ten. The reason for this is that the Roman calendar had ten months before the Caesars took over. Then they decided to create two new months to honor Julius and Augustus Caesar. You can guess which months these were. The subsequent months were pushed further along to make room for them.

5. This problem combines perimeter calculations with elementary algebra and the idea of a function and its inverse. The numerical parts should help students see patterns in the algebraic parts.

   (a) $5 \cdot 12 + 34 = 94$ inches

   (b) $P = 5s + 34$

   (c) $1\frac{1}{2}$ times the base must be equally divided among the other four sides, so each short side is $\frac{51}{4} = 12.75$ inches.

   (d) In this case, if students can't see how to get the formula first, have them try to find the answer for the particular case of 90 inches, then develop the formula by substituting P for 90 in their calculations, like this: $\frac{90 - 34}{4} = 14$ inches is the length of one short side in this particular case, so $s(P) = \frac{P - 34}{4}$.

NOTES

Published by IT'S ABOUT TIME, Inc. © 2000 MATHconx, LLC

(d) The result of part (c) doesn't look quite right. In order to try different perimeters, she writes a formula for the length *s* of each short side of design (2) as a function of its perimeter, *P*. What is the formula? Try it out by finding the side length for a perimeter of 90 inches.

6. Trace or sketch each polygon in Display 1.14 and label its vertices, starting wherever you like. Then make a list of all the vertices, sides, and angles. Do you think that everyone will label the figures in the same way? Do you think that everyone will get the same list of parts? Check with some of your classmates to see if your answers agree.

(a)

(b)

(c)

Display 1.14

Published by IT'S ABOUT TIME, Inc. © 2000 MATHconx, LLC

23

6. It doesn't matter where the students start naming the vertices, as long as they use the same letters and go in order around the figure in either direction. The lists of vertices, sides, and angles will all come out the same, except for the possible reversals of side segment endpoints or the outer endpoints of angle segments. That is, you should not be able to tell from the lists which students started labeling at which vertex.

(a) vertices: A, B, C, D
   sides: AB, BC, CD, DA
   angles: ∠ABC, ∠BCD, ∠CDA, ∠DAB

(b) vertices: A, B, C, D, E, F
   sides: AB, BC, CD, DE, EF, FA
   angles: ∠ABC, ∠BCD, ∠CDE, ∠DEF, ∠EFA, ∠FAB

(c) vertices: A, B, C, D, E, F, G
   sides: AB, BC, CD, DE, EF, FG, GA
   angles: ∠ABC, ∠BCD, ∠CDE, ∠DEF, ∠EFG, ∠FGA, ∠GAB

NOTES

1.3 Symmetry

Learning Outcomes

After studying this section, you will be able to:

Identify symmetry about a line;

Identify an equilateral triangle by symmetry;

Construct the perpendicular bisector of a given line segment;

Find the shortest path from a point to a line.

Symmetry is a fundamental idea of nature, art, and science. There are many kinds of symmetry. The kind you are going to study in this section is symmetry about a line. The idea is that if you take the part of the figure that lies on one side of the line and fold it over to the other side, you want it to match the other half of the figure exactly. We might also call this "inkblot symmetry." Think about putting a drop of ink or finger paint on a piece of paper and folding the paper along a line through the drop. If you squish the folded paper down, and then open it, you will get a blot that is symmetric about the line of the fold, as in Display 1.15.

Display 1.15

The line of the fold is called the **line of symmetry** or **axis of symmetry**. This line divides the figure in half, so that the half on one side of the axis is a "mirror image" of the half on the other side. Sometimes you can find an axis of symmetry of a figure by tracing it onto a piece of paper. Then use trial and error to see if you can find a way to fold it so the two halves line up. If you succeed, the crease in the paper where you folded it will be the axis of symmetry.

24

1.3 Symmetry

This section deals with symmetry about a line, sometimes known as reflection symmetry. Understanding symmetry requires both imagination and spatial visualization skills. To check a plane figure for this kind of symmetry, you have to imagine "flipping it over" (rotating it 180° around the line) and visualize what the outcome will be. Learning to do this is much more important than learning the names of various special polygons. For many students it is a difficult process that is not learned instantly.

No amount of words will substitute for physical and dynamic experience with symmetry. Early on, engage your students in discussion to estimate their current ability at spotting symmetries. If they are having difficulty, try to provide lots of experience by using tools such as

- Miras, mirrors or other aids to seeing symmetries as reflections,

- patty paper or other see through foldable paper that students can fold along a suspected line of symmetry and actually see how the two halves line up, and

- overhead transparencies, often in identical pairs, that you can flip over right before their eyes.

Additional Support Materials:

Assessments	Qty
Form (A)	1
Form (B)	1

Blackline Masters	Qty

Extensions	Qty

Supplements	Qty
Symmetry	4

For each of the four drawings in Display 1.16:

1.18

1. Find all axes of symmetry of its outline (its shape as if it were just a shadow).

2. Find all axes of symmetry of the drawing itself. For any drawing that is *almost* symmetric, say what keeps it from being exactly symmetric.

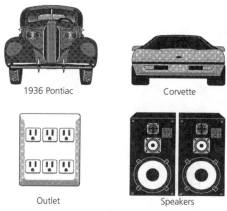

1936 Pontiac   Corvette

Outlet   Speakers

Display 1.16

Display 1.17 shows two boxplots.

1.19

1. Is either one symmetric about the horizontal line through its whiskers? Are they both?

2. Is either one symmetric about the vertical line through its median? Are they both?

3. What (if anything) can you say about the distribution of data if its boxplot is symmetric about its median line?

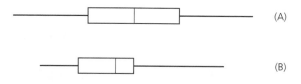

(A)

(B)

Display 1.17

25

This is an exercise in visualization, to help you judge how well your students see symmetry about a line.

1. All four outlines have a vertical axis of symmetry. In addition, the outline of the outlet box has a horizontal axis of symmetry.

2. The Corvette is the only one of the actual pictures that has an axis of symmetry. It is symmetric about a vertical line.

   The steering wheel prevents the 1936 Pontiac from being perfectly symmetric about its vertical axis.

   The outlet box has a vertical axis of symmetry except for the fact that the two vertical slots in each of the six outlets are not the same size.

   Considered as a pair, the speakers are symmetric except for the square grid in the upper right of each speaker. Considered separately, the grid is still exceptional, as is the perspective representation of the top of the speaker box.

These departures from symmetry are large enough that your students should be able to see them. At the same time, all the pictures do have a high degree of symmetry; students who find them symmetric should feel mostly right, rather than wrong.

These two boxplots are quite different from each other.

1. *All* boxplots are symmetric about the horizontal line through the whiskers.

2. Boxplot (A) symmetric about its median line; boxplot (B) is not.

3. Not much. A symmetric distribution would give rise to a symmetric boxplot, but other distributions can do so, as well. All that is required is that the following pairs be equidistant from the median: the first and third quartiles, and the maximum and minimum data values.

NOTES

....

....

....

....

Many geometric figures have axes of symmetry. Display 1.18 shows three copies of a triangle, $\triangle ABC$, with its three axes of symmetry marked.

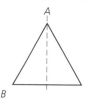
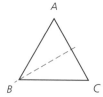

Display 1.18

a
1.20

Trace the first copy of $\triangle ABC$ onto a piece of paper. Fold it along its line of symmetry through vertex *A*. What do you notice about sides *AB* and *AC*?

When you can put a copy of one segment on top of another so that the two match exactly, we say the two segments are **congruent**. In particular, the endpoints of the two segments must match up, so the two segments must have the same length. In fact, two segments are congruent *whenever* their lengths are equal.

b
1.21

These questions refer to Display 1.18.

1. What does the axis of symmetry through vertex *C* tell you about the sides?

2. What does the axis of symmetry through vertex *B* tell you about the sides?

3. What special property of $\triangle ABC$ follows from your answers to questions 1 and 2?

Display 1.18 also illustrates some other important ideas.

c
1.22

Look again at your copy of $\triangle ABC$ that you folded along the line of symmetry through *A*. Label the point where the fold intersects *BC* as *M*. What can you say about the lengths of *MB* and *MC*? Why?

The **midpoint** of a segment is a point of the segment that is the same distance from each end. You can find it by measuring or by folding, as you just did. (Point *M* is the midpoint of *BC*.)

26

Published by IT'S ABOUT TIME, Inc. © 2000 MATHconx, LLC

1.20

Sides *AB* and *AC* match up perfectly, so they have the same length.

1.21

This set of observations is setting up a general approach to regular polygons by means of axes of symmetry.

1. Sides *AC* and *BC* are congruent, so they must have the same length.

2. Sides *AB* and *BC* are congruent, so they must have the same length.

3. Triangle *ABC* (in fact, any triangle with three axes of symmetry) must have all its sides congruent and hence all the same length. This means that $\triangle ABC$ is an equilateral triangle.

MB and *MC* are congruent (they match up exactly), so their lengths are equal.

1.22

NOTES

_____

You can also find the midpoint of a line segment with an unmarked straightedge and a compass. This is a particularly accurate method. A procedure for creating a geometric object with straightedge and compass is called a **geometric construction**. Work through the following steps to see how this midpoint construction works.

- Take out a piece of paper. Draw a line segment on it, somewhere near the middle, and label its endpoints *A* and *B*. Its exact length is not important, but make it a convenient size to work with. Somewhere between 2 and 4 inches will work pretty well.

- Set your compass to a distance that is longer than half the length of *AB*. Setting it to the full length of *AB* will work, but is not necessary. Use that setting to draw two arcs, one centered at each endpoint. Be sure to keep the same compass setting for both arcs. Draw enough of each arc so that they intersect above and below *AB*, as in Display 1.19(a).

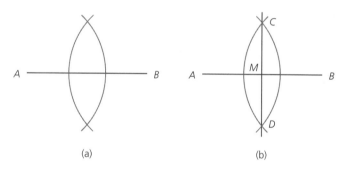

(a)   (b)

Display 1.19

- Label the two points where the arcs intersect *C* and *D*. Draw line *CD*. Line *CD* intersects *AB* at its midpoint, *M*. Your completed constructions should look like Display 1.19(b). Check– Does *AM* = *MB*? It should.

> **On your diagram, choose a point *P* somewhere along *CD*. Draw *AP* and *BP*. Now fold your diagram along *CD*.**
>
> **1. What do you observe about segments *MA* and *MB*?** 1.23
>
> **2. What do you observe about ∠*AMC* and ∠*AMD*?**

1.23

Encourage your students to do the actual folding, rather than just look at the diagram. Most people learn far more effectively from the combination of observation and kinesthetic activity than from observation alone.

1. Segments *MA* and *MB* coincide when the paper is folded, so they are congruent.

2. ∠*AMC* and ∠*AMD* coincide when the paper is folded. They are also congruent. We haven't formally defined *congruent angles* yet, but it means the obvious thing. If your students automatically use that terminology in this case, that's fine. However, *coincide* or some equivalent expression is good enough.

NOTES

3. **What do you observe about segments *PA* and *PB*? Explain why your observation would be true, no matter where along *CD* you chose *P*.**

4. **Rephrase your answer to part 3 as a statement about all points of the line *CD*.**

About Words

The prefix *bi-* means two. The rest of *bisector* comes from the same root as *section*. A section is a piece of something. To *bisect* means to cut into two equal pieces.

The folding exercise you just did illustrates that the line *CD* is an axis of symmetry for the segment *AB*—in fact, for the entire diagram in Display 1.19(b). It is called the **perpendicular bisector** of *AB*. This means that *CD* intersects *AB* at right angles and cuts it into two equal parts.

When two intersecting lines form matching angles next to each other, the angles are called **right angles**. Lines that form right angles are said to be **perpendicular**. Part 2 asks you to notice that ∠*AMC* and ∠*AMD* are right angles; they coincide when the diagram is folded along *CD*. Your answer to part 4 is an important property of perpendicular bisectors. (What was it?)

A perpendicular bisector can be used to construct the shortest path from a point to a line, usually called "dropping a perpendicular" from a point to a line. To see where this name comes from, look at Display 1.20(a). Think of line *L* as floor level. From point *P* above it, you want the shortest path to *L*. Imagine holding a weighted string at *P* (like a surveyor's plumb line) so that the bottom of it just touches the floor. That's the perpendicular path from *P* to *L*, but is it the shortest? Yes! Just think of swinging the weighted string back and forth like a pendulum, as in Display 1.20(b). The string touches the floor *only* at the perpendicular ("straight down"); any other path from *P* to *L* would have to use more string. That is, the perpendicular distance is the shortest distance from *P* to *L*.

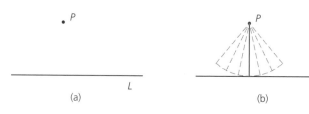

(a)

(b)

Display 1.20

Published by IT'S ABOUT TIME, Inc. © 2000 MATHconx, LLC

3. Segments *PA* and *PB* coincide when the paper is folded, so they are congruent. Since points *A* and *B* coincide when the paper is folded along *CD*, a segment drawn to *A* from *any* point along *CD* also will coincide with a segment drawn to *B* from that point.

4. This is an important conclusion for students to reach and understand. Every point on *CD* is equidistant from *A* and *B*, the endpoints of the original segment.

NOTES

The geometric construction of a perpendicular from a point to a line is an easy extension of the perpendicular bisector process. Look at Display 1.20(a) again. If P were the same distance away from two points, say A and B, on L, then the line of symmetry that matches segments PA and PB would have to be the perpendicular bisector of AB. Can you justify this statement? We'll ask you again in the problem set. So the problem is solved if we can find two points on L that are the same distance away from P.

Thinking Tip

Work backwards.
Sometimes it helps to think about a problem by working backwards from what you want to what you have.

1. Draw a copy of Display 1.20(a). Then use a compass to locate two points on L that are the same distance away from P. Label them A and B.

1.24

2. Now finish constructing the perpendicular from P to L.

Problem Set: 1.3

1. The figure in Display 1.21 is called a **pentagram**. It was a special symbol of the Pythagoreans in ancient Greece. Its outline is the familiar five pointed star that appears on the flag of the United States.

   (a) Draw a careful copy of this figure as a polygonal path without lifting your pencil from the paper. How many line segments are in your path?

   (b) Is the pentagram a polygon? If so, how many sides does it have? If not, why not?

   (c) Is the outline of the pentagram a polygon? If so, how many sides does it have? If not, why not?

   (d) How many axes of symmetry does the pentagram have? Draw them all on your copy of this figure.

   (e) How is a pentagram related to a pentagon?

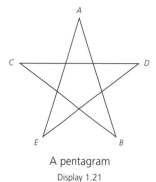

A pentagram
Display 1.21

1.24

The two parts of this construction are illustrated in Display 1.1T.

1. A compass set to any length larger than the perpendicular distance from P to L will make an arc that intersects L in two places, A and B.

2. This part is straight mimicry of the perpendicular bisector construction described in the student book.

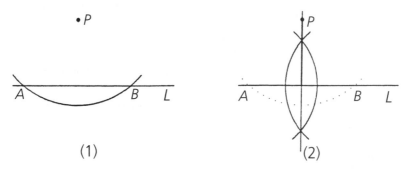

Display 1.1T

Problem Set: 1.3

1. (a) This can be drawn as a polygonal path of five segments, just by connecting the lettered vertices in order.
   (b) It is not a polygon. Even if you draw it as a polygonal path with many segments that don't actually cross each other, there will be vertices joining more than two endpoints, which is not allowable by the definition of a polygon.
   (c) Yes, its outline is a decagon (a ten-sided polygon).
   (d) It has five axes of symmetry, one through each vertex.
   (e) It is not itself a pentagon, but the shape inside it is a pentagon.

NOTES

2. The figure in Display 1.22 is called a **hexagram**. It is a traditional symbol of Judaism, called "the Star of David." A form of this figure appears on the flag of the Republic of Israel.

   (a) Is this figure a polygonal path with six sides? Is it a polygonal path at all? (That is, can it be drawn completely without lifting your pencil from the paper?)

   (b) Is the hexagram a polygon? If so, how many sides does it have? If not, why not?

   (c) Is the outline of the hexagram a polygon? If so, how many sides does it have? If not, why not?

   (d) Describe all axes of symmetry for this figure.

   (e) How is a hexagram related to a hexagon?

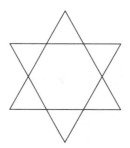

A hexagram

Display 1.22

3. Symmetry is important in decorative designs. Find all axes of symmetry for the designs in Display 1.23.

Display 1.23

2. The hexagram is a good tool for exploring how your students process geometric diagrams. For example, it could be looked at as two equilateral triangles, in which case there are six different sides, or as a hexagon with six triangular hats, in which case it has 18 different sides. You might poll the class on how many line segments make up this figure. Encourage students to find as many different ways of looking at it as possible. There is no right way; the goal is to learn to see more than one way.

(a) Whether or not this figure is a polygonal path depends on some particular way of dividing it up into sides. If you think of the hexagram as two overlapping triangles, then it is not a polygonal path. If you try to lay out an easy, six-sided path as we did for the pentagram, you will find yourself restricted to just one of the two triangles, with no way to get to the other one. Thus, it is not a polygonal path *with six sides*. However, it *is* possible to draw it as a single polygonal path if you think of it as having a vertex at each crossing point and 18 separate segments.

(b) It is not a polygon. See the corresponding part of the pentagram problem.

(c) Its outline is a 12-sided polygon.

(d) The hexagram has six axes of symmetry. Three of them go through pairs of opposite peaks of the perimeter; the other three go through pairs of opposite valleys.

(e) It is not itself a hexagon, but the shape inside it is a hexagon.

3. Left to right in the top row of Display 1.23, the first design has four axes of symmetry (like a square), the second has a vertical axis of symmetry, and the last has two axes of symmetry (like a rectangle). In the second row, the first has no axes of symmetry, the second has two (like a rectangle), and the third has a vertical axis of symmetry.

NOTES

4. Many letters of the alphabet are symmetric, although the details depend on the particular font. Display 1.24 shows the letters of a popular sans-serif font. Find all axes of symmetry for each letter.

ABCDEFGHI
JKLMNOPQR
STUVWXYZ

Display 1.24

5. The set of symbols in Display 1.25 is actually a typesetting font called "Zapf Dingbats" (a registered trademark of International Typeface Corporation). For each symbol, say *how many axes* of symmetry it has.

Display 1.25

6. (a) Justify the claim that *any* axis of symmetry of *any* triangle must pass through a vertex of that triangle.

   (b) Is it possible for a triangle to have two axes of symmetry, but not three? Justify your answer.

7. Justify this statement:

   If a point P not on a line L is the same distance away from two points on L, say A and B, then the line of symmetry that matches segments PA and PB must be the perpendicular bisector of AB.

Published by IT'S ABOUT TIME, Inc. © 2000 MATHconx, LLC

31

Chapter 1

4. This font exercise and the next may appeal to your more artistic or literary students. The fonts shown here are standard PostScript fonts used with Macs, Windows, and OS/2. If you have access to a PostScript printer, you can print out large versions of individual letters from these fonts (and others, if you want) and make transparencies for classroom discussion. The plainest fonts generally have the most symmetry. The font in Display 1.24 is Helvetica, a registered trademark of Linotype-Hell AG.

In Helvetica, A, H, I, M, O, T, U, V, W, X, and Y have symmetry about a vertical axis. D, E, H, I, O, and X have symmetry about a horizontal axis.

5. Here are the numbers of axes of symmetry for each symbol, row by row.

4, 4, 4, 4, 4, 4, 6, 6, 1
8, 8, 0, 6, 8, 8, 12, 16, 0
8, 3, 4, infinitely many, 4, 2, 4, 4, 0
0, 1, 1, 1, 3, 4, 1, 4, 0
0, 0, 4, 1, 4, 3, 4, 1, 1

6. (a) If a line passes through a triangle and does not go through a vertex, then two vertices of the triangle must be on one side of the line and one vertex must be on the other. Thus, the two sides of the line cannot be mirror images of each other, so the line is not an axis of symmetry.
   (b) No. By part (a), an axis of symmetry must pass through a vertex. As we saw in the work related to Display 1.18, the sides on each side of that vertex must be congruent. If there are two axes of symmetry, one of the sides in each case must be the same, since there are only three sides in all. Therefore, all three sides are congruent, so the triangle is equilateral. This means that it has a third axis of symmetry.

7. This line of symmetry must cross L somewhere. Call that crossing point Q. Then, folding over on the line of symmetry makes QA and QB coincide because A and B coincide and Q is on the edge of the fold. Thus, QA is congruent to QB, so Q is the midpoint of AB. Also, $\angle AQP$ and $\angle BQP$ coincide, so they must be right angles. This means that the line of symmetry (the fold line) is the perpendicular bisector of AB.

Published by IT'S ABOUT TIME, Inc. © 2000 MATHconx, LLC

1.4 Regular Polygons

Learning Outcomes

Learning Outcomes

After studying this section, you will be able to:

Identify congruent angles;

Classify quadrilaterals as squares, rectangles, parallelograms, and rhombi;

Identify regular polygons;

Show by example that the converse of a true statement need not be true.

In this section, we will apply the idea of symmetry to polygons. In particular, we shall study a special kind of polygon called a *regular polygon*. We could define a **regular polygon** as a polygon with as much symmetry as possible. This definition comes close to explaining the reasons why these polygons are important in the first place. However, it is a little hard to apply. How do we know when we have as much symmetry as possible? For that reason, you will also see how to describe regular polygons in terms of their sides and angles.

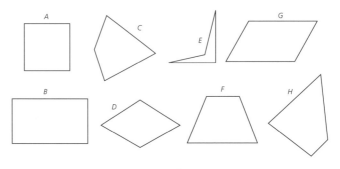

Some quadrilaterals

Display 1.26

Some quadrilaterals appear in Display 1.26.

1. Why are these figures called *quadrilaterals*?

2. How many axes of symmetry does each quadrilateral have?

3. Choose the quadrilateral you think has the *most* symmetry. How are the sides of your chosen quadrilateral related? Which of the other quadrilaterals also have this property?

4. How are the angles of your chosen quadrilateral related? Which of the other quadrilaterals also have this property?

Published by IT'S ABOUT TIME, Inc. © 2000 MATHconx, LLC

32

1.4 Regular Polygons

This section is an exercise in self restraint for you, the teacher. You need to avoid rushing to characterize regular polygons in terms of the measures of the sides and angles. While this is a handy way to identify them, it fails to get to the heart of what makes these polygons special — their symmetry. So, the purpose of the section is to continue to develop a sense of symmetry in the students and to let them come up with their own characterization of regular polygons—both in terms of symmetry and in terms of what we can measure.

This exercise is a first attempt at quantifying symmetry.

1.25

1. The figures are called quadrilaterals because they have four sides. There is nothing profound here; it's just a reminder.

2. The square (*A*) has four axes of symmetry; the rhombus (*D*) and the rectangle (*B*) each have two; and the kite (*C*), the boomerang (*E*), and the trapezoid (*F*) each have one.

3. The square has the most symmetry in the sense of being symmetric about more axes. The square has all its sides congruent; so does the rhombus.

4. The square has all of its angles congruent; so does the rectangle.

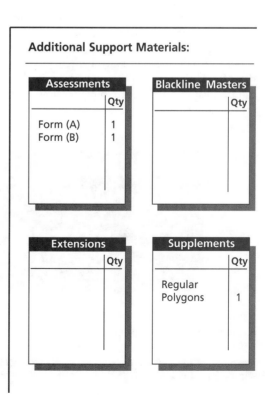

Additional Support Materials:

Assessments	Qty
Form (A)	1
Form (B)	1

Blackline Masters	Qty

Extensions	Qty

Supplements	Qty
Regular Polygons	1

Symmetry isn't just nice to look at —it's practical. Once you have made a design for one side of an automobile grille or a bicycle helmet, it's easy to do the other side if you have symmetry. A symmetric load on a big truck is less likely to cause the truck to tip over on a sharp corner. If you want to fence in a polygonal area, a regular polygon will give you the largest enclosed area for the least amount of fencing. We begin our study of polygons with lots of symmetry by reviewing what we know about symmetries of the fewest-sided polygons of all—triangles.

In the previous section, we looked at the symmetries of an equilateral triangle. See Display 1.18 to refresh your memory, if you want. We found that a triangle with three axes of symmetry has all its sides congruent. Of course, if the sides match up when the triangle is flipped over, then so do the angles formed by those sides. Thus, a triangle with three axes of symmetry must have all its *angles* congruent, too.

We need to be a little careful about what we mean by angles being congruent. A polygonal path is made up of segments and angles that are interrelated. If you take away the segments, the angles disappear too! An angle is not so much an object, like a segment, as a relationship between two objects. An angle is the way in which two segments come together. When we talk about congruent angles, we are saying that certain segments come together in the same way. In other words, two angles are congruent if one can be placed on the other so that their corners match up, regardless of the lengths of the segments that form them. Here is another way to think about it: If you start with any angle, you can cut the sides off shorter and they will still come together in the same angle. You can do this over and over. No matter how short the sides may get, the angle remains unchanged.

33

NOTES

a

1.26

1. In Display 1.27, all but one of the *angles* are congruent. Which angle is *not* congruent to the others?

2. In Display 1.27, three of the *polygonal paths* are congruent to each other. None of the others are congruent. Which are the three congruent paths?

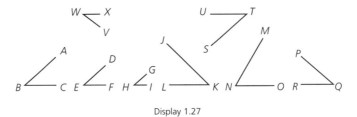

Display 1.27

You have seen that a triangle with all of its sides congruent also has all of its angles congruent, and vice versa. A triangle with all of its angles congruent has all of its sides congruent. Four-sided polygons are not so simple. A quadrilateral with all its sides congruent (and therefore all the same length) is called a **rhombus**. If you have more than one, they are called **rhombi**.

b

1.27

Find all the axes of symmetry of the rhombus in Display 1.28. Are any of the angles congruent to one another? Are *all* the angles congruent to one another?

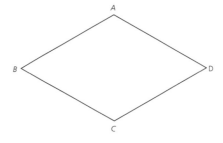

A rhombus

Display 1.28

1.28

How can you use axes of symmetry to show that the diagonals of a rhombus are perpendicular bisectors of each other? Do it, if you can. *Hint:* To illustrate your answer, draw or trace a rhombus, and then fold it along its axes of symmetry.

Published by IT'S ABOUT TIME, Inc. © 2000 MATHconx, LLC

34

1.26

The point of these questions is to contrast congruence of angles with congruence of figures. The display is deliberately a bit crowded, so that students will have to look carefully and maybe even do some measuring or tracing. This can be a good small group activity in class. Students who disagree on their choices will have to find ways to persuade each other.

1. For congruence of angles, neither side length nor orientation matters. The one noncongruent angle is $\angle MNO$. This can be confirmed by tracing, if necessary.

2. For congruence of figures (polygonal paths), segment length matters, but again orientation does not. The three congruent paths are ABC, PQR, and STU. This can be confirmed by either tracing or measuring, if necessary.

1.27

The rhombus has two axes of symmetry, one through each pair of opposite vertices. If your students are having trouble visualizing axes of symmetry, you might have them trace this figure onto a piece of patty paper and then fold it through the opposite vertices. Then they can check for themselves that all the sides are congruent. The two pairs of opposite angles are congruent, but an angle in one of these pairs is not congruent to an angle in the other.

1.28

This exercise uses symmetry to establish an important property of rhombi. It also reinforces the symmetry based definition of right angle from the previous section: "Whenever two crossing lines form matching angles next to each other, the angles must be right angles."

- By folding the rhombus along its two axes of symmetry, students can see that the four angles formed by the crossing folds are congruent, so they must all be right angles.

- The segments of the fold lines between the vertices of the rhombus are the diagonals. Again, symmetry shows that each fold divides the other diagonal into two congruent segments. That is, each diagonal bisects the other one.

NOTES

_____

_____

_____

_____

_____

_____

The corners of the rhombus in Display 1.28 came in two flavors. ∠*ABC* is congruent to ∠*ADC* but not to the other two angles. Those other two angles, ∠*BCD* and ∠*DAB*, are congruent. This makes a rhombus a somewhat special kind of quadrilateral. A quadrilateral may have no angles that are congruent, or it may have just two, or it may have more.

> These questions refer to Display 1.26, which appears at the beginning of this section.

a
1.29

> 1. Find all the quadrilaterals in that display that have no congruent angles.
>
> 2. Find all the quadrilaterals in that display that have exactly one pair of congruent angles.
>
> 3. Find all the quadrilaterals in that display that have two pairs of congruent angles but not all four angles congruent.
>
> 4. Find all the quadrilaterals in that display that have all four angles congruent.
>
> 5. Can a quadrilateral have three congruent angles, but not four? If so, explain how to make one. If not, explain why not.

Unlike the rhombus in Display 1.28, *all* the angles of a square or a rectangle are congruent. They are right angles. In fact, a **rectangle** is *defined* as a quadrilateral with four right angles.

> Find all the axes of symmetry of the rectangle in Display 1.29. How are the sides of a rectangle related?

b
1.30

A   D

B   C

A rectangle

Display 1.29

Published by IT'S ABOUT TIME, Inc. © 2000 MATHconx, LLC

35

1.29

These questions serve to heighten students' awareness of the properties that we shall be using in the next few pages to classify rectangles. They also provide practice in visual perception.

1. *H*

2. *C* and *E*

3. *D*, *F*, and *G*

4. *A* and *B*

5. Yes. Draw a polygonal path containing three congruent, nonright angles that add up to more than 180° (two right angles), but less than 360° (four right angles). Extend the first and last segments of the path until they meet. For example, three 100° angles result in a quadrilateral with a fourth angle of 60°.

1.30

Again there are two axes of symmetry, but they don't go through the vertices. Each one goes through the midpoints of a pair of opposite sides. The pairs of opposite sides are congruent (the same length).

NOTES

_____

_____

_____

_____

_____

_____

_____

_____

_____

_____

Chapter 1

A square has four axes of symmetry. The square shown in Display 1.30 is symmetric about a vertical line, a horizontal line, and lines through opposite vertices.

1. **Is every square a rectangle? Why or why not?**

2. **Is every square a rhombus? Why or why not?**

1.31

3. **Use your answers to questions 1 and 2 to define a square.**

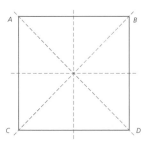

The axes of symmetry of a square

Display 1.30

Rectangles, rhombi, and squares all are special cases of *parallelograms*. A **parallelogram** is a quadrilateral in which both pairs of opposite sides are congruent, as in Display 1.31. This is a perfectly good definition, even though it doesn't say anything about "parallel." But it doesn't explain the name.

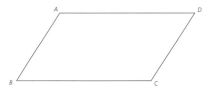

A parallelogram

Display 1.31

Another way to define a parallelogram is as a quadrilateral with both pairs of opposite sides parallel. To see if opposite sides are parallel, you can drop perpendiculars from both ends of one side to the line determined by the other side.

36

1.31

These questions ask students to anticipate some of the classification structure that is about to be described. They are marked as discussion questions because there is occasional disagreement about the answers to 1 and 2. Such disagreement usually results from students' unwarranted assumption that the definition of rectangle *excludes* the case of all sides equal and/or the definition of rhombus *excludes* the case of all angles equal. The sooner these misconceptions are identified and disposed of, the better.

1. Yes. Every square is a quadrilateral with four right angles.

2. Yes. Every square is a quadrilateral with four congruent sides.

3. A *square* is a rectangular rhombus. That is, it is both a rectangle and a rhombus.

Chapter 1

NOTES

(Do you remember how to drop a perpendicular from a point to a line?) If those perpendicular segments are the same length, then the sides are parallel. This definition is equivalent to the one we stated first. That is, any figure that satisfies either definition also satisfies the other one. We prefer the first one right now because it fits in better with our discussion of rectangles, rhombi, and squares.

> **Find all axes of symmetry for the parallelogram in Display 1.31. Find all congruent angles.**

1.32

Let's organize what we know about types of quadrilaterals. We have seen that a rhombus has all of its sides congruent, a rectangle has all of its angles congruent, a square has all of its sides *and* all of its angles congruent, and a parallelogram has opposite sides congruent. A diagram showing how these types are related appears in Display 1.32.

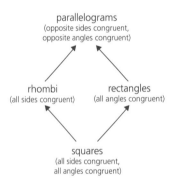

Types of quadrilaterals

Display 1.32

As you read from top to bottom, Display 1.32 goes from the more general type of quadrilateral to the more specialized. In particular,

- All rhombi are parallelograms.

- All rectangles are parallelograms.

- All squares are rhombi.

- All squares are parallelograms.

- All squares are rectangles.

Published by IT'S ABOUT TIME, Inc. © 2000 MATHconx, LLC

37

1.32 This parallelogram does not have any axes of symmetry. Both pairs of opposite angles are congruent.

NOTES

Besides knowing what these statements say, you should also know what they do *not* say! Sometimes it is easy to confuse a statement of the form

"All [something] are [something else]."

with its *converse*,

"All [something else] are [something]."

When you're talking about everyday things you know well, it's easy to keep the subject and the predicate straight. For instance, you wouldn't confuse:

"All parakeets are birds"

with

"All birds are parakeets."

The first statement is true, and the second one is false. But when you're studying less familiar things, such as polygons, the distinction between a statement and its converse may not be so obvious.

A statement like: "All parakeets are birds" is called a **universal statement.** It's a *guarantee* that anything of the first kind is also of the second kind. You can prove the statement is false just by finding a single example where the guarantee fails–in the case of: "All birds are parakeets" just find one bird that's not a parakeet—maybe a robin, a crow, a chicken, or a goldfinch. An example that proves a universal statement false is called a **counterexample.**

1.33

Here again are five true universal statements about quadrilaterals.

1. All rhombi are parallelograms.

2. All rectangles are parallelograms.

3. All squares are rhombi.

4. All squares are parallelograms.

5. All squares are rectangles.

Write the converse of each statement. Then decide if the converse is true or false. If you think it's false, find or draw a counterexample. If you think it's true, explain why.

Published by IT'S ABOUT TIME, Inc. © 2000 MATHconx, LLC

1.4 Regular Polygons

1.33

This exercise should make it clear that the converse of a true statement need not be true. In fact, you may want to ask your students a follow up question after they do these. Find an example of a true statement that has a *true* converse. Here's one. "All rectangles are equiangular parallelograms."

1. All parallelograms are rhombi. False; see Display 1.32.

2. All parallelograms are rectangles. False; see Display 1.32.

3. All rhombi are squares. False; see Display 1.28.

4. All parallelograms are squares. False; see Display 1.32.

5. All rectangles are squares. False; see Display 1.29.

Chapter 1

NOTES

We'll start you off. The converse of the first statement is "All parallelograms are rhombi." Do you think that's true? Can you find a counterexample?

We have seen that the various kinds of quadrilaterals may have various amounts of symmetry, measured by counting axes of symmetry. The square has the most (4) of any quadrilateral we considered, and it is an example of a regular polygon. We know that an equilateral triangle is also a regular polygon, but we still do not know how to recognize regular polygons in general. The following questions should help you to figure that out.

The figure in Display 1.33 is a *regular* pentagon.

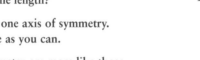

1.34

1. How many sides does this figure have? Are they all the same length?

2. The picture shows one axis of symmetry. Find as many more as you can.

3. These axes of symmetry are more like those of an equilateral triangle than like those of any quadrilateral. Explain this statement.

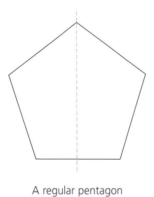

A regular pentagon

Display 1.33

1.34

Notice that the problem *tells* the student that this is a regular polygon. So far, we are able to see if one figure has *more* symmetry than another, but we do not have a criterion for determining whether it has as *much symmetry as possible*.

1. The figure has five sides, all the same length.

2. There are four more axes of symmetry, one through each of the other vertices.

3. Each of these axes of symmetry goes through one vertex and the midpoint of the opposite side, rather than through two vertices (as for a rhombus) or two midpoints (as for a rectangle).

NOTES

1.35

1. Use all the regular polygons you have encountered in the text to make a two column table. One column of the table should show how many sides the regular polygon has. The other column should show how many axes of symmetry it has.

2. Using this table, can you make a guess as to the relationship between these two numbers? Is your guess true for the two regular polygons in Display 1.34? Explain.

A regular octagon

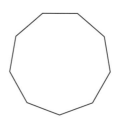

A regular nonagon

Display 1.34

Problem Set: 1.4

1. (a) When is a square a rhombus?
   (b) When is a square a rectangle?
   (c) When is a square a parallelogram?
   (d) When is a rectangle a rhombus?
   (e) When is a rhombus a rectangle?
   (f) When is a rectangle a parallelogram?

2. (a) Draw a rhombus that has four axes of symmetry.
   (b) Draw a rectangle that has four axes of symmetry.

3. A square has four axes of symmetry, while a rhombus has only two. A rectangle also has two axes of symmetry. Describe how the axes of symmetry for a rectangle differ from those for a rhombus.

4. (a) Is there a quadrilateral with exactly *one* axis of symmetry? If so, draw one. If not, explain why not.
   (b) Is there a quadrilateral with exactly *three* axes of symmetry? If so, draw one. If not, explain why not.

40

1.35

The evidence is a bit limited. So far, the text has only discussed regular (equilateral) triangles, quadrilaterals (squares), and pentagons (in the preceding questions). The relationship so far is pretty simple. There appear to be as many axes of symmetry as there are sides. These data suggest that we might *define* a regular *n*-gon as an *n*-gon with *n* axes of symmetry. Students should check this conjecture to see that it holds for the regular octagon and nonagon in Display 1.34. It does.

Problem Set: 1.4

1. (a) A square is always a rhombus.
    (b) A square is always a rectangle.
    (c) A square is always a parallelogram.
    (d) A rectangle is a rhombus when it is a square (and not otherwise).
    (e) A rhombus is a rectangle when it is a square (and not otherwise).
    (f) A rectangle is always a parallelogram.

2. (a) The only rhombus with four axes of symmetry is the square.
    (b) The only rectangle with four axes of symmetry is the square.

3. The axes of symmetry for a rhombus are diagonals going from one corner to the opposite corner. The axes of symmetry for a rectangle go from the middle of one side to the middle of the opposite side.

4. (a) A kite, a boomerang, and some trapezoids have only one axis of symmetry.
    (b) This would be difficult for your students to answer definitively. If they explore the question for awhile, perhaps in groups, they will probably come to believe that the answer is No, but they may well have a difficult time proving it.

NOTES

_____

_____

_____

_____

_____

_____

Chapter 1

5. A rhombus has an axis of symmetry through each pair of opposite vertices. Write an explanation of why a quadrilateral with two such axes of symmetry *must* be equilateral.

6. This problem refers to the figure in Display 1.35.

    (a) How many sides does this figure have?
        Are they all the same length?
    (b) What would you call this figure?
    (c) The picture shows one axis of symmetry.
        Find as many more as you can.
    (d) Do you think that this figure is a regular polygon?
        Explain.

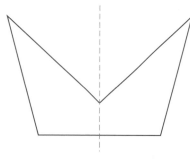

Display 1.35

7. Fred says that all equilateral polygons are regular polygons.

    (a) Can you give a counterexample to Fred's claim?
        That is, can you find an equilateral polygon that has
        less symmetry than another polygon with the same
        number of sides?
    (b) What is the converse of Fred's claim? Is it true?
        Give an explanation or a counterexample.

8. Freda says that all equi*angular* polygons are
   regular polygons.

    (a) Can you give a counterexample to Freda's claim?
        That is, can you find an equiangular polygon that has
        less symmetry than another polygon with the same
        number of sides?
    (b) What is the converse of Freda's claim? Is it true?
        Give an explanation or a counterexample.

Published by IT'S ABOUT TIME, Inc. © 2000 MATHconx, LLC

41

Chapter 1

5. Label the vertices A, B, C, and D in order around the rhombus. Symmetry around axis AC implies equal lengths as follows. $AB = AD$ and $BC = CD$. Symmetry around axis BD implies $AB = BC$ and $AD = CD$. Thus, we have $AD = AB = BC = CD$. "Things equal to the same things are equal to each other."

6. This problem shows that an equilateral pentagon need not be regular.
   (a) The figure has five sides, all the same length.
   (b) You could call it an equilateral pentagon.
   (c) There are no other axes of symmetry.
   (d) This is not a regular pentagon because it has less symmetry than the equilateral pentagon of Display 1.33.

7. This is an important problem.
   (a) See problem 6. Also, a rhombus has all of its sides congruent but it has less symmetry than a square.
   (b) The converse is, "All regular polygons are equilateral." This is true. A regular polygon is supposed to have as much symmetry as possible. When you flip a figure about an axis of symmetry, angles get matched to congruent angles and sides get matched to congruent sides. If any sides are not congruent to one another, this can reduce the potential for symmetry.

8. This is an important problem.
   (a) A rectangle has all of its angles congruent but it has less symmetry than a square.
   (b) The converse is, "All regular polygons are equiangular." This is true. A regular polygon is supposed to have as much symmetry as possible. When you flip a figure about an axis of symmetry, angles get matched to congruent angles and sides get matched to congruent sides. If any angles are not congruent to one another, this can reduce the potential for symmetry.

NOTES

9. (a) How are the angles of a regular polygon related?
    (b) How are the sides of a regular polygon related?

10. Find an example of an "All *A* are *B*" type of sentence in the text, or make one up.

    (a) Find the converse of your chosen statement.
    (b) Find the converse of the converse.
    (c) Do you notice anything? Explain.

11. Find all axes of symmetry for the 11 polygons in Display 1.36 and determine which are regular.

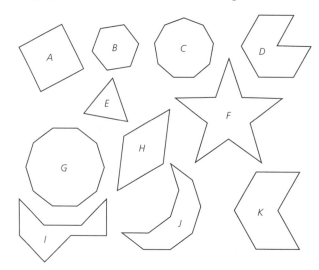

Display 1.36

12. The converse of "If a triangle has all its sides congruent, it also has all its angles congruent" is "If a triangle has all its angles congruent, it also has all its sides congruent."

    (a) Is the original statement true? Explain or give a counterexample.
    (b) Is the converse true? Explain or give a counterexample.
    (c) What are the analogous statements for a quadrilateral?
    (d) Is either of these analogous statements true? Are they both true? Explain or give counterexamples.

Published by IT'S ABOUT TIME, Inc. © 2000 MATHconx, LLC

Chapter 1

9. (a) All the angles of a regular polygon must be congruent.
   (b) All the sides of a regular polygon must all be congruent.

10. The converse of the converse is the original statement.

11. See Display 1.2T, in which each polygon is labeled with the number of axes of symmetry it has and is labeled regular if it is. This exercise allows you to engage your class in additional discussion of the properties of regular polygons. For example, they are convex and equiangular, though we have not yet discussed convexity or angle measurement. Encourage your students to use their own words in describing these aspects of the figures.

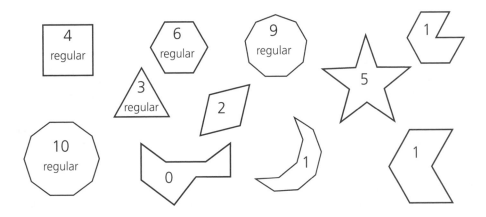

Display 1.2T

12. (a) True. Every equilateral triangle is equiangular (by symmetry).
    (b) True. Every equiangular triangle is equilateral (by symmetry).
    (c) "If a quadrilateral has all its sides congruent, it also has all its angles congruent" is "If a quadrilateral has all its angles congruent, it also has all its sides congruent."
    (d) Neither analogous statement is true. A nonsquare rhombus is a counterexample for the first one; a nonsquare rectangle is a counterexample for the second.

1.5 Areas of Right-Angled Figures

In previous sections you learned about the perimeter of a polygon. Another important property of figures and surfaces is *area*. If you think of perimeter as a measure of the boundary of a piece of land, you can think of area as a measure of how much land lies within the perimeter. You need to know the area of a lawn or garden if you want to buy fertilizer for it. If you want to paint or paper the walls of a room, their area tells you how much paint or paper to buy. If you want to cover a floor with tile or carpet or linoleum, you need to know its area.

Describe some other situations in which you need to know (or find) the area of a polygonal region.

1.36

Euclid School has a Photography Club. The school is going to let the club members make a darkroom in an unused storage space. They need to cover the floor with tile to protect it from possible spills of darkroom chemicals. One of the custodians gave them a sample square tile of the kind they need. He says he will try to get the club members enough tile to cover the floor if they will let him know how many tiles they need. Display 1.37 is a picture, drawn to scale, of the tile the custodian gave the students and of the floor they want to cover.

Learning Outcomes

After studying this section, you will be able to:

Find the area of a rectangular region by tiling it with square units of various sizes;

Approximate the areas of other regions by tiling with square units of various sizes;

Find the area of a rectangular region by measuring its sides and using a formula;

Find the area of a right triangular region by measuring its sides and using a formula.

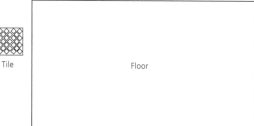

Tile   Floor

Display 1.37

43

1.5 Areas of Right-Angled Figures

1.5 Areas of Right-Angled Figures

In this section, the emphasis on measurement as the repeated application of a unit is extended to area measure. The work with rectangular regions is the foundation for later discussions of area. Repeatedly applying a unit to an object to be measured, increasing accuracy by using a smaller unit, and decomposing an object into smaller, more tractable pieces are the key ideas of the chapter. Formulas that appear along the way are useful, but *they are not the primary goal!* At the risk of being offensively insistent, we remind you that memorized formulas are *not* evidence of mastery of the key ideas.

Even as these materials are being written, changes are taking place in the elementary and middle school curricula which will give future high school students a better grasp of these fundamental ideas. If your students have already benefited from these changes, you may be able to move quickly through some parts of this section and others. If your students are weak in such intuitions, however, you will need to move more slowly. If your students are already "formulaholics" who don't want to do an area problem without being given a formula, concentrate on examples for which there are no formulas (and never will be)—cloud shaped regions, arbitrary polygons, etc. It is *essential* that students get beyond the reliance on memorized area formulas to an understanding of how *any* area computation relies on the repetition of square units, sometimes by ingenious means.

1.36

This need not take much time. Its purpose is to focus students' attention on the question at hand.

Additional Support Materials:

Assessments	Qty
Form (A)	1
Form (B)	1

Blackline Masters	Qty
Student p. 46	1
Student p. 53	1

Extensions	Qty
An Optimal Rectangle	1

Supplements	Qty
Areas of Right-Angled Figures	4

Chapter 1

Sometimes "simple" and "easy" are not the same thing.

1.37

1. What's the simplest way to figure out how many tiles are needed? Can you think of a way that would make sense to a typical six year old child?

2. What's the easiest way to figure out how many tiles are needed? How would you do it if you were in that club?

3. How many tiles are needed? Explain why you will get the same answer the simplest way and the easiest way.

4. Can you think of any reason to know the simplest way if you know an easier way?

The floor-tiling example you just did is an area problem. In that case, the tile was the unit of area measure. The most common units of area are 1 by 1 squares based on some unit of length measure. This creates an important link between measuring length and measuring area. We might choose a unit of area that is one inch or one centimeter or one wobbit on a side. Then we would call the area unit a **square inch**, a **square centimeter**, or a **square wobbit**. See Display 1.38. (A few units of area, such as the acre, do not have such a simple relationship to a length unit.)

Area measurement is easiest for a rectangle. In that case, a simple formula lets you find the number of square units you need without counting tiles. Just measure the length and width, and then multiply.

The square inch   The square   The square wobbit
                         centimeter

Units of area

Display 1.38

Published by IT'S ABOUT TIME, Inc. © 2000 MATHconx, LLC

Chapter 1

1.37

Caution: It is very important *not* to take the easy way out here! These questions connect tiling (which your students may have done in elementary school) with area calculations. The value of this exercise lies in questions 3 and 4, *if* you steer the discussion carefully enough to bring out the ideas they set up for you.

1. The simplest way is to tile the floor with copies of the tile you are given. That is, mark off how many times it fits in the room by marking out adjoining copies of it on the floor, one at a time. When you are finished marking, count up the squares. A typical six year old can outline the squares and count them up, but cannot do multiplication.

2. The easiest way is to measure an edge of the tile, see how many times it fits into the length of the room and into the width of the room, and multiply those two numbers.

3. Since Display 1.37 is drawn to scale, students can measure it to get the numbers they need. The floor is 9 tile sides by 5 tile sides, so $9 \cdot 5 = 45$ tiles will do the job. Lead your students to explain that the answer by multiplying will be the same as the answer by counting because $9 \cdot 5$ represents 5 rows of 9 tiles each.

4. If they immediately say No, ask them how they would approach the problem if the floor were some kind of funny shape—perhaps with a built-in cabinet, or two or three posts in the middle of the room. The point to bring out here is that tiling and counting is *always* a reasonable approach to *any* area problem. Formulas that make the job easier are useful shortcuts when the situation is nice enough, but their limited applicability makes them useless in some situations. This is an underlying theme of the chapter.

NOTES

Another room is available as a possible darkroom for the Euclid School Photography Club. It measures 8 feet by 6 feet.

1.38

1. Find the area of this room. What unit of measure are you using?

2. Is the area of this room more, less, or the same as the area of the original room? (Why can't you answer this question?)

3. We forgot to tell you that the size of the custodian's sample tile is 1 foot by 1 foot. Now, which room has more area?

4. Find the perimeter of this room. Is it more, less, or the same as the perimeter of the original room? What unit of measure are you using?

5. Write a formula for finding the area of a rectangle. Be sure to say what each variable means and how the units of measure are related.

6. Write a formula for finding the perimeter of a rectangle. Be sure to say what each variable means and how the units of measure are related.

You can find the area of a rectangle by counting squares or by using a formula. Each approach has advantages and disadvantages. The formula is easy to use (if you remember it), but it works only for rectangles. Counting is very simple and works for any shape. However, most shapes cannot be covered exactly with a whole number of unit squares. (See Display 1.39 for some examples.) In such cases, we need to estimate fractions of a unit.

Published by IT'S ABOUT TIME, Inc. © 2000 MATHconx, LLC

1.38

Among other things, we want to emphasize that area and perimeter are measured with different *kinds* of units. These questions also serve to refresh students' memories of the simple area and perimeter formulas for rectangles.

1. 48 square feet. The unit is one square foot.

2. This question can't be answered until you know the size of the custodian's sample tile, which was never stated. This question emphasizes the significance of the unit of measure.

3. The new room has more area. The area of the original room is 45 tiles, which is 45 square feet.

4. The perimeter of the new room is $6 + 8 + 6 + 8 = 28$ feet. The perimeter of the original room is $9 + 5 + 9 + 5 = 28$ feet. They both have the same perimeter. The unit is one foot.

5. For the formulas in this part and the next, it doesn't matter what letters the students choose for the variables. It *matters a lot* that they tell you what each letter represents. We use the traditional ones: l for length, w for width, and A for area. $A = l \cdot w$. The lengths l and w must be measured with the same unit; the area is expressed in squares of that unit length.

6. Using l for length, w for width, and P for perimeter, this formula can be expressed in several different ways, all correct.

$$P = l + w + l + w \qquad P = 2l + 2w \qquad P = 2(l + w)$$

Note that you might pause here to show students how each of these forms can be derived from the others by associativity, commutativity, and/or distributivity. All three measurements must be based on the same unit length.

NOTES

_____

Chapter 1

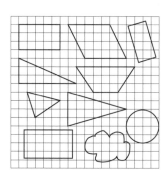

Display 1.39

1.39

1. Some of the figures in Display 1.39 are covered by whole unit squares and parts of unit squares. How might this affect the way you find the area of a shape? Explain.

2. Estimate the area of each of the ten shapes in Display 1.39. Rate each of your estimates as "exact," "pretty close," or "pretty rough."

Here's a way to estimate the area of *any* shape and to get an idea of the accuracy of the estimate. We'll use the circle in Display 1.39 as an illustration.

1.40

1. There are four small squares completely inside the circle. Is 4 square units a good estimate of the area inside the circle? We'll call this an *inner estimate*. Is it too low or too high?

2. You can get another estimate of the area of the circle by counting all the small squares that are wholly *or partly* inside the circle. How many of these are there? Is this a good estimate of the area inside the circle? We'll call this an *outer estimate*. Is it too low or too high?

3. Make inner and outer estimates for the area of the cloud shape in Display 1.39. Save your answers for use in problem 6 at the end of this section.

Thinking Tip

Try to improve estimates. Any time you make an estimate, try to find some way to make a *better* one.

Once we have these two estimates (inner and outer), we know the true area must be somewhere between them. If the estimates are close to one another, we know we have a fairly accurate idea of the area. If the two estimates are far apart, we know we only have a rough idea of the area.

46

1.39

The first part invites a fairly open-ended discussion. The second part is more straightforward, but students might benefit from small group work on their estimates.

1. Guide the students to think about fractional area units. In particular, lead them to see the difference between such things as half of a length unit squared and half of a square unit.

$$\frac{1}{2} \text{ sq. in.} = \frac{1}{2} \cdot (1 \text{ sq. in.}) \quad \text{but} \quad \left(\frac{1}{2} \text{ in.}\right)^2 = \frac{1}{4} \text{ sq. in.}$$

2. Display 1.3T shows reasonable approximations of the areas, in square units. If you use the Blackline Master provided for this exercise, the areas are in square centimeters. Your students' answers should agree for the rectangle in the top left corner, but their answers for the other shapes may vary. Indeed, you might want to gather data from the class and make some sort of display to see how much variability there is. The cloud should be the hardest to estimate. If you have any outliers, you might check to see if someone is misapplying a formula, rather than counting squares. A good way to convince students that they have made a mistake is to trace the figure in question and slide it over another figure whose area is close to either the right or the wrong answer for comparison.

Some students may find ways of determining the areas of certain regions that are quite exact. One student might trace the nice rectangle and slide it over the trapezoid. This should make it pretty clear that they have the same area. Another student might decide that the right triangle has half the area of a 2 by 7 rectangle. Yet another might remember the area formula for a circle and use that. Encourage students to do these things and to share their ideas with others. Be receptive to any formulas they may already know, but gently point out that we want to develop methods that will apply to regions (such as the cloud) for which there are no formulas.

Display 1.3T

1.40

This is marked "Do this now" because it is essential to the flow of ideas in this section. It probably should be done as a brief all class discussion.

Chapter I

Find inner and outer estimates for the three rectangles in Display 1.39. Describe any differences in accuracy among the estimates for these three rectangles. Can you suggest a way to combine the two estimates for a single figure to get a new and more accurate estimate? If you can, apply it to these rectangles.

1.41

For rectangles, of course, the area formula gives you an exact result *provided that* you know the lengths of the sides exactly. In Display 1.39, the grid tells you the exact length and width of one of the rectangles but not of the other two. The accuracy of their areas calculated by any formula depends on how accurately you measure the sides of these rectangles.

We can also find the area of triangles with a formula. The formula for triangles is based on the area formula for rectangles. That's because every rectangle can be divided into two triangles by connecting opposite vertices (see Display 1.40) *and* any triangle can be related to one or two rectangles in this way.

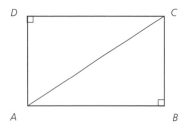

Display 1.40

To see how this works, notice first that each of the triangles in Display 1.40 includes a right angle that is also a corner of the rectangle. (In a diagram, a right angle often is identified by putting a little square inside it.) A triangle that has a right angle as one of its three angles is called a **right triangle.** We realize that this probably is not a great surprise to you; it is stated here to make sure that all the terms we use are clearly defined.

Is it possible to make a triangle that has two right angles? If it is, draw one. If not, explain why it cannot be done.

1.42

This relationship between right triangles and rectangles leads to a simple area formula for right triangles. When we break a rectangle into two right triangles, as in Display 1.40, the triangles are related in a special way: they are *congruent*. So far, we have only defined congruence for segments and for angles. Now we extend this idea to planar figures of all kinds.

Published by IT'S ABOUT TIME, Inc. © 2000 MATHconx, LLC

1. This is a poor estimate; the four squares fall far short of covering the circle. Notice that there are 8 other squares that are *almost* entirely inside the circle. It should be obvious that an inner estimate can never be too high, but may sometimes be too low.

2. There are 12 border squares. Taking these together with the 4 squares entirely inside the circle, we get an area estimate of 16 squares. This estimate clearly is too high. In general, an outer estimate will sometimes be too high, but never too low.

3. The inner estimate is 6 squares; the outer estimate is 25 squares.

1.41

Display 1.4T shows the inner (black squares) and outer (gray squares plus black squares) estimates for all the figures except for the rectangle that used to be in the upper left corner.

"nice" rectangle: 15 inner, 15 outer; difference = 0

tilted rectangle: 3 inner, 18 outer; difference = 15

misaligned rectangle: 10 inner, 28 outer; difference = 18

There is perfect accuracy for the nice rectangle, but accuracy is very poor for the other two because they are not aligned appropriately with the grid. One is tilted and one is shifted over so that none of its corners are at points where the grid lines cross.

One common way to improve inner and outer estimates is to average the two. This can be a good strategy, but all we can say with confidence is that the average will be better than the *worse* of the original two estimates. For these three rectangles, the average estimates are: nice—15, tilted—10.5, misaligned—19. In these cases, averaging gives reasonable accuracy. It would not work so well for something like a long skinny snake that crossed many squares on the grid but actually covered very little area. You might have your students check this out. Determining the "true" area of the snake may be problematical, but that should reinforce the idea that we do not have a formula for every occasion.

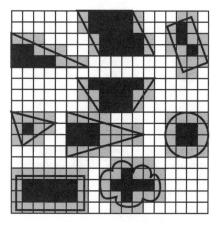

Display 1.4T

1.42

There are no triangles in Euclidean plane geometry with two right angles. In a Euclidean plane, two lines that form right angles with another line must be parallel. Students can see this intuitively by doing some drawing experiments, if it is not obvious to them.

Two figures are **congruent** if you can place (a copy of) one on top of the other in such a way that they match up exactly. They are alike except for their positions in the plane. For polygons, this means that all their sides and all their angles must be congruent. It also means that they must have equal areas!

1.43

These questions refer to Display 1.40.

1. Are you convinced that △ *ABC* and △ *CDA* are congruent? How would you check?

2. How are the areas of △ *ABC* and △ *CDA* related to each other? To the area of the entire rectangle?

3. Explain how to find the area of one of the triangles if you know the area of the entire rectangle.

4. Do you know the area of the entire rectangle? How could you find it?

5. Find the area of the rectangle and the area of each triangle.

But what if you have only one right triangle? How do you find its area?

1.44

Explain how Display 1.41 shows you a way to find the area of any right triangle. That is, supply the words that go with this picture.

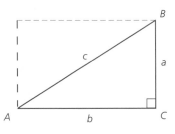

Display 1.41

The longest side of a right triangle is called the **hypotenuse**. It is also the side opposite the right angle. The other two sides are called the **legs** of the right triangle. Display 1.41 illustrates some customs that many people use when they label a right triangle:

Chapter I

The parenthetical qualification about Euclidean geometry is primarily a reminder for you at this stage. In **MATH** *Connections* Year 3, students will see a form of plane geometry, a non-Euclidean type modeled by a sphere, in which there are triangles containing two (and even three) right angles.

1.43

These questions set up the formula for the area of a right triangle, which is done next.

1. The most direct way to check is to trace one of the triangles and move the tracing around until it fits right on top of the other triangle. Encourage students to do this if they seem at all doubtful about the congruence of these two triangles. That congruence is the basis for the entire derivation of the triangle area formula!

2. The areas are the same because the triangles are congruent. The area of the rectangle is the sum of the areas of the two triangles. Since the triangles have the same area, the area of each triangle is half the area of the rectangle.

3. Divide the area of the rectangle by 2.

4. Measure the length and width of the rectangle and multiply them together.

5. The actual area of this rectangle depends on the size of the printed figure. Our original rectangle measured 44 mm by 27 mm, so its area was 1050 sq. mm, making the area of each triangle 1188 sq. mm. If the figure in your book is not printed to scale, you'll have to make the obvious adjustments.

1.44

The details of this idea will be explained shortly in the text. However, most students should get it right from the visual suggestion of the picture, coupled with the rectangle example they just worked through. Try to get them to explain it on their own before moving on, so that they "own" it. The explanation in the text will be reinforcement of an idea they already understand.

The idea, of course, is to complete the rectangle with another copy of the given right triangle. The area of the right triangle is half the area of this rectangle; that is, the area is half the product of the two sides that form the right angle.

- The vertices are labeled with capital letters, *A*, *B*, and *C*, with *C* at the vertex of the right angle.

- The sides are labeled with lowercase letters that represent the lengths of the sides. The lowercase letter used for a side usually corresponds to the capital letter used for the opposite vertex.

This isn't the only way to label a right triangle, but it's very common. Knowing this custom will make it easier for you to deal with other mathematics books and with standardized tests.

Using this notation, we can write a formula for the area of *any* right triangle. The lengths of the legs are *a* and *b*, so the area of the triangle must be half the area of the rectangle with side lengths *a* and *b*. That is, the area *A* of the right triangle is

$$A = \frac{ab}{2}$$

The edges of a right triangular sail measure 7.2 ft., 9.6 ft., and 12 ft. What is the area of the sail?
Hint: **Draw a sketch and think about rectangles.**

1.46

We now have area formulas for rectangles and right triangles. In Section 1.7 you will see how to generalize these ideas to get a formula for the area of *any* triangle. Formulas can be a handy shortcut for finding the areas of some common geometric figures. But there are so many different figures in the world that we cannot memorize a formula for every one. For those many, many other figures, you still need the simple underlying principle from which we started.

Area is based on tiling a region with a unit square.

Thinking Tip

When you learn a formula or put one in your notes, be sure to include the information you need in order to use it correctly:

- What do all the variables stand for?
- To what does the formula apply? For example, this area formula applies to *right* triangles.

49

Published by IT'S ABOUT TIME, Inc. © 2000 MATHconx, LLC

1.45 In this notational scheme, AB is a side (a segment) and c is its length (a number). Opinion is still divided on how important it is to require students to be explicit about this distinction.

1.46 This is a straightforward reinforcement exercise. As noted above, the longest side of a right triangle is the hypotenuse, so the area must be half the area of the rectangle formed by the other two sides.

$$\text{Area of sail} = \frac{7.2 \cdot 9.6}{2} = 34.56 \text{ sq. ft.}$$

NOTES

....

....

....

....

....

....

....

....

....

....

....

....

....

1.47 Find the areas of regions *A* through *I* of Display 1.42 by counting how many times you can fit the given unit into each region. (Is it useful to learn a formula for each different shape?)

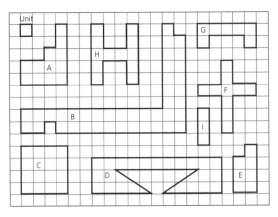

Display 1.42

Problem Set: 1.5

1. This problem refers to Display 1.43. Answer these questions about triangles 1–6.

   (a) Which triangles are congruent to triangle 0?

   (b) Of the triangles congruent to triangle 0, which are "flipped over"?

   (c) Of the triangles that are *not* congruent to triangle 0, which are congruent to one another?

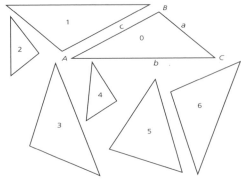

Display 1.43

1.47

A: 12, *B*: 40, *C*: 16, *D*: 25, *E*: 7, *F*: 10, *G*: 7, *H*: 12, *I*: 3. These shapes are fairly easy to do by counting. However, most of them cannot be done by directly applying a single formula.

Problem Set: 1.5

1. This exercise can be done in a variety of ways. We suggest tracing (using patty paper or some other see through paper) as the easiest, most efficient, most reliable approach.
   (a) 0, 1
   (b) 1
   (c) 2 and 4; 3 and 6

NOTES

Chapter 1

2. (a) There are ten centimeters in a decimeter. How many square centimeters are in a square decimeter? (*Hint*: Draw a diagram.)

   (b) There are 100 centimeters in a meter. How many square centimeters are in a square meter?

   (c) How many millimeters are in a centimeter? How many square millimeters are in a square centimeter?

   (d) How many millimeters are in a meter? How many square millimeters are in a square meter?

3. (a) There are three feet in a yard. How many square feet are in a square yard? (Make a scale drawing.)

   (b) How many inches are in a foot? How many square inches are in a square foot?

   (c) There are 1760 yards in a mile. How many square yards are in a square mile?

   (d) To find out how many square feet are in a square mile, should you multiply your answer to part (c) by 3, by 6, by 9, or by 12?

   (e) Check your answer to part (d) by answering these questions: How many feet are in a mile? How many square feet are in a square mile? What do you get when you divide this number of square feet by your answer to part (c)? Why should this answer be the same as your answer to part (d)?

4. (a) It takes one can of prepared frosting to cover the top of an 8 inch square cake. (An 8 inch square cake is 8 inches on each side.) Mr. Cardullo is making a 16 inch square cake for his daughter's birthday party. How many cans of frosting will he need to cover the top?

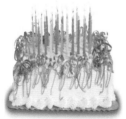

   (b) Makeda wants wall-to-wall carpeting for her living room floor, which is rectangular and measures 14 feet by 18 feet. The carpeting she wants is sold by the square yard. How many square yards will she need?

Published by IT'S ABOUT TIME, Inc. © 2000 MATHconx, LLC

51

2. (a) $10^2 = 100$
   (b) $100^2 = 10,000$
   (c) $10; 10^2 = 100$
   (d) $1000; 1000^2 = 1,000,000$

3. (a) 9
   (b) $12; 12^2 = 144$
   (c) $1760^2 = 3,097,600$
   (d) by 9
   (e) There are 5280 feet in a mile. There are $5280^2 = 27,878,400$ sq. ft. in a square mile. Dividing by the answer to part (c), you get 9. That is, this answer is 9 times the answer to part (c) because there are 9 square feet in one square yard.

4. (a) 4 cans
   (b) $\dfrac{14 \cdot 18}{9} = 28$ sq. yd.

NOTES

5. Here are the measurements of the walls and windows of a room.

   Wall 1. 14 ft. by 11 ft., one door

   Wall 2. 10 ft. by 11 ft., one window

   Wall 3. 10 ft. by 11 ft., one window

   Wall 4. 14 ft. by 11 ft., no windows

   The windows are 4 ft. by 2.5 ft. and the door is 8 ft. by 2.5 ft.

   (a) Find the total wall area.
   (b) Paint comes in cans that cover 300 square feet each. How many cans of paint will be needed?

6. We found that covering a shape with squares in order to find its area may not give accurate results. One way to overcome this problem is to use smaller squares. This problem asks you to try that approach on the cloud shape from Display 1.39. An enlargement of that shape is shown in Display 1.44. The square at the lower left represents the original unit; the new units (the small squares of the grid) are one third as long on each side.

Display 1.44

   (a) Make two estimates of the area of this figure

Published by IT'S ABOUT TIME, Inc. © 2000 MATHconx, LLC

5. (a) Assuming that you do not paint over the windows or the door, there are 488 sq. ft. that need paint.
   (b) This will require 2 cans of paint. You will use a little less than $\frac{2}{3}$ of the paint in the second can.

6. (a) These answers may vary slightly, since it is not always easy to tell from the diagram whether the figure intersects some of the squares.
   (i) inner estimate: 105 squares   (ii) outer estimate: 150 squares
   (b) Divide by 9 (because there are 9 small squares in each larger one). The area is between 11.7 and 16.7 of the original units.
   (c) Using the original squares back in 1.40, the inner estimate was 6 and the outer estimate was 25. The new estimate certainly is an improvement, but it's still not very accurate.
   (d) To get greater accuracy, use even smaller squares.

NOTES

Chapter 1

by counting smaller squares that are

(i) completely inside the cloud;

(ii) completely or partly inside the cloud.

(b) Convert your estimates to the original units.

(c) Compare your new estimates to the ones you did before. Which gives greater accuracy?

(d) If this is still not accurate enough, what can you do?

7. Display 1.45 is another picture of our old friend, the rhombus. Your teacher will give you a copy of this figure to use for this problem.

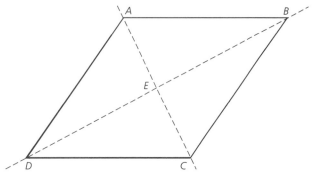

Display 1.45

(a) Find four triangles in the figure that are all congruent to one another. How do you know that they are all congruent?

(b) Justify the claim that these four triangles are right triangles.

(c) Next to each of these four triangles, draw another congruent copy with the same hypotenuse, as in Display 1.40. When you are done, you should have a big rectangle. Give a formula for the area of this rectangle in terms of the length of the diagonals *AC* and *BD*.

(d) Use your result from part (c) to write a formula for the area of a rhombus in terms of the lengths of its diagonals.

(e) Can you give a formula for the area of a rhombus in terms of just the length of its sides? If so, do it. If not, explain why.

53

7. The point of this problem is in parts (d) and (e).

   (a) △ABE, △ADE, △CBE, and △CDE Their congruence is most easily established by paper folding at this stage. Also, in 1.28 of Section 1.4, students showed that the diagonals of a rhombus are perpendicular bisectors of each other. That guarantees that all corresponding sides of these triangles are congruent.

   (b) This is true because the diagonals of a rhombus are perpendicular bisectors of each other (1.28).

   (c) See Display 1.5T. If we let s be the length of diagonal AC and l be the length of diagonal BD, then the area of the rectangle is $s \cdot l$.

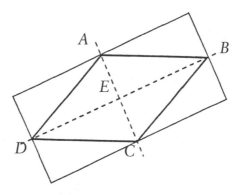

Display 1.5T

   (d) If s and l are the lengths of the two diagonals, then the area of the rhombus is $\frac{sl}{2}$.

   (e) The area of a rhombus is not determined by the length of its side. For example, Display 1.6T shows three rhombi with the same side length, but with very different areas.

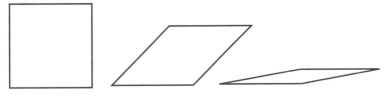

Display 1.6T

8. (a) Graph the equation $y = 5$ on an xy coordinate plane.

   (b) Determine the missing coordinates for the points $(2, ?)$ and $(10, ?)$ on the line of part (a). Label these points M and N, respectively.

   (c) Now locate the points $(10, 0)$ and $(2, 0)$ on your graph. Label these points O and P, respectively.

   (d) Find the area of rectangle $MNOP$.

9. (a) Graph the equation $y = \frac{2}{3}x$ on an xy-coordinate plane.

   (b) Determine the missing coordinates for the points $(6, ?)$ and $(9, ?)$ on the line of part (a). Label these points R and S, respectively.

   (c) Now locate the points $(9, 0)$ and $(6, 0)$ on your graph. Label these points T and U, respectively.

   (d) Find the area of the polygon $RSTU$.

Published by IT'S ABOUT TIME, Inc. © 2000 MATHconx, LLC

8. (a) See Display 1.7T.
   (b) (2, 5) and (10, 5)
   (c) See Display 1.7T.
   (d) $(10 - 2) \cdot 5 = 40$ sq. units

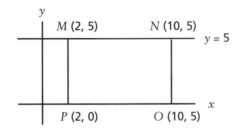

Display 1.7T

9. (a) See Display 1.8T.
   (b) (6, 4) and (9, 6)
   (c) See Display 1.8T.
   (d) polygon = rectangle + triangle

   Area $= 4 \cdot 3 + \dfrac{1}{2} \cdot 2 \cdot 3 = 15$ sq. units

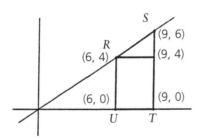

Display 1.8T

NOTES

1.6 Area and Algebra

In your past studies you have seen how drawing a picture or a diagram can help you to understand an idea better. We can use pictures to connect the geometric idea of area to some of the laws of algebra that you studied earlier in **MATH** *Connections*. In particular, the areas of rectangles can be used to show how the Distributive Law works.

First we need to review what is meant by "an algebraic law." In this section, we shall consider only laws that are expressed as equations. Of course, not every equation deserves to be called a law of algebra. See if you can figure out what we mean by a law from the following questions and examples.

These questions are about equations in one variable.

1.48

1. **What does it mean to "solve" an equation? Can an equation in one variable have more than one solution?**

2. Solve the equation $x - 2 = 0$. How many solutions are there? Describe them all.

3. Solve the equation $x^2 = 9$. How many solutions are there? Describe them all.

4. Solve the equation $2x = x + x$. How many solutions are there? Describe them all.

5. Solve the equation $\frac{x}{x} = 1$. How many solutions are there? Describe them all.

6. Two of these four equations are different from the other two in some essential way. Which are alike and which are different? In your own words, what's the key difference?

How did you do? Did you see a difference that separates the four equations above into two different kinds? Here's the idea we want you to see. Some equations are true for some numbers and false for others, but other equations are true for *all* numbers for which the equation makes any sense at all.

Published by IT'S ABOUT TIME, Inc. © 2000 MATHconx, LLC

Learning Outcomes

After studying this section, you will be able to:

Identify algebraic identities and equations with particular solutions;

Use areas of rectangles to illustrate an important law of algebra;

Use a diagram to set up an algebra problem in terms of area.

55

1.6 Area and Algebra

This section unites the geometric idea of area with some of the algebra from **MATH** *Connections* Year 1 by interpreting the Distributive Law geometrically. It begins by distinguishing algebraic identities from other equations, first in one variable, then in two variables.

1.48

This should be done right away. It is marked as Discuss this because there is much to be gained here from having students build on each others' thoughts and suggestions. In parts 1 and 6, try to mold and guide students' answers until they accurately describe the main ideas in their own words.

1. Solving an equation means finding one or more numbers which, when substituted for the variable, make the equation a true statement. Yes, it can have more than one solution, as some of the following examples will show.

2. $x = 2$ is the only solution.

3. There are exactly two solutions, 3 and -3.

4. Any number makes this a true statement; there are infinitely many solutions.

5. Any number except 0 makes this a true statement; there are infinitely many solutions.

6. Try to get your students to see the difference between an equation that is true for *some* (few) numbers (of a certain kind) and an equation that is true for *all* numbers (of a certain kind). This is the key idea. It is made explicit in the text that follows. From this point of view, $x - 2 = 0$ and $x^2 = 9$ are alike, but are different from $2x = x + x$ and $\frac{x}{x} = 1$.

Published by IT'S ABOUT TIME, Inc. © 2000 MATHconx, LLC

For instance, putting any number into

$$x - 2 = 0$$

gives us a statement that's clearly either true or false, but we get a false statement for every substitution except $x = 2$. On the other hand,

$$2x = x + x$$

not only makes sense for every number, it is true for all of them. The equation

$$\frac{x}{x} = 1$$

doesn't make sense for $x = 0$ because division by 0 doesn't make sense. However, for every other number, it makes sense *and* it's true.

1.49 We call the set of all numbers for which an equation makes sense (is either true or false) its **domain**. (This is like the domain of a function.) An equation that is true for *all* numbers in its domain is called an **identity**. Thus, the equations

$$2x = x + x \text{ and } \frac{x}{x} = 1$$

are identities, but the other two (in questions 2 and 3) $x - 2 = 0$ and $x^2 = 9$ are not.

 Which of the following are identities? For those that are not, see if you can find *any* values for x that make the equation true.

1.50

1. $x + 4 = 0$
2. $x + 0 = x$
3. $3x - 7 = 2$
4. $x^2 - x^2 = 0$
5. $x^2 + x^2 = 0$

6. $x^2 - x = 0$
7. $(x^2 + 7) - (x^2 + 3) = 4$
8. $x^2 - 4 = 0$
9. $x^2 + 4 = 0$
10. $2x + 4 - 2(x + 1) = 2$

1.51 We can apply this same distinction to equations involving two or more variables. The equation

$$x \cdot (y - 4) = 0$$

is not an identity. It is true if $x = 2$ and $y = 4$, but it is not true for $x = 2$ and $y = 3$. (In fact, there are infinitely many numbers for which it is true and also infinitely many numbers for which it is false. Do you see why?) On the other hand, the equation

$$xy - xy = 0$$

is an identity because the equation is always true, no matter what numbers are substituted for x and y.

56

Published by IT'S ABOUT TIME, Inc. © 2000 MATHconx, LLC

Chapter 1

1.49 Although we are being a bit informal here, this usage of *domain* actually agrees with its usage for functions. You can think of an equation in x as a function from the set of all numbers for which the equation makes sense to the set {*true, false*}. Similarly, an identity in two variables is a function from all ordered pairs of its domain numbers to the set {*true, false*}. From this point of view, an *identity* (equation) is just the constant function that matches every domain number (or pair) with *true*. You probably should not present this formality to your students unless their questions force the issue.

1.50 The emphasis here is not on equation solving skills but on thinking about what each equation says.

1. Not an identity. $x = -4$

2. An identity.

3. Not an identity. $x = 3$

4. An identity.

5. Not an identity. $x = 0$

6. Not an identity. $x = 0$ or $x = 1$. You might encourage students to use the Distributive Law to rewrite this as $x \cdot (x - 1) = 0$ and then ask them, "When is the product of two numbers 0?"

7. An identity. Trying a lot of numbers should convince students that this is a good candidate. They or you can confirm their suspicions with the obvious algebraic manipulation.

8. Not an identity. $x = 2$ or $x = -2$

9. Not an identity. There are no real solutions because the square of a real number is never negative.

10. An identity.

1.51 We didn't insert a formal question for students here because we didn't want to interrupt the contrast between this equation and the next one. However, once the distinction is made, you might want to come back and pursue this parenthetical question. Students' experience to date might give them the erroneous impression that equations are either identities or have only one or two solutions. Here we have a nonidentity with infinitely many solutions. Most of the formulas used in applications, such as area and volume formulas, have infinitely many solutions and infinitely many nonsolutions.

This equation illustrates the fact that a product is 0 if, and only if, one of its factors is 0. If $x = 0$, then any value of y is a solution. If $y = 4$, then any value of x is a solution. No other values for x and y are solutions.

We can continue to find identities and solutions to equations for any number of variables. Practical problems in industry may involve thousands of variables. However, if you understand the pattern for a few variables, you can handle any number. This is the power of patterns.

> **Which of the following equations are identities? Do any of the identities have names? If so, what are they? Find at least one solution and one nonsolution for each equation that is not an identity.**

1.52

1. $(x - 1) y = 0$

2. $x + y = y + x$

3. $(xy - 1) + (xy + 1) = 2xy$

4. $(x - 4)^2 + (y + 3)^2 = 0$

5. $x + yz = xy + z$

6. $(x \cdot y) \cdot z = x \cdot (y \cdot z)$

In algebra, a **law** is an identity that people consider important. Most identities are not important enough to be called laws of algebra. For example,

$$10^{-1} \cdot 34.96^0 x = 0.1x$$

is an identity, but not one worth memorizing. On the other hand, the various forms of the Distributive Law come up and are used all the time. It is worth knowing such laws.

Now that you have a better idea of what algebraic laws are, we can investigate an example that shows a useful connection between the area of a rectangle and the Distributive Law.

$$x \cdot z + y \cdot z = (x + y) \cdot z$$

Several years ago, Ms. Bocciarelli inherited a small piece of land in a popular vacation area. She has been saving to build a little summer cottage on this land. Yesterday she received a letter from her neighbors. They have a small cottage on the property next to hers. Now they are going to retire and build a house on their property. They were going to tear down their old summer cottage, but they thought Ms. Bocciarelli might like to buy it. They have offered to sell her the cottage and a small part of their land that the cottage sits on.

Published by IT'S ABOUT TIME, Inc. © 2000 MATHconx, LLC

57

1.52

Note in passing that *any* letters can be used in equations of more than one variable. There is nothing special about *x, y,* and *z.*

1. Not an identity. Like the preceding example in the text, this equation has many solutions and many nonsolutions.

2. An identity, the Commutative Law for Addition.

3. An identity. Encourage students to work out the simple algebra.

4. Not an identity. How can two nonnegative numbers add up to zero? They must both *be* zero! That happens here when $x = 4$ and $y = -3$, and not otherwise. This is what we mean by thinking about what the equations *says*.

5. Not an identity. It is easy to find nonsolutions. Solutions are a little harder to find, but there are infinitely many, too. For instance, if $y = 0$ or 1, then choosing any number the same for both x and z works.

6. An identity, the Associative Law for Multiplication.

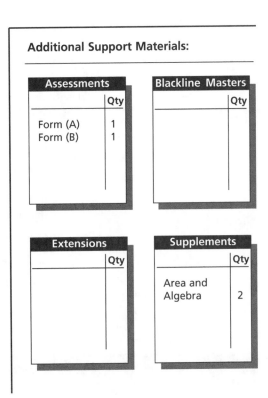

Additional Support Materials:

Assessments	Qty
Form (A)	1
Form (B)	1

Blackline Masters	Qty

Extensions	Qty

Supplements	Qty
Area and Algebra	2

Chapter 1

Display 1.46 is a map of these two pieces of land.

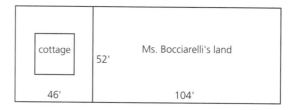

Display 1.46

Ms. Bocciarelli's original property is a 104' by 52' rectangle. The land her neighbors have offered to sell her is an adjoining rectangle measuring 46' by 52'. She wants to buy the cottage, but the sale has to be approved by the local zoning board. They want to know the total area of the land involved.

a
1.53

1. **Find the area of Ms. Bocciarelli's original piece of land, in square feet.**

2. **Find the total area of the land Ms. Bocciarelli will own after she buys the neighbors' cottage lot. Express your answer in square feet.**

How did you calculate the total area of the combined lot? There are two ways to do it.

• You could think of her land as made up of two separate lots, one 104' by 52', the other 46' by 52'. You could find the area of each lot separately and add them up.

• You could add the two horizontal lengths to get the total length of one side of the combined lot, 104' + 46' = 150'. Then you could multiply that by the width, 52', to get the total area.

Which did you do?

b
1.54

Use your calculator to do the following two computations. Be sure to key them in exactly as shown.

104 * 52 + 46 * 52   (104 + 46) * 52

How do the two results compare? What happens if you leave out the parentheses?

58

Chapter 1

1.53

These are straightforward arithmetic questions that set up the discussion to follow.

1. 5408 sq. ft.

2. 7800 sq. ft.

1.54

If you key accurately, you get the same result, 7800, either way. If you leave out the parentheses, you get 2496, which is off by about a factor of four. The same errors that get students into trouble in doing algebraic manipulations also get them into trouble when using the calculator. However, the problems are a little harder to spot and diagnose since there is no paper trail. Estimating helps here. It makes no sense that the combined lot should be smaller than the small lot.

NOTES

In measuring areas, it is easy to see that we should get the same result for either $104 \cdot 52 + 46 \cdot 52$ or $(104 + 46) \cdot 52$. In fact, we should get the same result both ways regardless of the particular sizes of the lots. We could replace 104, 52, and 46 with any other positive numbers. This general statement is the Distributive Law,

$$x \cdot z + y \cdot z = (x + y) \cdot z$$

In terms of Ms. Bocciarelli's property, the Distributive Law says we can find the area of the lot two ways.

- The $x \cdot z + y \cdot z$ way amounts to finding the area of each piece of the lot and adding those areas.

- The $(x + y) \cdot z$ way amounts to finding the dimensions of the new lot first, and then finding its area.

A practical difference between these two methods is that the first requires two multiplications while the second requires only one. This makes the second method easier if you have to do the calculation without a calculator. You might think that we don't have to worry about that with today's technology, but the fact is that the use of computers has led to *more* concern about the speed of an algorithm. Generally, multiplications take so much longer than additions on a computer that computer scientists just count the number of multiplications needed and ignore the number of additions. If we can use the Distributive Law to cut the number of multiplications in a long calculation in half, that would be a big timesaver.

The map of Ms. Bocciarelli's property is a geometric illustration of a form of the Distributive Law. You don't need the cottage or the story, of course. The figure itself is a geometric interpretation that can strengthen your understanding of the law and show how it applies to geometry. The following questions will help you review and extend these ideas.

Published by IT'S ABOUT TIME, Inc. © 2000 MATHconx, LLC

59

NOTES

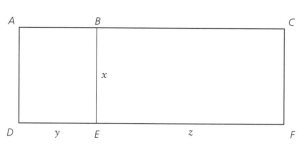

Display 1.47

1.55

These questions refer to the rectangles in Display 1.47. In that diagram, x is the length of BE, y is the length of DE, and z is the length of EF. State your answers in terms of x, y, and z.

1. How long are the segments AB, AD, BC, and AC?

2. What are the dimensions of the large rectangle, $ACFD$? What is its area?

3. What are the dimensions of the small rectangle, $ABED$? What is its area?

4. What are the dimensions of the rectangle, $BCFE$? What is its area?

5. Use your answers to questions 2, 3, and 4 to explain how Display 1.47 illustrates the Distributive Law. Be sure to state the law in algebraic form as part of your explanation.

6. Does this diagram illustrate the Distributive Law for all numbers of its domain, or only for some numbers? Explain your answer.

When Ms. Bocciarelli took her plan to the zoning board, they told her that she could not have a cottage on her land unless she owned at least $\frac{1}{5}$ of an acre. Her plan does not give her a big enough piece of land.

1.56

1. An acre is 43,560 square feet. How many square feet of land does Ms. Bocciarelli need all together?

2. She wants to see if she can buy from her neighbors a strip of land that is long enough to satisfy the zoning board. To figure out how much she needs, she draws the diagram shown in Display 1.48.

60

Note that the figures in Display 1.47 are stated to be rectangles.

1.55

1. Lengths: $AB = y$, $AD = x$, $BC = z$, $AC = y + z$

2. Dimensions x by $y + z$; area: $x \cdot (y + z)$ or $(y + z) \cdot x$

3. Dimensions x by y; area xy or yx

4. Dimensions x by z; area xz or zx

5. Either the left or right form of the Distributive Law works here, but be careful that your students don't just copy the letters from the previous discussion. In this instance, the roles of x and z have been interchanged (deliberately). The area of the large rectangle is the sum of the areas of the smaller rectangles into which it has been divided. That is,

$$x(y + z) = xy + xz \quad \text{or} \quad (y + z)x = yx + zx$$

6. This diagram is a good illustration of the law for all *positive* numbers because lengths are always positive. However, the Distributive Law holds for negative numbers, as well, a fact that cannot be illustrated by such a diagram.

You might have to lead some of your students through part 3, but most should be able to handle the process on their own.

1.56

1. $\frac{1}{5} \cdot 43{,}560 = 8712$ sq. ft.

2. $A(y) = (y + 104) \cdot 52$ sq. ft.

3. Solve $8712 = 52 \cdot (y + 104)$ for y, as follows.
    $8712 = 52 \cdot (y + 104)$
    $8712 = 52y + 52 \cdot 104$
    $8712 - 52 \cdot 104 = 52y$
    $3304 = 52y$
    $63.54 = y$
    Thus, she needs a strip of land 64 feet long to satisfy the zoning board.

4. The Distributive Law was used in the second equation step, to break out the y term from the constant term. Let students express this in their own words.

Chapter 1

Express the total area of the big rectangle as a function of y. What is the unit of measure here?

3. Use your answers to parts 1 and 2 to find out how long a strip of land Ms. Bocciarelli would need to buy from her neighbors. Round your answer *up* to the nearest foot. Why up?

4. Did you use the Distributive Law? If so, how?

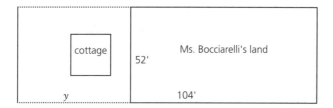

Display 1.48

The neighbors don't want to sell that much land to Ms. Bocciarelli because it would put the boundary too close to the house they plan to build. She decides to forget about the cottage. She can get a break on her taxes and insurance if her property is $\frac{1}{10}$ of an acre or less, so now she is thinking of selling the neighbors a strip off the 52 ft. edge of her property to reduce the area to $\frac{1}{10}$ of an acre. That will be enough to camp on once in a while.

How much land must Ms. Bocciarelli sell?

1. Suppose she sells a strip w feet wide. Express the area of the remaining piece of land as a function of w.

1.57

2. Use algebra, including the Distributive Law, to solve Ms. Bocciarelli's latest problem. Point out where you use the Distributive Law.

In this latest problem, you used a form of the Distributive Law that relates multiplication to subtraction. There are quite a few forms of the Distributive Law, but not as many as there seem to be. Most of them are just variations of one another. The important thing about *any* form of the Distributive Law is that it relates *two* operations. The first one we used in this section relates multiplication to addition.

61

1.57

Here the students are asked to adapt what they have just done to a situation involving subtraction. This is a good exercise for small groups.

1. $A(w) = 52 \cdot (104 - w)$

2. $\frac{1}{10} \cdot 43{,}560 = 4356$. Solve
   $4356 = 52 \cdot (104 - w)$
   $4356 = 52 \cdot 104 - 52w$ (Distributive Law)
   $52w = 5408 - 4356$
   $52w = 1052$
   $w = 20.23$ (approx.)
   Thus, Ms. Bocciarelli must sell off a strip about $20\frac{1}{4}$ ft. wide.

NOTES

Chapter 1

Here's another example of how areas of rectangles can help you understand algebraic expressions. Do you believe that

$$(x + 3)^2 = x^2 + 6x + 9$$

is an identity? Maybe, maybe not. One way to convince yourself is to work out the algebra, step by step, until the two sides of the equation are identical. But first let's look at a picture that should make the answer clear.

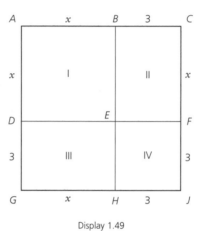

Display 1.49

This refers to Display 1.49, in which all the angles are right angles.

1.58

1. Write an algebraic expression to represent each of the following objects:

   (a) the lengths of *AC* and *AG*

   (b) the area of square *ACJG*

   (c) the area of square *ABED* (region I)

   (d) the area of rectangle *BCFE* (region II)

   (e) the area of rectangle *DEHG* (region III)

   (f) the area of square *EFJH* (region IV)

2. Relate your answers for the previous part to the equation
   $$(x + 3)^2 = x^2 + 6x + 9$$

   Is this equation an identity? Why or why not?

Published by IT'S ABOUT TIME, Inc. © 2000 MATHconx, LLC

1.58

This is another good small group activity.

1. (a) $x + 3$ for both
   (b) $(x + 3)^2$
   (c) x^2
   (d) $3x$
   (e) $3x$
   (f) 3^2 (or 9)

2. The right side of the equation represents the area of the big square, $ACJG$. This area is the sum of the areas of regions I, II, III, and IV. That sum is

$$x^2 + 3x + 3x + 3^2$$

which equals $x^2 + 6x + 9$. Since this argument didn't depend on x in any way, the equation must be true for every number x, which means it is an identity.

NOTES

It may not be obvious to you that this example is related to the Distributive Law, but it is. In fact, you might think of Display 1.49 as a picture of how the Distributive Law works in this case.

You know that $(x + 3)^2$ is shorthand for $(x + 3) \cdot (x + 3)$, right? Now think of the first copy of $(x + 3)$ as a single thing, t. Then, by the Distributive Law, we have

$$(x + 3)^2 = t \cdot (x + 3) = t \cdot x + t \cdot 3$$

Now, put back $(x + 3)$ for t. You get

$$(x + 3)^2 = (x + 3) \cdot x + (x + 3) \cdot 3$$

Use the Distributive Law again on each piece of this sum.

$$(x + 3)^2 = x \cdot x + 3 \cdot x + x \cdot 3 + 3 \cdot 3$$

Finally, tidy up the right side of this equation, using the fact that addition and multiplication are commutative.

$$(x + 3)^2 = x^2 + 3x + 3x + 9$$

Of course, $3x + 3x = 6x$, so there you have it!

$$(x + 3)^2 = x^2 + 6x + 9$$

This example also teaches us something about when distributivity does *not* work. Exponentiation is *not* distributive over addition. That is, you CANNOT rewrite $(x + 3)^2$ as $x^2 + 3^2$ and expect to get the same thing. Display 1.49 should convince you of that. $(x + 3)^2$ is the entire area of the large square, but $x^2 + 3^2$ is just the area of regions I and IV, two smaller squares. The two rectangular pieces of the regions II and III have been left out.

Can you generalize the two approaches you just saw to products that are not perfect squares? Try it. Consider the expression $(x + 2) \cdot (x + 5)$.

1.59

1. Draw a diagram like Display 1.49 that illustrates what you should get when you convert this expression to the form $\_x^2 + \_x + \_$.

   Hint: You'll need to start with a rectangle.

2. Use the Distributive Law to multiply out this expression. Does your result agree with what you got in part 1? It should.

Published by IT'S ABOUT TIME, Inc. © 2000 MATHconx, LLC

1.59

This pushes students to generalize a bit on their own. It might be quite demanding for some classes, but the payoff in understanding usually is worth the effort. Help if you must, but not too much and not too soon.

1. See Display 1.9T. The area of the entire rectangle is $(x + 2) \cdot (x + 5)$. The areas regions I, II, III, and IV are, respectively, x^2, $5x$, $2x$, and 10.

2. Here are the main algebraic steps. The Distributive Law is used in the first two.

$$(x + 2) \cdot (x + 5) = (x + 2) \cdot x + (x + 2) \cdot 5$$
$$= x{\cdot}x + 2 \cdot x + x \cdot 5 + 2 \cdot 5$$
$$= x^2 + 2x + 5x + 10$$
$$= x^2 + 7x + 10$$

Chapter I

	x	5	
x	I	II	x
2	III	IV	2
	x	5	

Display 1.9T

NOTES

Problem Set: 1.6

1. Which of the following equations are identities? Do any of the identities have names? If so, what are they? Find at least one solution and one nonsolution for each equation that is not an identity.

   (a) $2y + 8 = 0$

   (b) $y(y + 3) = 3y + y^2$

   (c) $9 - y^2 = 5$

   (d) $(y^2 - y) - (y^2 - 9) = 8$

   (e) $(y^2 - 1) - (y^2 - 9) = 8$

   (f) $4(y + 5) = 2y + 2(y + 10)$

2. For each part, find the areas of rectangular regions I, II, III, and IV. Then use these areas to express the area of the large square algebraically in two different ways.

   (a)

	8	12
8	I	II
12	III	VI

   (b)

	r	12
r	I	II
12	III	VI

   (c)

	2x	5
2x	I	II
5	III	VI

   (d)

	7s	3p
7s	I	II
3p	III	VI

Published by IT'S ABOUT TIME, Inc. © 2000 MATHconx, LLC

Problem Set: 1.6

1. (a) Not an identity; -4 is the only solution.
   (b) An identity.
   (c) Not an identity; 2 and -2 are the only solutions.
   (d) Not an identity. 1 is the only solution.
   (e) An identity.
   (f) An identity.

2. (a) I: 64; II: 96; III: 96; IV: 144; Area: $(8 + 12)^2 = 64 + 96 + 96 + 144$
   (b) I: r^2; II: $12r$; III: $12r$; IV: 144; Area: $(r + 12)^2 = r^2 + 24r + 144$
   (c) I: $(2x)^2$; II: $10x$; III: $10x$; IV: 25; Area: $(2x + 5)^2 = 4x^2 + 20r + 25$
   (d) I: $(7s)^2$; II: $21sp$; III: $21sp$; IV: $(3p)^2$;
   Area: $(7s + 3p)^2 = 49s^2 + 42sp + 9p^2$

NOTES

_____

_____

_____

_____

_____

_____

_____

_____

_____

_____

_____

_____

3. For each part, make a diagram that will help you write an equivalent form of the given expression. Then use the Distributive Law to show algebraically that the two forms are equivalent.

   (a) $(y + 10)^2$

   (b) $(k + r)^2$

   (c) $(2z + 4)^2$

   (d) $(x + 7)(x + 5)$

4. Draw a diagram to explain to a friend why $(x + y)^2 \neq x^2 + y^2$. What is the difference between the two sides of this expression? Describe that difference both geometrically and algebraically.

5. Mrs. Alvarez has a long, rectangular room, 12 ft. by 30 ft., that serves as a living room and a dining area. She wants to put wall-to-wall carpeting in the dining area at one end of the room. How big can she make the dining area and still leave 210 sq. ft. of living room space uncarpeted? Draw a diagram to illustrate your work. Be sure to define any variables you use.

6. Display 1.50 is an illustration of $(x + 3y + 5)^2$. It is subdivided into nine rectangular regions. Expressions for three of these areas have been filled in.

   (a) Copy this diagram and fill in expressions for the rest of the areas.

   (b) Use your answers for part (a) to rewrite $(x + 3y + 5)^2$ in a form that doesn't need parentheses. Write your new expression with as few separate terms as possible.

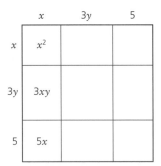

Display 1.50

Published by IT'S ABOUT TIME, Inc. © 2000 MATHconx, LLC

65

Chapter 1

3. Since each of these involves at least one variable, the precise positions of the crossing lines are irrelevant.

(a)

	y	10
y	y^2	$10y$
10	$10y$	100

$$(y + 10)^2 = (y + 10) \cdot y + (y + 10) \cdot 10$$
$$= y \cdot y + 10 \cdot y + y \cdot 10 + 10 \cdot 10$$
$$= y^2 + 20y + 100$$

(b)

	k	r
k		kr
r	kr	r^2

$$(k + r)^2 = (k + r) \cdot k + (k + r) \cdot r$$
$$= k \cdot k + r \cdot k + k \cdot r + r \cdot r$$
$$= k^2 + 2kr + r^2$$

(c)

	$2z$	4
$2z$	$(2z)^2$	$8z$
4	$8z$	4^2

$$(2z + 4)^2 = (2z + 4) \cdot 2z + (2z + 4) \cdot 4$$
$$= 2z \cdot 2z + 4 \cdot 2z + 2z \cdot 4 + 4 \cdot 4$$
$$= 4z^2 + 16z + 16$$

(d)

	x	7
x	x^2	$7x$
5	$5x$	35

$$(x + 7)(x + 5) = (x + 7) \cdot x + (x + 7) \cdot 5$$
$$= x \cdot x + 7 \cdot x + x \cdot 5 + 7 \cdot 5$$
$$= x^2 + 12x + 35$$

4.   See Display 1.10T. The difference is the two rectangular side panels, each of which has area xy. That is, the difference between $(x + y)^2$ and $x^2 + y^2$ is $2xy$.

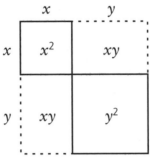

Display 1.10T

5. See Display 1.11T. If x represents the extent of the dining area, then $30 - x$ is the extent of the living room area, and $210 = 12 \cdot (30 - x)$. Solve this for x.

$$210 = 12 \cdot (30 - x) = 12 \cdot 30 - 12 \cdot x = 360 - 12x$$

so

$$x = \frac{360 - 210}{12} = 12.5 \text{ ft.}$$

dining area	12 living room
x	$30 - x$

Display 1.11T

Chapter 1

6. (a) See Display 1.12T.
   (b) $(x + 3y + 5)^2 = x^2 + 10x + 6xy + 30y + 9y^2 + 25$. The order of the summands is not important.

	x	$3y$	5
x	x^2	$3xy$	$5x$
$3y$	$3xy$	$9y^2$	$15y$
5	$5x$	$15y$	25

Display 1.50 completed

Display 1.12T

NOTES

1.7 Triangles and Triangulation

Learning Outcomes

After studying this section, you will be able to:

Construct a triangle from the lengths of its sides;

Construct all three altitudes of a triangle;

Find the area of any triangle by breaking it down into right triangles;

Explain and use a formula for finding the area of any triangle;

Find the area of any polygon by dividing it into triangular regions.

The first thing you will learn in this section is how to use a compass and a straightedge to make accurate drawings of various triangles. There are many reasons why this is a valuable skill. If you want to discuss a geometric figure in general terms, a rough sketch may be good enough. If you want to determine axes of symmetry or try to figure out if a certain angle is a right angle, you will need an accurate drawing. If you want to solve a real world problem by making a scale drawing and measuring its parts, you need a *very* accurate drawing!

There are many uses for accurate drawings outside of school, as well. Buildings and mechanical parts are usually made from accurate scale drawings. Many paintings and graphic designs start out with careful line drawings to which color or paint are added later. There is even an algorithm for using accurate scale drawings to find the area of an irregular region.

As a first example, we'll construct a triangle whose three sides are 3, 4, and 5 wobbits long. Do you remember the wobbit? We use wobbits, instead of inches or centimeters, because we want to discourage you from measuring lengths with a ruler. Measuring involves too much "eyeball" approximating to be as reliable as the construction process we use.

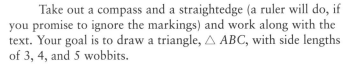

The wobbit, a unit of length

Display 1.51

Take out a compass and a straightedge (a ruler will do, if you promise to ignore the markings) and work along with the text. Your goal is to draw a triangle, $\triangle ABC$, with side lengths of 3, 4, and 5 wobbits.

1. Start by drawing a line segment more than 5 wobbits long. (Estimate.) Choose one end as a vertex of the triangle and label it *A*. Then use your compass to mark off five wobbits along the line, starting from *A*. Use the official wobbit in Display 1.51 to set your compass. Label the fifth wobbit point *B*. At this stage, your drawing should look like

66

Chapter 1

1.7 Triangles and Triangulation

This section begins with a compass and straightedge construction of a triangle; students will need the appropriate tools. This construction leads to the important idea that two triangles are congruent whenever the three side lengths of one equal the three side lengths of the other. The main theme of this section is that the area of any polygon can be found by triangulating it and adding up the areas of its component triangles. On the way to that result, we define the altitudes of a triangle and derive the familiar formula for finding the area of a triangle from an altitude and its base.

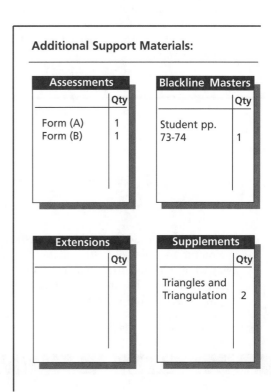

Additional Support Materials:

Assessments	Qty
Form (A)	1
Form (B)	1

Blackline Masters	Qty
Student pp. 73-74	1

Extensions	Qty

Supplements	Qty
Triangles and Triangulation	2

Display 1.52, but larger. (The text displays are much smaller than the actual triangle you are constructing.)

Display 1.52

2. Now use the marked line to set your compass at 3 wobbits. Put the point of the compass at *A* and mark off an arc of points that are 3 wobbits from *A*, as in Display 1.53.

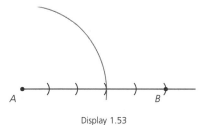

Display 1.53

3. Next, set your compass for 4 wobbits, put the point at *B*, and draw an arc of points 4 wobbits from *B*, as in Display 1.54. This arc should cross your arc centered at *A*. (If it doesn't, back up a step or two and extend the two arcs until they cross.) Label that crossing point *C*. (Actually, if you extend the arcs far enough, they'll cross at *two* points, one above the line *AB* and one below it. Either one will do for what we want.)

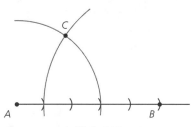

Display 1.54

4. Notice that *C* is exactly 3 wobbits away from *A* (because it is on the arc centered at *A*), and it is exactly 4 wobbits away from *B*. (Why?) Use your straightedge to draw segments *AC* and *BC*, and you're done! △ *ABC* has side lengths of 3, 4, and 5 wobbits.

Published by IT'S ABOUT TIME, Inc. © 2000 MATHconx, LLC

NOTES

Chapter 1

a
1.60

Use the procedure just described to construct triangles with the following side lengths:

1. 4 wobbits, 2 wobbits, and 3 wobbits

2. 2 wobbits, 5 wobbits, and 4 wobbits

3. 4 wobbits, 3 wobbits, and 5 wobbits

4. 5 wobbits, 3 wobbits, and 3 wobbits

Are any of these triangles the same as the triangle of Display 1.54? If so, in what way are they the same? Explain.

Suppose you are given *a triangle* and need to construct a new triangle congruent to the old one. This might happen in an artistic or engineering drawing if you want to repeat the same triangle in several places. You can construct the new triangle without using a ruler to measure the sides. Just use the given triangle to set your compass.

b
1.61

Construct a triangle congruent to the one in Display 1.55. Write down your steps in order. When you're finished, check with some of your classmates to see if you all have the same triangle. Did you all start your construction with the same side? Did you all use the same sequence of steps?

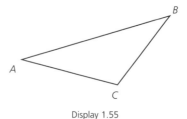

Display 1.55

Now you know how to construct a triangle from the lengths of three sides, either by copying another triangle or by measuring off the sides in terms of a unit length. But an important question remains unanswered. Is it ever possible to construct two *different* triangles from the same three side lengths?

1.60

In one sense, the triangle of part 3 is the same as the one in Display 1.54 because it also has side lengths of 3, 4, and 5 wobbits, albeit in a different order. This makes the two triangles congruent, an important fact that will be emphasized shortly. However, depending on your students' constructions, the orientation of this triangle may differ from that of the triangle in Display 1.54. If orientation is considered important, then the two triangles are not "the same." Draw out your students a little on this, so that they can see that "sameness" needs to be defined a little more carefully before this question really makes sense.

1.61

Many different sequences of steps can lead to the same triangle. In Display 1.55, the placement of $\triangle ABC$ is deliberately skewed to make it less likely that all students will make the same choices of construction steps in the same order. If students construct their triangles on patty paper or some other transparent paper, they can check the results by superimposing their triangle over the one in the text. This also leads to the question of whether the three side lengths really *determine* a unique triangle, up to congruence.

NOTES

_____

Is it? Before you rush to answer the question, it needs some sharpening.

1.62

1. Think of a meaning for *different* which allows you to answer Yes. Then give an example of two triangles with the same three side lengths that are different according to your meaning of the word.

2. What if *different* means not *congruent*? Are there two triangles with the same three side lengths that will not match, no matter how one is placed on top of the other? If so, give an example. If you don't think that's possible, justify your opinion with a persuasive argument.

Triangles occupy a special place in the world of polygons. They are the only polygons whose size and shape are completely determined by the lengths of their sides. You already figured that out, didn't you? Moreover, any polygonal region can be broken into triangular regions, as you will see later in this section. This means that, if we can find the area inside *any triangle*, we will also know how to find the area inside *any polygon*.

In Section 1.5 you learned how to find the area of a right triangle. Now we combine that skill with constructing a perpendicular from a point to a line (from Section 1.3) to find the area of *any* triangle. The key to the process is a line segment called an *altitude*.

About Words

The *altitude* of a plane in flight is its vertical distance above sea level.

Words to Know: An **altitude** of a triangle is a line segment that is drawn from one vertex to the line of the opposite side and which meets that line at right angles. If the altitude lies within the triangle, then the opposite side is called the **base** for this altitude.

Display 1.56 illustrates an altitude and base for a typical triangle. It also shows you why we are interested in this line: It divides this triangle into two right triangles, which we already know how to handle.

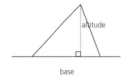

Display 1.56

1.62

This is an *essential* discussion! It is imperative that students become convinced that three side lengths determine a triangle up to congruence.

1. If *different* means in *different places* or *oriented differently*, the answer clearly is Yes. Students should be able to draw two triangles that cannot be matched up unless one of them is "flipped over." This is the orientation distinction, which is important in some parts of mathematics.

2. If *different* means *not congruent*, the answer is No. Any two triangles with the same three side lengths necessarily are congruent. We do not suggest a formal proof here. Instead, we strongly suggest that you allow and/or guide your students to present arguments that convince *them*. If they are having trouble coming to grips with the question, you might supply them with two identical sets of three straight sticks that can form a triangle. Have one student make a triangle with one set of sticks; then have other students try to form a noncongruent triangle with the other set of sticks. This activity should provoke the kind of persuasive discussion needed.

Note that from this point on, it is assumed that students are comfortable with the fact that a triangle is determined up to congruence by the lengths of its three sides.

NOTES

Chapter 1

1.63 Do you think that altitude and base are good names for these line segments? Can you think of other names that you would like better? Defend your answers.

A triangle actually has three altitudes, one for each vertex. Sometimes an altitude actually lies outside the triangle. Display 1.57 shows the three altitudes for △ *RST*, two of them outside the triangle.

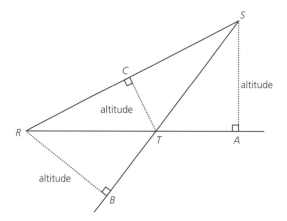

Display 1.57

It is not possible for all three altitudes to lie outside the triangle. If you use the longest side as the base, the altitude will always be inside. This means, for any triangle, there is always at least one altitude that divides it into two right triangles, as in Display 1.56. We use this altitude for the diagram that leads to the general formula for the area of a triangle.

Since you already know how to do all the pieces of this process, we'll let you put them together. The following questions guide you step by step.

70

1.63

There is not a unique right answer here, of course. The point of the question is to help students see the connection between the length of the altitude and the height of the triangle when its base is at the bottom of the picture. This discussion should also draw attention to the fact that an altitude is a *segment*, not a number!

NOTES

Chapter 1

1. On a blank sheet of paper, use a compass and a ruler to construct a triangle, $\triangle ABC$, with side lengths as follows: $AB = 7.5$ cm, $AC = 10$ cm, and $BC = 5$ cm. Put side AC at the bottom (horizontally), so that vertex B is above it. Put the drawing in the middle of your paper, with lots of room all around it.

1.64

2. Draw the altitude from vertex B, using the construction method for dropping a perpendicular from a point to a line. (See Section 1.3 if you need to refresh your memory.) Label as D the point at which the altitude meets the base.

3. For reference, mark each segment of your figure with a lowercase letter to stand for its length, as shown in Display 1.58.

4. Measure your figure as accurately as you can to find the lengths of d, e, and h. (You should already know the lengths of a, b, and c. What are they?) Notice that $d + e$ should equal b. Does it? If not, check your measurements.

5. Express the areas of $\triangle ABD$ and $\triangle BCD$ in terms of the letters of your diagram. Explain why your answers make sense. Then calculate these two areas from your measurements.

6. Calculate the area of $\triangle ABC$ from your numerical answers to part 5.

7. Use the Distributive Law to show how your algebraic answers to part 5 say that the area of $\triangle ABC$ is $\frac{1}{2}bh$.

Keep this diagram. You will need to use it again soon.

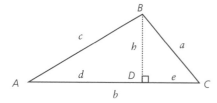

(Note: This is a labeling guide only, not drawn to exact scale.)

Display 1.58

Published by IT'S ABOUT TIME, Inc. © 2000 MATHconx, LLC

1.64

This is the derivation of the standard formula for the area of a triangle, done with a prototypical example. When your students are finished with their step-by-step responses to these questions, get them to review what they did so that they understand the big picture and how the major pieces fit together.

1. This reviews and uses the construction process just learned. It is also an exercise in following written instructions! Please resist the temptation to spare them from having to cope with reading carefully. It's an essential skill for all students to learn. Encourage them to put their drawing in the middle of the paper, so that they have extra room around it for extending lines, labeling, etc.

2. This reviews the construction process from Section 1.3.

3. Display 1.58 is not drawn to size or to exact scale. It is a labeling guide only. Measuring this figure is *not* a valid substitute for measuring their own drawings.

4. *a, b,* and *c* are the three sides of the triangle; they are 5 cm, 10 cm, and 7.5 cm, respectively. Reasonable approximations for the other measurements are $d = 6.5$ cm, $e = 3.5$ cm, $h = 3.6$ cm.

5. This part is the key. Because $\triangle ABD$ and $\triangle BCD$ are right triangles, the area of each is half the area of the rectangle formed from its legs. That is: area of $\triangle ABD = \frac{1}{2}dh = 11.7$ sq. cm   area of $\triangle BCD = \frac{1}{2}eh = 6.3$ sq. cm. Of course, the numerical answers are approximations based on the measurements of part 4.

6. $11.7 + 6.3 = 18.0$ sq. cm (approximately).

7. Make sure that your students understand the easy steps here.
   Area of $\triangle ABC$ = (area of $\triangle ABD$) + (area of $\triangle BCD$)
   $$= \frac{1}{2}dh + \frac{1}{2}eh$$
   $$= \frac{1}{2}(d + e)h \text{ (Distributive Law, twice)}$$
   $$= \frac{1}{2}bh$$

Chapter 1

People following the same directions can come up with very different results from measuring and approximating, even when they are careful. In such cases, the tools of data analysis can help make the results more reliable.

a
1.65

1. Gather the answers for the area of $\triangle ABC$ from everyone in the class. Make a stem-and-leaf plot and a boxplot of these data.

2. Find the mean and standard deviation of these data.

3. In this case, do you think the mean or the median is a better measure of the actual area of a triangle with side lengths of 5 cm, 10 cm, and 7.5 cm? *Hint:* Ask yourself: Are there any outliers in this data set? If so, how do they affect the mean and the median?

A Fact to Know: The area of a triangle can be found by calculating $\frac{1}{2}bh$, where h is the length of any altitude and b is the length of the base for that altitude.

Now that you have worked this formula out for yourself, you should be able to explain how it comes from finding the areas of right triangles and rectangles. That will help you to remember what the formula says and to know how to use it.

There's just one problem here: Our development of this formula depended on having an altitude *inside* the triangle. But the statement of this formula says that h can be "the length of any altitude." What if the altitude is outside the triangle? Does the formula still work?

b
1.66

Take out the paper with your construction of $\triangle ABC$ on it.

1. Construct the altitude from vertex C by extending side *AB* and dropping a perpendicular to it. See Display 1.57 for help in visualizing this.

   (a) What is the base for this altitude?

   (b) Measure this altitude and its base carefully. Then calculate the area of the triangle, applying the formula to these two lengths.

72

1.65

This is a relevant application of data analysis from **MATH** *Connections* Year 1. Besides reviewing those concepts, it emphasizes the variability and unreliability of measurement in geometric arguments. This is particularly true for such things as area computations, in which small variations in length measurement are compounded by the multiplication.

The answer to part 3 is not clear-cut; it depends, in part, on the data from your class. If there are no outliers or if the outliers balance out, then there will be little difference between the mean and the median. On the other hand, one or two outlying answers can shift the mean, but not the median.

1.66

This is a good exercise for small groups. Some students have difficulty visualizing external altitudes; peer explanations can be very effective in clarifying their thinking.

1. (a) This base is the segment *AB*; it is *not* the extension from *A* to the foot of the altitude!
   (b) A reasonable measurement for this altitude is about 4.8 cm. The base is *AB*, which is given as 7.5 cm. The area is $\frac{1}{2} \cdot 7.5 \cdot 4.8 = 18$ sq. cm.

NOTES

Chapter 1

(c) Does your result agree with your previous answer for this area? If not, do you think it is close enough to be within measurement error?

2. Now construct the altitude from vertex A, measure it and its base, and use the area formula again. Does your result agree with your previous answers? Explain any differences.

In the previous example you saw that the area formula for triangles works even if the altitude you choose is outside the triangle. Problem 8 at the end of this section guides you through an algebraic proof of the fact that this always works. Now it's time to consider polygons with more sides.

Let's review what we have done so far with area. We found that rectangles are easy to deal with. Then we found that we could handle any *right* triangle by relating it to a rectangle. Finally, we found we could handle *any* triangle by relating it to a right triangle (and thus to a rectangle). Now we will see how to find the area of *any* polygon by breaking it up into triangles. Display 1.59 shows the example we will work with.

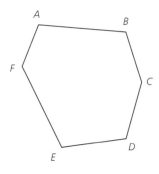

Display 1.59

How many sides does the polygon in Display 1.59 have? What would you call it? Is it regular?

1.67

We can use an algorithm—a step-by-step procedure—to divide the polygon in Display 1.59 into triangles.

73

1.7 Triangles and Triangulation

(c) The answers should agree within a reasonable tolerance for measurement error.

2. A reasonable measurement for the altitude from vertex A is about 7.2 cm. Its base is BC, which is 5 cm long. Thus, the area is $\frac{1}{2} \cdot 5 \cdot 7.2 = 18$ sq. cm.

   Again, the answers should agree within a reasonable tolerance for measurement error.

1.67

The polygon has six sides, so it is a hexagon. It is not regular. In everyday language, people often use *hexagon* to mean a *regular* hexagon, but of course we do not do that in mathematics. The purpose of these questions is to draw students' attention to this distinction and to make sure they are with us when we call *FBCDE* a pentagon.

NOTES

a
1.68

Here's how the algorithm works. Your teacher will give you a larger copy of Display 1.59. Use it to follow the steps listed below. As you do each step, copy and complete the corresponding item in the Results column.

Steps	Results
1. Pick a starting vertex.	1. I chose vertex _____ as my starting vertex.
2. Pick a direction to walk around the polygon.	2. I chose to begin walking toward vertex _____ .
3. Walk around the polygon to the second vertex past the starting vertex.	3. I stopped at vertex _____ .
4. Draw the diagonal from that vertex to the starting vertex.	4. I drew the diagonal _____ .

Display 1.60 shows how one of the authors worked through these steps. If you made different choices, your diagram may look different. (That's OK.)

Results
1. I chose vertex *F* as my starting vertex.
2. I chose to begin walking toward vertex *A*.
3. I stopped at vertex *B*.
4. I drew the diagonal *BF*.

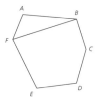

Display 1.60

We started with the hexagon *ABCDEF*. Now we have broken it into a *FAB*ulous triangle (we know how to find its area) and the polygon *FBCDE*.

b
1.69

How many sides does *FBCDE* have? What is this kind of polygon called? Is it regular? What letters name the corresponding polygon in your diagram? How many sides does it have?

14

1.68

The activities for the rest of this section lead students through a triangulation algorithm to the ultimate goal of finding the area of the polygon by summing the areas of the triangles. The algorithm is fairly simple; students should catch on quickly. Once you have finished, you may want to ask students whether they would expect this algorithm to work with polygons of different sizes. It will. You might also ask them to come up with their own algorithm for triangulating a polygon.

Students' results *should* vary. Part of the message here is that the algorithm works, regardless of what step-by-step choices are made.

1.69

This polygon has five sides, so it is a pentagon. It is not regular. Students' letter strings may vary, but they should have pentagons. There is an implicit induction step here. We reduce the number of sides of the polygon with the most sides by one at each step. We eventually get it down to three sides, a number small enough to deal with directly.

NOTES

Now we ignore the triangle we cut off (for the time being) and focus on the remaining polygon. We cut off another triangle by applying the same algorithm as before.

Apply the steps listed to your remaining pentagon. As you do each step, copy and complete the corresponding item in the Results column.

1.70

Steps	Results
1. Pick a starting vertex.	1. I chose vertex _____ as my starting vertex.
2. Pick a direction to walk around the polygon.	2. I chose to begin walking toward vertex _____ .
3. Walk around the polygon to the second vertex past the starting vertex.	3. I stopped at vertex _____ .
4. Draw the diagonal from that vertex to the starting vertex.	4. I drew the diagonal _____ .

Display 1.61 shows how one of the authors worked through these steps.

Now we have two triangles and a quadrilateral, *BCDE*. (Your quadrilateral may have a different name.)

Results
1. I chose vertex *E* as my starting vertex.
2. I chose to begin walking toward vertex *F*.
3. I stopped at vertex *B*.
4. I drew the diagonal *BE*.

Display 1.61

What do you think we should do next? How many choices do we have for a starting point? After we choose a starting point, how many choices do we have for a direction to go in? How many choices in all? Are there really that many ways to divide this quadrilateral into triangles? Explain.

1.71

Published by IT'S ABOUT TIME, Inc. © 2000 MATHconx, LLC

75

Again, students' results should vary. Nevertheless, all students should end up with two triangles and a quadrilateral.

1.70

Students should see by now that the obvious next step is to divide the quadrilateral into triangles. There are four possible starting points, with two directions from each, for a total of eight possible choices. However, there are only two different ways to divide the quadrilateral into rectangles, one for each diagonal.

1.71

NOTES

Chapter 1

Display 1.62 shows one way of dividing the quadrilateral *BCDE*.

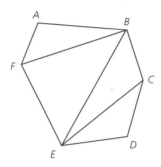

Display 1.62

The process of dividing a polygon into nonoverlapping triangles is called **triangulation**. The algorithm we have been using is a triangulation algorithm. Its purpose is to divide a polygon into triangles. Each time it is applied, one triangle is "sliced off" the remaining polygon. (You will see a slightly different triangulation algorithm in a later chapter.)

One important feature of an algorithm is some way to tell when you are done. For this algorithm, you are done when the remaining polygon is itself a triangle. We are done.

1.72

1. How many times did we need to apply this algorithm to our hexagon?

2. How many times would you need to apply this algorithm to a pentagon? To an octagon? To a decagon?

3. How many times would you need to apply this algorithm to an *n*-gon? Explain.

4. What would happen if you applied the algorithm to a triangle?

Now you can find the area of any polygon. All you have to do is triangulate the polygon, find the area of each triangle, and add.

76

1.72

This is a brief exercise in pattern recognition.

1. 3 times

2. 2 times; 5 times; 7 times

3. $n - 3$ times. Each application reduces by 1 the number of vertices in the remaining polygon. An n-gon has n vertices, and you are done when you have reduced it to 3 vertices (a triangle). Therefore, you need to apply the algorithm $n - 3$ times.

4. Nothing, really. The diagonal segment called for by the algorithm would just be one side of the triangle.

Chapter 1

NOTES

_____

....

....

....

....

....

....

....

....

....

....

....

....

1. Use your diagram to find the area of each triangle in your triangulation of the hexagon. Add up these areas to find the area of the hexagon.

1.73

2. Compare your answer with those of your classmates. Do you see a pattern? Is it what you expected? If so, explain why you expected this pattern. If not, explain how things are not as you expected.

Problem Set: 1.7

Note that in these problems, *construct* means *use a compass and a straightedge to draw.*

1. Construct a triangle with side lengths 4, 5, and 6 wobbits. Is it a right triangle? If so, which angle is the right angle?

2. (a) Construct a triangle with side lengths 12, 5, and 13 cm. Is it a right triangle? If so, which angle is the right angle?

   (b) Construct a triangle with side lengths 8, 5, and 13 cm. Does anything troublesome happen? How can you spot a problem like this in the future?

   (c) Construct a triangle with sides of lengths 7, 5, and 13 cm. Does anything troublesome happen? How can you spot a problem like this in the future?

3. Construct two congruent copies of the triangle in Display 1.63 in such a way that they share the same segment as their longest side and together form a parallelogram.

Display 1.63

4. Two radar stations are 130 miles apart. They both spot a UFO directly above a line connecting them. According to the radar, the UFO is 120 miles from one station and 50 miles from the other.

   (a) Why don't these last two distances add up to 130 miles?

   (b) Make an accurate scale drawing of the situation.

   (c) About how high is the UFO flying?

Published by IT'S ABOUT TIME, Inc. © 2000 MATHconx, LLC

77

1.7 Triangles and Triangulation

Chapter 1

1.73

This is a long exercise. Part 1 requires students to review and apply the process of finding the area of a triangle four times. Each one involves dropping a perpendicular and measuring lengths carefully. We suggest that the measurements be done in centimeters (and/or millimeters) for accuracy and convenience.

1. The area of the hexagon on our Blackline Master is approximately 66.6 sq. cm. Assuming no distortion in the copying process, students' answers should be close to this.

2. This is actually a question about data. The pattern should be a grouping of the individual answers around a central value, with perhaps one or two outliers. You can have students use their calculators to find the mean and the standard deviation of the answers and draw a boxplot to see how close the class comes to agreeing on the answer.

Problem Set: 1.7

1. There are no right angles.

2. (a) The angle opposite the 13 cm side is a right angle.
    (b) The two circles used in the construction will be tangent to one another; they meet only in one point, which is on the line of the base side. Thus, the two shorter sides of the triangle fall on the longest side. You can spot the problem in the future if the length of the longest side is equal to the sum of the lengths of the other two sides.
    (c) This time the two circles do not intersect at all. You can spot this problem in the future because it happens when the longest side is longer than the sum of the lengths of the other two sides.

Parts (b) and (c) illustrate *triangle inequality*—the longest side of a triangle must be shorter than the sum of the lengths of the other two sides. This simple idea shows up in powerful ways in analysis and other parts of mathematics.

3. See Display 1.13T.

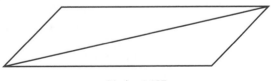

Display 1.13T

4. (a) This is an example of triangle inequality again. If those distances added up to 130 miles, the UFO would not be a *flying* object!
    (b) This is a 5-12-13 right triangle with its hypotenuse horizontal.
    (c) It is about 46 miles up.

5. In this section we divided a hexagon into triangles in stages. At each stage, we had a new polygon to divide. For example, after the first stage, we had the pentagon *FBCDE* to work with. *FBCDE* eventually was divided into three triangles. Complete the table in Display 1.64. Make sketches to help you visualize some cases, if you want. Can you see a pattern to put into the last line of the table? Can you justify it?

Name	No. of Sides	No. of Triangles
quadrilateral	4	
pentagon	5	3
hexagon	6	
octagon		
decagon		
n-gon	n	

Display 1.64

6. Construct an equilateral triangle with sides 2 inches long.

   (a) Construct three altitudes, one connecting each vertex to the opposite side. Do you notice anything interesting?
   (b) Measure the lengths of the altitudes. Do you get three different answers?
   (c) Use an altitude and its base to find the area of the triangle.

7. Construct a triangle with sides 8, 10, and 12 cm long.

   (a) Construct three altitudes, one connecting each vertex to the opposite side. Do you notice anything interesting?
   (b) Measure the lengths of the altitudes. Do you get three different answers?
   (c) Use each altitude and its base to find the area. Do you get three different answers?

8. To prove algebraically that the area formula for triangles works even if the altitude you choose is outside the triangle, consider the situation shown in Display 1.65. Angle C of $\triangle ABC$ is greater than a right angle, and the altitude from B meets the extension of side AC at D. The length of AC is b, the length of the extension CD is e, and the length of the altitude is h.

Published by IT'S ABOUT TIME, Inc. © 2000 MATHconx, LLC

5. See Display 1.14T. The pattern suggested by these few examples is that an *n*-gon can be divided into *n* − 2 triangles. However, it is not so easy to give a justification for the general case. Here is an approach that works for convex polygons.

   Choose one of the *n* vertices, say *A*. There is a diagonal from *A* to each of the other vertices except for the two adjacent to *A*; that is, there are *n* − 3 diagonals from *A*. Going around the vertices of the polygon clockwise from *A*, each of these diagonals cuts off a triangle from the remaining polygon. After the last diagonal is used, there is one triangle left. Thus, there are (*n* − 3) + 1 triangles.

6. (a) All three altitudes intersect at a single point.
   (b) All three altitudes are about 1.73 in. long.
   (c) The area is about 1.73 sq. in.

7. This exercise is meant to contrast with the previous one. Some things that are true for equilateral triangles are true for *all* triangles, even though other things may change.

   (a) All three altitudes intersect at a single point.
   (b) The lengths of the three altitudes are different.

Name	No. of Sides	No. of Triangles
quadrilateral	4	2
pentagon	5	3
hexagon	6	4
octagon	8	6
decagon	10	8
n-gon	*n*	*n* − 2

Display 1.64, completed

Display 1.14T

   (c) Probably the three answers will be slightly different, but only because of measurement and approximation error. Theoretically, the answers should be identical; after all, it's the same triangle in all three cases!

8. For students who are concerned about using a picture (Display 1.65) in a proof, you might point out that all the letters used are defined at the beginning in such a way that the picture is unnecessary. It's just there to help their visual imagination.

(a) In terms of these variables, how long is *AD*?

(b) Express the area of △ *ABC* as the difference of the areas of two right triangles, both of which contain the right angle at *D*.

(c) Express the area equation of part (b) algebraically, and then work out the algebra to complete the proof. Justify each step you take. When you get to your last step, explain how you know you're finished.

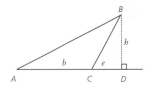

Display 1.65

9. A spider named Charlie is decorating the tracks of the Burlington Northern Railroad. Charlie ambles along one track and every 30 inches spins a spider web connecting the current location to two fixed points, *A* and *B*, on the other track. So far this morning Charlie has done this at ten locations, as shown in Display 1.66. The tracks are 56 inches apart.

(a) Does Charlie's pattern have any symmetry?

(b) Charlie made ten triangles. Each triangle has *A* and *B* as two of its vertices. The other ten vertices are labeled 1–10. Do any of these triangles appear to be right triangles?

(c) What is the approximate distance between *A* and *B*?

(d) Find the area of each of the ten triangles. (*Hint:* This part requires more thinking than calculation.)

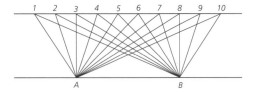

Display 1.66

Published by IT'S ABOUT TIME, Inc. © 2000 MATHconx, LLC

79

Chapter 1

(a) $b + e$

(b) Area of $\triangle ABC$ = area of $\triangle ABD$ − area of $\triangle CBD$

(c) Area of $\triangle ABC = \frac{1}{2}(b + e)h - \frac{1}{2}eh$ (areas of right triangles)

$$= \frac{1}{2}bh + \frac{1}{2}eh - \frac{1}{2}eh \text{ (Distributive Law, twice)}$$

$$= \frac{1}{2}bh \text{ (subtraction)}$$

We are finished because b is the length of the base for the external altitude from B and we have shown that the area of $\triangle ABC$ satisfies the area formula for this altitude and this base.

9. This fanciful tale includes an important result that may be surprising to your students: A large family of triangles that look quite different all have the same area! This is an "Aha!" problem that shows the power of abstract reasoning. Don't give away the punch line too soon.

(a) The figure is symmetric about the perpendicular bisector of AB.

(b) Triangles 3 and 8 appear to be right triangles with right angles at A and B, respectively. Triangles 4 and 7 also appear to be right triangles with right angles at 4 and 7, respectively.

(c) Since triangles 3 and 8 appear to be right triangles, the quadrilateral $A38B$ is (approximately) a rectangle. Thus, we can use the distance from point 3 to point 8 as an approximation of the length of AB. The length is
$$(8 - 3) \cdot 30 = 150 \text{ inches}$$

(d) All the triangles have AB as a base, and they all have an altitude of 56 in., so they must all have the same area! Thus, the area of each of the ten triangles is (approximately)
$$\frac{1}{2} \cdot 150 \cdot 56 = 4200 \text{ sq. in.}$$

NOTES

1.8 The Pythagorean Theorem

1.8 The Pythagorean Theorem

Learning Outcomes

After studying this section, you will be able to:

State the Pythagorean Theorem and its converse;

Explain how the Pythagorean Theorem is a statement about areas;

Use the Pythagorean Theorem to find lengths and areas;

Use the converse of the Pythagorean Theorem to construct right angles.

As you have seen, right triangles are very important building blocks in geometry. In this section you will study the most important fact about right triangles. In fact, it is probably one of the half dozen most important statements in all of mathematics. It's called the *Pythagorean Theorem*.

The theorem got its name from a community called the Pythagoreans, who lived in southern Italy during the 6th century, B.C. They were followers of Pythagoras, a teacher, scholar, and religious leader. Because they believed that everything could be explained by numbers, they were pioneers in applying mathematical ideas to the real world. For instance, they developed a mathematical theory of musical harmony, and they knew that the Earth was a sphere nearly 2000 years before Columbus sailed from Spain.

We really know very little about Pythagoras himself. Many legends about him have come down to us, but after 2500 years it is hard to tell fact from myth. One of the legends about Pythagoras says that he discovered the theorem named after him while contemplating a floor tile pattern like the one in Display 1.67.

This was a familiar pattern, but Pythagoras looked at it in a new way. Many discoveries are made this way. He noticed a relationship among three squares built on the sides of a right triangle. To show you how Pythagoras looked at this floor pattern, in Display 1.68 we have shaded the squares he concentrated on.

1.74

1. Find the areas of the three squares. Use one square tile as your area unit. Each small triangle is one quarter of a unit.

2. Pythagoras might have noticed *two* special relationships among these areas. What are they?

Published by IT'S ABOUT TIME, Inc. © 2000 MATHconx, LLC

1.8 The Pythagorean Theorem

There is absolutely no doubt that the Pythagorean Theorem is one of the most important statements in all of mathematics. Besides being a prominent part of Euclidean geometry and number theory, it lies at the very heart of coordinate geometry and trigonometry, and has powerful implications in many, many areas of advanced mathematics. This section is a gentle introduction to the Pythagorean Theorem, based on its traditional, literal interpretation in terms of areas of squares.

1.74

The second part works well as a short discussion question.

1. The area of each small square is 9 (square units); the area of the large square is 18.

2. (1) The area of the large square is twice the area of either small one, and (2) the sum of the two small areas equals the large one. Guide students to identify both of them. If you have students who like to pursue such things, you might ask them which of these two properties is more likely to generalize to triangles that aren't quite so *nice*. The text takes that approach after these questions. They might notice on their own that the first property necessarily depends on the legs of the triangle being equal, whereas the second one might not.

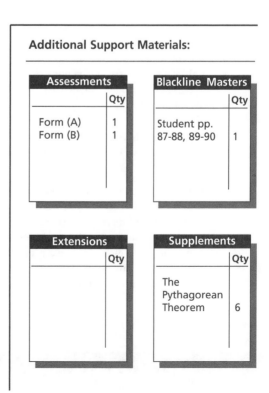

Additional Support Materials:

Assessments	Qty
Form (A)	1
Form (B)	1

Blackline Masters	Qty
Student pp. 87-88, 89-90	1

Extensions	Qty

Supplements	Qty
The Pythagorean Theorem	6

Chapter 1

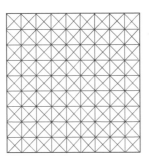

Display 1.67

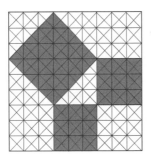

Display 1.68

The triangle in Display 1.68 is rather special. It is an *isosceles right* triangle. This means that it has two sides of the same length that form a right angle between them.

Do you think that the relationships Pythagoras noticed still hold if the right triangle is not isosceles? If it is isosceles, but not a right triangle? If it is neither isosceles, nor right? How can you find out?

1.75

Use whatever tools you want (ruler, compass, protractor) to draw and measure the following figures as precisely as you can.

1. Draw a right triangle that is not isosceles. Make the sides whatever length you want. Then draw a square on each side of your triangle. Measure the lengths of the sides carefully and compute the areas of the squares. Which of the two area relationships of Display 1.68 still holds? Do they both hold? Compare your results with those of your classmates.

1.76

81

Published by IT'S ABOUT TIME, Inc. © 2000 MATHconx, LLC

This is a thinking habit question. Spend just enough time on it to focus students' understanding of the questions and to get them to suggest the need for test case examples. This will make the more specific questions that follow meaningful.

1.75

This set of activities is worth some investment of time; it will sharpen and reinforce students' understanding of what the Pythagorean Theorem says and of the conditions under which it holds. The students' drawings need not be formal constructions, but they need to come close enough to drawing right angles (when appropriate) that their measurements and computations make their examples persuasive. The students' freedom to choose side lengths is important. By comparing their results for various sizes and shapes of triangles with each other, they should come to understand that the *defining conditions*, not the individual sizes, determine the results they are getting.

1.76

1. The sum of the areas of the square on the legs equals the area of the square on the hypotenuse. However, the smaller squares have unequal areas, so the other property cannot hold.

NOTES

Chapter 1

2. Repeat part 1 for an isosceles triangle that is not a right triangle.

3. Repeat part 1 for a triangle that is neither isosceles nor right.

4. What do you think the Pythagorean Theorem says?

This is what Pythagoras observed.

The **Pythagorean Theorem** (geometric version).
The square on the hypotenuse of a right triangle is equal to the sum of the squares on its legs.

Notice that we say "the square(s) *on*," rather than "the square(s) *of*." Pythagoras would have said "on" because he was thinking of the actual squares and their areas. To Pythagoras, a square was a geometric figure, not a number. And when he said "equal," he meant it that the two smaller squares could actually be cut up and put together to form the big square. He didn't think or write in the language of algebra. In fact, algebraic notation would not be invented for another 2000 years!

Nowadays we often think of the Pythagorean Theorem algebraically. This makes it more useful for many things that Pythagoras never even dreamed about. Using the fact that a square of the side length s has area s^2, we can restate the theorem like this.

The **Pythagorean Theorem** (algebraic version).
If $\triangle ABC$ is a right triangle with hypotenuse of length c and legs of lengths a and b, then

$$a^2 + b^2 = c^2$$

In the algebraic version, $\angle C$ is the right angle of $\triangle ABC$. It's the angle opposite the hypotenuse.

1.77

1. What if you change the triangle by making $\angle C$ bigger than a right angle? How should the algebraic statement change? Does it help if you visualize the geometric form of the theorem?

2. What if you make $\angle C$ smaller than a right angle? How should the algebraic statement change?

82

2. Neither property holds. Of course, the squares on the two equal sides have equal areas.

3. Neither property holds.

4. For some students who have never heard of the Pythagorean Theorem before, this may not be quite as obvious as you think. They might want to say something about *isosceles* right triangles here. Guide them to see that (a) a theorem is more valuable if it applies to a wider class of things, and (b) the answers to parts 1, 2, and 3 suggest that something worthwhile can be said about *all* right triangles, even if they are not isosceles. At this point, students should be able to formulate the correct statement pretty clearly.

1.77

These questions provide a good illustration of how the algebraic and geometric interpretations of the Pythagorean Theorem complement each other.

1. If you visualize pulling apart sides AC and BC to make $\angle C$ more than a right angle, you can almost see the square on the side opposite $\angle C$ grow while the other two squares stay the same size. This tells you that the algebraic statement should become

$$a^2 + b^2 < c^2$$

2. Similarly, as sides AC and BC are squeezed together to make $\angle C$ less than a right angle, the square on the side opposite $\angle C$ shrinks while the other two squares stay the same size. Thus, in this case the algebraic statement should become

$$a^2 + b^2 > c^2$$

You can use Geometer's Sketchpad or similar software to set up a nice demonstration of this, but it takes a bit of careful preparation. The squares must be constructed in just the right way so that the square on the hypotenuse grows without distortion as you move the other sides of the triangle.

The Pythagorean Theorem is a statement about *all* right triangles. It says that *every* right triangle has this special relationship between the squares of its sides. What about its converse? Roughly speaking, its converse says that any triangle with this special relationship between the squares of its sides must be a right triangle.

The converse of the Pythagorean Theorem

If $\triangle ABC$ has sides of lengths a, b, and c such that

$$a^2 + b^2 = c^2$$

then the angle opposite the side of length c must be a right angle.

As you have seen, a true statement can have a false converse. However, in this case, the converse is true, too. Moreover, it is a very convenient tool for identifying right triangles.

Use the converse of the Pythagorean Theorem to determine which of the triangles with the following side lengths are right triangles. For the ones that are not, say whether the angle opposite the longest side must be greater than or less than a right angle. Explain.

1.78

1. 3 cm, 10 cm, 11 cm

2. 5 cm, 12 cm, 13 cm

3. $\frac{3}{10}$ m, $\frac{2}{5}$ m, $\frac{1}{2}$ m

4. 0.5 m, 2.1 m, 2.5 m

5. 0.9 km, 2.6 km, 2.7 km

6. 0.7 km, 2.4 km, 2.5 km

The converse of the Pythagorean Theorem was used by surveyors in ancient Egypt. They measured by using ropes with knots at regular intervals. They knew that if they marked off a 3–4–5 triangle, it would contain a right angle. The ancient Chinese knew that the theorem itself is true for isosceles right triangles. The contributions of the Greeks was to prove that it holds for any right triangles. The Pythagorean Theorem is a statement about areas. But many applications are more concerned with the lengths of the sides than the areas of the squares on them, as in the following example.

Published by IT'S ABOUT TIME, Inc. © 2000 MATHconx, LLC

83

1.78

The Yes or No part of this is a routine computational exercise. For the cases that are not right triangles, knowing the relative size of the largest angle depends on understanding the ideas in discussion 1.77 and adapting them to this converse situation.

1. Not a right triangle. The angle opposite the 11 cm side is greater than a right angle because $3^2 + 10^2 < 11^2$.

2. A right triangle.

3. A right triangle.

4. Not a right triangle. The angle opposite the 25 m side is greater than a right angle because $0.5^2 + 2.1^2 < 2.5^2$.

5. Not a right triangle. The angle opposite the 27 km side is less than a right angle because $0.9^2 + 2.6^2 > 2.7^2$.

6. A right triangle.

NOTES

Joel, a ham radio operator, wants to put up a 42 foot antenna pole. If the antenna leans to one side or another, it might fall over in a high wind. For that reason, he wants to build it at right angles to the ground. He plans to use support wires to hold the antenna upright. The antenna, the ground, and each support wire form a right triangle. We consider only one wire at a time; they all can be handled in the same way. A mathematical model of this situation is a right triangle, $\triangle ABC$ in Display 1.69.

Each support wire will be attached to the antenna 40 feet above the ground, right near the top. To know how much wire to buy, Joel needs to know the length of each support. He decides to anchor one wire to the ground 30 feet from the base of the antenna. Then he uses the formula from the Pythagorean Theorem.

$$a^2 + b^2 = c^2$$

In this case, $a = 40$ ft. and $b = 30$ ft., so

$$40^2 + 30^2 = c^2$$

This tells him that $c^2 = 2500$.

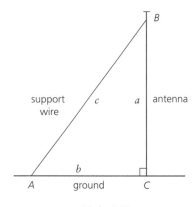

Display 1.69

1.79

1. How long is this support wire? What is its unit of measure?

2. Joel doesn't have enough room to put one of the support wires 30 feet from the base. He has to anchor it 22 feet from the base. How long is this support wire? Round your answer to one decimal place.

84

Chapter 1

1.79

This typical, commonplace application of the Pythagorean Theorem requires students to understand and calculate square roots.

1. This part uses *nice* numbers, to reinforce recognition of 3–4–5 right triangles and to help students see what the answer ought to be. The numbers in the next part are not so nice. The wire is 50 feet long. The unit of measure is the foot, not the square foot.

2. Make sure students can identify what a and b are in this case. Matching the story to the diagram may be a source of trouble for some students. The reference to 30 ft. in this part of the story is a deliberate tactic to help you identify students who plug in numbers blindly without understanding what they read. In this case,

$$a = 40 \text{ and } b = 22, \text{ so } 40^2 + 22^2 = c^2$$

Thus, the wire is $\sqrt{2084}$ ft. long, approximately 45.7 ft.

NOTES

If you know the length of *any* two sides of a right triangle, the Pythagorean Theorem tells you the length of the third side. In the previous example, it was used to find the length of the hypotenuse from the lengths of the other two sides. In this next example, the hypotenuse and one other side are known.

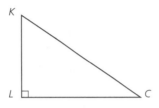

Display 1.70

Charlie Brown finally has his kite off the ground in the school parking lot. He has 100 feet of string stretched out to the kite, and he wants to know how high off the ground it is. Lucy measures the distance from where Charlie is standing to a point, *L*, at which she is directly under the kite. This is 75 feet.

1.80

1. Is Display 1.70 a good mathematical model for this situation? What do the letters represent? What simplifying assumptions are we making when we use this model?

2. How high is Charlie's kite, according to the model in Display 1.70? Round your answer to the nearest foot.

3. How might you modify your answer to part 2 in order to account for the assumptions of this model?

Sometimes, but not often, *all three* side lengths in an application of the Pythagorean Theorem are whole numbers. The two most common examples, which you have seen already, are

3, 4, 5 and 5, 12, 13

There are many others, but they are not always easy to find. Curiosity about such numbers has led people to search for more examples and to investigate what special properties such triples of numbers might have. They even gave these numbers a special name: Three positive whole numbers *a*, *b*, and *c* such that $a^2 + b^2 = c^2$ are called a **Pythagorean triple**. If the sides of a triangle form a Pythagorean triple, then we know (from the converse of the Pythagorean Theorem) that the triangle must contain a right angle opposite its longest side. This is a handy shortcut in some situations.

Published by IT'S ABOUT TIME, Inc. © 2000 MATHconx, LLC

85

1.80

The discussion parts of this exercise are 1 and 3. Part 2 is a straightforward application of the Pythagorean Theorem.

1. It's a pretty good model for getting a rough idea of how high the kite is. *C, L,* and *K* represent the locations of Charlie Brown, Lucy, and the kite, respectively. Students should notice at least two simplifying assumptions implied by this diagram: (1) the kite is in one place; and (2) the string is straight and does not stretch. We might reasonably assume the kite is virtually stationary at the instant Lucy is right under it. However, the string probably stretches and sags under its own weight. This last factor probably has the largest effect on the accuracy of the calculation.

2. Since the hypotenuse represents the length of the string, the Pythagorean Theorem tells us that
    $$75^2 + h^2 = 100^2$$
    where *h* is the height of the kite above the ground. You may have to help students to set this up. However, if you do this as a discussion problem, some students should be able to come up with it themselves and explain it to anyone who doesn't understand. Now guide them to solve for h^2 and then take the square root. Students should see these steps as natural, easy algebraic simplifications, not as some arcane procedure.

    $$h^2 = 100^2 - 75^2 = 4375$$
    $$h = \sqrt{4375} = 66 \text{ ft. (approximately)}$$

3. This is mostly an exercise in using common sense. It's impossible to account for the movement of the kite, of course. The main issue is the string, which probably sags a lot more than it stretches. Because of that, the answer in part 2 probably is too high. It would be reasonable to reduce it to somewhere between 50 and 60 ft.

NOTES
....
....
....
....
....
....
....

1.81

1. Which of the following are Pythagorean triples? Justify each answer.

   (a) 15, 36, 39   (d) 8, 12, 16

   (b) 7, 9, 11   (e) 20, 30, 40

   (c) 7, 24, 25   (f) 30, 40, 50

2. Check that all of the following are Pythagorean triples.

   3, 4, 5   6, 8, 10   9, 12, 15   12, 16, 20

   In your own words, what's the pattern here?

3. We can state the pattern of part 2 algebraically, like this: If *n* is a natural number, then *3n, 4n, 5n* is a Pythagorean triple. Prove it. *Hint:* Use the Distributive Law and a little algebra.

We end this section with one more important use of the Pythagorean Theorem. In a rectangular coordinate system, it is the key to finding the distance between two points by using their coordinates. Display 1.71 shows a typical example of this. The line segment between the points (2, 1) and (6, 4) is the hypotenuse of a right triangle with its legs parallel to the coordinate axes. Its length is the *distance*, *d*, between the two points. The right angle vertex is (6, 1).

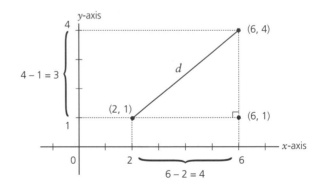

The distance between (2,1) and (6,4)

Display 1.71

Notice that the right angle vertex is on the same horizontal line as (2, 1), so it has the same *y*-coordinate, 1. It is on the same vertical line as (6, 4), so it has the same *x*-coordinate, 6.

86

1.81

The first two parts are routine. Part 3 challenges students to apply a little of the algebra they have learned.

1. (a) Yes   (b) No   (c) Yes   (d) No   (e) No   (f) Yes

2. Every multiple of 3, 4, 5 by a positive integer is a Pythagorean triple.

3. The first challenge is setting up the question algebraically. We must prove that $(3n)^2 + (4n)^2 = (5n)^2$. Then, starting with the left side of this equation, we have

$$(3n)^2 + (4n)^2 = 3^2 \cdot n^2 + 4^2 \cdot n^2$$
$$= (3^2 + 4^2) \cdot n^2$$
$$= 5^2 \cdot n^2$$

because 3, 4, 5 is a Pythagorean triple. But $5^2 \cdot n^2 = (5n)^2$, so we are done.

NOTES

This means that the length of one leg of the triangle is $6 - 2$, the difference in the x-coordinates of the original two points. The length of the other leg is $4 - 1$, the difference in the y-coordinates of the original two points. Now apply the Pythagorean Theorem to find the length of the hypotenuse.

$$d^2 = (6 - 2)^2 + (4 - 1)^2$$

$$d^2 = 4^2 + 3^2$$

$$d^2 = 25$$

$$d = \sqrt{25} = 5$$

Use the Pythagorean Theorem to find the distance between the following pairs of points in the coordinate plane. Draw a sketch in each case, and give the coordinates of the vertex of the right angle.

1.82

1. **(0, 0) and (5, 12)**

2. **(8, 3) and (2, 10)**

3. **(−4, 1) and (5, −5)**

You will see many uses for the Pythagorean Theorem as you learn more about mathematics and science. It is fundamental to any technological or industrial society. In fact, many years ago there was a plan to use it to try to communicate with life on other planets by drawing a *very* large copy of the figure with the triangle and the three squares, many miles wide in a desert. The theory was that any advanced civilization, regardless of how they communicated, would have to know the idea of the Pythagorean Theorem. They would recognize the figure and know that there is intelligent life on this planet, too.

Problem Set: 1.8

1. According to the Pythagorean Theorem, if you draw squares on the sides of a right triangle, the sum of the areas of the squares on the legs will be the same as the area of the squares on the hypotenuse. Does that also work with shapes other than squares? This problem asks you to explore a part of that question. Your teacher will give you a copy of a right triangle with squares drawn on its sides to help you answer the following questions. Use the centimeter as your unit of length.

87

1.82

These can be done by mimicking the example of Display 1.71. The only fussy part is keeping the order of the coordinates straight. Drawing a sketch and identifying the third vertex should help the students with that. Some practice with square roots and negative numbers is built into these exercises.

Vertex of right angle: (5, 0) or (0, 12); distance: 13 (a Pythagorean triple!)

Vertex of right angle: (8, 10) or (2, 3); distance: $\sqrt{85} = 9.2$ (approx.)

Vertex of right angle or (5,1) : (-4, -5); distance: $\sqrt{117} = 10.8$ (approx.)

Problem Set: 1.8

1. A Blackline Master for this problem is supplied. Parts (a), (b), and (c) are routine drawing, measurement, and calculation exercises to reinforce what the Pythagorean Theorem says about areas and to link its algebraic expression with its geometric meaning. Part (d) is more challenging.

NOTES

_____

(a) Measure the sides of $\triangle ABC$. Then measure the sides of the squares on each side and calculate their areas. In this case, is it true that $a^2 + b^2 = c^2$?

(b) Extend each square by 2 cm along the dashed lines to form a rectangle. The dimensions of your rectangle on side BC should be a and $a + 2$.

   (i) In terms of b and c, what are the dimensions of the rectangles on the other two sides?

   (ii) Calculate the areas of these three rectangles. Is it true that the sum of the areas of the rectangles on the legs equals the area of the rectangle on the hypotenuse?

(c) Extend each of these rectangles further along the dashed lines, so that the long side of each is twice as long as the side of the original square.

   (i) In terms of a, b, and c, what are the dimensions of these new rectangles?

   (ii) Calculate the areas of these three rectangles. Is it true that the sum of the areas of the rectangles on the legs equals the area of the rectangle on the hypotenuse?

(d) Try to generalize these examples to make up a rule that describes when the area-sum property holds for rectangles on the sides of a right triangle. If you're really feeling adventuresome, try to prove your rule algebraically, based on your expressions for the dimensions of the rectangles in parts (b) and (c). *Hint:* It has something to do with the Distributive Law.

2. Two empty lots have been put up for sale, and Ms. Bocciarelli is thinking about buying them. The real estate agent said they are both rectangular lots. He claimed the small lot is 50 feet wide by 120 feet long and the large lot is 320 feet wide by 400 feet long. Ms. Bocciarelli went out and checked the measurements. They were what the agent said. She also measured the distance from one corner of each lot to the opposite corner. She got 130 feet for the small lot and 540 feet for the large lot. Then she knew something was wrong. What is it? How is it likely to affect the value of the property?

3. A right triangle has legs of lengths 8 mm and 15 mm long. How long is the hypotenuse? Find the area and the perimeter.

88

(a) This is a 3 cm by 4 cm by 5 cm right triangle, so it clearly fits the Pythagorean Theorem.

(b) (i) b by $b + 2$ and c by $c + 2$
   (ii) $3 \cdot 5 = 15$ sq. cm; $4 \cdot 6 = 24$ sq. cm; $5 \cdot 7 = 35$ sq. cm
       No; $15 + 24 \neq 35$

(c) (i) a by $2a$, b by $2b$, and c by $2c$
   (ii) $3 \cdot 6 = 18$ sq. cm; $4 \cdot 8 = 32$ sq. cm; $5 \cdot 10 = 50$ sq. cm
       Yes; $18 + 32 = 50$

(d) A correct conjecture can take many forms. The main idea is that increasing the side lengths by *multiplying* the original side lengths by the same number works, but *adding* the same number to each side length doesn't work. An algebraic proof works like this: If rectangles are formed by multiplying each original side length by k to get the other side of the rectangle, then the sum of the areas on the legs is $a \cdot ka + b \cdot kb$. Now,

$$a \cdot ka + b \cdot kb = k \cdot (a^2 + b^2) \quad \text{[by the Distributive Law]}$$
$$= k \cdot c^2 \quad \text{[by the Pythagorean Theorem]}$$
$$= c \cdot kc \quad \text{[by associativity and commutativity]}$$

A similar argument for an added constant shows where the process breaks down.

$$a(a + k) + b(b + k) = a^2 + ak + b^2 + bk$$
$$= (a^2 + b^2) + (a + b)k$$
$$= c^2 + (a + b)k$$

This does not equal $c(c + k)$ unless $a + b = c$. But then you would not have a triangle!

2. The small lot is rectangular. The sum of the squares of the sides equals the square of the diagonal. The large lot is not rectangular. The sum of the squares of the sides is 262,400. The square of the diagonal is 291,600. A rectangle with sides of 320 ft. and 400 ft. would have a diagonal of 512.25 ft.

   If the large lot is not rectangular, then its area is likely to be *less* than the $320 \cdot 400 = 128,000$ sq. ft. that the agent implied. How much less? Your students have the tools to construct a triangle with sides of 320, 400, and 540 units and finds its area, which represents half the area of the lot. The area of the lot is 124,200 sq. ft. That's a discrepancy of 3800 sq. ft., about 3% less area than claimed.

3. $8^2 + 15^2 = 289$, so $c = 17$ m. The area is $\frac{1}{2} \cdot 8 \cdot 15 = 60$ sq. m; the perimeter is $8 + 15 + 17 = 40$ m. Note that we have another Pythagorean triple here. 8, 15, 17.

Published by IT'S ABOUT TIME, Inc. © 2000 MATHconx, LLC

4. A right triangle has one side 27 yd. long and a hypotenuse 40 yd. long. How long is the other side? Round your answer to one decimal place. Find the area and perimeter.

5. In the western flatlands there is a rectangular tract of prairie bounded on all four sides by almost perfectly straight dirt roads. Two roads run north–south; two run east–west.
   The tract of land measures 10 miles by 12 miles. A car and a horseback rider start from its southeast corner at the same time, both headed for its northwest corner. The car must drive on the dirt roads and can average about 35 mph. The horse can cut across the prairie and can average about 25 mph. Who will get to the northwest corner first, and by how much time?

6. Ms. Bocciarelli is building a two-story house. The second floor is 8 feet above the first floor. She plans a staircase from the first floor to the second that would cover 11 feet horizontally.

   (a) How long does the banister for the staircase need to be?
   (b) The lumberyard works in inches. How much banister stock should Ms. Bocciarelli order at the lumberyard? Make careful calculations; banister stock is expensive.

7. Can there be a Pythagorean triple with 1 in it? If so, find one. If not, explain why not.

8. Prove that, if n is a natural number and a, b, c is a Pythagorean triple, then na, nb, nc is also a Pythagorean triple. *Hint:* Use the Distributive Law.

9. A triangle in the coordinate plane has vertices (1, 2), (7, 10), and (26.2, -4.4). Is it a right triangle? Why or why not? Find its perimeter and its area. *Hint:* Start by finding the lengths of its sides.

10. Over the centuries, the Pythagorean Theorem has been proved in hundreds of different ways. Here is a proof from about 900 A.D. by an Arab scholar. The main idea of the proof, illustrated by Display 1.72, is this.

    Starting with a square on the side of the hypotenuse, cut away two copies of the original right triangle. Then glue them back on to the remaining odd pentagon in such a way that they clearly form the shape of the other two squares, side by side.

Published by IT'S ABOUT TIME, Inc. © 2000 MATHconx, LLC

Chapter 1

4. $40^2 - 27^2 = 871$, so the other side is $\sqrt{871} = 29.5$ yd. (approximately). Thus, the area is $\frac{1}{2} \cdot 29.5 \cdot 27 = 398.25$ sq. yd., and the perimeter is $27 + 29.5 + 40 = 96.5$ yd.

5. This is a hypotenuse computation problem with a time factor complication. The diagonal (the hypotenuse) is $\sqrt{10^2 + 12^2} = 15.62$ miles (approximately). The horse can cover this distance in about $\frac{15.62}{25}$ hours, which is about 37.5 minutes. The car has to travel $10 + 12 = 22$ miles, which it can do in about $\frac{22}{35}$ hours, which is about 37.7 minutes. The horseback rider probably gets there first, but only by about 12 seconds. It's a virtual tie.

6. (a) Ms. Bocciarelli will need 13.6 ft. of banister stock.
   (b) This is just 0.2 in. more than 13 ft., 7 in., so she can get by with buying 163 in. of banister stock if she has a really careful carpenter.

7. No. If there were, it obviously couldn't represent the hypotenuse because there are no natural numbers a and b such that a^2 and $b^2 = 1$. Therefore, we would have $1^2 + b^2 = c^2$ for some natural numbers b and c. That is, $1 = c^2 - b^2$. But there are no natural numbers whose squares differ by 1, so this can't happen.

8. This is a generalization of parts 2 and 3 of 1.81. Even if you don't assign this problem, it would be a good idea to make sure that your students understand what it says. Here's a proof.
   Since a, b, c is a Pythagorean triple, we know that $a^2 + b^2 = c^2$. We must show that $(na)^2 + (nb)^2 = (nc)^2$. Start with the left side of this equation.

   $$\begin{aligned} (na)^2 + (nb)^2 &= n^2 \cdot a^2 + n^2 \cdot b^2 \\ &= n^2 \cdot (a^2 + b^2) \quad \text{[Distributive Law]} \\ &= n^2 \cdot c^2 \quad \text{[original Pythagorean triple]} \\ &= (nc)^2 \text{ as required.} \end{aligned}$$

9. This requires finding three distances in the coordinate plane, and then thinking about what you have.

   Between $(1, 2)$ and $(7, 10)$: $\sqrt{(7-1)^2 + (10-2)^2} = \sqrt{100} = 10$. This could also be done by recognizing 6, 8, 10 as a Pythagorean triple.
   Between $(7, 10)$ and $(26.2, -4.4)$: $\sqrt{(26.2-7)^2 + (-4.4-10)^2} = \sqrt{576} = 24$
   Yes, this is a right triangle. The short justification is to recognize that 10, 24, 26 is a Pythagorean triple. It's $2 \cdot 5, 2 \cdot 12, 2 \cdot 13$. See problem 8. Otherwise, use the converse of the Pythagorean Theorem and calculate $10^2 + 24^2 = 26^2$.
   Its perimeter is $10 + 24 + 26 = 60$ units. Since it's a right triangle, its area is $\frac{1}{2} \cdot 10 \cdot 24 = 120$ square units.

10. The main idea of this proof is fairly easy to visualize. Of course, a number of details must be checked to make sure that the visual argument is not

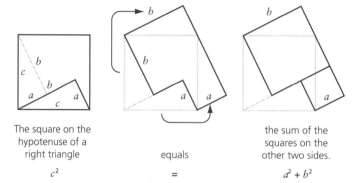

The square on the
hypotenuse of a
right triangle

equals

the sum of the
squares on the
other two sides.

c^2

$=$

$a^2 + b^2$

The Pythagorean Theorem

Display 1.72

(a) Your teacher will give you a sheet of paper with two square figures on it. The top one is for this part. It shows two congruent copies of a right triangle inside a square with side length the same as the hypotenuse of the triangle. Cut out the two triangles. Then reassemble the three pieces to form the sum of the squares on the other two sides of the triangle, as shown in Display 1.72.

(b) Is the cut-and-paste demonstration of part (a) a convincing proof of the Pythagorean Theorem? There is a danger in believing such things without checking the details. For instance, look at the bottom square of the handout sheet. It is an 8 by 8 square, measured in half-inches that are clearly marked all the way around it. Cut out the square. Then cut it carefully along the dotted lines to make four pieces. Reassemble the four pieces into a 5 by 13 rectangle. Then explain what's wrong with what you just did. *Hint:* What is the area of the square? Of the rectangle?

90

misleading. Part (a) gives students hands-on experience with the argument. Part (b) illustrates why such demonstrations must be checked with care. Checking the actual steps of the proof requires more formal geometric machinery than we have at this stage.

(a) If the pieces are assembled properly, the dotted line(s) should connect and show the separation between the two squares, as in the third diagram of Display 1.72.

(b) By matching the 3 unit side of each triangle with the 3 unit side of one of the quadrilaterals, you get two longer right triangles that can be put together so that the boundary is a 5 by 13 rectangle. This visually persuasive process is misleading, however. The area of the 8 by 8 square is 64 square units, whereas the area of a 5 by 13 rectangle is 65 square units! There is a long, thin hole in the middle of this rectangle, resulting from the fact that the hypotenuse of each assembled long triangle is not a straight line. Thus, it would be a mistake to accept the cut and paste argument of part (a) as a proof of the Pythagorean Theorem without supporting each step by a formal justification.

NOTES

1.9 It Varies With the Square

Mrs. Chi is preparing a birthday party for Fan. She knows that he and his friends are really crazy about Cliff's Famous Homemade Chocolate Ice Cream. It's pretty expensive and comes only in pints, but birthdays are special occasions. Mrs. Chi figures a pint will serve two hungry teenagers.

1. How many hungry teenagers can be served with 10 pints of ice cream? With 12 pints? With 15 pints?

2. Write an equation for the number, T, of hungry teenagers that can be served with p pints of Cliff's Famous Homemade Chocolate Ice Cream.

3. Graph this equation on your calculator. What shape do you get? Describe its location in the coordinate plane.

1.83

Learning Outcomes

After studying this section, you will be able to:

Recognize situations in which one variable varies directly or inversely as another or as the square of another;

Express direct and inverse variations algebraically;

Describe real world situations using direct or inverse variation.

You have just seen a typical example of direct variation, a particularly nice relationship between two variables. As one variable increases, so does the other, and they increase "in step," so to speak. Similarly, as one variable decreases, so does the other. In the ice cream example, for instance, if you double the number of people, you double the number of pints you need; if you triple the number of people, you triple the number of pints you need, and so on.

Phrases to Know: A variable y **varies directly as** a variable x if there is a positive constant k, such that $y = kx$. This situation is also described by saying that y is **directly proportional to** x. The number k is called the **constant of proportionality**.

Sometimes the constant of proportionality is called the *scaling factor*, particularly when we are talking about changing the size of a picture or a geometric figure. This simpler phrase will appear often in the next chapter, where we talk about scaling geometric shapes.

Published by IT'S ABOUT TIME, Inc. © 2000 MATHconx, LLC

1.9 It Varies With the Square

The previous section made extensive use of the squaring function to find areas and made use of its inverse, the square root function, to find lengths. This section uses these two functions as it explains direct and inverse variation. Although it is geometrically motivated, much of this section describes spatial or physical relationships algebraically. The problems give students opportunities to practice solving algebraic equations in geometric and physical contexts. Some of this material is related to the **MATH** *Connections* Year 1 chapters on functions and coordinate geometry.

1.83

This exercise presents a simple, typical example of direct variation, which is about to be defined.

1. 20; 24; 30

2. $T = 2p$

3. It is a straight line with slope 2 that that goes through the origin.

Chapter 1

Additional Support Materials:

Assessments	Qty
Form (A)	1
Form (B)	1

Blackline Masters	Qty

Extensions	Qty

Supplements	Qty
It Varies With The Square	4

a
1.84

1. What shape is the graph of a direct variation equation? Describe its position in the coordinate plane as specifically as you can.

2. What is the constant of proportionality in the ice cream example?

3. Does the perimeter of a square vary directly as its side length? If so, what is the constant of proportionality? If not, why not?

4. Does the side length of a square vary directly as its perimeter? If so, what is the constant of proportionality? If not, why not?

5. Does the area of a square vary directly as its side length? If so, what is the constant of proportionality? If not, why not?

6. For a given number *n* of sides, is the perimeter of a regular *n*-gon directly proportional to its side length? If so, what is the constant of proportionality? If not, why not?

Are Fahrenheit degrees directly proportional to Celsius degrees? Why or why not?

1.85

A close relative of direct variation is important in dealing with variables, particularly in geometric settings involving area. Here is a simple example.

b
1.86

The legs of an isosceles right triangle are the same length.

1. What is the area of an isosceles right triangle with leg length 4 cm? 5 cm? 7 cm? 10 cm? 20 cm? 100 cm? Make a small table of these data.

2. Write a formula for the area, *A*, of an isosceles right triangle with leg length *x*.

3. Graph your formula on your calculator. Is it a straight line? Where does it touch the axes?

4. As *x* gets larger, does *A* get larger? Does *A* vary directly as *x*? If so, what is the constant of proportionality? If not, why not?

In this latest example, *A* (which is measured in square units) is equal to a constant times the *square* of *x* (which is

92

Published by IT'S ABOUT TIME, Inc. © 2000 MATHconx, LLC

1.9 It Varies With the Square

1.84

You may have to sharpen the first question, depending on students' initial responses. The second question should be obvious.

1. It's a straight line with a positive slope, i.e., it goes up from left to right, and it *must* go through the origin.

2. 2

3. Yes. $P = 4s$, so the constant of proportionality is 4.

4. Yes. $s = \frac{1}{4}P$, so the constant of proportionality is $\frac{1}{4}$. This and part 3 together illustrate that there is an implicit order in the language of the definition which affects the value of the constant, but not the fact that two variables are in direct proportion.

5. No. $A = s^2$, so A is not equal to a *constant* times s.

6. This question uses the alternative phrasing to give students experience with both forms. Yes. $P = \frac{1}{4}ns$. Since n is given, it is a constant, and it must be positive. Thus, n is the constant of proportionality.

1.85

No. This might make for a short, profitable exchange of student opinions. You might have to help students remember that the relationship between Fahrenheit degrees and Celsius degrees is given by the equation $F = \frac{9}{5}C + 32$. This would be a direct proportion if the scales had the same origin—that is, if 0° C and 0° F coincided. But they don't. A direct variation graph must go through (0, 0). Informally, this implies that, as one variable gets very small, then a variable that varies directly with it must be getting very small, too.

1.86

This extends part 5 of 1.84

1. 8 sq. cm; 12.5 sq. cm; 24.5 sq. cm; 50 sq. cm; 200 sq. cm; 5000 sq. cm

2. $A = \frac{1}{2}x^2$

3. It is not a straight line. It is a curve (a parabola, actually, but they need not know this) that crosses the axes at (0, 0).

4. Yes. No, because A is not a *constant* multiple of x.

measured in units of length). This kind of situation comes up often enough to have a name of its own.

Phrases to Know: A variable y **varies directly as the square** of a variable x if there is a positive constant k, such that $y = k \cdot x^2$. This phrase is sometimes shortened to "y *varies directly as* x^2." The number k is again called the **constant of proportionality**.

1. Write a formula expressing the length d of the diagonal of a square in terms of its side length s.

2. Does the diagonal vary directly as the side length, or does it vary directly as the square of the side length? What is the constant of proportionality? Explain.

1.87

In some situations, as one variable increases, another *decreases*. This often comes up in a situation where the variables represent conflicting goals. As temperature decreases, the cost of heating increases; as the price of a product increases, demand for it (usually) decreases. In a state lottery, it is attractive to have as many prizes as possible and prizes as large as possible. However, it is difficult to increase the number of prizes without reducing their value!

Phrases to Know: A variable y **varies inversely as** a variable x if there is a positive constant k, such that $y = \frac{k}{x}$. This situation is also described by saying that y is **inversely proportional** to x. As before, the number k is called the **constant of proportionality**.

You are the director of a state lottery. In a typical week, ticket sales total $6 million. Of that, $3 million goes to the state budget and $1 million goes toward the expenses of running the lottery, leaving the state with $2 million to give away each week. You are considering various ways of splitting up the prize money. Your goal is to sell as many tickets as possible.

1.88

1. One plan is to give five prizes of equal value. If you follow that plan, what will each prize be worth?

Published by IT'S ABOUT TIME, Inc. © 2000 MATHconx, LLC

1.87

This one is a bit tricky. Handle with algebraic care.

1. By the Pythagorean Theorem, $d = \sqrt{s^2 + s^2} = \sqrt{2s^2}$

2. The form in which we left the formula in part 1 may lead some students to believe that the diagonal varies with the square of the side length. This is *not* the case. One more algebraic simplifying step shows why.

$$d = \sqrt{2s^2} = \sqrt{2} \cdot \sqrt{s^2} = \sqrt{2} \cdot s$$

You may have to help your students with this algebraic manipulation. Thus, d varies directly as s. The constant of proportionality is $\sqrt{2}$. The intuitive tipoff is that both the side and the diagonal are measured in units of length; neither is measured in square units. If students are skeptical or confused, have them calculate diagonals for squares with four or five different side lengths and plot the data points.

1.88

Selecting an appropriate scale and appropriate points to plot is not easy in this situation.

1. $400,000 each

2.

Number of Prizes	Value of Each Prize
1	$2,000,000
2	$1,000,000
5	$400,000
10	$200,000
50	$40,000
100	$20,000
1000	$2,000
10,000	$200

Display 1.15 T

Chapter 1

2. You are also considering seven other plans, each with prizes of equal value. How large can each prize be if you give 1, 2, 10, 50, 100, 1000, or 10,000 prizes? Make a table of these data.

3. Which of these eight plans would *you* find most attractive if you were thinking of buying a ticket?

4. Define some variables and write an equation describing these situations.

5. Graph the equation on graph paper using the same scale on both axes. Try letting both variables vary between 0 and 10,000. You may need to compute more data points.

6. Can you find any symmetry in the graph?

7. Make the same graph on your graphing calculator. Is this graph better or worse than the one you made by hand for studying this function? Explain.

Sometimes as one variable increases, its square determines the rate at which another decreases. This often comes up in a situation where something—such as light, sound, or magnetic attraction—spreads out from a source.

Phrases to Know: A variable y **varies inversely as the square** of a variable x if there is a positive constant k, such that $y = \frac{k}{x^2}$. This phrase is sometimes shortened to "*y varies inversely as x^2.*" The number k is called the **constant of proportionality**.

1.89

The amount of light from a point source varies inversely as the square of the distance away from the light source. Have you ever seen anyone trying to take flash pictures at a school play or graduation? The flash on a simple camera provides the right amount of light about 8 feet from the camera. For a particular flash, the law is

$$L = \frac{256,000}{d^2}$$

where L is the amount of light (in units of light) and d is the distance (in feet) from the flash to the subject.

3. This is purely a personal opinion question to engage students with the scenario.

4. For v as prize value and n as the number of prizes, $v = \frac{2{,}000{,}000}{n}$. Reversing the two variables in this equation is also legitimate. There is no clear-cut independent or dependent variable in this situation.

5. Have students use the same scale on both axes in order to avoid distorting the shape and symmetry of the graph. They should get a curve that approaches both axes asymptotically.

6. The graph is symmetric about the line $y = x$.

7. Some graphing calculators can be forced to use the same scale on both axes (for the TI-82 (TI-83), use the ZSquare option on the ZOOM menu, but the low resolution of the graphics still distorts the symmetry.

1.89

The answers below are based on slide film. With print film, you will not see much difference except for the graduation picture. Any differences you do see are likely to be the result of the processing machine trying to compensate for bad exposure. For the graduation shot, quality will depend entirely on the stage lighting; the effect of the flash will be negligible.

Note that a fixed, but unspecified, unit of light is used here to avoid a messy explanation of exactly how light is measured relative to a particular camera and a particular kind of film.

NOTES

1. How much light is available at 8 feet? Assume that this is just the right amount of light for taking pictures with this camera.

2. How much light is available at 6 feet, the minimum recommended distance for this flash? What percent is this of the amount available at 8 feet? How do you think a picture taken at 6 feet will look?

3. How much light is available at 10 feet, the maximum recommended distance for this flash? What percent is this of the amount available at 8 feet? How do you think a picture taken at 10 feet will look?

4. Suppose you take this camera to your friend's graduation and from 50 feet away, take a picture of her receiving her diploma. How much light is available at 50 feet? What percent is this of the amount available at 8 feet? How do you think a picture taken at 50 feet will look? What's the message here?

Problem Set: 1.9

1. Display 1.73 shows a spring. If you pull on the ends of the spring, the amount the spring stretches varies directly as the force with which you pull. Springs like this are used to make simple scales. (Some scales for weighing fish or produce are made like this.) If you turn the spring vertically and hang a weight on one end, the amount it stretches is directly proportional to the weight. This enables us to read the weight on a length scale.

Display 1.73

(a) A particular spring stretched 1.28 inches when we hung a 32 pound weight on it. Find the constant of proportionality.

(b) How far would the spring stretch if you hung a 50 pound weight on it?

(c) We want to make a scale with this spring with marks every 5 pounds. How far apart should the marks be, in inches?

(d) The scale is 4 inches long. What is the heaviest weight the scale will measure?

Published by IT'S ABOUT TIME, Inc. © 2000 MATHconx, LLC

95

1. Proper exposure requires 4000 units of light.

2. At 6 feet, you get 7111 units of light. This is 178% of what you get at 8 feet, 78% too much. The picture will look washed out.

3. At 10 feet, you get 2560 units of light. This is 64% of what you get at 8 feet, 36% too little. The picture will look dark.

4. At 50 feet, you get 102.4 units of light. This is 2.56% of what you get at 8 feet, 97.44% too little. The picture will look like a close up of a black hole unless there is enough light on stage to save it. The message is to refrain from popping all those flashes in the eyeballs of the graduates.

Problem Set: 1.9

1. The mathematical model is known as Hooke's Law. It is fairly accurate if you do not stretch the spring too far.

   (a) This kind of question was not asked in the section, but it requires only a simple algebraic step from what is known. Since the stretch s in inches is directly proportional to the weight w in pounds, then there is a constant of proportionality, k, such that $s = kw$. Since k is *constant*, it is the same for all weights. We are told that $1.28 = k \cdot 32$, so $k = 0.04$. That is, the spring stretches 0.04 inches per pound.
   (b) $s = 0.04 \cdot 50 = 2$ inches
   (c) $0.04 \cdot 5 = 0.2$ inches apart
   (d) $4 = 0.04 \cdot w$, so $w = 100$ pounds

NOTES

2. The amount of fuel needed to keep a house warm in winter is directly proportional to the difference in temperature between the inside and outside. We shall measure fuel usage in terms of dollars of fuel cost. (Assume that the price of fuel stays the same all winter.) It costs $4 per day to heat a particular house when the inside temperature is 68°F and the (average) outside temperature is freezing (32°F).

   (a) Write an equation for the relationship between the fuel cost per day, c in dollars, and the difference between the indoor and outdoor temperatures, d in degrees Fahrenheit. (You will have to find the constant of proportionality from the data given.)

   (b) What will it cost for a day when the average outside temperature is 0°? 50°? –10°? Round your answers to the nearest cent.

   (c) Copy the table in Display 1.74. In the second column, fill in the costs that you calculated in part (b). Then calculate and fill in the costs for the indoor temperatures of 62° and 72°.

   (d) If you were living in this house and paying for the fuel, what temperature would you maintain indoors? Why?

Outdoor Temp.	Indoor Temperature		
	68°	62°	72°
50°			
32°	$4.00		
0°			
–10°			

Daily heating cost

Display 1.74

3. (a) Explain the following two statements:

   (i) Saying that varies directly as x is the same as saying that $\frac{y}{x}$ is a fixed number.

   (ii) Saying that y varies inversely as x is the same as saying that xy is a fixed number.

Published by IT'S ABOUT TIME, Inc. © 2000 MATHconx, LLC

2. (a) $c = kd$. For the data given, $d = 68 - 32 = 36$, so $4 = k \cdot 36$, implying $k = \frac{4}{36} = \frac{1}{9}$. Thus, the equation is $c = \frac{1}{9}d$.

    (b) $c = \frac{1}{9} \cdot (68 - 0) = \$7.56$

    $c = \frac{1}{9} \cdot (68 - 50) = \$2.00$

    $c = \frac{1}{9} \cdot (68 - (-10)) = \$8.67$

    (c) See Display 1.16T.

    (d) This is a personal opinion question.

Outdoor Temp.	Indoor Temperature		
	68°	62°	72°
50°	$2.00	$1.33	$2.44
32°	$4.00	$3.33	$4.44
0°	$7.56	$6.89	$8.00
−10°	$8.67	$8.00	$9.11

Daily heating cost (problem 2)

Display 1.16T

Note that deciding whether it is worth it to you to turn down the thermostat to save money is a personal decision. Most people making that decision do not have any idea of the actual savings involved for their particular house and climate. If most of your students live in homes where their families control and pay for their own heat, this problem might be expanded into an interesting, individualized project. You could have each student find out how much his/her family paid for heat over some period of time, get the average daily temperature for that period and the normal indoor temperature (thermostat setting) for their home. This would enable each student to calculate the constant of proportionality for his/her own home and then make out a table similar to Display 1.74 to see how changing the indoor temperature would affect the heating bill for his/her own family.

3. (a) This is an easy exercise in getting students to recognize what algebraic equations say.

    (i) Saying that y varies directly as x means $y = kx$ for some constant k. A constant is a fixed number. Divide both sides of $y = kx$ by x, so $\frac{y}{x} = k$.

    (ii) Similarly, saying that y varies inversely as x means $y = \frac{k}{x}$ for some constant k. Multiply both sides of $y = \frac{k}{x}$ by x, so $xy = k$.

(b) Write the analogous two statements for direct and inverse *square* variations.

4. If you ignore air resistance, the distance that a free falling object travels varies directly as the square of the time that it is falling. This basic law of physics was discovered by Galileo in the 17th century. In particular, a rock dropped from the top of a 19.5 meter tower will hit the ground in exactly 2 seconds.

(a) Write an equation for this relationship between the distance fallen, in meters, and the time of the fall, in seconds. Be sure to define the variables you use. (Find the constant of proportionality from the data given.)

(b) The tallest unbroken vertical drop of Niagara Falls is 51 meters. How long does it take a drop of water to fall from the edge of the Falls to the pool at its base? Round your answer to the nearest tenth of a second.

(c) Victoria Falls, on the Zambezi River in south central Africa, was discovered by a European, David Livingstone, in 1855. To estimate the height of the Falls, Livingstone might have timed how long it took a log going over the falls to drop from the edge to the river below. It would have taken the log $4\frac{3}{4}$ seconds. How high is this waterfall? Round your answer to the nearest meter.

(d) Write an equation for the relationship between distance fallen, *in feet*, and the time of the fall, *in seconds*. Be sure to define the variables you use. Round your value for the constant of proportionality to the nearest integer. One meter equals 39.37 inches.

(e) A careless mechanic leaves a small wrench in the wheel well of a cargo plane. As the plane is flying at 30,000 feet, the wrench falls out. How far (in feet) does the wrench fall in 5 seconds? In 10 seconds? How long does it take to hit the ground? Round your answer to the nearest tenth of a second.

5. A special case of Newton's Law of Gravity says that the weight of an object on Earth varies inversely as the square of its distance from the center of the Earth. For this problem, assume that the distance from sea level to the center of the Earth is 4000 miles. It actually varies from place to place on the globe, but this estimate will work well enough for us.

Published by IT'S ABOUT TIME, Inc. © 2000 MATHconx, LLC

97

(b) Saying that y varies directly as the square of x is the same as saying that $\frac{y}{x^2}$ is a fixed number.

Saying that y varies inversely as the square of x is the same as saying that $x^2 y$ is a fixed number.

4. A little history and geography are casually dropped into this problem. The heights given here are approximately correct for the longest free fall drops of these waterfalls.

(a) Using D for distance in meters and t for time in seconds, $D = kt^2$. According to the data, $19.5 = k \cdot 2^2$, so $k = 4.875$. Thus, the equation is $D = 4.875t^2$.

(b) $51 = 4.875t^2$, so $t^2 = \frac{51}{4.875} = 10.46$ (approx.); therefore, $t = 3.2$ sec.

(c) $D = 4.875 \cdot 4.75^2 = 110$ meters.

(d) This starts with a bit of unit conversion practice. By calculating $\frac{39.37}{12}$, students should see that there are 3.28 feet in a meter. Now, either by converting the old constant directly or by converting the given distance of 19.5 m into 64 ft. and recalculating, they should get the equation $d = 16t^2$, where d is the distance in feet and t is the time in seconds. This equation might be familiar to some students from physics or science class.

(e) $d = 16 \cdot 5^2 = 400$, so the wrench falls 400 ft. in 5 sec. It falls 1600 ft. in 10 sec. Solve $30,000 = 16 \cdot t^2$ to see how long it takes to hit the ground: $t^2 = 1875$, so $t = 43.3$ sec.

NOTES

(a) Mount Everest, located in the Himalayas between Nepal and Tibet, is the world's tallest mountain. Its top is 29,028 feet above sea level. Kumar weighs 200 pounds at sea level. If he is transported to the top of Mount Everest (so that he doesn't burn off any weight getting there), how much less will Kumar weigh at the top of this mountain? Round your answer to the nearest tenth of a pound.

(b) A rocket at Cape Canaveral is starting to lift a 900 pound lunar satellite into space. The farther up it goes, the less the satellite will weigh. How much will the satellite weigh 50 miles up? 100 miles up? 200 miles up? Round your answers to the nearest pound.

(c) How high above the Earth will the satellite of part (b) weigh only 100 pounds?

Published by IT'S ABOUT TIME, Inc. © 2000 MATHconx, LLC

5. Each of these parts requires students to set up the problem, make the appropriate distance conversion, and solve the equation on their own. It also gives them practice with handling large numbers. These are good exercises for small groups.

(a) Using w for weight and d for distance from the center of the Earth, $w = \dfrac{k}{d^2}$. To find k, solve $200 = \dfrac{k}{4000^2}$, so $k = 3{,}200{,}000{,}000$.

In scientific notation (if you want to give your students practice with it), $w = \dfrac{3.2 \times 10^9}{4005.5^2}$

There are 5280 ft. in a mile so Mt. Everest is about 5.5 miles high. Thus, the person's weight at the top is

$w = \dfrac{3.2 \times 10^9}{4005.5^2} = 199.5$ lb. (approx.)

That is, Kumar will weigh about half a pound less at the top of Mt. Everest.

(b) This equation requires a different constant of proportionality because it is based on a different sea level weight. In this case,

$900 = \dfrac{k}{4000^2}$, so $k = 1.44 \times 10^{10}$. This means that the equation is

$$w = \frac{1.44 \times 10^{10}}{d^2}$$

At 50 miles up: $w = \dfrac{1.44 \times 10^{10}}{4050^2} = 878$ lb.

At 100 miles up: $w = \dfrac{1.44 \times 10^{10}}{4100^2} = 857$ lb.

At 200 miles up: $w = \dfrac{1.44 \times 10^{10}}{4200^2} = 816$ lb.

(c) The same constant of proportionality as in part (b) is used here. The algebra of this part is a little more challenging. Solve for d.

$100 = \dfrac{1.44 \times 10^{10}}{d^2}$

$d^2 = \dfrac{1.44 \times 10^{10}}{100}$

$d^2 = 144{,}000{,}000$

$d = 12{,}000$

That's the distance from the *center* of the Earth. Thus, the satellite has to be 8000 miles above the surface of the Earth.

1.10 Volume

A building has been demolished, leaving a big hole in the ground. Measuring the perimeter of the top of the hole tells you how far it is to walk around the hole. Measuring the area of the top of the hole tells you how much plywood you would need to cover the hole so that no one falls in. Measuring the *volume* of the hole tells you how much stuff you need to fill it up. We use a unit segment to measure length, a unit square to measure area, and a unit cube to measure volume.

The size of a unit cube depends on the unit of length you choose. A **unit cube** is a cube that measures one unit of length along each edge. A **cubic inch** is a cube with each edge one inch long, a **cubic meter** is a cube with each edge one meter long, and so on. The **volume** of a three dimensional object is the number of unit cubes (of some unit length) needed to fill up the space the object occupies.

1. How many unit cubes does it take to fill each of the boxes with the dimensions (in cm) given in Display 1.75? Copy and complete that table.

2. Which of the five boxes in the table of Display 1.75 is pictured in Display 1.76?

3. Use the data from your table to determine the number of cubes that are needed to fill a box of any dimensions. You may want to build boxes of other dimensions for additional data.

a

1.90

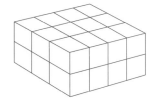

Display 1.76

Box	Length	Width	Height	No. of Cubes
A	4	2	2	
B	4	3	2	
C	4	4	2	
D	4	4	3	
E	4	4	4	

Display 1.75

Will your formula tell you how many unit cubes it takes to fill a box even if the dimensions of the box are not whole numbers? Explain.

b

1.91

99

Learning Outcomes

After studying this section, you will be able to:

Find the volume of a rectangular box by filling it with unit cubes;

Find the volume of a rectangular box measuring its sides and using a formula.

1.10 Volume

This chapter ends as it began—by counting units of measure. In Section 1.1 we developed the idea of a unit length as the basis for measuring linear figures. In Section 1.5 we extended that idea to unit squares as the key to measuring areas. Now we extend this same idea by one more dimension, to unit cubes as the key to measuring volumes. This fundamental concept will be used a little in Chapter 2 and more in Chapter 5 (on three dimensional geometry). The focus of this short section is on what *volume* means, rather than on formulas for special shapes. If your students become comfortable with the idea of approximating volumes with unit cubes and with getting closer approximations by using smaller unit cubes, then you and we have done our jobs in this section.

1.90

These questions are straightforward. They lead to the standard formula for the volume of a rectangular prism.

1. *A*: 16   *B*: 24   *C*: 32   *D*: 48   *E*: 64

2. Box *B*. This picture is here mainly as an aid for students whose visual imagination needs some prompting. Students should be able to visualize the locations of all 24 unit cubes in this configuration.

3. Here students are being asked to recall from middle school that the volume of a rectangular box (a rectangular prism) is given by $V = lwh$ and to connect that idea with filling the box with unit cubes. If your students don't know or have trouble remembering this formula, you might need to spend some time having them use actual cubes to build solid boxes of various dimensions and then count the number of cubes they used. On the other hand, if your students are already comfortable with this formula, you can just move on.

1.91

Do not pass over this question lightly! The literal answer is *NO*. Think of actually filling the box with unit cubes, rather than just finding its volume. Side lengths that are not integers will not allow you to fit the proper number of cubes in the box to completely fill it up, unless you can break up or grind up the unit cubes. This is a nontrivial issue. Make sure that your students understand the problem here.

They should also understand the way to fix the problem, at least for dimensions that are rational numbers: Choose a smaller unit of length, and hence a smaller size of unit cube. This is a good opportunity to review common denominators. For instance, if the dimensions are 9.2 cm by 7.6 cm by 3.5 cm, then 1 mm unit cubes will work. Of course, the answer will then be the number of 1 mm cubes that fill the box. If the dimensions are $5\frac{1}{2}$ in. by $3\frac{2}{3}$ in. by $2\frac{1}{5}$ in. then unit cubes of edge length $\frac{1}{30}$ will work and the answer will be in terms of cubes of that size. This kind of reasoning connects the arithmetic with the conceptual framework.

EXPLORATION

We shall explore how volume is related to area by designing cake pans.

SETUP

Take out a sheet of graph paper and cut out an 18 by 18 square, as shown in Display 1.77. Don't worry about the corner markings yet. This represents a piece of sheet metal, 18 inches on a side. The Kingpin Cakepan Company (KCC) wants to make cake pans out of these sheets of metal. They want the pans to hold as large a volume as possible. They are not sure how to do this, so they have hired your class to help them figure it out.

To make a cake pan, you cut out a square at each corner, then fold up the four sides to make the pan. Display 1.77 shows the sheet marked for cutting four different sizes of squares out of the corners: 1 by 1, 2 by 2, 3 by 3, and 4 by 4. Your teacher will divide the class up into teams. Team 2 will cut out a 2 by 2 square, make a pan, and find its volume. Team 3 will cut out a 3 by 3 square, make a pan, and find its volume—and so on. We'll be Team 1, to provide examples for you along the way. We'll refer to you as Team _n_, where _n_ is a number from 2 through 8.

QUESTIONS

1. What is the perimeter of the entire metal sheet? What is its area?

2. Cut an _n_ by _n_ square out of each corner. What is the perimeter of the sheet that's left? What is its area? Team 1 cut a 1 by 1 square out of each corner. The area that's left is 320 sq. in.

3. Fold up the sides of the pan. What is the height of each side? What is the length? What is the area of the bottom of the pan? Each side of Team 1's pan is 1 inch high and 16 inches long. The area at the bottom of its pan is 256 sq. in.

4. How many 1 inch cubes can fit into your cake pan? This is its volume. Team 1's pan holds 256 1 inch cubes.

5. If your pan were filled with unit cubes, how many layers would there be? How many cubes would be in each layer? Team 1's pan contains one layer of 256 cubes.

Published by IT'S ABOUT TIME, Inc. © 2000 MATHconx, LLC

As long as all side lengths are *rational* numbers, the common denominator approach justifies the formula $V = lwh$. A subtler, more difficult problem arises if one or more of the side lengths is irrational. We suggest that you finesse this issue, either by (a) avoiding it entirely, or (b) observing that an irrational number can be approximated within any desired degree of accuracy by a rational number, so the rational number approach gets us an approximation of the volume that is as close as we please. A more rigorous disposition of this question involves the concept of limit and a careful definition of irrational numbers.

1.92 Our field testing has shown this to be an effective small group exploration. Divide your class into seven teams, numbered 2 through 8. Team n will cut n by n squares from each corner of its sheet. The book uses Team 1 to provide examples along the way, so you don't need (or want) a Team 1 in your class.

Your students will need at least one sheet of graph paper for each team. Ordinary graph paper ($\frac{1}{4}$ inch grid) works fine. Be sure that your students' 18 by 18 squares include *complete* grid squares all around. Most graph paper sheets are trimmed so that partial squares occur around the edges.

1. The perimeter is 72 in. The area is 324 sq. in.

2. The perimeter is still 72 in. The area depends on n. For Team n, it is $324 - 4n^2$. Note that in this and subsequent parts, answers given in terms of n are for your use only. Students should not be dealing with this exploration at that level of generality yet. We shall introduce them to it shortly.

3. For Team n, the height is n, the side length is $18 - 2n$, and the bottom area is $(18 - 2n)^2$. See Display 1.17T.

4. For Team n, the volume is $n \cdot (18 - 2n)^2$. See Display 1.17T.

5. For Team n, there would be n layers, each layer containing $(18 - 2n)^2$ cubes. Help students to visualize the volume in this way.

NOTES

....

....

....

....

....

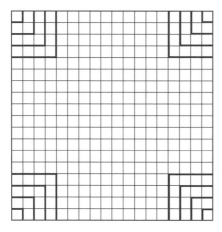

Display 1.77

Make a table of the results from the whole class. Include the side length, height, bottom area, and volume of each cake pan. Do you find any patterns in the table? Which team has the pan with the largest volume?

1.93

You probably have a winning team—one team with the biggest pan volume. However, before you turn the results in to KCC, you want to check and make sure they are correct. After all, if one of the results is really just a big mistake, it may seem like the biggest volume. Besides, you haven't checked cutout sizes that are not integers. Maybe one of them gives you a bigger volume.

One way to check your results is to make a graph. If the points lie on a line or a smooth curve, that gives you more confidence that your results are correct. If you find a pattern with one exception, you may want to check the exception.

To make the graph with your graphing calculator, you need to express the volume as a function of one variable, x. In this case, let x be the side length of the cutout squares.

1.94

1. Express the height of the cake pan in terms of x.

2. Express the length of the cake pan in terms of x.

3. Express the width of the cake pan in terms of x.

4. Express the volume of the cake pan in terms of x.

1.93

See Display 1.17T. We have also included the hypothetical Teams 0 and 9 whose cake pans hold no cake, as an extension of the pattern. There are several patterns in the table that your students might notice. The most important observation is that the volume of these cake pans is the product of the height and bottom area, which is the same as the product of length, width, and height. Results for Team 3 should be the largest volume.

Team	Height (in.)	Side Length (in.)	Bottom Area (sq. in.)	Volume (cu. in.)
0	0	18	324	0
1	1	16	256	256
2	2	14	196	392
3	3	12	144	432
4	4	10	100	400
5	5	8	64	320
6	6	6	36	216
7	7	4	16	112
8	8	2	4	32
9	9	0	0	0

Display 1.17T

1.94

This exercise presents and uses the algebraic description of the Exploration process.

1. Height $= x$

2. Length $= 18 - 2x$

3. Width $= 18 - 2x$

4. Volume $= x \cdot (18 - 2x)^2$

Chapter 1

5. Now graph the volume function on your calculator. Use the information that the class collected as a guide for setting your window.

6. Does the volume that your team got agree with the graph? Check by using a menu choice on the calculator to find the value for your *n*.

7. Does there appear to be a maximum volume? For what value of *x*? Does it agree with what one of your teams got?

REFLECT

This chapter traced the study of geometry back to its roots. The tap root—the most basic root of all—is the idea of a line segment and a unit of length. Everything has grown from that central, fundamental idea. Except for this last section, you have studied *plane* geometry, the geometry of flat surfaces. You learned how to make and measure polygons, and how to classify them by symmetry. You saw how areas can be described in terms of unit squares, which are based on unit lengths. The huge variety of polygons became more manageable when they were broken into triangles by triangulation. This made it important to know how to find areas of all kinds of triangles, which we did by constructing altitudes and finding a formula: $A = \frac{1}{2} bh$, where h is the length of an altitude and b is the length of its base. You learned about the *Pythagorean Theorem*, one of the oldest and most powerful statements in all of mathematics; and finally, you saw how measuring volume in three dimensional space is based on unit lengths and unit squares.

The next chapter is about changing size without changing shape. It shows how proportionality is the key to understanding angles and how to measure them. We shall take closer looks at scaling figures to different sizes, at congruence of triangles, and at the relationship between angles and parallel lines. Triangulation will allow us to extend our results about triangles to other polygons, and you will see how unit squares and cubes help us understand how scaling affects the areas and volumes of two and three dimensional shapes.

Published by IT'S ABOUT TIME, Inc. © 2000 MATHconx, LLC

5. Good WINDOW settings are from 0 to 9 for X and from 0 to 450 for Y.

6. It should agree.

7. The lack of labels on the axes makes it difficult to instantly see where the maximum is on the calculator graph, but we can find the approximate coordinates of the peak by using the calculator's TRACE function. This will show the peak at $x = 3$, as the students should have found, and not at some intermediate point between integer values.

Additional Support Materials:

Assessments	Qty
Form (A)	1
Form (B)	1
Chapter Test (A)	1
Chapter Test (B)	1

Blackline Masters	Qty

Extensions	Qty

Supplements	Qty
Volume	4

Problem Set: 1.10

1. You now have a long-term consulting contract with Kingpin Cakepan Company. They have a new loaf pan that measures 4 inches by 5 inches by 9 inches.

   (a) Find the volume of this new pan in cubic inches.

   (b) KCC needs your result in quarts. There are 57.75 cubic inches in a quart. How many quarts will the pan hold? Round your answer to two decimal places.

   (c) KCC is still not satisfied. To get the best results, you should only fill the cake pan three-quarters full. If you do that, how many quarts will the new cake pan hold? How many cubic inches?

2. KCC needs a cake pan that holds 200 cubic inches when filled to the top.

   (a) Find five possible length, width, and height combinations that could be used for such a pan. For simplicity of design, stay with measurements in whole numbers of inches.

   (b) For each possibility you consider, find the size of the rectangular piece of sheet metal you would need to make the pan and the size of the corners that must be cut out before it is folded up.

   (c) Which of your five designs uses the least sheet metal? Who would be interested in this question?

   (d) Do you think there is an even smaller sheet size that will give you the same volume? Why or why not?

3. In the text you saw that the volume of a rectangular cake pan can be expressed in terms of the area of its base,

$$V = lwh \text{ or } V = Ah$$

   where A is the area of the bottom of the pan. This second formula extends to cake pans (and similar shapes) whose bases are not rectangular.

   (a) KCC makes heart shaped cake pans for Valentine's Day. The area of the bottom is 85 square inches. The pan is 1.5 inches deep. What is its volume? How many quarts of batter will the pan hold when it is three-quarters full? (See problem 1.) Round your answers to two decimal places.

   (b) KCC also makes small cake pans in the shape of triangular prisms, for use by pastry chefs who need parts for special order cakes with fancy designs. The bottom of the pan is an isosceles right triangle with

Problem Set: 1.10

1. (a) 180 cu. in.
   (b) 3.12 quarts.
   (c) 2.34 quarts; 135 cu. in.

2. (a) There are many possibilities, including some unrealistically silly ones, such as 1 by 1 by 200. Some relatively reasonable ones are listed in Display 1.18T, along with the sizes of their rectangular sheets and corner cuts.

   (b)

Length	Width	Height	Corner Cutout	Sheet Size	Area Before Cuts (in.^{2})	Area After Cuts (in.^{2})
10	10	2	2×2	14×14	196	180
10	5	4	4×4	18×13	234	170
10	4	5	5×5	20×14	280	180
8	5	5	5×5	18×15	270	170
5	8	5	5×5	15×18	270	170
5	5	8	8×8	21×21	441	185
20	5	2	2×2	24×9	216	200
25	4	2	2×2	29×8	232	216
25	2	4	4×4	33×10	330	266

Display 1.18T

   (c) This is not straightforward. The answer before the corners are cut out differs from the answer after they are cut out. This is deliberately left ambiguous to fuel responses to the next question. The KCC would be interested in which design uses the least sheet metal because that represents a manufacturing cost to them. The before cutout size may not be the only significant one if there is a way to reuse the corners. This could lead to tiling questions and become very complicated!

   (d) The question of minimum sheet size is important to notice, but very difficult to settle at this level of sophistication. This is an open-ended chance for students to explore, speculate, and reason. You can leave it unresolved.

   You can extend this into a classroom activity by gathering a list of possibilities from students and posting them on the board. Since there are three variables (l, w, and h), we cannot easily graph a function, but we can gather lots of data. Once students have exhausted whole number

4 inch legs, and the pan is 3 inches high. What is its volume? How many quarts of batter will it hold when it is three-quarters full? (See problem 1.) Round your answer to two decimal places.

4. The Fixit family renovated an old part of their house. They had a trailer full of old plaster, lath, wood ends, and wallboard pieces to dispose of. Their trailer is 5 ft. by 8 ft. with 2 ft. high sides, and it was completely filled.

   (a) When they got to the town waste disposal center, they found out that it costs $15 per cubic yard (or fraction thereof) to dump this trash. How much did they have to pay?

   (b) After the Fixits dumped their trash, they picked up a load of cut and split firewood, which sells for $120 a cord. The woodcutter filled their trailer completely and charged them $80. A cord of wood is usually measured as a 4 ft. by 4 ft. by 8 ft. stack. Did the Fixits get a good deal, a fair deal, or a poor deal?

5. The Armstrong Aquarium has a dolphin tank that is 40 ft. by 30 ft. by 15 ft. deep. Its owners need to clean it out and repaint it. The directions on the cleaner say that they should completely fill the tank with water and add one box of cleaner for each 10,000 gallons of water in the tank.

   (a) Find the volume of the tank in cubic feet.

   (b) How many inches are in a foot? How many square inches are in a square foot? How many cubic inches are in a cubic foot?

   (c) How many cubic inches are in the dolphin tank?

   (d) A gallon contains 231 cubic inches. How many boxes of cleaner should the Armstrong Aquarium owners buy?

   (e) After cleaning the tank, they want to paint its inside walls and floor. Find the area they want to paint.

   (f) The paint they need is sold only in gallons. One gallon covers 400 sq. ft. How many gallons must they buy?

Published by IT'S ABOUT TIME, Inc. © 2000 MATHconx, LLC

solutions, they can add to the table by picking arbitrary numbers for two of the variables and then calculating the third from $lwh = 200$.

For minimizing sheet size before cutouts, the first possibility in Display 1.17T is about as good a solution as is likely to be found by trial and error. However, to show your students that problems do not always have integer answers, you might ask them to check out a pan that is $9.29 \times 2.32 \times 2.32$ inches. It is just a tad better. How did we get it? We won't go into all the details, but the two related optimization problems actually have the same solution: the pan should be square with a height one fourth the width. We could say that the cake pan that solves the current problem is geometrically similar to the cake pan that solves the problem in the text. Similarity is discussed in Chapter 2. For the current problem, the $10 \times 10 \times 2$ pan is close to optimal with the height/width ratio of $\frac{1}{5}$, but we could do better by making the pan a bit narrower and a bit taller. Your students can investigate this by trial and error.

You can further extend this into a field project, if you want, by asking students to measure cake pans at home or in stores and see if they are anything like optimal from the minimum sheet size viewpoint. You should find that a very common size for a square pan is $8 \times 8 \times 2$! Its sides are not quite vertical, however—they are tapered a bit so that you can get the cake out of the pan.

3. The principle in this problem greatly extends the kinds of solids for which students can find volumes.
   (a) 127.5 cu. in.; 2.21 qt.
   (b) 24 cu. in.; 0.42 qt.

4. (a) $45. One cubic yard is $3^3 = 27$ cu. ft. Their trailer holds $5 \cdot 8 \cdot 2 = 80$ cu. ft., so they have almost 3 cu. yd. of trash.
   (b) They were overcharged by $5. A cord contains 128 cu. ft. The Fixits' trailer holds 80 cu. ft., and $\frac{80}{128} = 0.625$. The woodcutter charged them for $\frac{80}{120}$ of a cord, which equals 0.667. The correct cost should have been $0.625 \cdot \$120 = \$75$.

5. (a) 18,000 cu. ft.
   (b) 12; 144; 1728
   (c) 31,104,000
   (d) The tank holds 134,649.35 gallons of water. This requires 13.46 boxes, so they should buy 14.
   (e) The area of the floor is 1200 sq ft. There are four walls with a total area of
   $$15 \cdot 2 \cdot (40 + 30) = 2100 \text{ sq. ft.}$$
   (the perimeter of the tank times its depth). Thus, the total area to be painted is 3300 sq. ft.
   (f) This is another roundup question. $\frac{3300}{400} = 8.25$, so they have to buy 9 gallons of the paint.

Chapter 2

Chapter 2 Planning Guide

Chapter 2 Similarity and Scaling: Growing and Shrinking Carefully

This chapter is long and rich. It uses similarity and scaling factors to explain and unify a wide range of important topics, including angle measurement, the relationships among angles formed by cutting parallels, congruence of triangles, the effect of scaling on areas and volumes, and the utility of rotations and reflections. It interweaves geometry and algebra via proportionality. By using the calculator's TAN function keys to convert between slope and degree measure of angles, it illustrates the idea of inverse functions and foreshadows the next chapter.

Assessments Form A (A)	Assessments Form B (B)	Blackline Masters
Quiz 2.1-2.2(A), Quiz 2.3-2.4(A) Quiz 2.5-2.6(A) Quiz 2.7-2.8(A) Quiz 2.9-2.10(A) Chapter Test(A)	Quiz 2.1-2.2(B) Quiz 2.3-2.4(B) Quiz 2.5-2.6(B) Quiz 2.7-2.8(B) Quiz 2.9-2.10(B) Chapter Test(B)	Student pp. 128-129, 139, 186

Extensions	Supplements for Chapter Sections	Test Banks
Following 2.10 Build It Up & Tear It Down: A Problem Solving Strategy	2.1 The Same Shape — 5 Supplements 2.2 Similar Triangles and Rectangles — 4 Supplements 2.3 How to Measure Angles — 3 Supplements 2.4 Finding Angle Size Efficiently — 3 Supplements 2.5 Parallel Lines and the Angle Sum of a Triangle —3 Supplements 2.6 Parallelograms and Congruent Triangles — 4 Supplements 2.7 Other Tests for Congruent Triangles — 1 Supplement 2.8 Other Polygons — 1 Supplement 2.9 Stretching and Shrinking Angles and Areas — 3 Supplements 2.10 Stretching and Shrinking Volumes — 1 Supplement	To be released

Pacing Range 6-8 weeks including Assessments
Teachers will need to adjust this guide to suit the needs of their own students. Not all classes will complete each chapter at the same pace. Flexibility — which accommodates different teaching styles, school schedules and school standards — is built into the curriculum.

Teacher Commentary is indexed to the student text by the numbers in the margins (under the icons or in circles). The first digit indicates the chapter — the numbers after the decimal indicate the sequential numbering of the comments within that unit. Example:

2.9

Student Pages in Teacher Edition

2.9

Teacher Commentary Page

Observations

Kathleen Bavelas
Manchester Community
Technical College, CT

"I have found that it is really important for you to do the problems yourself, before you assign them. Often I'll look at a problem and I'll say to myself, 'Oh, that looks nice and juicy,' but when I get into it, I realize that this problem should be done *in* class. The students will need the advantages of the group work as well as some directed guidance.

"Also, I suggest that when students show a predisposition to want to know something that you go there with them — even if it means you have to throw out your plan for the day. The idea is that if they're excited about it, that's the place to go. And this material is going to offer lots of those opportunities as you go on with the Explorations."

Errol Libby
Oxford Hills Comprehensive
High School, ME

"Chapter 2 is about scaling — how things are made larger or smaller but stay the same shape. All the problems presented are embedded in reality and I find that the students end up mastering the material better because they are engaged in the problems and understand how they are applied. I often hear comments like 'This class goes by so fast,' and I never get the feeling that these students are 'suffering through' something.

"The Profiles at the beginning of each chapter are terrific examples of how people are really using the math they learned to make a living."

The Profiles are where students will meet people in various careers and professions who use mathematics in their everyday work.

The Profiles point out to students how many different and diverse professions utilize mathematics as a key building block. This is an excellent opportunity to open up class discussions and will lead to an increased knowledge of the value of mathematics in the real world. Students come to realize the importance of mathematics in many more of the professions, occupations and careers than they might have previously thought.

Brad Bower
Movie Magic

They have been seen in almost all action movies ever made. They even star in music videos. Months are spent making sure they look as real as they can. And then, in a flash, most are trashed, smashed, sunk, run over or blown up. Ah, the life of a motion picture special effects created model.

Brad Bower is manager of the Creative Studio Model Shop for Universal Studios Recreation Group. He has been building models professionally since 19. "I look forward to every day on the job," says Brad. "After all, who doesn't like entertainment?"

Brad started out building models at the Walt Disney Company. He rose to manager of their special effects department, then was hired by Universal. "Models can be created to replicate existing structures and environments. Or, they can be three dimensional blueprints of future projects," Brad explains. "But in both cases, precision is the key and math is the tool."

Every Universal Studio's model starts its "life" on paper, in the design department. Next, rough drawings of the design concept are sent to the Creative Studio Model Shop. Here's where Brad's group of model-builders, painters and sculptors start their creative work. Often, the model-builders are working from drawings that are still in progress. "As the design becomes more fully developed, they produce more accurate scale models that include more details."

"Math is something I enjoyed in school from the start," says Brad. "We use math every day in all different forms. Each scale model must be a perfectly accurate representation of its full-sized counterpart. Its dimensions, proportions, location and function must be precise."

"The challenge for the model-builder," Brad continues, "is to maintain the intent of the original design throughout the project."

Even if that means hearing the director yell "ACTION!" and watching your prized creation go up in smoke!

106

Chapter 2 — Similarity and Scaling: Growing and Shrinking Carefully

Preliminary Note. This chapter is quite long. Many different ideas from plane geometry, as well as some from algebra and trigonometry, appear here. The material has been kept within a single chapter to preserve its thematic unity. As you plan your time, it would not be unreasonable to allow six to eight weeks for this chapter. The many opportunities for class discussion provide a way to tailor the coverage to fit your schedule, *provided that you do not seriously underestimate how much time you will need.*

The idea of uniform stretching and shrinking is the point of departure for this chapter. We presume that students know from Chapter 1 how to measure length, area, and volume, know the Pythagorean Theorem, and have seen a variety of polygons.

The chapter interweaves several distinct themes, some of which may not be obvious from the titles of the sections.

- Proportionality, including scaling factors, scale drawings, and the effect of proportional change on area and volume. This leads to the consideration of scaling as a function.

- Angle measure, including both degree measure and slope as ways of measuring angles, and the use of the calculator's TAN and TAN^{-1} keys to switch back and forth between the two. This discussion also provides an example of inverse functions and serves as a precursor to the trigonometry chapter. Radian measure is introduced in a later chapter, after examining properties of circles.

- Some standard plane geometry involves transversals of parallel lines and congruence of triangles. These facts are applied to a variety of theoretical and practical situations.

- Rotation as a useful kind of transformation. This is combined with the discussion of reflection (line symmetry) in Chapter 1 to add to students' understanding of transformations as geometric tools.

- Some algebraic techniques. In particular, the discussion of cross multiplication in Section 2.1 can be used to reinforce and extend students' ability to handle equations in which each side is a fractional expression. We begin with a simple comparison of numerical fractions; in later sections, this technique is used to solve proportion equations for an unknown value.

- A "habit of thought" theme has been suggested, but not emphasized, in earlier chapters: What is the minimal information needed to determine a figure? This is reflected in the various congruence criteria for triangles and other figures. Encourage your students to interpret a congruence statement as: "If I have this much information about a figure, then I should be able to find *all* its other size and shape properties." For example, the so-called SAS theorem for triangles means that, if you just know two sides and the included angle of a triangle, then you can find the measures of the other sides and angles, the perimeter, the altitudes, the area, etc.

Chapter 2

Similarity and Scaling: Growing and Shrinking Carefully

CHAPTER

2

2.1 The Same Shape

"One side will make you grow taller, and the other side will make you grow shorter."

"One side of *what*? The other side of *what*?" thought Alice to herself.

"Of the mushroom," said the Caterpillar, just as if she asked it aloud; and in another moment it was out of sight.

Alice remained looking thoughtfully at the mushroom for a minute, trying to make out which were the two sides of it; and, as it was perfectly round, she found this a very difficult question. However, at last she stretched her arms round it as far as they would go, and broke off a bit of the edge with each hand.

Published by IT'S ABOUT TIME, Inc. © 2000 MATHconx, LLC

107

2.1   The Same Shape

The main point of this section is the development of a workable, intuitively comfortable definition of *similarity* in terms of ratios. Capturing the idea of same shape but different size with an unambiguous definition that quantifies the size change and conforms to the students' visual imagination is a surprisingly fussy process. Our approach rests on a somewhat informal treatment of similarity as a transformation. It can be generalized in later courses to a more formal transformational approach. That is not necessary (and, in our view, not desirable) at this stage. This first section focuses on the idea of a *scaling factor*, a constant that measures the amount of stretching or shrinking.

Note that actually, we're fudging the opening dictionary definition just a bit. This definition, as it appears in *Webster's New World Dictionary* (*2nd College Edition,* 1980), does not include the word *necessarily* and is thereby inaccurate. However, a discussion of that issue probably would be more distracting than helpful here.

Chapter 2

Additional Support Materials:

Assessments	Qty
Form (A)	1
Form (B)	1

Blackline Masters	Qty

Extensions	Qty

Supplements	Qty
The Same Shape	5

2.1 The Same Shape

"And now which is which?" she said to herself and nibbled a little of the right-hand bit to try the effect: the next moment she felt a violent blow underneath her chin; it had struck her foot!

She was a good deal frightened by this sudden change, but she felt that there was no time to be lost, as she was shrinking rapidly; so she set to work at once to eat some of the other bit. Her chin was pressed so closely against her foot, that there was hardly room to open her mouth; but she did it at last, and managed to swallow a morsel of the left hand bit.

—Lewis Carroll, Alice in Wonderland

This section is about growing and shrinking. More precisely, it is about similarity. A dictionary defines the geometric meaning of *similar* as "having the same shape, but not [necessarily] the same size or position." This isn't a bad description of the idea, *provided that* you know what "same shape" means. Do you?

2.1

What do *you* think it means to say that two things "have the same shape"? Test your opinion with these examples.

1. Do all triangles have the same shape? If you say Yes, explain why. If you say No, draw two triangles that have different shapes. Also draw two triangles with the same shape but different sizes.

2. Do all rectangles have the same shape? If you say Yes, explain why. If you say No, draw two rectangles that have different shapes. Also draw two rectangles with the same shape but different sizes.

3. Do all squares have the same shape? If you say Yes, explain why. If you say No, draw two squares that have different shapes. Also draw two squares with the same shape but different sizes.

4. Do all automobile tires have the same shape? Defend your answer.

108

2.1

This is an important first question to discuss thoroughly. It's well worth some open discussion time to sharpen students' understanding and appreciation of the phrase *similar figures* in geometry. The everyday use of *similar* as "having some resemblance; alike but not identical" makes its mathematical meaning potentially confusing. Many nontechnical books (not just dictionaries) describe its geometric meaning by saying something like *same shape*. The good news is that this is a pretty good short expression of the intuitive idea, and it contrasts well with *same size*. The bad news is that *shape* is not a well defined concept; different people may legitimately interpret the word differently.

These examples are intended to bring out such differences, to let students focus on the aspects of shape that are important in the concept of similarity. Until same shape is defined more carefully, *either* a Yes or a No answer is defensible in most of these cases.

1. In the sense that they are all triangles, the answer is Yes. However, most students will say that there are lots of different shapes of triangles. They should be able to draw triangles that look very different from each other and articulate the difference in some way. It is helpful, but not essential at this point, if they can describe those differences informally in terms of both angular measure (sharper corners) and linear measure (long and skinny vs. short and fat).

2. Again, all rectangles have the same generic shape (rectangular), but there are different shapes of rectangles. As in the case of triangles, this is not a question of right or wrong; rather, it's a matter of the *shape* concept becoming more useful as it is refined to distinguish among different types of rectangles. Angles are no longer an issue here, of course. The intent is to focus students on the issue of uniform change in both (all) directions. You might refine part of the question by asking for examples of rectangles that are *the same size* but different in shape. If you do this, take the time to discuss what same size means in this context. It's not obvious or uniquely determined; you can probably use any reasonable suggestion from the class as an operative definition for the moment.

3. In this case, the answer should be Yes from everyone. If not, ask for examples of squares that are the same size but different shapes. See the comment about "same size" in the previous part.

4. As you move to questions of three dimensional objects in the real world, matters are not so clear. That's why this part is here. If someone observes that there are tires with the same wheel size but different widths (or different profiles, if you have more sophisticated auto buffs in your class), this will probably lead them to an answer of No. Uncertainty in this case is an acceptable outcome.

Chapter 2

5. Do all boxes of Kellogg's Corn Flakes have the same shape? Go to a supermarket and look at the 12 oz., 18 oz., and 24 oz. boxes of this cereal. Measure them, if you like. Then explain whether or not these boxes have the same shape.

In some sense, these questions are unfair. The idea of "same shape" has not been carefully defined, so there is no reliable way for you to justify your answers. But that was the point of asking. We want you to see the need for a careful definition of *similar figures*.

Look at Carroll's description of Alice nibbling on the magic mushroom. How does your imagination picture the shrinking Alice? Which part of Display 2.1—(a) or (b)—comes closer to what you "see" in your mind's eye? Do you see her squashed down as in (a), almost all head and feet? Do you think that was what Carroll imagined when he wrote,

"Her chin was pressed so closely against her foot, that there was hardly room to open her mouth"?

From these words, it seems so. But that would be a strangely distorted Alice, hardly fit for her next adventure, in which she is an ordinary little girl—except that she's 9 inches tall! In spite of his chin and foot comment, Carroll probably imagined something more like Display 2.1(b). He probably thought of Alice as growing and shrinking "proportionally," so that she always stayed the same shape. In this case, her chin would be just as far from her foot, relatively speaking, as it had been when she was large. That is, if the distance from her chin to her foot was twice her arm's length when she was big, then that distance should still be twice her arm's length when she was small!

(a)

(b)

Display 2.1

109

5. This example is somewhat richer than the previous ones. It may be even more confusing at first, but it suggests some important ideas. The answer Yes is defensible from the viewpoint of generic classification (they all are boxes), but if the class is beginning to focus on uniform change in all directions, the answer is by no means obvious, at least until some fairly careful measurements are taken. The boxes look to be about the same shape proportionally, but they're not.

In the event that you don't want your students invading the local supermarket to measure corn flakes boxes, here are the measurements (to the nearest $\frac{1}{8}$ in.) for three common sizes.

Size	Height	Width	Thickness
12 oz.	$11\frac{1}{2} = \frac{92}{8}$ in.	$7\frac{1}{2} = \frac{60}{8}$ in.	$2\frac{5}{8} = \frac{21}{8}$ in.
18 oz.	$12\frac{1}{8} = \frac{97}{8}$ in.	$8\frac{1}{8} = \frac{65}{8}$ in.	$3\frac{3}{8} = \frac{27}{8}$ in.
24 oz.	$13\frac{1}{4} = \frac{105}{8}$ in.	$10 = \frac{80}{8}$ in.	$3\frac{1}{4} = \frac{26}{8}$ in.

Once your students have these measurements, the critical question is "How can they be used to settle the question of shape?" Let your students wrestle with that for a while, then leave it unsettled and come back to it later, if need be. The key idea, of course, is that the ratios of the corresponding sides must be the same, an idea that the text is about to discuss. If your students choose this method of comparison on their own, so much the better. However, you need not *expect* them to do some now. By this method of comparison the boxes are *not* exactly the same shape.

About Words

The Latin term *per cent* expresses a ratio; it means for each hundred or: out of one hundred.

To make the idea of same shape precise, we need to begin with the idea of a **ratio**, which is a way of measuring one quantity in terms of another. A ratio is usually (but not always) expressed as a fraction. For example, if Pat Pivot, the star center on the basketball team, has made 42 of her 60 foul shots, we say that she is "42 for 60." We can express this relative measurement as a fraction, $\frac{42}{60}$, or as a *percent*, which is just a special kind of fraction—a fraction with an implied denominator of 100.

2.2

1. **Express Pat Pivot's foul shot record of 42 out of 60 as a percent. Then explain how your process can be used to express any fraction as a percent.**

2. **Jeannie Jumpshot has made 28 of her 49 foul shot attempts. At this rate, if she has a total of 91 attempts during the season, how many would she make? Explain how to find this number *without* expressing her foul shot ratio as a percent.**

Here is an example of how ratios are used. Display 2.2 from the March 1994 issue of *Railroad Model Craftsman* is a drawing of a boxcar. Notice what it says in the lower left corner.

$$\text{O scale: } \tfrac{1}{4}" = 1' - 0"; \; 1:48$$

This line explains O *scale*, a size ratio used by many model railroaders. The scale factor $\frac{1}{4}" = 1' - 0"$ part tells you that $\frac{1}{4}$ inch in the model represents 1 foot in real life. The next part, 1 : 48, actually says the same thing. Because there are 48 quarter-inches in 1 foot, each quarter-inch of the model represents 48 quarter-inches of the real boxcar. That is, the model-to-real-length ratio is 1 to 48. The numbers of a ratio may be written with a colon between them or in fraction form. Both 1:48 and $\frac{1}{48}$ represent the ratio 1 to 48.

110

2.2

These should be review exercises for most students. They are intended to lead into proportions—equality between two ratios.

1. One obvious way to do this is simply to divide 60 into 42, then move the decimal 2 places to the right. A more general approach, which is better suited to our purpose here, is to solve the equation

$$\frac{42}{60} = \frac{x}{100}$$

Either way is acceptable, of course, and provides the answer 70%. The point of the next question is to more or less force students to think of the second way.

2. $\frac{28}{49} = \frac{x}{91}$. By cross multiplication, $49x = 28 \cdot 91$, so $x = 52$.

NOTES

Chapter 2

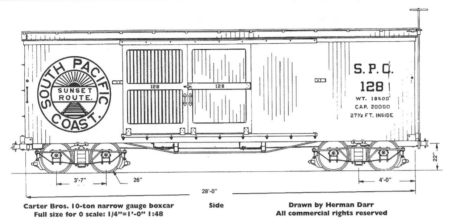

Carter Bros. 10-ton narrow gauge boxcar　　　**Side**　　　**Drawn by Herman Darr**
Full size for 0 scale: 1/4"=1'-0" 1:48　　　　　　　　**All commercial rights reserved**

Display 2.2

"Carter Bros. 10-ton Narrow Gauge Boxcar (side view)," drawn by
Herman Darr, page 66. Copyright © March 1994 by *Railroad Model
Craftsman*, Carstens Publications Inc. Reprinted with permission.

The measurement given in the drawing states that the
boxcar shown in Display 2.2 is 28 feet long.

2.3

1. How long is an O scale model of this boxcar?

2. If HO scale is defined by the ratio 1 : 87, how long
   is an HO scale model of this boxcar? (Round your
   answer to the nearest 10th of an inch.)

3. If N scale is defined by the ratio 1 : 160, how long
   is an N scale model of this boxcar? (Round your
   answer to the nearest 10th of an inch.)

If you were building an O scale model of the boxcar in
Display 2.2, you'd need to know how wide to make the sliding
double door. That's not one of the measurements marked on
the drawing. How can you figure it out from the picture?
An easy way is to use a **proportion**, an equality between
two ratios, like this:

• From the answer to question 1, just before this, we know that
  an O scale model of this boxcar would be 7 inches long.

• Measure that length on the picture in the book (which is
  not a full-size picture of the model). Using a ruler marked
  in centimeters and millimeters, find the length of the boxcar
  in the picture, about 12.4 cm.

Published by IT'S ABOUT TIME, Inc. © 2000 MATHconx, LLC

2.3

These questions, along with the text immediately after them, are intended to lead students to a working idea of how to compute proportions. Note that especially for those with students who are model railroaders, "Scales" in model railroading are commonly called *gauges*; O scale and O gauge mean the same thing. We have opted to use the term *scale* here because it generalizes to other common uses of ratios.

1. This part should be easy. If each foot in real life is $\frac{1}{4}$" in the model, then an O scale model of the 28 foot boxcar should be exactly 7 inches long.

2. This part requires students to use the ratio with a little care. If the answer is to be in inches, then 28' must be converted to inches (336") before the ratio is applied.

    $$336 \cdot \frac{1}{87} = 3.9 \text{ inches}$$

3. This part is similar to part 2. $336 \cdot \frac{1}{160} = 2.1 \text{ inches}$

NOTES

....

....

....

....

....

....

....

....

....

....

....

Chapter 2

2.1 The Same Shape

- Next measure the double door width in the picture. It is about 4.1 cm. This means that the ratio of the double-door width to the boxcar length is 4.1 : 12.4; in fraction form, it is $\frac{4.1}{12.4}$.

- Now because the ratio $\frac{\text{door width}}{\text{boxcar length}}$ should be the same in the model as it is in the picture, set up the equation

$$\frac{\text{door width}}{\text{boxcar length}} = \frac{4.1}{12.4} = \frac{x}{7}$$

The solution to this equation is the proper door width *in inches* for the O scale model.

Solving this equation depends on a fact about fractions that you probably already know. Two fractions are equal if, and only if, you get the same product both ways when you "cross multiply."

For example,

$$\frac{2}{3} = \frac{6}{9} \text{ because } 2 \cdot 9 = 3 \cdot 6$$

Using this process on our proportion, we get

$$\frac{4.1}{12.4} = \frac{x}{7}$$
$$12.4x = 4.1 \cdot 7$$
$$x = \frac{28.7}{12.4}$$
$$x = 2.3 \text{ inches (approx.)}$$

 Cross multiplication is a handy way to test whether or not two fractions are equal. Why does it work? That is, how is this process related to the equality of two fractions? (*Hint:* Start by answering these simpler questions.)

2.4

1. How do you know whether or not two fractions with the *same denominator* are equal?

2. What's a sure way to find a common denominator (not necessarily the least) for two fractions?

 1. Suppose you compute the width of the sliding double doors by repeating the process just described, but use a ruler marked in inches (and fractions of inches), rather than in centimeters. Will you get the same final answer? Why or why not? Try it. Does it come out the way you thought it would?

2.5

112

2.4

This discussion question is important for future algebraic work, as well as for a commonsense understanding of fractions. It is worth some class discussion time to make sure that this principle is well understood. It might also be a good idea to refresh this discussion when cross multiplication is encountered again.

For some classes, you might need to start the discussion at a more primitive stage than the first question, perhaps at the stage of "What is a fraction?" The Latin writers of the Middle Ages introduced the terms *numerator* (numberer—how many) and *denominator* (namer—of what size) because they suggested to people who know Latin what fraction notation meant. *It is critically important for students to understand that the denominator of a fraction specifies the size of a piece of the unit measure that is being counted, and the numerator counts how many of them are being used.* This principle drives the answers to the two preliminary questions and to just about everything else connected with fractions.

1. Since the denominators are the same, the fractions represent the same quantity if and only if the numerators are the same. Both fractions are counting the same size pieces, so the number of pieces [the numerator] must be the same.

2. A common denominator that *always* works is the product of the two denominators. This way of finding a common denominator can be used to set up an algorithm because it doesn't require any *ad hoc* investigation of common factors.

Now student discussion should be guided to put these facts together, perhaps via numerical examples, to see that the cross multiplication equation is just the equality of the two numerators when the fractions have been converted to the sure fire common denominator. In general,

$$\frac{a}{b} = \frac{c}{d} \text{ if and only if } \frac{ad}{bd} = \frac{bc}{bd} \text{ if and only if } ad = bc$$

2.5

Besides illustrating a fundamental fact about proportions, the computation explained here and the related problems provide review and practice in handling fractions and solving simple equations.

1. Yes, you would get the same final answer, except perhaps for some roundoff error due largely to the eyeball approximations of lengths using relatively crude measuring devices (standard rulers). The double door width in the picture is about $1\frac{5}{8}$ in. and the boxcar length is about 5 in. This yields the proportion

    $$\frac{1.625}{5} = \frac{x}{7}$$

    which resolves to $x = 2.3$, rounded to the nearest tenth of an inch.

Chapter 2

2. What is the width of the sliding double doors on the real boxcar?

3. Use the method just described to figure out the height of the sliding door on the O scale model, and also on the real boxcar. Can you use either a centimeter-marked or an inch-marked ruler?

4. How high off the rails will the top of the boxcar's roof be in O scale? In real life?

Now we are ready to tackle the question of describing more carefully the idea of *similar* objects. You go first.

How can the ideas of ratio and proportion be used to make a useful definition of what it means to say that two shapes are similar? Once you have a definition you like, test it by looking at Display 2.3. Are any of the figures (b), (c), or (d) similar to (a)? Are more than one of them similar to (a)? What does *your* definition tell you?

2.6

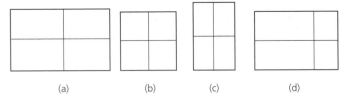

(a)   (b)   (c)   (d)

Display 2.3

Now it's our turn. First, here is a useful term that occurs often in mathematics— constant. A **constant** is a particular number that doesn't change throughout an entire example or discussion. Sometimes we know that a number is a constant, but we don't know or don't want to write down its exact value. In such cases, we can represent it by a letter and just say that this letter is a constant.

A Word to Know: Two objects are **similar** if there is a constant k such that the distance between any two points of one object is k times the distance between the corresponding two points of the other.

Published by IT'S ABOUT TIME, Inc. © 2000 MATHconx, LLC

113

2. This doesn't really require a formal proportion equation. The model to real scale is 1:48, so the real double door is about 2.3 · 48 inches long; that is, 9.2 feet.

3. Yes, you can use either inches or centimeters for measurement; the scaling factor is relative to the unit of measure. The approximate height in the picture is 2.8 cm ($1\frac{1}{8}$ in.). Thus, the proportion

$$\frac{2.8}{12.6} = \frac{x}{7} \ \text{ or } \ \left(\frac{1.125}{5} = \frac{x}{7}\right)$$

produces the required height, approximately $x = 1.6$ in. (in either case).

4. These measurements are taken from the top of the rail to the top of the catwalk on the roof; they do *not* include the brake wheel at the top right of the picture. The approximate height in the picture is 4.4 cm ($1\frac{3}{4}$ in.). Thus, the proportion

$$\frac{4.4}{12.6} = \frac{x}{7} \ \text{ or } \ \left(\frac{1.75}{5} = \frac{x}{7}\right)$$

produces the required height, approximately $x = 2.5$ in.

2.6

Don't expect closure on this question. It's here primarily to get students to think more about ratio and proportion in visual terms, so that they will better understand the definition about to be presented. This question is worth 5–10 minutes of class discussion, but no more (unless your students really get into it). It might also be useful to come back on the ideas they propose in this discussion *after* you cover the text's definition, so that they can see how the formal idea of constant ratio captures the visual intuition of same shape.

In Display 2.3, students should come to recognize that (c) is similar to (a), but (b) and (d) are not. The challenge, of course, is getting their definitions specific enough to make these distinctions. The purpose of (d) is to get students to see the need for dealing with *all* pairs of corresponding points in any proportionality comparison, not just a preselected subset such as the frame of the picture. They should develop the intuition that a similarity transformation is uniform in some obvious visual sense.

One issue that might arise here is how you know which points of one object actually correspond to which points of another. That question is raised and dealt with at the beginning of the next section. If a student raises it here, acknowledge that it's an important question, but for now just rely on intuition in these early examples to indicate which points obviously correspond.

Chapter 2

We call the constant k a **scaling factor.** Sometimes it is also called the *constant of proportionality.* Similar objects are also said to be in *proportion* to each other. The scaling factor tells you the relationship between the two different sizes. For example, the note at the bottom left of Display 2.2 says that the scaling factor for an O scale model of the boxcar is $\frac{1}{48}$. This means that the distance between any two points of the model should be exactly $\frac{1}{48}$ times the distance between the corresponding two points of the real boxcar.

2.7

Look at Display 2.2.

1. **What is the scaling factor for an HO scale model of this boxcar?**

2. **Think of the O scale model of the boxcar as the first object in the definition of *similar* and think of the real boxcar as the second. What is the scaling factor?**

Here's a simple example: The two rectangles in Display 2.4 are similar. Because a rectangle is determined by its four vertices (corner points), we can check similarity just by comparing the distances between corresponding vertices. In this case, the distance WX must be k times the distance AB for some scaling factor k and the distance XY must be k times the distance BC for the same k.

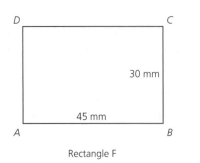

Rectangle F

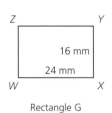

Rectangle G

Display 2.4

2.7

Question 1 is a routine reinforcement of the example just presented in the text. It requires only that the student recognize that the HO scale ratio — shown in Do this part 2 right after Display 2.2 — is the scaling factor: $\frac{1}{87}$ in fraction form. Question 2 illustrates that, when two similar figures are considered in reverse order, the scaling factor is inverted. In this case, the ratio is 48:1, so the scaling factor is 48. This idea will recur in some of the exercises.

NOTES

Chapter 2

Using the measurements (in millimeters) from Display 2.4, we have

$$24 = k \cdot 45 \quad \text{and} \quad 16 = k \cdot 30$$

That is, the ratios $\frac{24}{45}$ and $\frac{16}{30}$ both must equal the same number, k. Do they? You can check this in either of two ways:

1. simplify the two fractions and see that you come out with the same value for k; or

2. check that the two fractions are equal by cross-multiplying.

The second way often is more efficient, particularly when you don't need to know the value of the scaling factor. Here we see that

$$\frac{24}{45} = \frac{16}{30}$$

because

$$24 \cdot 30 = 45 \cdot 16$$

(Did you check our arithmetic to make sure?) In other words, the ratios of the corresponding side lengths form a proportion.

These questions refer to Display 2.4.

2.8

1. Use the Pythagorean Theorem to compute the length of the diagonal *AC* of rectangle *F*. Check your answer with a ruler.

2. Use a proportion to compute the length of the diagonal *WY* of rectangle *G*. Check your answer with a ruler.

3. Use the Pythagorean Theorem to compute the length of the diagonal *WY* of rectangle *G*. Compare your answer with your answer for part 2.

4. Because these two rectangles are similar, you can multiply the distance between two points of rectangle *F* by a scaling factor to find the distance between the corresponding two points of rectangle *G*. What is the numerical value of this scaling factor?

5. You can also multiply the distance between two points of rectangle *G* by a scaling factor to find the distance between the corresponding two points of rectangle *F*. What is the numerical value of this scaling factor? How is it related to your answer for part 4?

Published by IT'S ABOUT TIME, Inc. © 2000 MATHconx, LLC

115

2.8

This set of questions links practicing proportions with the Pythagorean Theorem and the use of measurement to check that a computed answer is at least approximately correct. Questions 4 and 5 focus on the two way nature of the similarity relationship and the fact that the two scaling factors are reciprocals of each other, an idea that comes up again in the exercises. Of course, students should be encouraged to use their calculators to do the arithmetic.

1. $\sqrt{45^2 + 30^2} = \sqrt{2925} = 54$ mm (approx.)

2. $\frac{30}{16} = \frac{54}{d}$, so $30d = 16 \cdot 54$ which is 16 times 54, implying $d = 28.8$ mm (approx.) Other proportions can be used in this way to get the same result.

3. $\sqrt{24^2 + 16^2} = \sqrt{832} = 28.84$ mm (approx.)

4. The scaling factor for *F* to *G* lengths is $\frac{16}{30} = \frac{8}{15}$. If students are confused about which number should be the numerator and which should be the denominator, encourage them to relate the fact that the rectangle is getting smaller indicating the need for a scaling factor less than 1.

5. The scaling factor for *G* to *F* lengths is $\frac{30}{16} = \frac{15}{8}$. The fact that the rectangle is getting larger requires a scaling factor greater than 1.

Chapter 2

NOTES

....

....

....

....

....

....

....

....

....

2.1 The Same Shape

Problem Set: 2.1

1. A photocopier has reduced a diagram by a scaling factor of 60%.

   (a) If two points are 5 inches apart on the original diagram, how far apart are they on the copy?

   (b) If two points are 1 inch apart on the original diagram, how far apart are they on the copy?

   (c) If two points are 2 inches apart on the original diagram, how far apart are they on the copy?

   (d) If two points are 3 inches apart on the copy, how far apart are they on the original diagram?

   (e) If two points are 1 inch apart on the copy, how far apart are they on the original diagram?

   (f) If two points are 2 inches apart on the copy, how far apart are they on the original diagram?

   (g) The person who received the reduced copy of the diagram wants to blow it back up to its original size. What scaling factor should she use?

2. Both American football and Canadian football are played on rectangular fields, but the sizes of the fields are different:

   - The American field is $53\frac{1}{3}$ yards wide, 100 yards long from goal line to goal line, and has an extra 10 yards of end zone at each end.

   - The Canadian field is 65 yards wide, 110 yards long from goal line to goal line, and has an extra 10 yards of end zone at each end.

   (a) Make a sketch of each field and label it with the appropriate dimensions.

   (b) The two playing fields, without the end zones, are not proportional. How wide would the 100 yard American field have to be in order for it to be proportional to the Canadian field?

   (c) Are the two playing fields, including the end zones, proportional? Justify your answer.

   (d) The end-zone sizes are not proportional when compared with the lengths of the playing fields between them. How long would the Canadian end zone have to be in order for it to be proportional to the American one?

116

Problem Set: 2.1

1. Parts (a), (b), and (c) ask the same question for three different numbers, starting with an integer answer, then a unit length answer, and finally an answer involving fractions or decimals. Parts (c), (d), and (e) do the analogous thing in reverse. Part (g) focuses on the invertible nature of scaling.

   (a) 3 in.

   (b) .6 in.

   (c) 1.2 in.

   (d) 5 in.

   (e) $1\frac{2}{3}$ in.

   (f) $3\frac{1}{3}$ in.

   (g) $\frac{5}{3}$

2. (b) $\frac{100}{110} = \frac{x}{65}$ implies by cross multiplication that $110x = 6500$; that is, $x = 59.1$ yds.

   (c) No. If they were, then the ratio of the lengths would equal the ratio of the widths.

   But $\frac{120}{160} \neq \frac{53.33}{65}$, which can be verified by cross multiplication. $(7800 \neq 8532.8)$

   (d) $\frac{100}{110} = \frac{10}{x}$ implies $100x = 1100$; that is $x = 11$ yds.

   (e) Because the Canadian field is wider, there is much more room for running and passing to the outside. Because the Canadian end zone is longer (deeper), there is more room for pass plays near the goal line. Other strategic differences may be suggested. Two differences in rules are: (1) Canadian football has 12 players to a side, whereas in the United States football has 11; and (2) in Canadian football, a team has only 3 downs, instead of 4, to make 10 yards. Both of these might be ways of counterbalancing the more wide open game that a wider field allows.

Chapter 2

(e) How might the differences in field sizes affect the strategy of the game? Do you know of any major rule differences between the two games? How (if at all) are they related to the different field sizes?

3. Display 2.5 shows scale drawings of the front and side views of the Snydertown, PA, railroad depot. The drawing shows the length, width, and height of the real depot, and the scaling information is given in its upper right corner.

(a) If you were building an HO scale model of this depot and working with a metric ruler, what would be the length, width, and height of your model? Round your answer to the nearest millimeter.

(b) If you were building an HO scale model of this depot and working with a ruler marked in inches, what would be the length, width, and height of your model? Round your answer to the nearest 100th of an inch.

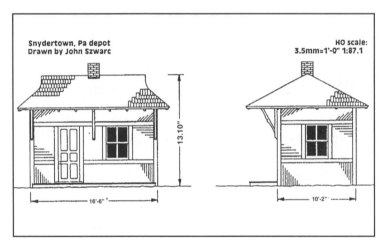

"Snydertown, PA depot," drawn by John Szwarc, page 85. Copyright© March 1994 by *Railroad Model Craftsman*, Carstens Publications, Inc. Reprinted with permission.

Display 2.5

Published by IT'S ABOUT TIME, Inc. © 2000 MATHconx, LLC

117

3. This is simultaneously an exercise in several different skill areas—
systems of measurement, ratio and proportion, fractions, rounding.
(a) length = 58 mm; width = 36 mm; height = 48 mm.
(b) length = 2.27 in.; width = 1.40 in.; height = 1.91 in. This can be
done by converting from mm to inches, but it might be more instructive
and more accurate if it were done directly from the scaling ratio 1:87.1.

NOTES

4. Many model railroaders think of HO scale as "half-O."

   (a) Using this meaning, what is the scaling factor for HO scale? Express it as a ratio and also as a fraction.

   (b) What is the difference in length between a scale model of a 40 foot boxcar using the half-O ratio versus a model of the same boxcar using the other HO scale ratio, 1:87?

5. You have completed a precision drawing that just fits on an 11 by 17 inch piece of paper, with no room to spare on any edge.

   (a) You need a reduced copy that will fit inside a 6 by 10 inch box in a report that is being prepared. What is the largest scaling factor you can use when setting the copying machine? Round your answer down to the nearest percent. Why round *down*?

   (b) Your drawing is so well liked that it's going to be made into a wall poster. The shorter side of the rectangular poster must be 2 feet long; the other length can be cut exactly to your specifications. If you don't want to leave any extra margin, what scaling factor should you use? How long will the longer side of the poster be? Round your answer to the nearest tenth of an inch.

Published by IT'S ABOUT TIME, Inc. © 2000 MATHconx, LLC

4. The intent of this exercise is to give the students experience in dealing with ratios as scaling factors, and in seeing how a larger second number (denominator) is related to a smaller measurement.

   (a) O scale is defined in the text as $\frac{1}{4}$ inch to 1 foot; that is, a scaling ratio of 1:48. Half O, then, would have a scaling ratio of 1:96; that is, a scaling factor of $\frac{1}{96}$.

   (b) A half O scale model of a 40 foot boxcar would be 5 inches long; a 1:87 HO scale model of the same boxcar would be just a little more than 5.5 inches long.

5. (a) The smaller of the fractions $\frac{6}{11}$ and $\frac{10}{17}$; that is, 54%. You round down because rounding up might result in a picture that's just a little too large to fit inside the box.

   (b) The scaling factor is $\frac{24}{11}$. The longer side will be $\frac{24}{11} \cdot 17 = 37.1$ inches long.

NOTES

Chapter 2

6. This problem refers to Display 2.4. Begin by tracing or copying this figure on a plain piece of paper.

   (a) On side *DC* of rectangle F, mark the point that is 30 mm to the right of *D*. Call this point *P*. Then find and mark the corresponding point, *P'* ("*P* prime"), on rectangle G.

   (b) On side *DA* of rectangle F, mark the point that is 15 mm below *D*. Call this point *Q*. Then find and mark the corresponding point, *Q'*, on rectangle G.

   (c) Use the Pythagorean Theorem to compute the distance between *P* and *Q* on rectangle F. Round your answer to the nearest mm. Check your result by measuring. Do you get the same answer? If not, explain what went wrong.

   (d) Find the distance between *P'* and *Q'* on rectangle G in three different ways,
      • using the Pythagorean Theorem,

      • using the scaling factor, and

      • by measuring.

      Round your answer to the nearest mm. Which way was easiest for you? Which way do you think is the most accurate? Which way do you like best? Why?

   (e) On side *ZY* of rectangle G. mark the point that is 10 mm to the right of *Z*. Call this point *R'*. Then find and mark the corresponding point, *R'*. on rectangle F.

   (f) On side *YX* of rectangle G. mark the point that is 12 mm below *Y*. Call this point *S'*. Then find and mark the corresponding point, *S*. on rectangle F.

   (g) Find the distance between *R* and *S* by measuring and by one other way. Round your answer to the nearest mm. Do you get the same answer both ways? If not, explain what went wrong.

Published by IT'S ABOUT TIME, Inc. © 2000 MATHconx, LLC

6. This exercise elaborates on the fact that the vertex correspondence and the scaling factor determine all the other pairings of corresponding points of two similar rectangles. In this case, recall that the scaling factor k is $\frac{16}{30} = \frac{8}{15}$.

   (a) D and Z are corresponding vertices, as are C and Y. Thus, P' must be $k \cdot 30$ mm ($= 16$ mm) to the right of Z on ZY.

   (b) D and Z correspond, as do A and W. Thus, Q' must be $k \cdot 15$ mm ($= 8$ mm) below Z on ZA.

   (c) $33.54 = 34$ mm (both ways).

   (d) 18 mm, all three ways. In this case, there's not much difference in accuracy. In general, measurement is probably the least accurate, but may be the easiest. This question provides an opportunity for a discussion about how rounding affects accuracy, but it may not be worth the class time it takes, unless you have some to spare.

   (e) This part and the next emphasize the reversibility of scaling. The students should see that they need to undo the previous scaling by multiplying by the reciprocal of the scaling factor to get these corresponding points. Thus, $\frac{1}{k} = \frac{15}{8}$ is the reverse scaling factor, so R is 18.75 mm to the right of D.

   (f) Similarly, S is $\frac{15}{8} \cdot 12 = 22.5$ mm below C.

   (g) There is a small trap here. The answer to part (e) is *not* the length of one side of the relevant right triangle; you want the length of the rest of that side! Apart from that, a routine application of the Pythagorean Theorem, and possibly the reverse scaling factor, yields (approximately) 35 mm.

NOTES

Chapter 2

7. Is the drawing of Alice in Display 2.6 out of proportion? How can you tell? Relate your explanation to our mathematical definition of proportion.

Display 2.6

7. This is a writing exercise; it can also be used for a class discussion, if you like. Display 2.6 is one of John Tenniel's original illustrations for the episode of *Alice in Wonderland* just before Alice meets the White Rabbit. See Martin Gardner's *The Annotated Alice*. New York: Bramhall House, 1960. Yes; it's out of proportion.

The most striking distortion is the length of Alice's neck. It's about twice as long as her head is high; it is about the same as the distance from her shoulders to her waist. In a proportional drawing of *any* size, both of these measurements should be far more than the length of her neck.

Here are some other, less obvious considerations. If Alice were a real little girl, she would probably be about $3\frac{1}{2}$ to 4 feet tall. Her shoes would be 6 or 7 inches long; her face would be about 6 inches wide; she would measure about 15 inches (more or less) across the shoulders. If we compare her real height to her height in the drawing (which measures about $3\frac{1}{2}$ in.), we get a scaling factor of about $\frac{1}{12}$. But this means that, in the picture, her shoes should be about $\frac{1}{2}$ inch long; her face should be about $\frac{1}{2}$ inch wide; she should measure about $1\frac{1}{4}$ inches across the shoulders. Since these other measurements don't match, the proportions are not correct.

Chapter 2

NOTES

_____

2.2 Similar Triangles and Rectangles

There's a lot of information packed into the definition of similarity, along with a hidden difficulty. Let's unpack it carefully. Do you remember what it says? Here it is again, with two key words missing. Can you fill them in?

> Two objects are **similar** if there is a constant k such that the distance between _____ two points of one object is k times the distance between the _____ two points of the other.

The first missing word is *any*. It means that you can't control the choice of points when you apply this definition. No matter which two points *anybody* picks, the same constant k must work for them. The difficulty is hiding in the second missing word. Do you know what the word is? Can you describe the difficulty? Try to figure it out as you answer the following questions.

2.9

These questions refer to the two triangular regions, F and G, in Display 2.7.

2.10

1. Can you tell just by looking at these triangular regions *exactly* which point of region F should correspond to point A of G? What about point B?

2. Find one point of G for which, just by looking, you know the exact corresponding point of F. Can you find two points of G for which you know the corresponding points of F? Three? Four? Explain your answers.

3. Suppose you know that these two triangular regions are similar. How can you find which point of F corresponds exactly with point A of G? Do it if you can, and describe your method. Will your method work for point B? Why or why not?

4. What is the difficulty in applying the definition of similarity?

Learning Outcomes

After studying this section, you will be able to:

Copy triangles and rectangles to various scales by using a scaling factor to find the distances between vertices;

Decide whether or not two triangles or rectangles are similar by comparing the ratios of their side lengths;

Estimate and compute the scaling factor needed to fit a given triangle or rectangle into a particular space.

Published by IT'S ABOUT TIME, Inc. © 2000 MATHconx, LLC

2.2 Similar Triangles and Rectangles

Applying the definition of similarity to arbitrary figures leads into relatively deep logical water. Because the definition is a universal statement, formally verifying that two figures actually are similar would require checking (somehow) the distance between each of the infinitely many pairs of points in one figure and their counterparts (assuming that you knew what they were) in the other figure. This section begins by pointing out these logical difficulties; then it works around them for the time being by restricting attention to triangles and rectangles.

The missing word is corresponding. Deciding exactly which points of two objects correspond or ought to correspond is not at all easy. In the questions of 2.10 we focus the students' attention on vertices as points for which correspondence is easily recognizable. If there's any justice in the world, corners ought to correspond to corners, right?! Thus, the issue becomes simpler for polygons because the correspondence of the vertices will determine whether or not the figures are similar. The more general problem of correspondence is handled in a later section.

2.10

The main object of these questions is to focus the students' attention on the vertices of the figures as particularly well behaved points. You should at least guide the students to appreciate the fact that the corners are the critical points in determining the shape of a polygon, even if you don't get around to answering these specific questions in detail.

1. No to both. Approximations can be made, but if you were testing for similarity using these points, the approximations wouldn't be good enough to give you a reliable ratio.

2. Any vertex will do. Thus, you can easily find by observation three dependable points, but not four.

3. You can take the ratio of the lengths of the two base sides or of any pair of corresponding sides and compare it to the ratio of distances between A and one vertex of the base and length of the corresponding segment of F. This process does not work for B because B is not on a side. It is possible to find the exact location of the point corresponding to B by using comparative distances from the vertices, but this is quite awkward.

4. The difficulty is setting up some sort of one-to-one correspondence between the points of the two figures. You might mention that a *one-to-one correspondence* is a special kind of function, and functions were discussed in Ch. 6 of **MATH** *Connections* Year 1.

Assessments   Blackline Masters   Extensions   Supplements

For Additional Support Materials see page T-249

Chapter 2

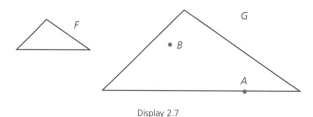

Display 2.7

2.11

Two drawings are shown in Display 2.8. Make a copy of each one that is twice the size of the original. That is, make copies that have a scaling factor of 2. Which one is easier to do, (a) or (b)? Why?

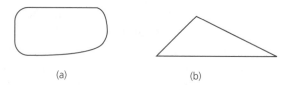

(a)   (b)

Display 2.8

Did the questions about Displays 2.7 and 2.8 help you to see the difficulty in using the definition of similar figures?

The problem is deciding which points of one figure really correspond to which points of the other.

For triangles, the process is easy. A triangle is determined by its vertices (its corners). Once you know where all three vertices are, only one triangle will fit. But sometimes figuring out which vertices of one polygon correspond to which vertices of another is not so simple. In many situations you just have to be told what the correspondence is. There are two common ways to do this.

• Corresponding vertices of two figures often are labeled with the same letter, but with different subscripts to indicate which figure the vertex is in. For instance, when we write two triangles as $\triangle A_1B_1C_1$ and $\triangle A_2B_2C_2$, we mean that the vertex A_1 of the first triangle corresponds to the vertex A_2 of the second triangle, B_1 corresponds to B_2, and C_1 corresponds to C_2.

• Sometimes the order in which the vertices are listed is intended to tell you the correspondence between the vertices of two polygons. (This often is the case on standard tests.) For instance, if two similar triangles are written as $\triangle ABC$ and $\triangle DEF$, you are expected to assume that A corresponds to D, B corresponds to E, and C corresponds to F.

122

2.2 Similar Triangles and Rectangles

2.11

This hands-on activity is worth a little class time. Again, the key idea here is that the vertices (corners) and straight sides of (b) makes it *much* easier to reproduce than (a). In fact, it is virtually impossible to produce an accurate double size copy of (a) without using some fairly sophisticated ideas about projections which we don't expect the students to know. On the other hand, (b) can be doubled fairly easily using ruler and compass.

- Measure the length of each side and draw a new segment to represent one side, let's say the base, twice as long as the original base.

- To find the location of the third vertex, set the compass to twice the length of another side and mark an arc for it, using one end of the base as the center. Repeat this process for the remaining side. The third vertex is at the intersection of these two arcs.

- Connect the third vertex to each of the two base vertices.

Again, the message here is that the location of the vertices determines a triangle (and hence a triangular region). This makes triangles particularly *nice* figures to use and helps to explain why triangulating more complicated polygons seen earlier is a worthwhile thing to do.

Chapter 2

Additional Support Materials:

Assessments	Qty
Form (A)	1
Form (B)	1

Blackline Masters	Qty
Student pp. 128-129	1

Extensions	Qty

Supplements	Qty
Similar Triangles and Rectangles	4

2.2 Similar Triangles and Rectangles

The first of these ways is clearer, but the second way is simpler. This book usually uses the simpler method, unless it is likely to be confusing. Unless you are told otherwise, assume that the order in which the vertices of two polygons are listed tells you the correspondence between them.

Because the vertices of a triangle determine its size and shape, two triangles are similar if the distances between the vertices of one triangle are proportional to the distances between the corresponding vertices of the other. That's a lot of words to express a very simple idea. It's easier and clearer with symbols, as follows.

(2.12)

Triangles $A_1B_1C_1$ and $A_2B_2C_2$ are similar if all three ratios of the lengths of their corresponding sides are equal. In symbols,

$$\frac{A_1B_1}{A_2B_2} = \frac{B_1C_1}{B_2C_2} = \frac{A_1C_1}{A_2C_2}$$

To show you how assuming the correspondence of vertices from their listing order makes it easier to read and write such expressions, we restate this important principle without using subscripts.

$\triangle ABC$ and $\triangle DEF$ are similar if $\dfrac{AB}{DE} = \dfrac{BC}{EF} = \dfrac{AC}{DF}$

Which of these two forms do *you* think is easier to understand?

1. Are all three of the triangles in Display 2.9 similar? Use a ruler to help you justify your answer.

2.13

2. Can you draw two triangles, *ABC* and *DEF*, for which

$$\frac{AB}{DE} = \frac{BC}{EF}$$

but the triangles are *not* similar? If you can, do it. If not, explain why it cannot be done.

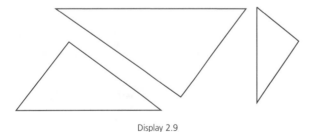

Display 2.9

2.12 In this book we make no notational distinction between a segment and its length. That is, *AB* may represent either the line segment between points *A* and *B* or the length of that line segment, depending on context. This simplifies notation without sacrificing clarity in almost every situation. In the few cases where there is a chance of confusion, we explicitly state how the symbol is to be interpreted.

Caution. Some other books and some standardized exams distinguish notationally between a line segment and its length. There are various ways of doing this. Here are some common ones.

- Line segment (set of points): $\overline{AB}$; length of segment: *AB*

- Line segment (set of points): $\overline{AB}$ or *AB*; length of segment: $m(\overline{AB})$ or *m(AB)* (*m* for measure)

- Line segment (set of points): $\overline{AB}$ or *AB*; length of segment: *d(A, B)* (*d* for distance)

Please alert your students to these notational devices as soon as you think it is appropriate, so that they are not confused by them in standard exam situations or in consulting other books.

2.13

1. Yes. The ratios of the corresponding sides are proportional. The important thing here is to see that students check by comparing ratios of measurements. Of course, the measurements will be subject to the usual errors and approximations of that process, so it is perhaps better to say that the answer is *probably similar*.

2. Yes. Take any triangle and multiply the lengths of two of its sides by any scaling factor *k*. Construct a new triangle using sides of these scaled lengths *but changing the angle between them*. The resulting triangle will satisfy the given proportion, but will not be similar to the original triangle. Display 2.1T shows an example of this.

$$\frac{AB}{DE} = \frac{BC}{EF} = \frac{1}{2}$$

but the ratio of the lengths of the third sides is quite different.

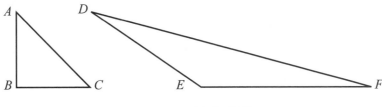

Display 2.1T

Chapter 2

For rectangles, there is an even easier test for simplicity. Two rectangles have the same shape if the ratio of their lengths equals the ratio of their widths. In symbols, two rectangles *ABCD* and *EFGH* (as shown in Display 2.10) are similar if

$$\frac{AB}{EF} = \frac{BC}{FG}$$

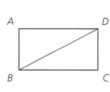
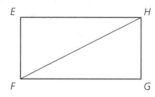

Display 2.10

 The test for similar rectangles checks only three of the four corner points. What about the fourth one? Refer to Display 2.10 as you answer these questions.

2.14

1. Suppose $\frac{AB}{EF} = \frac{BC}{FG} = k$ (where *k* is the scaling factor). Why must the ratios of corresponding sides that meet at *D* and *H* also equal *k*?

2. Why must the lengths of the corresponding diagonals also have the same ratio?
   Hint: Use the Pythagorean Theorem.

124

2.14

These questions set the stage for scaling with Cartesian (rectangular) coordinates.

1. The length of each of those sides equals that of one of the sides in the given proportion because the parallel sides of a rectangle are the same length.

2. Here's a somewhat formal but very straightforward argument using a little algebra. Call the length, width, and diagonal of the first rectangle l_1, w_1, and d_1, respectively. Call the length, width, and diagonal of the second rectangle l_2, w_2, and d_2, respectively. Since the scaling factor is k, we know that $l_2 = k \cdot l_1$ and $w_2 = k \cdot w_1$. By the Pythagorean Theorem,

$$
\begin{aligned}
d_2 &= \sqrt{l_2{}^2 + w_2{}^2} \\
&= \sqrt{(k \cdot l_1)^2 + (k \cdot w_1)^2} \\
&= \sqrt{k^2 l_1{}^2 + k^2 w_1{}^2} \\
&= \sqrt{k^2 \cdot (l_1{}^2 + w_1{}^2)} \\
&= k\sqrt{l_1{}^2 + w_1{}^2} \\
&= k \cdot d_1
\end{aligned}
$$

If your students are not up to this level of manipulative algebra on their own, you might show them this argument to demonstrate how algebra can be used to verify a geometric fact.

Chapter 2

NOTES

The principle in question 2 is very important:

If two rectangles are similar, with scaling factor k, then the ratio of their corresponding diagonal lengths also equals k.

We can use this fact to see how similarity works for a rectangular coordinate system in a plane. Suppose you have two points—say A and B—anywhere in the plane. If you stretch or shrink the plane by the same scaling factor in both coordinate directions, then *the distance between A and B will also stretch or shrink by that same scaling factor*.

Display 2.11 shows how this fact follows from the statement about rectangles. The two points, A and B, can be considered as the diagonally opposite corners of a rectangle with sides parallel to the coordinate axes. When the plane is stretched by the scaling factor—in this case, 3—in both coordinate directions, the length and width of the rectangle are multiplied by 3. This means that the diagonal distance is also multiplied by 3.

These questions refer to Display 2.11.

2.15

1. Suppose that point A of the left rectangle is 1 cm to the right of and 1 cm above the origin. What measurements describe point A of the right rectangle?

2. Suppose also that $l = 4$ cm and $w = 2$ cm.

   (a) What measurements describe point B of the left rectangle?

   (b) What measurements describe point B of the right rectangle?

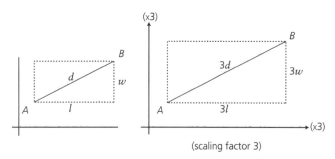

(scaling factor 3)

Display 2.11

125

2.15

These should be routine calculations, if the students understand Display 2.11. If they have trouble with this, finding out why should help you clear up any misconceptions about the basic idea of uniform stretching.

1. 3 cm to the right and 3 cm above the origin

2. (a) 5 cm to the right and 3 cm above the origin
   (b) 15 cm to the right and 9 cm above the origin

NOTES

Chapter 2

Here is a handy way to test whether two right triangles are similar.

Two right triangles are similar if the ratio of the legs of one triangle equals the ratio of the legs of the other.

In other words, suppose that $\triangle ABC$ and $\triangle DEF$ are two right triangles with right angles at C and F. If

$$\frac{BC}{AC} = \frac{EF}{DF}$$

then the two triangles must be similar.

2.16 Why does this similarity test for right triangles work? *Hint:* Start by drawing a diagram and labeling it carefully. Then look at how we dealt with similarity of rectangles. How are right triangles related to rectangles?

2.17 Suppose you stretch the coordinates in a plane by 5 in the x direction and 2 in the y direction. Will the distance between any two points in the plane stretch by a predictable constant amount? If so, what is that amount? If not, explain why not.

When you walk away from something, it seems to get smaller; when you walk toward it, it seems to get larger. For instance, suppose you take a picture of a house from 1000 feet away, then walk toward the house until you are 200 feet away and take another picture of it. The image of the house in the first photo would be much smaller than its image in the second, right? But all the dimensions of the house would change by the same scaling factor, so the house would look the same; that is, the two images would be similar. "Zooming" with a graphing calculator or a computer works like that. Zooming in makes it look as if you are walking toward the object being graphed; zooming out makes it look as if you are walking away from it.

Graphing calculators use scaling factors for zooming. Most graphing calculators allow you to choose the horizontal and vertical scaling factors separately. However, the default setting uses the same factor for both coordinate axes.

2.16

This is an important, useful fact that will be used later. If you choose not to use this question for a student exercise or a class discussion, you should at least draw your students' attention to the principle and give them a brief explanation of it.

To see why this test works, begin by observing that right triangles are *diagonal halves* of rectangles. Then, by the principle in question 2 of 2.14, if the length ratios of the corresponding legs of the two right triangles are the same, the ratio of the lengths of the hypotenuses will agree with that value. Thus, all we need to show is that

$$\frac{BC}{EF} = \frac{AC}{DF}$$

But cross multiplication of this proportion and cross multiplication of the given proportion yield the same equation! Therefore, this proportion is true whenever the given proportion is true.

2.17

A formal answer to this question may be a bit sophisticated for the average student, but if you allow some discussion, you might be surprised by which students have accurate intuitive ideas about this!

The answer is No. The amount of stretching depends on the direction of the segment connecting the two points relative to the coordinate system. Since one coordinate direction is being stretched more than the other, the effect on the diagonal distance between the two points will depend on how closely the points align with one coordinate direction, rather than the other. This means that there is no single constant scaling factor that works for all pairs of points.

NOTES

Chapter 2

The following questions should help you see how zooming works on your graphing calculator. Begin by putting these four equations into the equation list.

2.18

$$Y_1 = X \qquad Y_2 = X - 1 \qquad Y_3 = -X \qquad Y_4 = -X + 1$$

1. Find the menu in which the zoom factors appear and make a note of the way they are set now.

2. Graph the four functions together, using a standard WINDOW setting. Then use the ZOOM menu to zoom in and describe what happens. Relate your description to the zoom factors. What happens if you zoom in twice?

3. Return to the standard setting. Then zoom out and describe what happens. Relate your description to the zoom factors. What happens if you zoom out twice?

Reset the X and Y zoom factors to half of their original settings. Then, starting from the standard setting, zoom in and zoom out. Now reset the zoom factors as follows. Set the X factor to 6 and the Y factor to 2. Then, starting from the standard setting, zoom in and zoom out. Try the same thing with the X and Y settings reversed.

4. Which X and Y zoom factors give you similar pictures?

5. Why do you think the default setting for your calculator uses the same zoom factor for both the x-axis and the y-axis?

Caution: In discussing zooming, we have been talking about *appearance*—whether a figure *looks* larger or smaller. If you think of the figures as graphs, you don't really change the coordinates of any point because the scale on the axes is changed by the scaling factor, too. (For instance, when you zoom in by a factor of 2, the spacing of the tick marks on the axes doubles.) This gives the impression that the object you are zooming on is still the same object, only viewed closer up (zoom in) or from farther away (zoom out).

127

2.18

The relationship between zooming and similarity can be a bit tricky, particularly when it comes to scaling factors. If students experiment a little with their calculators, it should become much clearer to them.

1. For the TI-82 (TI-83) calculators, these settings appear in the ZOOM MEMORY menu as 4:Set Factors.... The default setting is 4 for both.

2. Seeing these equations at work should remind students about slopes and y-intercepts. If some students get an error message when they try to graph these equations, check first to see if they used the correct negative sign, $(-)$, in front of the X in equations 3 and 4.

    Students should see that zooming in makes the picture appear n times as large, where n is the zoom factor for both axes. For the TI calculator default settings, it would be 4 times as large. Zooming in twice makes the picture appear n^2 times as large (16 times, for the TI calculators).

3. Zooming out makes the picture appear smaller. The scaling factor in this case is $\frac{1}{n}$ (for the TIs, $\frac{1}{4}$, where n is the zoom factor. Zooming out twice applies a scaling factor of $\left(\frac{1}{n}\right)^2$ (for the TIs, $\frac{1}{16}$).

4. Similar pictures occur if and only if the X and Y zoom factors are equal. Otherwise, the new picture is a distortion of the old one.

5. This is a corollary of the previous answer. The same zoom factor is used for both to avoid distorting the graph.

Chapter 2

NOTES

_____

....

....

....

....

....

....

....

Problem Set: 2.2

1. A local company is running a contest for a new logo design. Your design sketch, shown in Display 2.12, has made it into the final round. Now the company wants you to submit it in two different sizes, to judge how it might look

    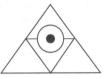

    Display 2.12

    *   on posters: The base of the large triangle must be 24 cm long.

    *   on stationery: The base of the large triangle must be 18 mm long.

    The base of the large triangle in your sketch is exactly 3 cm and its altitude is 2 cm.

    (a) What scaling factor should you use to make the poster-size version of your design?

    (b) What will be the height (the altitude) of the poster size version of your design?

    (c) Will the poster-size version fit on a standard 8.5×11 inch sheet of paper?

    (d) What scaling factor should you use to make the stationery-size version of your design?

    (e) What will be the height (the altitude) of the stationery size version of your design?

    (f) To reproduce this sketch in these sizes, you go to your local copy shop to have it photocopied. When you get there, you discover that the machine's size control recognizes only percents. Express the two scaling factors you need as percents.

2. Each row of the table in Display 2.13 refers to two triangles, $\triangle 1$ and $\triangle 2$. (Your teacher will give you a copy of this table.) In each case, $\triangle 1$ has sides of lengths a, b, and c. The corresponding sides of $\triangle 2$ have lengths d, e, and f, respectively.

    *   Draw a sketch of such a situation. Label the corresponding sides of the two triangles as they are given here.

Published by IT'S ABOUT TIME, Inc. © 2000 MATHconx, LLC

Problem Set: 2.2

1. Besides being a question about similarity, this question is intended to give students practice with using different measurement units (inches, centimeters, millimeters) and with expressing ratios as percents.

    (a) 8

    (b) 16 cm

    (c) Yes, provided you turn it sideways (in landscape orientation).

    (d) $\frac{18}{30}$, which is $\frac{3}{5}$ or 0.6.

    (e) 12 mm

    (f) 800% and 60%.

    Here is an interesting follow up question to part (f), once the students have correctly found the 800% answer.
    (g) The clerk at the copy shop says, "Our machine enlarges only up to 200%, but I'll just use that setting four times to get your 800% size. OK?" Is it OK? Explain. No, but *three* applications of the 200% enlargement will do the trick.

2. The sketch called for here should be generic, not referring to any particular pair of triangles. Its purpose is just to get visually oriented students focused on the situation represented by a line of the table. Note that each line of the table is a separate scaling exercise, independent of the rest. You can have your students do as many or as few rows as you choose. The answers appear in Display 2.2T.

	Triangle 1			Triangle 2			Scaling
	a	*b*	*c*	*d*	*e*	*f*	Factor
(a)	8.0	10.0	14.0	32.0	40.0	56.0	4.0
(b)	1.2	5.5	6.4	4.5	20.625	24.0	3.75
(c)	20.5	27.6	45.0	90.2	121.44	198.0	4.4
(d)	3.58	4.56	6.08	20.227	25.764	34.352	5.65
(e)	7.25	10.85	15.55	24.2875	36.3475	52.0925	3.35
(f)	12.5	4.8	8.0	7.8125	3.0	5.0	0.625

Display 2.13, filled in

Display 2.2T

Chapter 2

- In each row, the lengths of some of the sides have been given (in inches). Find values for the missing entries so that △1 and △2 are similar. Also find the scaling factor (from △1 to △2) in each case. You may copy the table onto your own paper and fill it in, if that helps you organize your work. Use your calculator whenever you want.

| | Triangle 1 | | | Triangle 2 | | | Scaling Factor |
	a	b	c	d	e	f	
(a)	8	10	14	32			
(b)		5.5	6.4	4.5	20.625		
(c)	20.5			90.2	121.44	198	
(d)	3.58		6.08		25.764	34.352	
(e)		10.85		24.2875	36.3475	52.0925	
(f)	12.5	4.8	8		3		

Display 2.13

3. The Make More Money Dept. of the U. S. Postal Service has decided to market a set of commemorative ceramic tiles displaying popular stamp designs of the 1990s. The tiles will be 6 inch squares, suitable for decorating kitchen counters, shower stalls, patio walks, etc. The stamps to be copied come in 4 different sizes (including allowance for a border).

   (a) regular issue: 20 x 22 mm

   (b) standard commemorative: 42 x 22 mm

   (c) oversize commemorative: 28 x 36 mm

   (d) special issue (love stamps, etc.): 27 x 20 mm

   For each stamp size, find the scaling factor that will make its design as large as possible on the tile. Then find the dimensions of the scaled tile design. Round your final answers to the nearest tenth of an inch. (*Hint:* In each case, one of the dimensions should be 6 inches.)

4. Little League baseball is similar to major league baseball in many ways. A major league baseball diamond is a square 90 feet on a side and the distance from the pitcher's mound to home plate is 60.5 feet. A Little League baseball diamond is a square 60 feet on a side.

   (a) Using your ruler, draw a square to represent a major league baseball diamond and then draw a proportional square representing a Little League baseball diamond.

Published by IT'S ABOUT TIME, Inc. © 2000 MATHconx, LLC

129

3. There is a unit conversion question involved in stating the scaling factor. If the ratio is stated properly as mm to in., it can be used to find the scaled dimensions for each stamp without explicitly going through the extra step of converting from metric to English measure. It will be automatically included in the scaling factor. However, if you want the scaling factor to be a unit free ratio, the metric English conversion (25.4 mm = 1 inch) will be necessary. You can decide how accurate you want your students' scaling factor answers to be. You might get them to decide this question after checking their results using the scaling factors.

In each case, the longer of the measurements must be scaled to 6 inches. This determines the scaling factor, which is used to find the other scaled dimension. The answers appear in Display 2.3T.

Type	Ratio	Scaled Dimensions	Scaling Factor
(a) regular issue	1 mm to $\frac{6}{22}$ in.	5.5 by 6 in.	6.927
(b) standard commem.	1 mm to $\frac{6}{42}$ in.	6 by 3.1 in.	3.629
(c) oversize commem.	1 mm to $\frac{6}{36}$ in.	4.7 by 6 in.	4.233
(d) special issue	1 mm to $\frac{6}{27}$ in.	6 by 4.4 in.	5.644

Display 2.3T

4. (b) 40.33 ft.

   (d) 50.42 ft.

   (e) The official distances are a few feet longer in each case. This is probably a safety factor; it gives younger players just a little more time to see and react to a pitched ball.

NOTES

2.2 Similar Triangles and Rectangles

(b) Use your calculator to find the proportional distance from the pitcher's mound to home plate in Little League, assuming that the two diamonds are in proportion.

(c) Another baseball league is called the Intermediate League. This league's diamond is a square 75 feet on a side. Using your ruler, draw a square representing an Intermediate League diamond that is proportional to your drawings of the other two diamonds.

(d) Use your calculator to find the proportional distance from the pitcher's mound to home plate in the Intermediate League, assuming that its diamond is proportional to the major league diamond.

(e) The official distances from the pitcher's mound to home plate are 46 feet in Little League and 54 feet in Intermediate League. They should *not* agree with the answers you got in parts (b) and (d). Are the official distances longer or shorter than the proportional ones? Why do you think this is the case?

5. The General Crunchies Co. is beginning a series of cutout models for the back of its breakfastfood boxes, starting with a camping theme. The first cutout is to be for a pup tent 7 feet long, 4 feet wide at the base, and 3 feet high at the peak. A sketch of the cutout pattern for this pup tent is shown in Display 2.14. The dashed lines are for folds, and the striped pieces are tabs for gluing the model together.

Unfortunately, the person who made this sketch was not very careful; some of the lengths and corners are not exactly right. Your job: Make an accurate pattern for this cutout, to a scale of $\frac{1}{2}$ inch to 1 foot. The measurements shown give you enough information to determine the rest of the shape. A ruler and a compass are the only tools you should need. Here are some questions to help you as you make your drawing.

(a) What is the scaling factor for this model?

(b) What are the dimensions of each slanted wall of the tent? How can you figure that out?

(c) Each front flap is a right triangle. If they are cut and folded accurately, they will close the front of the tent with no overlap. What are the side lengths of these triangles? How do you know?

130

5. Students will need a plain piece of paper (stiff paper preferred, but not necessary), a ruler, and a compass for this problem.

(a) The model to real scaling factor is $\frac{1}{24}$. Knowing this explicitly is not a prerequisite for the rest of the problem, but it serves to reinforce the idea of scale.

(b) The length of each side is (of course) the length of the tent, 7'. The width of a slanted side (the distance between the two dashed lines) is equal to a side length (other than the base) of the back. That can be found by the Pythagorean Theorem; it's the hypotenuse of a right triangle that has legs 3' (the height of the tent) and 2' (half the floor width). Thus, each side panel has width $\sqrt{13} = 3.6'$ (approx).

(c) The front flaps are right triangles of the same dimensions as in the previous part: 3', 2', $\sqrt{13}'$. Each is half of the back, divided down the middle.

(d) The width of a side determines the point between the two flaps. Once this is found, a compass can be used to draw an arc of 1.5 in. (3' scaled) centered at that point, and an arc of 1 in. (2' scaled) centered at the base corners of the side. The intersection point of these arcs is the vertex of the right angle corner.

(e) A good, practical choice for convenience in folding and gluing would be $\frac{1}{4}$ in. to $\frac{1}{2}$ in.

(f) The entire pattern will fit within a 6 inch square, small enough for the back of almost any standard breakfast food box.

Chapter 2

NOTES

_____

....

....

....

....

....

....

....

....

(d) How can you use a compass to find the correct position of the right angle corners of the front flaps?

(e) How wide should you make the glue tabs? This is a free choice, within reason.

(f) Will your pattern fit on the back of a cereal box? What are its maximum length and width?

Draw your pattern on a plain piece of paper. Then cut it out, fold it up, and glue or tape it together. Does your pattern work?

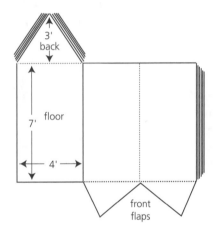

Display 2.14

6. The second in the series of General Crunchies cutout models is a lean-to. It is 8 feet from side to side, 7 feet from front to back, with a low back wall 3 feet high. The front opening is 6.5 feet high, and the roof overhangs about 6 inches in each direction. A sketch of the cutout pattern for this lean-to is shown in Display 2.15. The dashed lines are for folds, and the striped pieces are tabs for gluing the model together.

Using ruler and compass, make an accurate pattern for this cutout on a sheet of plain paper, to a scale of $\frac{1}{2}$ inch to 1 foot. Draw your pattern on a piece of plain paper. Then cut it out, fold it up, and glue or tape it together.

Published by IT'S ABOUT TIME, Inc. © 2000 MATHconx, LLC

131

6. This is a much easier cutout pattern than the pup tent because there are no diagonal distances to compute. In fact, this one can be done with only a ruler, provided that you have a sheet of paper with a reliably square corner. The pattern will fit on a standard 8.5 × 11 inch sheet. In fact, it fits inside a 6.5 × 11 inch rectangle; that's a minimum size for the back of the cereal box.

NOTES

Chapter 2

If your pattern were to be put on the back of a cereal box, how big would that back have to be?

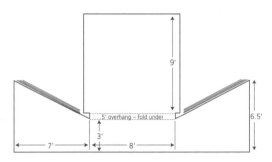

Display 2.15

7. Suppose you are drawing a new triangle that is similar to one you are given.

   (a) If the scaling factor is greater than 1, will the new triangle be larger or smaller than the given one?

   (b) If the scaling factor is positive but less than 1, will the new triangle be larger or smaller than the given one?

   (c) If the scaling factor is 1, what will the new figure look like?

   (d) If the scaling factor is 0, what will the new figure look like?

   (e) Does it make sense to have a negative scaling factor? Why or why not?

8. Show that the similarity test for rectangles,

$$\frac{AB}{EF} = \frac{BC}{FG}$$

   does not work for all quadrilaterals. That is, draw two quadrilaterals, *ABCD* and *EFGH*, that are not similar, but for which this equation is true. Verify these conditions by measuring your drawing.

9. Give a convincing argument to justify the following statement. Two right triangles are similar whenever the ratios of the lengths of *any two* pairs of their corresponding sides are equal.

Published by IT'S ABOUT TIME, Inc. © 2000 MATHconx, LLC

7. The first three parts of this question set up the idea that congruence is a special case of similarity. This will be discussed explicitly in a later section.

    (a) bigger
    (b) smaller
    (c) It will be exactly the same size and shape as the original triangle.
    (d) a single point!
    (e) No. The scaling factor adjusts distances between points, and distances are always nonnegative.

8. Display 2.4T shows one such drawing. The left and bottom sides of the two quadrilaterals are the same as those of the rectangles in Display 2.10, so the proportion still holds. However, the other two sides have been changed so that the figures are not similar.

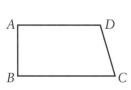 

Display 2.4T

9. This fact is the basis for much of right angle trigonometry. Besides being an important result for later work, this problem serves to reinforce and extend the ideas introduced in the last half of the section. It might be too challenging for some students to attack on their own. This question can also be used for class discussion.

    Probably the best way to begin is to draw an appropriate picture and introduce some notation. Let ABC and DEF be the right triangles, with the right angles at C and F, and represent the length of the side opposite each angle by the corresponding lowercase letter, as shown in Display 2.5T. According to the text, these triangles are similar if

    $$\frac{c}{f} = \frac{a}{d} = \frac{b}{e}$$

    Actually, there are three equality statements rolled into one here. Now, if we know

    $$\frac{a}{d} = \frac{b}{e}$$

    then the fact that $\frac{c}{f}$ equals the same scaling factor follows from treating c and f as the diagonals of rectangles and applying the principle of question 2 of 3.14.

    On the other hand, if we know $\frac{c}{f} = \frac{a}{d}$, then we can use an argument similar to the one used in question 2 of 2.14. Let k represent this common ratio. Then $c = kf$ and $a = kd$, so the Pythagorean Theorem yields

$$b = \sqrt{(c)^2 - (a)^2}$$
$$= \sqrt{(k \cdot f)^2 - (k \cdot d)^2}$$
$$= \sqrt{k^2 f^2 - k^2 d^2}$$
$$= \sqrt{k^2 \cdot (f^2 - d^2)}$$
$$= k \cdot \sqrt{f^2 - d^2}$$
$$= k \cdot e$$

That is, the ratio $\frac{b}{e}$ also equals k. The argument for the remaining case is exactly analogous to this one.

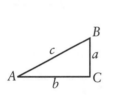 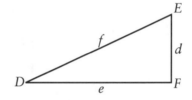

Display 2.5T

NOTES

2.3 How to Measure Angles

You have seen that similarity depends on knowing corresponding points of objects. You have also seen that the easiest corresponding points to identify are the "corner points," the vertices of angles. Usually, all the vertices (and some other points) in a diagram are labeled with letters. This makes it easy to name and keep track of angles. Sometimes the vertex alone is enough to identify the angle. When several different angles have the same vertex, other points are used to identify the sides, as you saw in Chapter 1.

You also saw that two angles are **congruent** if one can be placed on top of the other so that their vertices match and their corresponding sides lie along the same rays.
(A **ray** is part of a line that starts at a particular point and extends infinitely far in one direction.)

In Display 2.16, ∠A is congruent to exactly one of the other angles. Which one is it? How would you convince a friend who doesn't believe you that your choice is correct?

2.19

Display 2.16

Why do you think we say *ray*, instead of *line*, in the description of congruent angles? If we substitute *line* for *ray* in this description, can you find a counterexample? That is, can you find an example of two angles that fit the new description, but obviously are not the same size?

2.20

Comparing angles by placing one on top of the other is a simple and clear idea, but it's not always practical. The corner of a building, the peak of a roof, and a switch in a railroad track are just a few of the many, many cases of angles that can't just be traced or picked up and superimposed. To compare angles like that, we need a way to measure them.

Learning Outcomes

After studying this section, you will be able to:

Identify and construct congruent angles in various ways;

Measure angles in several different ways using degrees and slope;

Describe, construct, and measure angles in terms of rotation.

About Words

The word *angle* comes from the Latin word for corner, which is *angulus*.

2.3 How to Measure Angles

The concept of *angle* is surprisingly complex. Many distinct, but related, ideas come together in this single mathematical entity. This section discusses two ways of viewing angles—as corners and as rotations. Measurement provides the connection between these two viewpoints.

An important goal of the section is to get students to see that there are many different ways to measure angles, and our *choice* of how to do it is based on convenience, rather than on necessity. This is just like choosing a unit length for linear measure, a unit region for area measure, etc. In the case of angles, it's an important idea to get across in preparation for radian measure.

2.19

The correct answer is ∠C. This is an exercise to get students to ignore side length when they think about the size of an angle. It is essential to get students to see that the congruence of angles should *not* depend on the lengths of the sides, the location of the angle, or its orientation. None of these things affect the cornerliness of the angle, so to speak. We are so accustomed to thinking in this way that we might be tempted to pass over that as obvious, but it is not at all obvious to people who are just beginning to sharpen their intuitions about what an angle is.

Do not do this problem with a protractor. Remember that we haven't introduced degree measurement yet! Display 2.16 is deliberately designed to make the correct answer difficult to find with confidence because the student's justification strategy is important. Students should see that superposition is a reasonable way of deciding that two angles are the same size. Here's a reasonable approach to this problem.

> Take a piece of tracing paper or any paper you can see through and trace ∠A on it. Now put it on top of each of the other angles, in turn, so that one side of your traced angle lies along the same ray as one side of the other angle and the vertices match. The two angles are the same size if their other sides also lie along the same ray.

2.20

This question is intended to sharpen the students' understanding of both congruence and angles. When two lines intersect, the two angles on one side of a line satisfy this requirement, but they are not congruent unless the lines are perpendicular. See Display 2.6T.

Display 2.6T

Assessments   Blackline Masters   Extensions   Supplements
For Additional Support Materials see page T-275

Chapter 2

About Words

The prefix *super-* means *above* or *over*. The verb *impose* means *put on*. So *superimpose* means put on from above.

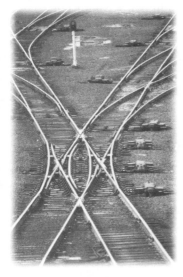

But what shall we measure? To compare the angles, the important thing to measure is how fast the rays from the sides of the angle diverge (move away from each other). For instance, picture two mice walking along the (inner) rails away from the vertex of a railroad switch. How fast are they moving away from each other?

Railroads actually measure the angles of their switches this way. (They don't use mice, of course!) They measure the distance, say y, between the inner rails at some point and then they measure the distance, say x, from that place to the vertex of the switch. The ratio $\frac{x}{y}$ is called the *number* of the switch. It's the number of feet of track *for each foot of separation*, assuming that the tracks keep running straight away from the turnout in each direction. For instance, a #12 switch is an angle that provides 1 foot of separation for every 12 feet of track. The diagram in Display 2.17 shows how switch size is determined. (In this display, the switch is called a "turnout" because it comes from a model railroading book. Track switches are called turnouts by model railroaders to distinguish them from electrical switches.)

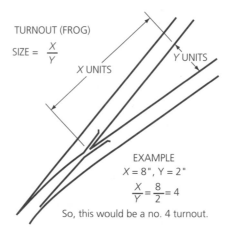

TURNOUT (FROG)

SIZE = $\frac{X}{Y}$

X UNITS

Y UNITS

EXAMPLE
$X = 8", Y = 2"$
$\frac{X}{Y} = \frac{8}{2} = 4$

So, this would be a no. 4 turnout.

DETERMINING
TURNOUT SIZE

From *Practical Guide to HO Model Railroading* by *Model Railroader Magazine.*
Copyright © 1986 by Kalmbach Publishing Company. Reprinted with permission.

Display 2.17

Note that we haven't put an About Words note about *congruent* in the student text, but some of your students might like to know where it comes from. It's a curious combination of the Latin prefix *con-* (meaning "with" or "together") and an Indo-European root meaning "collapse" or "topple." The meaning of *congruent* in everyday English is "in agreement" or "harmonious"; that is, things are congruent if they "fall together"!

Chapter 2

Additional Support Materials:

Assessments	Qty
Form (A)	1
Form (B)	1

Blackline Masters	Qty
Student p.139	1

Extensions	Qty

Supplements	Qty
How to Measure Angles	3

The Moosehead Lake Railroad wants to lay new track near its eastern terminal. They want a side track to run parallel to the main line, but 20 feet away from it, to bypass a loading platform.

2.21

1. If they use a #12 switch, how far will it be from the vertex of the switch until the inner rails are 20 feet apart?

This switch is on a main track for express trains. This railroad, like many others, uses the number of a switch as a guide for the maximum safe train speed through that switch—double the switch number, in miles per hour. This means that the maximum safe train speed over a #12 switch is only 24 mph. They would like the switch to handle trains safely at about 40 mph.

2. What number switch do they need?

3. How far would it be from the vertex of the switch until the inner rails are 20 feet apart?

Their surveyors say that the distance from the end of the platform to the switch vertex cannot be more than 360 feet.

4. What is the largest size switch they can use?

5. What is the maximum train speed over this switch?

Using a ratio to measure the rate of separation between lines should sound familiar. That's what *slope* is about. The slope of the wheelchair ramp at the Fuzzy Friends Toy Co. built earlier in **MATH** *Connections* measures its height relative to the horizontal distance from its low end. This rise-over-run ratio measures how fast the ramp line diverges from the parking lot level, the horizontal axis.

Published by IT'S ABOUT TIME, Inc. © 2000 MATHconx, LLC

2.21

These questions about railroad switches and train speeds provide some practice with using ratios and proportions in a realistic setting. Even the railroad name is more realistic than you might imagine. There is a real railroad in central Maine called the Belfast & Moosehead Lake RR. If your students need more practice with ratios and proportions, you can easily use this setting to make up similar practice exercises. Note that odd numbers are not used for switch sizes.

1. $12 \cdot 20 = 240$ feet

2. #20

3. $20 \cdot 20 = 400$ feet

4. This is easiest to see as a proportion, such as $\frac{360}{20} = \frac{x}{1}$. Solving by cross multiplication, we get $20x = 360$, so $x = 18$. There must be 1 foot of separation for every 18 feet, so this is a #18 switch.

5. 36 mph

NOTES

Chapter 2

2.22

Display 2.18 is a diagram of the wheelchair ramp. It is a straight ramp that rises 4 feet and has a horizontal length of 32 feet. The vertical line segments are the eight ramp supports. Each ordered pair tells you the location and length of a support. The first number is its horizontal distance from the left end of the ramp; the second number is its vertical length. If this ramp diagram is cut off at any one of these eight vertical segments, you have a right triangle.

1. Are all eight triangles similar? Justify your answer.

2. What does this have to do with the slope of the ramp line?

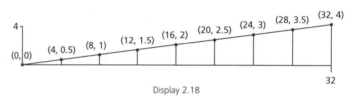

Display 2.18

The slope of a line in a coordinate system is a measure of the angle it makes with the horizontal axis. We can borrow that idea to measure angles, whether or not they are in a coordinate system. We can pick a point on one ray of an angle, measure the distance from that point to the vertex, and also measure the perpendicular distance from that point to the other ray. The ratio of that perpendicular distance divided by the distance to the vertex will be the same, no matter which point you pick. That makes the ratio a good measure of angle size; we'll call it the *slope measure* of the angle.

For instance, to find the slope measure of the angle made by the ramp and the ground in Display 2.18, we could begin by picking a point P on the ground under the ramp. If P is the point 16 feet to the right of the vertex, for example, then the slope measure of this angle is

$$\frac{\text{perpendicular distance from } P \text{ to ramp}}{\text{distance from } P \text{ to vertex}} = \frac{2}{16} = \frac{1}{8}$$

Here's another example. This one refers to Display 2.19. To find the (approximate) slope measure of $\angle AVB$, we can use a ruler to measure the segments AV and AB. Now, AV is about 3 inches long and AB is about 0.5 inches long, so

$$\text{approximate slope measure of } \angle AVB = \frac{AB}{AV} = \frac{0.5}{3} = \frac{1}{6}$$

We say approximate because the answer depends on measuring with a ruler, which is always only an approximation of actual length.

136

2.22

Yes, all eight triangles are similar. Any two of these triangles will be similar if the ratios of their two legs are equal. This is the principle stated right after Do this 2.15. This ratio is just the rise over run ratio of the second coordinate of the vertical segment's top point divided by its first coordinate. In each case, this ratio is the slope of the ramp line; therefore, all the ratios are the same. Thus, all eight triangles are similar.

NOTES

Chapter 2

These questions refer to Display 2.19.

2.23

1. Use a ruler to find the approximate slope measures of ∠AVC, ∠AVD, and ∠AVE.

2. Find the approximate slope measures of ∠BVC and ∠DVE. (Watch out! What do you have to measure? Measure carefully.)

3. How are the slope measures of ∠AVD and ∠AVE related?

4. When you add the slope measures of ∠AVD and ∠DVE, do you get the slope measure of ∠AVE? Do you think you should? Why or why not?

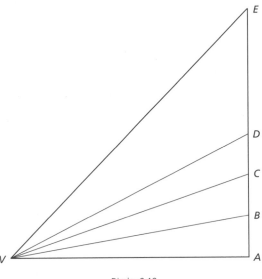

Display 2.19

The slope measure of an angle is very much like the way railroads measure switches, but it's not quite the same. What's different? (Look carefully at Displays 2.17 and 2.19.)

2.24

There are times when slope is a useful way to measure angles, but it applies easily only to angles smaller than a right angle. Also, as you may have noticed, slope measure does not behave very well with respect to addition and subtraction. We need to find a better way to measure angles.

Published by IT'S ABOUT TIME, Inc. © 2000 MATHconx, LLC

These questions have two objectives: (1) to give students experience with finding the slope measure of an angle, and (2) to suggest to students that slope measure does not behave very well arithmetically. Parts 1 and 2 will satisfy the first objective. Parts 3 and 4 lead the students to consider the additivity question.

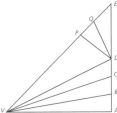

Two ways to measure $\angle DVE$ of Display 2.19

Display 2.7T

1. Slope measures $\angle AVC = \frac{1}{3}$; $\angle AVD = \frac{1}{2}$; $\angle AVE = 1$

2. The warning here refers to the fact that students need to measure the *perpendicular* distance from one line to the other in order to get the proper slope ratio. For each angle, there are two ways to do this, depending on which ray you start from. Display 2.7T illustrates two ways to measure $\angle DVE$.

   - If you use DV as the base segment and draw a perpendicular from it to EV (meeting it at Q), then the slope measure is $\frac{DQ}{DV}$, which is approximately $\frac{28}{85}$ when measured in millimeters.

   - But you could use EV as the base segment and measure the perpendicular distance *to* it, instead. If you draw a line from D perpendicular to EV at P, say, then the slope measure is $\frac{DP}{PV}$, which is approximately $\frac{27}{81}$ in millimeters.

   In either case, you get the same ratio (within measurement error): 0.33. The slope measure of $\angle BVC$ is approximately 0.16.

3. The slope measure of $\angle AVE$ is twice that of $\angle AVD$.

4. No. The slope measure of $\angle AVE$ is 1 and the measure of $\angle AVD$ is $\frac{1}{2}$, but the measure of $\angle DVE$ $\left(\frac{28}{85}\right)$ is clearly less than $\frac{1}{2}$. The student's opinion about "should" is less important than the reason. One could argue that it should because taking half of something away should leave half. But this *presupposes* that slope measure should behave in a nice arithmetic way, and there really is no reason (other than faith in the uniform simplicity of mathematical ideas) to make such an assumption.

This need not be an extended discussion, but two differences should be made clear. The obvious similarity comes from treating the railroad y-value (the spread between the inner rails) as the rise and the x-value as the run. However, if you do that, then the railroad switch numbers are the *reciprocals* of the corresponding slope numbers. There is another important, but less obvious difference. The distance between the rails is measured as if the rails formed an *isosceles* triangle with the switch vertex at its peak, whereas the slope measure treats one ray as a base line and measures the distance to the other ray by forming a *right* triangle.

Back in Chapter 1, you saw that any measurement system starts with choosing a *unit of measure*. Then everything is measured in terms of that unit. What shall we choose as a unit of measure for angles?

2.25 **Make up two different units of angle measure that nobody in the class has ever heard of before. Then decide which one you think is better. Give reasons to support your opinion.**

To measure angles, one unit of measure we might choose is a right angle. Right angles are easy to make, so there would be no confusion about how big the unit is. But a right angle is bigger than a lot of angles we might want to measure; we ought to make the unit smaller. How about using some fraction of a right angle as the unit? That's exactly what the French Academy of Sciences started to do back in 1791, when they were setting up the metric system. The metric system was based on powers of 10, so they thought about making $\frac{1}{100}$th of a right angle the unit of angular measure. They called this unit a *grade*. Thus, a right angle would be a 100 grade angle; folding a right angle in half, we would get two 50 grade angles; and so on.

Instead, the French Academy decided to measure angles with a different unit—the *radian*. We shall see more about radian measure later, after studying circles in Chapter 4. You will see then why the radian is such a useful unit for measuring angles.

For now, we'll use a unit of angle measure that comes from the Babylonians, several thousand years ago. That unit is the *degree*. The Babylonians divided a right angle into 90 equal parts.[1] Each of these 90 parts is a **degree**. We abbreviate "degree" with the same symbol used for temperature degrees, a small raised circle. Thus a right angle is a 90° angle; half of a right angle is a 45° angle; and so on. Display 2.20 shows you the size of a degree.

---

[1]For reasons related to astronomy, their calendar, and their system of counting, they divided the four right angles made by two perpendicular lines into a total of 360 equal parts.

2.25

The purpose of this discussion question is to emphasize two things in students' minds: (1) Angles can be measured in various ways, depending on the unit of measure that is used, and (2) a unit of angle measure is *chosen* for its convenience and utility, not dictated by some sort of mathematical necessity. Just as one can measure length in paperclips or pencils, instead of in inches, feet or meters, so one can measure angles using any of a variety of units. It is important that your students try to come up with a useful unit on their own, because then they will better understand what makes a good unit of angle measure. This prepares them to understand later that the use of radians, instead of degrees, is no big deal. It's just a change in the choice of unit, like using meters instead of feet to measure length.

Here are some ways to define a new unit of angle measure.

- Draw two crossing lines at random, then use the resulting angle as the unit. This has the disadvantage that the prototype would have to be reproduced and distributed before anyone else could use it. That's not awful; length measure is done exactly this way, using rulers, yardsticks, and tape measures. If students hit on this idea, you might ask them what kind of measuring tool they would design to be sure that everyone was using the same unit.

- Begin with a right angle, which is easily formed by folding paper, and subdivide it by repeated halving (again by folding), until a suitably small size is formed. With a little care in matching up crease lines, a standard size piece of paper can be folded and refolded to form an angle that is $\frac{1}{16}$th of a right angle. Dexterous students might do even better. This type of unit has the advantage of being reproducible without having to be copied from a prototype.

In defending their opinions of better or worse measures, students should be guided to see that at least two questions are relevant: (1) How easy is it to reproduce the unit? (2) Is the unit small enough so that one can measure approximately angles of moderate size by whole numbers of a (small) unit angle, rather than by always being forced to use fractions of a (large) unit angle? A third consideration might be: Is the unit of angle measure related to some other geometric fact, property, or figure? That's a difficult idea to get across at this stage and we do not recommend that you introduce this question yourself. However, if a student raises this issue, it should be encouraged and explored a little. After all, this kind of consideration is the basis for choosing radian measure over degree measure in many contexts.

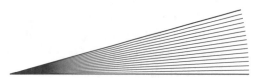

A 15° angle, measured in 1° steps.

Display 2.20

Display 2.21 shows ten angles. Estimate in degrees the measure of each one. (See if you can come within 5° of the exact size.)

a
2.26

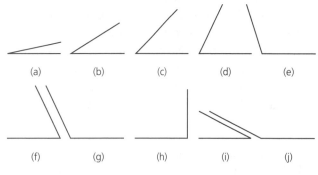

(a)　　　(b)　　　(c)　　　(d)　　　(e)

(f)　　　(g)　　　(h)　　　(i)　　　(j)

Display 2.21

Phrases to Know: The measures of some of the angles in Display 2.21 are less than one right angle. Such angles are called **acute angles**. Angles that have measure more than one right angle, but less than two, are called **obtuse angles**.

1. Which of the angles in Display 2.21 are acute? Which are obtuse?

2. Restate the definitions of *acute* and *obtuse* angles in terms of degrees.

b
2.27

3. Here are some other angle measures. Which of these angles are acute? Which are obtuse?

   (a) 48° (b) 84° (c) 148° (d) 95° (e) 3° (f) 180° (g) 179°

How would you describe an angle of exactly 180°? What do you think it should be called? Is it really an angle? Why or why not?

2.28

About Words

The words *acute* and *obtuse* come from the Latin words for sharpened and blunted, respectively.

139

2.26

This is an exercise in estimation, as well as in angle measure. You might not want to give your students the real measurements at this time. The comment about exact size is intended to goad them into thinking about how one finds the exact size. This leads directly into the forthcoming discussion of using a protractor to get a better measurement (but still not exact). Once they do the protractor measurements, they will be able to see for themselves whether their estimates fell within the 5° margin of error. Here, for your information, are the protractor assisted measurements of these angles, to the nearest degree.

(a) 11° (b) 31° (c) 45° (d) 63° (e) 108°
(f) 63° (g) 117° (h) 90° (i) 27° (j) 153°

2.27

These questions are routine terminology reinforcement exercises.

1. acute: (a), (b), (c), (d), (f), (i);   obtuse: (e), (g), (j)

2. An angle that measures less than 90° is acute. An angle that measures more than 90°, but less than 180°, is obtuse.

3. acute: (a), (b), (e); obtuse: (c), (d), (g)

2.28

This discussion question is desirable but not essential for moving on. It's two right angles put together, so it's a straight line. It *is* called a straight angle; see if students come up with this on their own.

The last part of this question is the most interesting because it provides a clear example of how a concrete idea is generalized by (a little) abstraction. If you think of an angle strictly as a corner, then a straight angle is not an angle at all. However, if you think of an angle as a separation between two rays that can be measured (in degrees or whatever), then there is no reason to rule out the case of a 180° separation—or more, for that matter! This latter viewpoint allows us to talk about angles of any number of degrees. This idea can lead to angles as measures of rotation more than once around, and the like. These are rich mathematical ideas, but such a discussion at this time can become a real time sink. Beware!

Chapter 2

To check your size estimates of the angles in Display 2.21, we need to measure the angles. The simplest tool for measuring angles is a **protractor**. Display 2.22 shows a picture of a protractor. Its basic shape is a semicircle resting on a straight base. The semicircle its divided into 180 equal (small) arcs, each one representing 1 degree. To measure an angle, put the center of the base at the vertex and align one side of the angle with the base line. The place at which the other side of the angle crosses the semicircle tells you the measure of the angle in degrees.

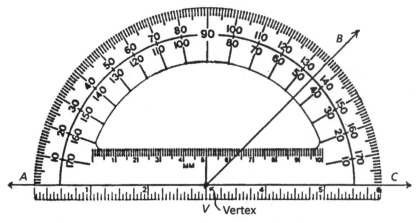

Measuring a 135° Angle and a 45° Angle With a Protractor

Display 2.22

Many protractors number the degree scale from both sides, so that an angle can be measured from either direction. That is, a side of the angle can be aligned with the base line either to the left or to the right of the vertex. In Display 2.22, for instance, the inner arch of numbers is used for measuring angles with base side to the right, while the outer arch of numbers measures angles with base side to the left. We sometimes say that the angles "open" to the right or to the left, depending on this alignment with the base. Thus, the ray that is heading up to the right (through B) is one side of a 45° angle, $\angle BVC$, that opens to the right; it is also one side of a 135° angle, $\angle AVB$, that opens to the left.

Published by IT'S ABOUT TIME, Inc. © 2000 MATHconx, LLC

NOTES

1. Use a protractor to measure, to the nearest degree, the ten angles shown in Display 2.21. Compare your measurements with your earlier estimates. Did you come within 5° each time?

   2.29

   Hint: If you don't have a protractor handy, use tracing paper to copy the angles of Display 2.21 and lay them out, one by one, on top of the protractor picture in Display 2.22. You may have to extend the sides of the angles a bit to make this work.

2. Use a protractor to draw an angle of each of these sizes.

   (a) 48°   (b) 84°   (c) 148°
   (d) 95°   (e) 3°   (f) 179°

   This question can also be answered by using tracing paper and Display 2.22.

   In English, the verb *protract* means "draw out or pull out." Explain why *protractor* is a good name for the tool shown in Display 2.22.

   2.30

Sometimes it is useful to think of angles in terms of rotation. That is, if we think of the sides of an angle as two arrows that pivot on the same endpoint (like the hands of a clock), then the size of an angle measures how far one arrow has rotated away from the other. It is customary to treat counterclockwise rotations as positive and clockwise rotations as negative.

From this viewpoint, there is no reason to stop measuring angles at 180°. We can measure all the way around the circle counterclockwise, getting larger and larger angles, until we get back to where we began. In fact, this is what the Babylonians had in mind when they defined the degree. They divided the entire circle into 360 equal parts. By rotating clockwise, we can get angles with negative measures. You might think of measuring such angles by using a double protractor, as in Display 2.23.

A Phrase to Know: An angle with a measure of more than 180° but less than 360° is called a **reflex angle.**

About Words

The root *flex* comes from the Latin word for bend, and the prefix *re-* means back. Thus, a *reflex* angle is one that bends back.

141

2.29 A Blackline Master of an enlarged copy of Display 2.21 is provided for your convenience. Although a real protractor is helpful here, it is not essential. The picture in the text will serve almost as well. However, a real protractor would make later work with angles much easier. The measurements of the angles in Display 2.21 are

(a) 11° (b) 31° (c) 45° (d) 63° (e) 108° (f) 63° (g) 117° (h) 90° (i) 27° (j) 153°

2.30 The act of extending the angle sides of Display 2.21 in order to answer question 1 of Do this now 2.31 should lead students to an appreciation of why the name protractor is appropriate for this tool.

NOTES

Chapter 2

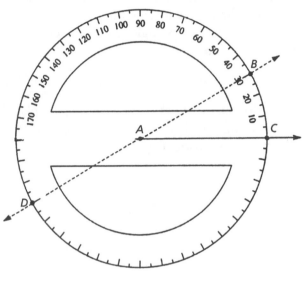

Display 2.23

2.31

These questions refer to Display 2.23. Think of ray *AC* as the starting side of each angle.

1. What is the measure of the counterclockwise angle with other side *AB*?

2. What is the measure of the counterclockwise angle with other side *AD*?

3. What is the measure of the clockwise angle with other side *AD*?

4. What is the measure of the clockwise angle with other side *AB*?

5. What is the measure of the counterclockwise angle with other side *AC*?

6. What is the measure of the clockwise angle with other side *AC*?

7. Which of the six angles just described are reflex angles?

8. What numbers should be used to label the next three of the longer hash marks beyond point *D* in the counterclockwise direction?

9. What numbers should be used to label the next three of the longer hash marks beyond point D in the clockwise direction?

142

2.31

These are routine reinforcement exercises for measuring angles considered as rotations.

(1) 30°

(2) 210°

(3   -150°

(4) -330°

(5) 360°

(6) -360°

(7) 210°

(8) 220, 230, 240

(9) If you stay with the numbering scheme in the figure: 200, 190, 180; if you number with respect to clockwise angle measure: -160, -170, -180.

Chapter 2

NOTES

A review of angle terminology using degree measure follows.
- An angle of measure less than 90° (but more than 0°) is an **acute angle**.

- An angle of measure 90° is a **right angle**.

- An angle of measure more than 90°, but less than 180°, is an **obtuse angle**.

- An angle of measure 180° is a **straight angle**.

- An angle of measure more than 180°, but less than 360°, is a **reflex angle**.

Problem Set: 2.3

1. (a) Copy Display 2.24a, add letters to it, and name all the angles. How many angles do you find?

   (b) Copy Display 2.24b, add letters to it, and name all the angles. How many angles do you find?

   (c) Copy Display 2.24c, add letters to it, and name all the angles. How many angles do you find?

   (d) If you were to copy Display 2.24d, add letters to it, and name all the angles, how many angles do you think you would find?

   (e) What would be the next step in this pattern?

   (f) Try to describe how this pattern works in general.

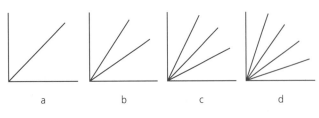

a   b   c   d

Display 2.24

2. Trace Display 2.24b on a piece of patty paper. Extend the four lines so that each one is at least 3 inches long. Label the vertex *V*, and label the other ends of the segments *P*, *Q*, *R*, and *S* in clockwise order, starting from the top.

   (a) There are five acute angles in this figure. List them in a column, using their three-letter names. Then measure each one with a protractor and write its degree measure next to its name. Round to the nearest degree.

   (b) Using a ruler, find the slope measure of each of these

Published by IT'S ABOUT TIME, Inc. © 2000 MATHconx, LLC

143

Problem Set: 2.3

1. This exercise is both a routine exercise in naming angles and a not so routine exercise in organized counting and pattern recognition. Parts (a)–(c) of this exercise are routine. Parts (d) and (e) are more challenging; part (f) is quite difficult. The students' answers to Parts (a)–(c) depend on their choices of labeling, so we do not list the angles by name here. There are 3 angles in (a), 6 angles in (b), and 10 angles in (c). There are 15 angles in (d), which the students can discover in a variety of ways, including counting them.

(e) The next step in the process is to add another segment to the figure. The next step in the pattern of how many angles you get is 21 (which you can get by counting). If you count the angles efficiently, you can see that the 21 comes from $6 + 5 + 4 + 3 + 2 + 1$. This leads to the answer for part (f).

(f) If you have n segments meeting at a common vertex, all within a right angle, just to keep the intuitive picture of angle comfortable, then the number of angles is $\frac{n(n-1)}{2}$.

2. The purpose of these questions is to give students practice in measuring angles, and also to get them thinking about the relative merits of slope or degree measure. If patty paper is not available, any paper thin enough to see through and trace on will do.

(a) and (b) See Display 2.8T. Measurements may vary a bit.

Angle	Degrees	Slope
$\angle PVQ$	34°	.67
$\angle PVR$	57°	1.50
$\angle QVR$	23°	.41
$\angle QVS$	55°	1.45
$\angle RVS$	32°	.64

Display 2.8T

five angles, and write that next to its degree measure. Round to two decimal places.

(c) How are $\angle QVR$ and $\angle RVS$ related to $\angle QVS$? How are their degree measures related? How are their slope measures related?

(d) What angle is formed by putting together $\angle PVQ$, $\angle QVR$, and $\angle RVS$? What is the sum of their degree measures? Do you get a similar result when you add their slope measures? What do we mean by similar?

(e) Write a paragraph comparing degree measure and slope measure. Which system is easier to use? Which behaves better in relation to arithmetic? Which do you like better? Give reasons to support your opinions.

3. Using just a pencil and a ruler, draw your best estimate of an angle of each of the following sizes. Try to get within 5° of the correct size. When you are finished, measure with a protractor to see how close you came. How many were within 5°? How many were within 3°? Did you get any to within 1°?

(a) 90°   (b) 45°   (c) 30°   (d) 60°   (e) 10°

(f) 180°   (g) 135°   (h) 100°   (i) 52°   (j) 175°

(k) 270°   (l) 225°   (m) 240°   (n) 300°   (o) 359°

4. Assume here that we are referring to a standard 12 hour clock and that the answers to these questions are not reflex angles.

(a) When a clock reads 3 p.m., what is the measure of the angle between the hour hand and the minute hand?

(b) When a clock reads 5 p.m., what is the measure of the angle between the hour hand and the minute hand?

(c) When a clock reads 6:30 p.m., what is the measure of the angle between the hour hand and the minute hand? Explain your answer.

(d) When a clock reads 9:30 p.m., what is the measure of the angle between the hour hand and the minute hand? Explain your answer.

(e) Is the process of finding the (nonreflex) angle between the hands of a clock a function? If so, what are its domain and range? If not, why not?

144

Published by IT'S ABOUT TIME, Inc. © 2000 MATHconx, LLC

(b) If you put together $\angle QVR$ and $\angle RVS$, you get $\angle QVS$. Adding their degree measures, we have $23° + 32° = 55°$, as expected. However, the slope measures don't work as well: $0.41 + 0.64 = 1.05$, which is nowhere near the 1.45 slope measurement of $\angle QVS$. This discrepancy is too large to be measure error, so slope measurement is not additive.

(c) You get the (apparent) right angle PVS. The degree measures actually add up to 89°, but that might be due to measurement or tracing error (or printing error). The slope measures only add up to 1.72, however, far short of the almost infinite slope of a nearly vertical line.

(d) Except for the observation that degree measure behaves better than slope with respect to putting together (addition), this is a wide open question. You should be looking for how well the students' reasons match up with their opinions.

3. This could be set up as an exercise between pairs of students, with each student checking the other's drawings, or as a contest between teams. Most (but not all) of the sizes listed here represent commonly used angles. You could add many more to the list, of course. Many of the sizes listed later relate to earlier ones, just in a different quadrant. Everyone should get (f) exactly right!

4. (a) 90°
   (b) 150° ($\frac{5}{6}$ of 180°)
   (c) 15°. Each hour marker is 30° which is $\frac{1}{12}$ of 360°. At 6:30, the hour hand is halfway between 6 and 7.
   (d) 105°. The same kind of explanation as in the previous part applies here.
   (e) Yes, this is a function. The domain is the set of all hand positions on the clock. The range is the set of all numbers between 0° and 180°, inclusive. Each hand position corresponds to exactly one angle.

NOTES

_____

....

....

....

....

Chapter 2

5. Assume here that we are referring to a standard 12 hour clock.

    (a) If the angle between the hour hand and the minute hand of a clock is 180°, what time is it? Can there be more than one correct answer to this question? Can there be more than two? Explain your answer.

    (b) If the angle between the hour hand and the minute hand of a clock is 120°, what time is it? Can there be more than one correct answer to this question? Can there be more than two? Explain your answer.

    (c) Is the process of finding the time from the (nonreflex) angle between the hands of a clock a function? This process is the reverse of the one described in question 4(e). If so, what are its domain and range? If not, why not?

6. (a) Draw five different triangles. For each one, measure its angles and add up the three numbers you get. Are your five sums related in any way? If so, how? Compare your results with those of two classmates.

Published by IT'S ABOUT TIME, Inc. © 2000 MATHconx, LLC

5. Parts (a) and (b) of this problem can be treated lightly, or they can be expanded into a major exercise in observation, estimation, and/or algebra, as you see fit. A light treatment of them is all that is required for part (c).

(a) It can be lots of different times, even if you restrict yourself to a single 12 hour period (a.m. or p.m.): 6:00, shortly after 7:05, shortly after 8:10, etc.

Finding out the *exact amount* of shortly after here and in part (b) are interesting problems. *If you choose* to expand on this, it can be done at several levels.
- Observation: How often does it happen? Does the size of the angle affect how often it happens?

- Estimation: About what time does it happen? How can we get closer and closer approximations to the exact answer?

- Algebraic Solution: A single, comprehensive algebraic solution probably would require some sophisticated modular arithmetic, but a case by case approach is well within the algebra and thinking skills of some students. For example, here is an outline of the argument for how the shortly after 7:05 time can be found.

Assume that 0° represents 12 o'clock, and let m and h represent the position (in degrees) of the minute hand and the hour hand, respectively. Measure time, t, in hours. As time progresses, the minute hand moves 360° per hour, and the hour hand moves 30° per hour. At 7 o'clock, $m = 0°$ and $h = 210°$. So at any time after 7:00,

$$m = 360t \quad \text{and} \quad h = 30t + 210$$

Now, we want $h - m = 180°$, so,

$$30t + 210 - 360t = 180$$
$$-330t = -30$$
$$t = \frac{1}{11} \text{ hour (approx. 5.45 min.)}$$

Thus, the hands are 180° apart at 7:05:27 (to the nearest second).

(b) This part is much like the previous one, except that there are even more different times at which this happens. Under the assumptions of the problem, this happens at 4 o'clock and 8 o'clock (since we are referring to the nonreflex angle, not the amount of rotation). It happens again shortly after 5:00 and shortly after 9:00, etc. This can lead to an extended investigation, along the lines sketched out in the previous part, if you choose.

(c) No, this is not a function. A single degree value corresponds to many different hand positions.

6. Students can do this using Geometer's Sketchpad. Alternatively, you can show them how these sums remain constant in a Sketchpad demonstration *after* they have done this exercise using a ruler and a protractor.

Caution. Sketchpad does *not* handle reflex angles well. If you draw a concave polygon, it will measure the nonreflex angle between any two given sides, regardless of whether it is an interior or an exterior angle of the polygon. Thus, you should stay with convex polygons in your demonstration.

(a) All the sums should be 180° (approximately, allowing for measurement error).

Chapter 2

(b) Draw five different quadrilaterals (four-sided polygons). For each one, measure its angles and add up the four numbers you get. Are your five sums related in any way? If so, how? Compare your results with those of two classmates.

(c) What should be the next group of questions in this sequence? Answer them.

(d) Can you see any sort of pattern here? If so, what?

7. (a) The real protractor used to make Display 2.22 was too big to be copied full size, so we reduced it. What scaling factor did we use (approximately)? How do you know?

(b) If we measured the angles of Display 2.21 using the real protractor instead of the one in Display 2.22, would we get different answers? If you say Yes, describe a way of converting one set of answers to the other. If you say No, explain why the measurements shouldn't change.

(b) All the sums should be 360° (approximately, allowing for measurement error).

(c) "Draw five different pentagons (five-sided polygons). For each one, measure its angles and add up the five numbers you get. Are your five sums related in any way? If so, how? Compare your results with those of two classmates." All the sums should be 540° (approximately, allowing for measurement error).

(d) The angle sum of a polygon appears to depend only on the number of sides, not on the shape. If a polygon has n sides, it seems that the sum of its angles is $(n - 2) \cdot 180°$.

7. This is an exercise to reinforce the connection between angle measure and similarity.

(a) Comparing either of the linear measurement scales in the picture with the actual size scale of a ruler, you will find that 6 in. was reduced to about 4.2 in. and 10 cm was reduced to about 7 cm. This means that the scaling factor was approximately 70%.

(b) No; the angle measure is unaffected by scaling. This is an important idea! Defending this conclusion might be difficult for most students, even the ones for whom the answer itself is obvious. Perhaps the best way to explain it here is to recall that one way of measuring angles is by slope, a ratio of two lengths. If the lengths are scaled by the same amount, then the scaling factor cancels out, since it is in both the numerator and the denominator, leaving the ratio unchanged.

Chapter 2

NOTES

2.4 Finding Angle Size Efficiently

In Section 2.3 we talked about two ways of measuring angles— by slope and by degrees. Here is an example from house building that shows how they are related.

33–11. An example of a nail-glued truss plan for a king-post truss with a 4-in:12 slope. This is one of the designs available from the American Plywood Association.

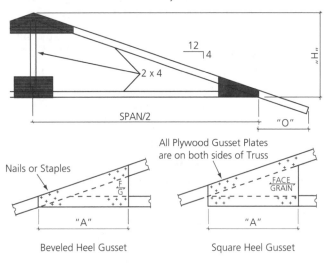

All Plywood Gusset Plates are on both sides of Truss

Nails or Staples

Beveled Heel Gusset   Square Heel Gusset

From *Carpentry and Building Construction*, 5th edition, page 483, by John L. Feirer, Gilbert R. Hutchings and Mark D. Feirer. Copyright © 1997 by Glencoe/McGraw-Hill. Reprinted with permission.

Display 2.25

Learning Outcomes

After studying this section, you will be able to:

Use the calculator functions TAN and TAN^{-1} to convert angle measures from degrees to slope, and vice versa;

Explain the meanings of the terms *supplementary* and *vertical* angles;

Apply the defining properties of vertical and supplementary angles in various settings.

Display 2.25 shows a diagram for a king-post truss— a type of roof support. The diagram contains most of the information needed for building this truss once you know the width of the house (the *span*). In particular, it tells you that the slope of the roof is 4 : 12. That is, the roof rises 4 inches for every 12 inches of span from side to center. This is the meaning of

in the upper part of the diagram.

Published by IT'S ABOUT TIME, Inc. © 2000 MATHconx, LLC

147

2.4 Finding Angle Size Efficiently

The goal of this section is to develop several key facts about angles from the viewpoint of a user, rather than a devotee, of mathematics. Specifically, the slope measure of an angle is related to its degree measure via the calculator functions TAN and TAN^{-1}, treating these simply as conversion functions whose theoretical underpinnings will be explained later, in the trigonometry chapter. These two functions also serve as a prototypical example of inverse functions. Vertical angles and supplementary angles are also introduced in this section.

Chapter 2

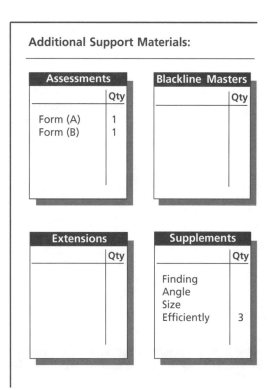

Additional Support Materials:

Assessments	Qty
Form (A)	1
Form (B)	1

Blackline Masters	Qty

Extensions	Qty

Supplements	Qty
Finding Angle Size Efficiently	3

Published by IT'S ABOUT TIME, Inc. © 2000 MATHconx, LLC

2.4 Finding Angle Size Efficiently

2.32 If the house is 30 feet wide (measured from the outsides of the walls), about how long is the vertical center post? Answer to the nearest foot. In actual construction, you would have to allow a few inches for the width of the beams. Along the sloped top beam, about how far is it from the peak to the outside wall? Don't include the overhang ("O" *as in Display 2.25*). Explain how you found your answers.

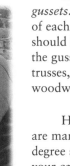

The lower half of Display 2.25 shows the shape of the *gussets*. These are the plywood supports that go on the sides of each joint. As you can see, the top edge of each gusset should be cut on an angle to match the slope of the roof. Often the gussets are cut from plywood sheets before assembling the trusses, using a table saw or a radial arm saw in a woodworking shop.

Here's the problem. Table saw settings for angle cuts are marked in degrees, not by slope. You need to know what degree setting corresponds to the roof slope. But that's OK— your calculator can tell you the degree value for any slope! You just have to know how to ask for it.

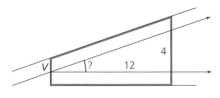

Display 2.26

The correspondence between the degree measure of an angle and its slope measure is a function. Each degree measurement has exactly one slope value. And if we restrict ourselves to angles that are less than 90° (as we would when building a roof), the opposite is also true. Each slope measurement has exactly one degree value.

- The process that turns the degree measure of an angle into its slope measure is called the **tangent function**; its calculator key is marked TAN.

- The reverse process, which turns slope measure into degree

Published by IT'S ABOUT TIME, Inc. © 2000 MATHconx, LLC

148

2.32

The slope is $\frac{4}{12} = \frac{1}{3}$; that is, the roof rises 1 foot for every 3 feet from wall to center (half the span). Half of the 30 foot span is 15 feet, so the center post is about 5 feet long (ignoring how the beam widths affect the top joint).
The Pythagorean Theorem can be used to find the length along the roof from center to outside wall,

$$\sqrt{15^2 + 5^2} = 15.8 \text{ feet (approx.)}$$

NOTES

Chapter 2

measure, is called the **inverse tangent function**; its calculator key is marked TAN⁻¹.

In general, a function that reverses the correspondence process of another function is called the **inverse** of that other function. Later you will see how trigonometry gives us an explanation of how the calculator is able to get each of these measurements from the other. You will also see then why the name *tangent* is used for this function. For now, we will concentrate on ways of using this handy tool.

To make the gusset shown in Display 2.26 with a table saw, we would need to know the measure of ∠V in degrees. To find this with your calculator, answer the following questions. (Before you start, make sure that your calculator is in Degree mode. This means that the calculator is using the degree as its unit of angle measure.)

2.33

1. What is the slope measure of ∠V?

2. Before calculating the degree measure of ∠V, estimate it by relating the picture to your idea of a right angle, as follows:

   (a) Is ∠V more or less than half a right angle?

   (b) Do you think that ∠V is more or less than a quarter of a right angle?

   (c) What is your best estimate of the degree measure of ∠V?

3. Which calculator function converts slope to degree measure? Use it to find the degree measure of ∠V to the nearest tenth of a degree. How does your answer compare with your estimate? If there is a difference of more than 10°, which answer do you trust more, the estimate or the computation?

4. Which calculator function converts degree measure to slope? Use it to check your answer. Do you get back the original slope? If not, what do you think went wrong?

149

2.33

This is a routine calculation, but one that needs a little care. Some of the questions are designed to get students comfortable with eyeballing the size of an angle, rather than just trusting the calculator. There is a button pushing trap in this process that can easily lead an unwary student to an erroneous answer, which will be far out of line with any reasonable estimate.

To check for Degree mode on a TI-82 (TI-83), look at the third line of the MODE menu to see that Degree, rather than Radian, is highlighted. The default is radian measure, so this menu item will have to be reset the first time the calculator is used for degree computation.

1. $\frac{4}{12}$, or $\frac{1}{3}$

2. This need not take much time, but it's a good idea to give students who are struggling some strategy for visual estimation. Comparison by successive halving of something familiar is such a strategy. For instance, they can crease a piece of paper to form a right angle, then fold that angle in half, crease the fold, and compare the picture with what they get. Then they can fold that angle in half again.

   (a) It's clearly less than half a right angle.
   (b) Not so clear; maybe a little less than a quarter of a right angle, maybe not.
   (c) A quarter of a right angle is 22.5°, so any answer in the 15°–25° range is reasonable.

3. You need the TAN⁻¹ function. On the TI-82 (TI-83), that is 2nd TAN. The correct answer is 18.4°. A student who gets 6.3° has fallen into the trap. That's much too small to be correct, as the eyeball estimate should indicate. Nevertheless, some students will prefer the (wrong) answer because it was computed by a machine. The last question of this part is designed, in part, to give them a second chance to recognize the error.

4. The TANGENT function applied to the correct degree answer should yield .333..., the original slope. The trap answer will return the value .11093657, far off the mark.

The button pushing trap here typifies a general calculator fussiness that students need to keep in mind. If they key in

$$2nd\ TAN\ 4 \div 12$$

the TI-82 (TI-83) will compute TAN⁻¹ 4 *before* dividing by 12. To get the correct answer, the entry line should read

$$2nd\ TAN\ (4 \div 12)$$

Chapter 2

a
2.34

1. Draw a horizontal line on a piece of paper. Then use a protractor to draw a line that makes a 30° angle with your first line.

2. Use your calculator to find the slope of the second line relative to the horizontal line. Explain how you do this.

3. How can you check this answer by measuring your drawing? Do it. Do your results agree? If not, can you explain what's wrong?

4. Draw a 30° angle on your calculator by graphing an appropriate equation. Does the angle in your graph look to be the same size as the one you drew? If not, can you explain what's wrong and how to fix it?

5. Is the slope made by a 60° angle double the slope made by a 30° angle? Check by whatever method you choose.

6. Think of a question related to this exercise that you would like to have answered.

Angles often occur in related groups, so that you can find the size of two or more angles by measuring just one of them. Here's a case where the measure of one angle determines the measure of four! When you draw two crossing lines to make an angle, you actually make four angles. (See Display 2.27.) The measures of each pair of these angles are related in one of two special ways. Can you see how?

b
2.35

Choose any two of the four numbered angles shown in Display 2.27. In what way are their measures related? Give a reason to justify your answer.

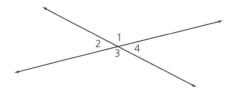

Display 2.27

150

2.34

These questions are classified as discussion because we believe that several students working together on them will be able to help each other iron out many small misunderstandings more efficiently than if each student were working alone. Some of them are routine; others plant seeds for further inquiry.

2. Find TAN 30°, which is approximately 0.58.

3. From some point on the slanted line, draw a vertical segment down to the horizontal one. Divide the length of that segment by the distance between its foot and the vertex of the angle. That should equal the slope, subject to measurement error.

4. The appropriate equation is $y = (TAN\ 30)x$. If the Standard WINDOW setting is used on a TI-82 (TI-83), the angle will appear to be narrower (smaller) than the hand drawn one because the vertical unit of window measure is smaller than the horizontal one. Setting the WINDOW to Square will make the two angles look to be the same size.

5. No. This plants a seed for further exploration. The crux of the matter here is that measuring an angle by slope does not just replace the degree by a different unit of measure; it's an entirely different process. Exactly how it is different, and whether or not there is *any* convenient relationship between multiples of each measure is a fertile area for independent exploration. It is nontrivial.

6. We have nothing specific in mind here, other than getting students into the habit of asking their own questions. If you are handling these questions as a small group exercise, you might encourage one group to try to answer the question(s) of another.

Sketchpad Exploration

It is not hard to set up a Geometer's Sketchpad diagram that would allow you or your students to vary an angle and see how the slope and the degree measure change. Here's how to do it.

1. Using the segment tool, draw a horizontal line segment, *AB*. It is horizontal if there are no kinks in it.

2. From the first point of your segment (*A*), draw another segment, *AC*, up and to the right, so that *C* is somewhere above segment *AB*.

3. Select all three points and choose Show Labels from the Display menu.

4. Select segment *AB* and point *C*, and Construct the Perpendicular Line.

5. Select that (vertical) line and segment *AB*, and Construct the Point at Intersection, *D*.

6. Select points *C, A, B* in that order, and Measure the Angle.

Chapter 2

7. Select segment *AC* and Measure the Slope. For this measurement to agree with the slope measure of the angle, it is critical that the segment you start with be horizontal. The next several steps emphasize what slope means by computing it directly, as a check and reinforcement.

8. Select points *C* and *D*, and Measure the Distance between them.

9. Select points *A* and *D*, and Measure the Distance between them.

10. Select the two Distance statements you just made, and Calculate

$$\text{Dist (C to D)} \div \text{Dist (D to A)}$$

Now your display is all set up; it should look like Display 2.9T. It shows the degree measure of the angle and the slope of segment *AC* (in two ways). By using the arrow-tool, you can select point *C* and move it around to form angles of different sizes and different segment lengths. The numerical displays will adjust as you move the point around.

2.35

This discussion is not difficult; it should not take much class time. It establishes the fundamental measurement properties of supplementary angles and vertical angles as simple, common sense ideas. No matter which pair is chosen, their measures either are equal (vertical angles) or sum to 180° (supplementary angles). Sketchpad can be used to demonstrate these relationships simply and persuasively, if you wish. In fact, they are included in the Sketchpad Exploration described right after 2.39 at the beginning of the next section.

Angle (*CAB*) = 30°

Slope (Segment *k*) = 0.58

Distance (*C* to *D*) = 1.33 inches

Distance (*D* to *A*) = 2.30 inches

$$\frac{\text{Distance (C to D)}}{\text{Distance (D to A)}} = 0.58$$

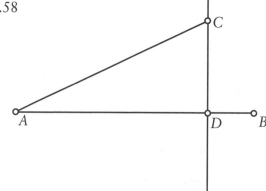

NOTES

A Phrase to Know: Two angles that are formed by two intersecting lines and do not have a side in common are called **vertical angles**.

How many pairs of vertical angles can you find in Display 2.27? What are they?

a
2.36

A Phrase to Know: Two angles with measures that add to 180° are called **supplementary angles**.

How many pairs of supplementary angles can you find in Display 2.27? What are they?

b
2.37

Each of these special pairs of angles has a useful property.

• Supplementary angles placed alongside one another so that their vertices and a single side coincide to form a straight angle (a straight line).

• The measures of vertical angles are equal.

We know that the first statement is true because the measure of a straight angle is 180°. The second statement can be approached in several ways. One simple way is to try an experiment. Draw two crossing lines at random on a sheet of scrap paper; then fold it through the crossing point so that the rays of the two different lines coincide. You will see that the vertical angles are congruent; they match exactly.

Here's another way of seeing that the measures of vertical angles are equal. It's a little more formal, but it's more reliable because it doesn't depend on a particular pair of lines or on your paper folding skill.

Form any pair of vertical angles—say ∠1 and ∠3, as in Display 2.27. Notice that ∠1 and ∠2 are supplementary, and ∠2 and ∠3 are also supplementary. That is,

$$∠1 + ∠2 = 180° \text{ and } ∠2 + ∠3 = 180°$$

This means that the two sums equal each other:

$$∠1 + ∠2 = ∠2 + ∠3$$

Subtracting ∠2 from both sides of this equation, we get

$$∠1 = ∠3$$

That is, the measures of the vertical angles must be equal.

Published by IT'S ABOUT TIME, Inc. © 2000 MATHconx, LLC

151

2.36

This question should be quick and routine. It just reinforces the term vertical angles. There are two pairs: $\angle 1$ and $\angle 3$; $\angle 2$ and $\angle 4$.

2.37

This is another quick, routine question to reinforce the term supplementary angles. Four: $\angle 1$ and $\angle 2$; $\angle 2$ and $\angle 3$; $\angle 3$ and $\angle 4$; $\angle 1$ and $\angle 4$.

NOTES

Chapter 2

2.38

1. How many pairs of supplementary angles can you find in Display 2.28? What are they? Justify your answer.

2. How many pairs of vertical angles can you find in Display 2.28? What are they? Justify your answer.

3. Draw a picture of vertical angles that are supplementary. What other property *must* such angles have? Justify your answer.

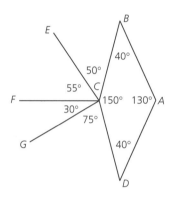

Display 2.28

Problem Set: 2.4

1. In this section you learned how to use the TAN and TAN⁻¹ functions of your calculator to convert the measure of an angle from degrees to slope and vice versa. Use your calculator to make the following conversions. Round your answers to two decimal places.

   (a) Convert from degrees to slope measure:

       30°   65°   46°   12°   89°   89.5°   1°

   (b) Convert from slope measure to degrees:

       $\frac{1}{2}$ 2 $\frac{6}{7}$ 1.25   23   1   10,000

Published by IT'S ABOUT TIME, Inc. © 2000 MATHconx, LLC

2.38

The first two parts focus on an important distinction in the defining conditions of supplementary angles and vertical angles. Supplementary angles are defined by their measure only, regardless of their location with respect to each other. Vertical angles, on the other hand, must share a common vertex and their rays must be opposite sides of the same two lines.

1. There are two pairs of supplementary angles: $\angle BCD$ and $\angle FCG$, which have a common vertex, but no common side; $\angle BAD$ and $\angle BCE$, which have neither vertex nor side in common. In both cases, the sum of the two angles is 180°.

2. There are no pairs of vertical angles because there are no crossing straight lines in the figure. Note that equal angles $\angle ABC$ and $\angle ADC$ are deliberately placed vertically, one over the other, to force students to distinguish between this situation and the one described in the definition of vertical angles.

3. Any two perpendicular lines form two pairs of such angles. Vertical angles that are supplementary must be right angles. Justification: Since they are vertical angles, they must be equal. Since they are supplementary, they must add up to 180°. This means that the measure of each angle must be half of 180°.

Problem Set: 2.4

1. (a) 0.58, 2.14, 1.04, 0.21, 57.29, 114.59, 0.02

   (b) 26.57°, 63.43°, 40.60°, 51.34°, 87.51°, 45°, 89.99°

2. These choices depend on knowing and using two facts.

NOTES

....

....

....

....

....

Published by IT'S ABOUT TIME, Inc. © 2000 MATHconx, LLC

Chapter 2

2. Answer these questions *without* using your calculator. Choose the larger angle in each of the following pairs. Give a reason to justify your choice.

   (a) $\angle A = 42°$; the slope measure of $\angle B$ is $\frac{7}{6}$

   (b) $\angle C = 53°$; the slope measure of $\angle D$ is 0.985

   (c) $\angle E = 100°$; the slope measure of $\angle F$ is 250

   (d) $\angle G$ is a right angle; the slope measure of $\angle H$ is 9000.09

   (e) $\angle J = 47°$; the slope measure of $\angle K$ is $\frac{7}{3}$

   (f) $\angle L = 73°$; $\angle M$ is its supplement

   (g) $\angle N = 98°$; $\angle P$ is its supplement

   (h) The slope measure of $\angle Q$ is 98; $\angle R$ is its supplement

3. Mr. Santos is painting his house. He needs to be able to rest the top of his ladder on the roof edge, which is 18 feet above the ground. His ladder, fully extended, is just 20 feet long, but it carries this warning.

   Do not exceed 70° angle of elevation between ladder and ground.

   (a) Why do you think the ladder carries this warning?

   (b) Can Mr. Santos safely use his ladder if it rests on the roof edge? Explain, using a mathematical argument. *Hints:* Draw a sketch. Use the Pythagorean Theorem. Think about the TAN function of your calculator.

   (c) If you were preparing a report for a consumer research group, what would you give as the maximum safe height (to the nearest inch) that this 20 foot ladder can reach? Why?

   Problems 4 and 5 are about sundials. The sundial is civilization's oldest timekeeping device. It doesn't require any moving parts, batteries, or electronics, and—unlike modern clocks—it constantly reminds us that time, as we humans define it, is based upon the movement of the Earth relative to the Sun. As the Earth rotates on its axis, the Sun appears in different places in the sky, causing the shadow of a fixed object on the Earth to change. This change is what marks the hours on a sundial.

Published by IT'S ABOUT TIME, Inc. © 2000 MATHconx, LLC

MATH *Connections*: A Secondary Mathematics Core Curriculum

(1) The slope measure of a 45° angle is 1.

(2) No matter how large the slope measure of an angle is, the angle must be less than a right angle.

Students should be aware of these facts from prior work. Parts of problem 1 serve as reminders of them.

(a) $\angle B$ is larger. Its slope is greater than 1, so its degree measure must be greater than 45°.

(b) $\angle C$ is larger. Since the slope of $\angle D$ is less than 1, its degree measure must be less than 45°.

(c) $\angle E$ is larger. The seemingly large slope measure of $\angle F$ simply means that it is very close to, but less than, a right (90°) angle.

(d) $\angle G$ is larger. See reason (2) above.

(e) $\angle K$ is larger. This requires a little estimation skill. Since $\angle J$ is close to a 45° angle, its slope measure must be close to 1. But the slope measure of $\angle K$ is greater than 2.

(f) $\angle M$ is larger. The sum must equal two right angles (180°). Since $\angle L$ is smaller than a right angle, its supplement must be larger than a right angle.

(g) $\angle N$ is larger. Since it is larger than a right angle, its supplement must be smaller than a right angle.

(h) $\angle R$ is larger. By reason (2) above, $\angle Q$ must be smaller than a right angle, so its supplement must be larger than a right angle.

3. This problem requires and reinforces some algebraic skills, particularly the use of square roots.

(a) The warning is to prevent the weight of a climber from overbalancing a nearly vertical ladder and causing it to fall away from whatever it's resting on.

(b) Yes. An appropriate sketch would show a right triangle with hypotenuse 20 ft. (the ladder), and angle elevation of 70° (the maximum safe angle), and a vertical leg representing the maximum safe height to be found. The key is to observe that the length of the vertical leg is tan 70° times the length of the horizontal leg (which is unknown). If we call the horizontal length x, the Pythagorean Theorem gives us

$$x^2 + ((\tan 70°)x)^2 = 20^2$$

From here on, it's routine algebra with the help of the calculator.

$$x^2 + (\tan 70°)^2 x^2 = 20^2$$
$$(1 + (\tan 70°)^2)x^2 = 20^2$$
$$8.55x^2 = 400$$
$$x^2 = 46.78$$
$$x = 6.84 \text{ (approx.)}$$

Only the positive root is of interest because x is a length. Thus, the maximum safe height is about $6.84 \cdot (\tan 70°) = 18.79$ ft., quite enough

Chapter 2

For more than 4000 years, sundials in many shapes and sizes have graced courtyards and cities, inspiring their users with such inscriptions as:

Carpe Diem (*Seize the day!*)

Tempus Fugit (*Time flies.*)

Utere, Non Numera (*Use them, don't count them.*)

Omnes Vulnerant, Ultima Necat (*Each one wounds, the last one kills.*)

Una Ex His Erit Tibi Ultima (*One of these will be your last.*)

Mach' es wie die sonnenuhr, zähl' die heiteren stunden nur (*Do as the sundial: count only the bright hours.*)

All but one of these quotes are shown in their original Latin.[1] Which one is the exception? In what language is it written?

The most surprising thing about sundials is that they work at all! As the seasons change, the sun rises and sets at different times and takes a higher or lower path across the sky. The daily shadow patterns are always changing. But *they change in a predictable way* that can be used to tell time! You just have to make exactly the right triangular shape and put it in exactly the right position, like this:

- Cut a right triangle (out of wood or metal or anything else rigid) so that the measure of one of its angles is exactly the latitude of the place where you are on the Earth. Do you know what *latitude* means? If not, look it up.

- Place the triangle upright on a flat surface in a sunny location, with its hypotenuse slanting upward, away from its latitude-angle vertex and headed toward the North Star.

Then the shadow cast by the slanted edge of the triangle at a particular time of day will lie along the same line on the surface every day of the year! It sounds like magic, but it's science. If you study astronomy, you'll see why this works as it does[†]. Sundials like this have the hours marked as lines on the

---

[1]Source: *Sundials: History, Theory, and Practice*, by René J. Rohr, (Toronto: University of Toronto Press, 1970).

[†]If you can't wait until then, you might look at *Sundials, Their Theory and Construction*, by Albert E. Waugh, (New York: Dover Publications, 1973).

154

for Mr. Santos' needs.

(c) Maximum safe height: 18 ft., 9 in. The computation of part (b) justifies this. The partial foot shown there, 0.79 ft., rounds down to 9 in. (0.75 ft.).

Notes on problems 4 and 5. The mathematical content of these problems focuses primarily on using the calculator's TAN function, but the setting supplies interesting connections with astronomy, geography, history, and language. You don't have to assign all parts of them to get most of the benefit, but the calculations are easy, once students see how to do the first one. The primary advantage of doing all parts is that the skill reinforcement occurs within a changing geographical context, thereby minimizing the sense of drill and creating a connection with another important subject. The last of the inscriptions is in German.

Chapter 2

NOTES

flat (horizontal) surface. The upright triangular piece is called a **gnomon**. For a sundial to work properly, the shape and position of its gnomon must be exactly right.

About Words

Gnomon is derived from the Greek word meaning one who knows.

4. (a) Hartford, Connecticut, is near 42° N latitude. The proper angle and position for a gnomon there is shown in Display 2.29 as ∠ BAC. Calculate the height of this gnomon for each of these horizontal (base) dimensions:

   (i) 4 in.   (ii) 7 in.   (iii) 11 in.

   Round your answers to the nearest tenth of an inch.

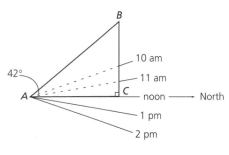

Display 2.29

(b) Using an 8.5" × 11" sheet of thick paper or cardboard, cut out a gnomon that would work for a sundial in Hartford.

(c) Find out the latitude of your home town (look on the edges of a road map) and make a sundial gnomon that will work there. Choose whatever base size you want.

(d) Repeat part (a) above for locations in Fairbanks, Alaska, at 65° N latitude and Miami, Florida, at 25° N latitude.

155

4. (a) Hartford, CT is near 42° north latitude, so the angle should be about 42°. The $\frac{\text{vertical}}{\text{horizontal}}$ ratio (the slope) is tan 42°. This value is multiplied by the base length to get the height of the vertical leg.

    (i) 4 in. by 3.6 in.   (ii) 7 in. by 6.3 in.   (iii) 11 in. by 9.9 in.

    (b) This part need not be done if you are going to do the next part.

    (c) Latitudes for towns in different states vary widely, as the next part shows. You can turn this into a project by having your students, individually or in groups, actually construct sundials and try out their gnomons.

    (d) Fairbanks: (i) 4 in. by 8.6 in. (ii) 7 in. by 15.0 in. (iii) 11 in. by 23.6 in.
    Miami: (i) 4 in. by 1.9 in. (ii) 7 in. by 3.3 in. (iii) 11 in. by 5.1 in.

NOTES

Chapter 2

5. (a) The Big Ben Sundial Co. exports sundials to major cities around the world. Their basic model has a right triangular gnomon with a 24 cm horizontal side. What is the proper height for this gnomon in each of the following cities? (Do you know the country of each one?)

Athens	Beijing	Berlin
Cairo	Calcutta	Lagos
London	Moscow	Mexico City
Panama City	Paris	Rome
San Juan	San Salvador	Singapore
Stockholm	Tel Aviv	Tokyo

Round your answers to the nearest mm. (You'll need to start with a globe, a world atlas, an encyclopedia, or a good map of the northern hemisphere.)

(b) Where in the northern half of the world are accurate gnomons shaped like *isosceles* right triangles? Locate at least one town or city in North America for which this is true.

(c) What would an accurate gnomon at the equator look like? What about at the North Pole?

Published by IT'S ABOUT TIME, Inc. © 2000 MATHconx, LLC

5. (a) There are too many cities listed to ask each student to do every one. You might have the students pick four or six of these cities that interest them most, or assign different sets of cities to different groups of students. These locations have been chosen to accommodate a wide range of geographical and ethnic interests and to provide interestingly different latitudes. See Display 2.10T for the answers. The north latitudes shown are to the nearest half degree.

City	Latitude	Ht., cm	City	Latitude	Ht., cm
Athens	38°	18.8	Panama City	9°	3.8
Beijing	40°	20.1	Paris	49°	27.6
Berlin	52.5°	31.3	Rome	42°	21.6
Cairo	30°	13.9	San Juan	18.5°	8.0
Calcutta	22.5°	9.9	San Salvador	13.5°	5.8
Lagos	6.5°	2.7	Singapore	2°	0.8
London	51.5°	30.2	Stockholm	59.5°	40.7
Mexico City	19.5°	8.5	Tel Aviv	32°	15.0
Moscow	55.5°	34.9	Tokyo	36°	17.4

Display 2.10T

(b) Gnomons shaped like isosceles right triangles are accurate any place along 45° north latitude. In North America, we can trace this line westward from about Bangor, ME, in the Northeast, across upstate New York (around Plattsburgh), across a bit of southern Canada between Ottawa and Toronto, through Minneapolis. Farther west, it divides Wyoming from Montana, forming the northern boundary of Yellowstone National Park, cuts through central Idaho, and meets the Pacific Ocean just below Portland, Oregon.

(c) Gnomons on the equator are just horizontal rods or rectangles pointing north. Gnomons at the North Pole are vertical rods.

NOTES

2.5 Parallel Lines and the Angle Sum of a Triangle

In Section 2.4 you saw some properties of angles formed by intersecting lines. Now we look at the case of lines that do not intersect. They don't form any angles by themselves, of course, but angles formed by crossing such lines with another line have some useful relationships. Let's begin with a reminder of a few basic facts that you may already know.

- In a plane, straight lines that never intersect, no matter how far they are extended, are called **parallel**.

- The perpendicular distance between two parallel lines is the same everywhere, no matter where you check it.

- If we put a coordinate system on the plane, parallel lines will always have the same slope.

Display 2.30(a) shows a line, *t*, that intersects two parallel lines, making eight angles. Which of these angles do you think are equal? Give reasons to support your answers.

2.39

Learning Outcomes

After studying this section, you will be able to:

Explain the meaning of the terms *corresponding*, *alternate interior*, and *complementary* angles;

Recognize and apply the equality of corresponding angles and alternate interior angles in relation to parallelism of lines;

Use in various settings the fact that the angle sum of any triangle is 180°.

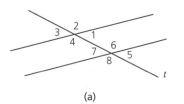

(a)

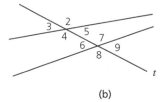

(b)

Display 2.30

The situation pictured in Display 2.30(a) is sometimes described as "parallel lines cut by a *transversal*". A **transversal** is a straight line that intersects two or more other straight lines at distinct points; *t* is the transversal in this figure.

About Words

Transversal is related to the verb *traverse*, which means go across. Traverse City is in northern Michigan. Can you find out how it got its name?

Published by IT'S ABOUT TIME, Inc. © 2000 MATHconx, LLC

157

2.5 Parallel Lines and the Angle Sum of a Triangle

This section connects angle congruence with parallelism. Parallel lines are characterized in several ways with the angles formed by a transversal. These facts lead to the main result of the section, the fact that the angle sum of every triangle is 180°. Although nothing is said about non-Euclidean geometries at this point, you might keep in mind this specific connection between parallelism and the angle sum of a triangle. The axiomatic introduction of nonEuclidean geometries—to be discussed in Year 3—normally proceeds from changing the Parallel Postulate. However, the three types of plane geometry can also be characterized locally by the angle sum of a triangle; only in Euclidean geometry is the angle sum exactly 180°. The dependence of the angle sum on the Parallel Postulate is made clear by the development in this section.

Note that when we talk about the angles of a polygon in this section and the next, we are referring to its interior angles. The term *interior angle* (in this sense) is not formally introduced until Section 2.6, to keep it separate from the phrase *alternate interior angles,* which occurs in this section.

2.39

This is an Exploration, but not a difficult one. It should be obvious, but not necessarily explicitly defensible, that if you slide the first intersection point along *t* until it coincides with the second, then all the angles will match up. Thus,

$$\angle 1 = \angle 5 = \angle 7 = \angle 3 \text{ and } \angle 2 = \angle 6 = \angle 8 = \angle 4$$

The interesting part of this discussion is seeing how the students justify the obvious invariance of the angles under translation. This can be pushed into a fairly deep discussion of invariance with some students, if you like, but such depth is not necessary for understanding the main ideas to come.

Sketchpad Exploration

Here is how to set up a Geometer's Sketchpad diagram that will display the eight angle measures in Display 2.30(a). As you vary the position of the transversal, all the measures change simultaneously, but (of course) only two different numbers appear at any one time. The display itself is shown in Display 2.11T; use this figure to guide the positioning of your choices.

1. Use the segment tool to draw a line segment, *AB*.

2. Use the point tool to draw a point, *C*.

3. Select segment *AB* and point *C*, and Construct the Parallel Line.

4. Use the point tool to draw a point, *D*, on the new line.

5. Use the arrow tool to select points C and D; then Construct the Segment, *CD*.

Assessments   Blackline Masters   Extensions   Supplements

For Additional Support Materials see page T-327

Chapter 2

The key to understanding parallel lines cut by a transversal is seeing that an angle at one crossing point should have the same measure as the angle in the same relative position at the other crossing point. For instance, in Display 2.30(a), ∠1 and ∠5 should have the same measure. In Display 2.30(b), ∠1 and ∠5 do not have the same measure because the two lines are not parallel. (Measure them with a protractor to convince yourself.)

One way to convince yourself of this fact is to make a picture on your graphing calculator. Set the window to include X from 1 to 10, Y from -5 to 5. Then graph the equations

$$y_1 = x - 3 \text{ and } y_2 = x - 6$$

The picture you get should look something like Display 2.30(a), with the x-axis as the transversal. The slope of each of the two parallel lines measures the angle it makes with the x-axis. But both lines have the same slope! (What is it?) Thus, they are congruent angles; they have the same measure.

A Phrase to Know: When two lines are crossed by a transversal, the two angles that are in the same relative position at the two crossing points are called **corresponding angles.**

Name the four pairs of corresponding angles in Display 2.30(a). Are the same pairs corresponding angles in Display 2.30(b)? Why or why not?

2.40

One use of corresponding angles is to see if two lines actually are parallel.

A Fact to Know: Two lines crossed by a transversal are parallel *if and only if* the measures of any pair of corresponding angles are equal.

A Phrase to Know: The phrase **if and only if** means that the two statements it connects are logically equivalent. If either one is true, so is the other.

If we know that two lines are parallel, then the corresponding angles formed by any transversal *must* be equal. In Display 2.30(a), the two unlabeled lines are parallel, so ∠1 = ∠5, ∠2 = ∠6, and so on.

158

6. Select the line *CD* (not the segment) and Hide it (using the Display menu).

7. Use the segment tool to draw the transversal line segment, *EF*, starting near the lower right corner of your picture and ending near the center, as shown.

8. Use the arrow tool to select segments *AB* and *EF*; then Construct the Point At Intersection, *G*.

9. Use the arrow tool to select segments *CD* and *EF*; then Construct the Point At Intersection, *H*.

10. Using the point tool, go to the Edit menu and Select All Points. Then go to the Display menu and Show Labels. At this stage, all the point labels should agree with the ones shown in Display 2.30(a).

11. All that remains to be done is the listing of the eight angle measures. In Display 2.11T they are listed in the order that agrees with the numbering in Display 2.30(a), but you may choose to list them differently. Each angle is done in the same way. Use the arrow tool to select the three defining points, in order, then Measure the Angle.

Your final display setup should look like Display 2.11T. By using the arrow tool, you can select point *F* and move it around so that the transversal crosses the parallel segments at different angles. The eight numerical displays will adjust automatically, graphically illustrating the angles that are equal and the angles that are supplementary.

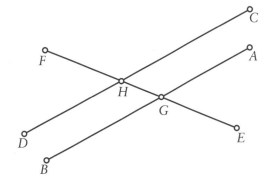

Angle (*CHE*) = 52°
Angle (*FHC*) = 128°
Angle (*FHD*) = 52°
Angle (*DHE*) = 128°
Angle (*AGE*) = 52°
Angle (*AGF*) = 128°
Angle (*FGB*) = 52°
Angle (*BGE*) = 128°

Display 2.11T

2.40 This is a routine check that students understand the term: ∠1 and ∠5, ∠2 and ∠6, ∠3 and ∠7, ∠4 and ∠8. Yes; the correspondence is the same, whether or not the lines that are cut by the transversal are parallel. However, the corresponding angles are not congruent unless the lines are parallel.

2.5 Parallel Lines and the Angle Sum of a Triangle

On the other hand, if two lines crossed by a transversal have an equal pair of corresponding angles, then the lines *must* be parallel. In Display 2.31(a), we can check to see if the lines are parallel by finding out if the two marked angles (or any other corresponding pair) are equal. In other words, knowing that two corresponding angles have the same measure guarantees that, no matter how far you extend these two lines in either direction, the distance between them will stay the same.

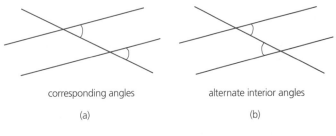

corresponding angles   alternate interior angles

(a)   (b)

Display 2.31

Display 2.31(b) illustrates another useful pair of angles that occur when two lines are crossed by a transversal.

A Phrase to Know: When two lines are crossed by a transversal, two angles with different vertices that are between the two lines and on opposite sides of the transversal are called **alternate interior angles**.

1. Name all the pairs of alternate interior angles in Display 2.30(a).

2. What do you think *alternate exterior angles* are? Make a sketch to illustrate your answer. Then name at least one pair of alternate exterior angles in Display 2.30(a).

2.41

Alternate interior angles can also be used to determine if two lines actually are parallel.

A Fact to Know: Two lines crossed by a transversal are parallel *if and only if* the measures of any pair of alternate interior angles are equal.

Published by IT'S ABOUT TIME, Inc. © 2000 MATHconx, LLC

159

2.41

Question 1 is another routine check that students understand the definition. There are only two pairs of alternate interior angles: ∠1 and ∠7; ∠4 and ∠6.

Question 2 asks students to focus on the meanings of the individual words in the phrase *alternate interior angles* and then use their sense of analogy. An appropriate description would be something like this.

> When two lines are crossed by a transversal, two angles with different vertices that are outside the two lines and on opposite sides of the transversal are called **alternate exterior angles.**

The two pairs of alternate exterior angles in Display 2.30(a) are ∠2 and ∠8; ∠3 and ∠5.

Chapter 2

Additional Support Materials:

Assessments	Qty
Form (A)	1
Form (B)	1

Blackline Masters	Qty

Extensions	Qty

Supplements	Qty
Parallel Lines and the Angle Sum of a Triangle	3

The parallel lines in Display 2.30(a) guarantee that $\angle 1 = \angle 7$ and $\angle 4 = \angle 6$. In Display 2.31(b), we can check to see if the lines are parallel by finding out if the two marked angles are equal.

How can the statement that relates alternate interior angles to parallels be derived from the statement that relates corresponding angles to parallels?

2.42

Let's pull together what we know so far about parallel lines and the angles formed by a transversal. For any two lines in a plane, the following statements are **equivalent**. That is, if we know that *any one* of them is true, then we know that *all* of them are true.

1. The lines are parallel.

2. The lines never meet, no matter how far they are extended.

3. The distance between the lines is the same everywhere.

4. For some transversals, two corresponding angles are equal.

5. For any transversal, all pairs of corresponding angles are equal.

6. For some transversals, two alternate interior angles are equal.

7. For any transversal, all pairs of alternate interior angles are equal.

A very important fact about triangles follows from 7.

A Fact to Know: The angle sum of any triangle is 180°.

That is, if we draw *any* **triangle** of *any* shape and add the measures of its three angles, the sum of the angles will *always* be 180°.

If a triangle contains a right angle, the sum of its other two angles must also be a right angle. Two angles that are related to each other in this way have many interesting, useful properties. This special case arises often enough to have a name of its own.

Published by IT'S ABOUT TIME, Inc. © 2000 MATHconx, LLC

2.42

This is an easy, but important, instance of a logical link between statements. Students should be guided to see that you can derive either of these statements from the other, by way of vertical angles. Using the notation of Display 2.30, the argument can be summarized like this.

∠7 = ∠5 (regardless of whether or not the given lines are parallel) because ∠7 and ∠5 are vertical angles. Thus, ∠1 = ∠7 if and only if ∠1 = ∠5. That is, the alternate interior angles have equal measures if and only if the corresponding angles have equal measures.

NOTES

Chapter 2

Words to Know: Two angles with measures that add to 90° are called **complementary angles**. Each one is called the **complement** of the other.

....

Answer these questions to see why the sum of the angles of a triangle is *always* 180°, regardless of the shape of the triangle. The questions refer to Display 2.32, which shows a triangle with a line through its top vertex, parallel to its base line.

2.43

1. Which three angles must you add to form the sum of the angles of this triangle?

2. What can you say about the two angles labeled 1? Why?

3. What can you say about the two angles labeled 2? Why?

4. What can you say about the angle formed by angles 1, 2, and 3 at the top of the figure? Why?

5. Are we done? Why or why not?

6. Do your answers to any of the preceding questions depend on knowing the measures of angles 1, 2, and 3?

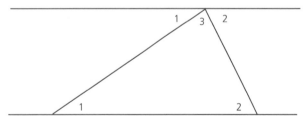

Display 2.32

In an earlier chapter you saw that polygons could be triangulated (subdivided into triangles). Use this fact to help you answer these questions.

2.44

1. What is the angle sum of a quadrilateral? Do all quadrilaterals have the same angle sum? Justify your answers.

161

2.43

These questions work well as a brief small group exercise. They take students step by step through an easy proof of the constancy of the angle sum. The argument depends on the fact about alternate interior angles which has just been introduced. Before letting the students answer these questions, make sure that they understand how Display 2.32 is made: One side (the base) of an arbitrary triangle is extended in both directions; then a line parallel to that base line is drawn through the opposite vertex. This can be done for any triangle of any shape. You might have the students reproduce this figure for any triangle they choose to draw.

1. ∠1, ∠2, and ∠3

2. They are equal because they are alternate interior angles of a transversal across two parallel lines.

3. They are equal because they are alternate interior angles of a transversal across two parallel lines.

4. They form a straight angle, so their sum must be 180°.

5. Yes. The sum of angles 1, 2, and 3 is the sum of the angles of the triangle. See question 1.

6. No. Nothing in Display 2.32 tells us the measure of any of these angles, but all the questions can be answered definitely.

Note that this result echoes problem 6(a) of Section 2.3, in which the students were asked to measure the angles of five different triangles and see if the angle sums were related. You might remind them of that exercise, or let them remind you of it.

Sketchpad Exploration

This is a good place for a simple, effective reinforcement Exploration about the angle sum of triangles. Your students can do this themselves, or you can show it to them.

1. Draw any triangle, △*ABC* (with the segment tool).

2. Use the arrow tool to highlight the three vertices in order; then choose Angle from the Measure menu to display the degree measure of ∠*ABC*.

3. Repeat step 2 to display the degree measures of ∠*BCA* and ∠*CAB*.

4. Highlight these three angle measures with the arrow tool. Then choose Calculate from the Measure menu.

5. Display the sum of the three angles by choosing each one in turn and putting + signs between them (using the displayed calculator button). The screen will show

Angle(ABC) + Angle(BCA) + Angle(CAB) = 180.00°

Chapter 2

2. What is the angle sum of a pentagon? Do all pentagons have the same angle sum? Justify your answers.

3. What is the angle sum of a hexagon? Do all hexagons have the same angle sum? Justify your answers.

4. If someone who was hiding a polygon told you the number of sides of that polygon, could you discover its angle sum? Would you bet $100 that you were right without seeing the polygon first? Explain.

2.45

1. When you cross parallel lines with parallel transversals, what kind of figure do you get? What is it called?

2. When this figure was defined in Chapter 1, did the definition use parallel lines? How would you define it, if you were making up your own definition?

3. Do you think that your definition and the definition in Chapter 1 always refer to exactly the same figures? Explain.

Problem Set: 2.5

1. (a) Draw a capital letter of the alphabet that is formed by a pair of alternate interior angles and one that is formed by a pair of vertical angles.

   (b) Why does each of these statements about some angle, ∠A, *not* make sense by itself? *Hint:* It's the same reason in each case.

   ∠A is a vertical angle.

   ∠A is an alternate interior angle.

   ∠A is a corresponding angle.

   ∠A is a supplementary angle.

162

6. Now use the arrow tool to drag one vertex of the triangle around, forming triangles of all different shapes. As you move the vertex around, the measures of the three separate angles will change on the screen, but the angle sum will stay the same.

7. To illustrate that displayed sums *can* change, you might display the sum of two of the angles under the sum of all three angles. This second sum will change as the shape of the triangle changes, emphasizing by contrast the constancy of the sum of all three angles.

2.44

These questions echo the pattern hinted at in problem 6(b–d) of Section 2.3. The answers all follow easily from two facts.
- The angle sum of a triangle is 180°, and an n-sided polygon can be triangulated into $n - 2$ triangles.

The latter statement, for quadrilaterals, pentagons, and hexagons, was established in Chapter 1. Its extension to the general case has not been explicitly stated, but the pattern can be observed from these early cases, then checked by example, at least. After making a few drawings to help their visual intuition, the students should recall that all the vertices of all the triangles used in the triangulation process are vertices of the original polygon. Therefore, the angle sum of the polygon can be obtained by adding up the angles of all the triangles. But this is just $180° (n - 2)$. In particular,

1. The angle sum of every quadrilateral is 360°.

2. The angle sum of every pentagon is 540°.

3. The angle sum of every hexagon is 720°.

4. Yes. Yes. Use the formula $180°(n - 2)$ to calculate the angle sum.

This question is to remind students about parallelograms.

2.45

1. Parallelograms were defined in Chapter 1 as quadrilaterals with both pairs of opposite sides congruent. Parallel lines were not used in that definition!

2. In many ways, it is much more natural to define parallelograms by saying that both pairs of opposite sides are *parallel*. You ought to lead students to that definition, if they don't get there by themselves.

3. The two definitions are logically equivalent. That is, any figure that satisfies one also satisfies the other. The notion of logical equivalence might be raised here with some classes, at least by way of attempted counterexamples.

Problem Set: 2.5

1. (a) N, Z, H; X
   (b) Each type named refers to a *pair* of angles. You cannot tell whether any of these applies to ∠A unless it is being related to another angle.

2. These questions refer to the roof truss diagrams in Display 2.33.

   (a) Truss B outlines two right triangles. To the nearest tenth of a degree, what is the size of each angle in these right triangles? Explain how you got your answers.

   (b) Suppose the vertical center post in Truss B is 5 feet long. Find the lengths of the other two sides of each right triangle. Round your answers to the nearest inch.

   (c) The top part of Truss C outlines two right triangles. To the nearest tenth of a degree, what is the size of each angle in these right triangles? Explain how you got your answers.

   (d) Suppose the vertical center post in Truss C is 9 feet long. Find the lengths of the other two sides of each right triangle. Round your answers to the nearest inch.

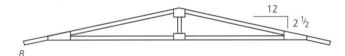

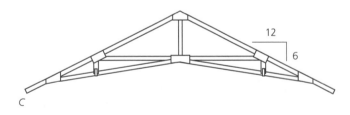

From *Carpentry and Building Construction*, 5th edition, page 487, by John L. Feirer, Gilbert R. Hutchings and Mark D. Feirer. Copyright © 1997 by Glencoe/McGraw-Hill. Reprinted by permission.

Display 2.33

Published by IT'S ABOUT TIME, Inc. © 2000 MATHconx, LLC

2. Parts (c) and (d) are identical in form to parts (a) and (b).

(a) The lower acute angles measure $\text{TAN}^{-1}\left(\frac{2.5}{12}\right) = 11.8°$ (approx.). Since these are right triangles, the other base angle is 90° in each case. Subtracting 90° + 11.8° from 180° leaves 78.2° as the measure of the top angle of each triangle.

(b) Using the rise over run proportion, we have $\frac{5}{x} = \frac{2.5}{12}$. Since 5 is twice 2.5, then x must be twice 12. Thus, the other leg of each right triangle is 24 feet long. The Pythagorean Theorem gives us the length of each hypotenuse.

$$\sqrt{5^2 + 24^2} = 24.52 = 24 \text{ ft. 6 in. (approx.)}$$

(c) The lower acute angles measure $\text{TAN}^{-1}\frac{6}{12} = 26.6°$ (approx.). Since these are right triangles, the other base angle is 90° in each case. Subtracting 90° + 26.6° from 180° leaves 63.4° as the measure of the top angle of each triangle.

(d) Using the rise-over-run proportion, we have $\frac{9}{x} = \frac{6}{12}$. Algebra (or mental arithmetic) yields $x = 18$, so the other leg of each right triangle is 18 feet long. The Pythagorean Theorem gives us the length of each hypotenuse.

$$\sqrt{9^2 + 18^2} = 20.12 = 20 \text{ ft., 1 in. (approx.)}$$

NOTES

Chapter 2

3. The diagram in Display 2.34 is a puzzle that has these properties,

   • *CDJK* is a rectangle.

   • ∠*F* and ∠*G* are right angles.

   • Triangles *ABN* and *HLN* are equilateral.

   • ∠*AML* and ∠*MLB* are supplementary angles.

   In this figure, 14 of the angles are congruent to ∠*BEH*, which is marked by a star. Without measuring anything, find at least five of them. Can you find ten? Can you find them all? Justify each angle you pick.

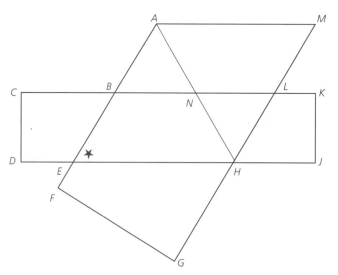

The measurements in this figure are not exact.

Display 2.34

4. (a) ∠*A* and ∠*B* have slope measures $\frac{2}{5}$ and $\frac{5}{2}$, respectively. Find their degree measures, rounded to one decimal place. Then find the sum of their degree measures and the product of their slope measures. How are ∠*A* and ∠*B* related?

   (b) ∠*C* and ∠*D* have slope measures 6.25 and 0.16, respectively. Find their degree measures, rounded to one decimal place. Then find the sum of their degree measures and the product of their slope measures. How are ∠*C* and ∠*D* related?

3. This exercise uses the concepts of vertical, corresponding, alternate interior, and supplementary angles to justify the various angle choices. All these angles are congruent to $\angle BEH$.

    $\angle NHL \quad \angle HNL \quad \angle HLN \quad \angle ANB \quad \angle NAB \quad \angle ABN \quad \angle EHN$
    $\angle EHG \quad \angle JHL \quad \angle KLM \quad \angle MAN \quad \angle AML \quad \angle DEF \quad \angle CBE$

    They can be found in a variety of orders and may be justified by a variety of reasons.

4. As they practice their measurement conversion skills with these questions, students are led to discover an interesting pattern that describes an important fact about complementary angles.

    (a) $\angle A = 21.8°$, $\angle B = 68.2°$. The sum is 90°. $\frac{2}{5} \cdot \frac{5}{2} = 1$. $\angle A$ and $\angle B$ are complementary angles.
    (b) $\angle C = 80.9°$, $\angle D = 9.1°$. The sum is 90°. $6.25 \cdot 0.16 = 1$. $\angle C$ and $\angle D$ are complementary angles.

NOTES

Chapter 2

(c) $\angle E = 33°$ and $\angle F = 57°$. Find their slope measures, rounded to two decimal places. Then find the sum of their degree measures and the product of their slope measures. How are $\angle E$ and $\angle F$ related?

(d) What pattern do you see in the information from parts (a) − (c)? Make up a general rule based on that pattern.

(e) What angle should be paired with a 72° angle to fit the pattern you see? Does your general rule work for these two angles? Explain.

(f) An angle has slope measure $\frac{3}{7}$. What is the slope measure of its complement? You should be able to find this *without* finding the degree measure of the angle.

(g) An angle has slope measure 3.58. What is the slope measure of its complement? You should be able to find this *without* finding the degree measure of the angle.

5. In Chapter 1 we saw that some figures can be used to tile an area. That is, copies of a figure can fill in an area completely, with no gaps between edges.

(a) Extend the top and bottom parallel lines in Display 2.32 to form a long strip. Then describe how the triangle in the figure can be used to tile the strip as far as you like in either direction. Draw a sketch to illustrate your description.

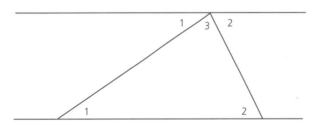

Display 2.32

(b) Draw a triangle of any shape you choose. Make it as weird as you like! Then show how the process you described in part (a) guarantees that your triangle can be used to tile a strip between two parallel lines.

(c) Explain and justify this statement. If you can tile a strip, you can tile a plane.

Published by IT'S ABOUT TIME, Inc. © 2000 MATHconx, LLC

(c) The slope measure of ∠E is 0.65; the slope measure of ∠F is 1.54. The sum is 90°. The product of these *approximate* slope measures is 0.65 · 1.54 = 1.001. You can compute the product of the exact slope measures by using the TAN function form: tan 33° · tan 57° = 1. ∠E and ∠F are complementary angles.

(d) The product of the slope measures of complementary angles always equals 1. In other words, the slope measures of complementary angles are reciprocals of each other.

(e) Its complement, an 18° angle. The slope measures rounded to two places are 3.08 and 0.32, respectively. 3.08 · 0.32 = 0.9856, which is not convincingly close to 1. However, the exact slope measures are tan 72° and tan 18°. Multiplying these two values with the calculator yields exactly 1.

(f) This leads students to recall and use the fact that fractions whose product is 1 are reciprocals of each other. The slope measure of the complement is $\frac{7}{3}$. Once the students have found their answers, you might ask them to check by converting to degree measure via the TAN⁻¹ function to see if they have complementary angles. They should get approximately 23.2° and 66.8°.

(g) This extends the previous part by getting students to find the reciprocal of a number that is not in fraction form. The slope measure of the complement is $\frac{1}{3.58} = 0.28$ (approx.). Once the students have found their answers, you might ask them to check by converting to degree measure via the TAN⁻¹ function to see if they have complementary angles. They should get approximately 74.4° and 15.6°.

5. (a) You may decide that a picture, without words, is sufficient to describe this idea. See Display 2.12T(a).

(b) Draw a line through any vertex parallel to the opposite side, then fit the triangles together as in part (a).

(c) A strip is determined by two parallel lines that are a certain distance apart. You can draw parallels to these two lines the same distance from them on either side, and repeat that process forever, dividing the entire plane into strips. Each one can then be tiled as above.

(d) Strips between parallel lines can be placed side by side in many different ways. Draw a picture of at least three of your triangle strips, running horizontally and arranged so that the corresponding vertices of the triangles are aligned vertically.

(e) Draw another picture of at least three of your triangle strips, running horizontally and arranged so that each side of each triangle lines up along a straight line with a side of another triangle.

(f) Parts (d) and (e) illustrate two different ways of using your triangle to tile a plane. Can you think of a third way? Which do you like best? Why?

6. Two English words that are pronounced in the same way but have very different meanings are *complement* and *compliment*. Look up these two words in a dictionary and write out a definition for each one (as a noun). Then explain why it makes sense to apply one of these words, but not the other, to angles.

166

(d) For this part and the next, we use the triangle of Display 2.32 to illustrate the idea. See Display 2.12T(b).

(e) See Display 2.12T(c).

(f) This part can be used, in part, as a writing exercise. There are lots of ways (infinitely many, in fact) to tile the plane by strips.

6. This is a short writing exercise that focuses students on the meaning of *complementary angles* and points out a common spelling error at the same time. It can be used as a brief, in class discussion, rather than as a writing exercise, if you prefer. The following definitions are taken from *The American Heritage Dictionary of the English Language*.

complement— Something that completes, makes up a whole, or brings to perfection.

compliment— An expression of praise, admiration, or congratulation.

An angle that makes a given angle into a complete right angle is appropriately called the *complement* of the given angle. The word *compliment* makes no sense at all in this context; one angle cannot praise, admire, or congratulate another.

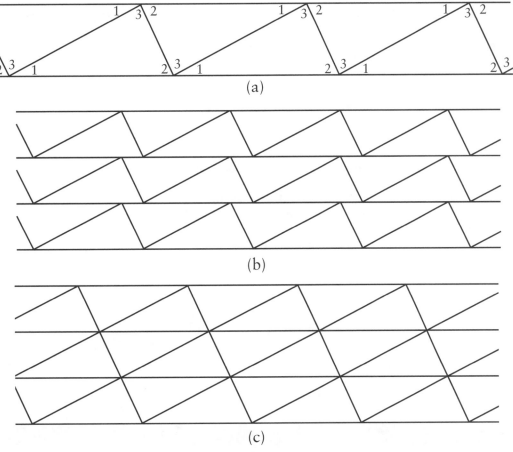

(a)

(b)

(c)

Display 2.12T

2.6 Parallelograms and Congruent Triangles

Polygons are figures made up of line segments and angles. In earlier chapters, we examined their side lengths and their symmetries. Now it is time to see what useful things can be said about the angles of polygons. There are many, many things that we *could* say about them—some interesting, some not, some useful, some not. To keep this section and the next two from being a hopeless clutter of details, they are built around a single theme question.

How much information is enough to determine a polygon?

This section and the next one focus on triangles. Section 2.8 extends our explorations and findings to other polygons.

In Chapter 1 you found that the lengths of the three sides are enough to determine a triangle—not its exact location, but its size and its shape. That is, any two triangles with sides of the same lengths must be congruent. This principle is abbreviated as SSS— which stands for side-side-side.

A Fact to Know: (SSS) If the three sides of one triangle have the same lengths as the three sides of another triangle, then the triangles are congruent.

So determine really should be understood in terms of congruence. A figure is **determined** if there is no doubt or ambiguity about its size or shape. Sometimes this is called "determined up to congruence". If a figure is determined by some information, there should be a way to find *any other* fact about its size or shape from that information. The way may not be obvious or easy, but if the figure is determined, *there has to be a way*!

Learning Outcomes

After studying this section, you will be able to:

Find the measures of all sides and all angles of a triangle if you know two sides and the included angle;

Find the measures of all the angles of a triangle if you know all three of its sides;

Explain and use a formula for finding the area of a parallelogram.

Published by IT'S ABOUT TIME, Inc. © 2000 MATHconx, LLC

2.6 Parallelograms and Congruent Triangles

This section begins with a thinking habit question that should become a recurring theme: "How much (or how little) information is enough to determine ...?" This notion of logical minimality is a habit of thought that is fundamental to many aspects of mathematics, including axiom systems and the construction of mathematical models. Indeed, many theorems of higher mathematics have stemmed from efforts to weaken the hypotheses of a known statement and prove the same conclusion. In applying mathematics to anything, it is important to know when you have enough information to specify a unique object.

This is particularly true in geometry and its applications. Standard examples abound.

- Two points determine a unique line.

- Three noncollinear points determine a unique circle (and a unique plane).

- Two intersecting lines determine a unique plane in space.

And so on. Most congruence theorems (SSS, SAS, ASA, etc.) are statements of this sort. At this stage, we want students to begin to think about this kind of inquiry as a natural question to ask in a variety of situations: When do I have enough information to determine the figure or shape or object I am dealing with? When do I have more than I need, and what can be discarded or ignored? What missing fact will give me enough to specify the object I'm dealing with? Some of these questions are raised explicitly in our discussion proposals and Problem Sets. Even if they are not posed in the text, however, feel free to guide students to think about such things.

In particular, if you have the time, you might begin this section by having the class try to build triangles by choosing side lengths and angles at random and seeing which combinations of their choices determine a triangle. A related, but much more elaborate, exercise of this sort is described at the end of the next section's Teacher Commentary. See **A GAME**.

Chapter 2

Assessments   Blackline Masters   Extensions   Supplements

For Additional Support Materials see page T-349

2.46 By SSS, there is only one triangle (up to congruence) with side lengths 4, 5, and 7 inches. Find each of the following facts about this triangle. Do as little drawing and measuring as possible, but do as much as you feel you need. In each case, explain your approach to the question. Find

1. its perimeter;

2. the length of the altitude from the 7 inch side to its opposite vertex;

3. the area enclosed by the triangle;

4. the size of each angle.

Why do you think we want you to do as little drawing and measuring as possible?

For part 2 of the previous question, how did you find the altitude of the triangle? Did you draw a diagram and measure it? That's OK, if you have a sharp pencil and are careful, but what if the triangle were 4 by 5 by 7 *miles*, instead of inches? Or, what if you don't have good measuring tools, or if you want a very precise answer? There is a way to find that altitude exactly, without measuring anything. Here's how.

1. Start with a sketch. You can draw your own or look at Display 2.35. Draw the altitude you want and call its length a. The foot of this altitude divides the 7 inch side into two pieces. If you call the length of one piece x, then the length of the other is $7 - x$.

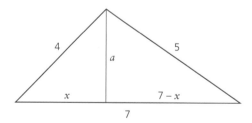

Display 2.35

2. Apply the Pythagorean Theorem on the two right triangles formed by this altitude.

$$x^2 + a^2 = 4^2 \quad \text{and} \quad (7 - x)^2 + a^2 = 5^2$$

168

2.6 Parallelograms and Congruent Triangles

2.46

This is a discussion question, rather than just a Do this now question, for several reasons. First of all, some parts of this are difficult. Secondly, it is intended to serve, in part, as a review and extension of material from Chapter 1, and a collective memory effort often is more productive than an individual one in such situations. Finally, it is expected that coping with this question will clarify any remaining student doubts about what *determine* means, and discussion might be needed to bring such doubts to the surface.

1. This is the (only) easy part. The perimeter is just the sum of the side lengths, 16 inches.

2. This part can be done by drawing and measurement. It can also be computed algebraically, but the tools needed to do that may not be things that your students do easily. An algebraic solution is described immediately after this question set. For less able students, this algebraic description could be omitted. The rest of the chapter can be done without it, except for problem 2 at the end of this section. However, good students should work their way through this process. It is a good illustration of how a couple of standard algebraic techniques come together to solve a geometry problem.

   If the students decide that they'll have to draw and measure, you might guide the discussion to the final question: Why should you do as little drawing and measuring as possible? This suggests the problem of measurement variability. Have the students decide on a way to maximize the dependability of their answer. This answer can be used to do the next part without any additional drawing or measuring, so it's important that it be as accurate as you can get it. Their drawing should be about 2.8 inches, rounded to the nearest tenth of an inch.

NOTES

Chapter 2

3. Each of these equations can be rewritten as
$a^2 = $ [**something**].

$$a^2 = 4^2 - x^2 \quad \text{and} \quad a^2 = 5^2 - (7-x)^2$$

4. You have two things equal to a^2, so they must equal each other.

$$4^2 - x^2 = 5^2 - (7-x)^2$$

5. Now just work out the arithmetic and solve for x.

$$4^2 - x^2 = 5^2 - (7^2 - 14x + x^2)$$

$$4^2 - x^2 = 5^2 - 7^2 + 14x - x^2$$

$$4^2 = 5^2 - 7^2 + 14x$$

$$16 - 25 + 49 = 14x$$

$$\frac{40}{14} = x$$

6. Now you can find a just by substituting $\frac{40}{14}$ for x in one of the first equations.

$$a^2 = 4^2 - \left(\frac{40}{14}\right)^2$$

Compute the numerical side of this equation with your calculator. Then take its square root to get a. What do you get? Does it agree with what you got before?

The problem about *The Daily Planet's* real estate taxes, at the end of this section, will give you a chance to use this technique in a real world situation.

The SSS test for congruent triangles can be used to get a handy formula for finding the area of a parallelogram.

2.47

1. Suppose that *ABCD* is a parallelogram, as in Display 2.36. Use SSS to make a convincing argument that the diagonal *BD* divides the parallelogram into two congruent triangles. *Hint:* Recall the definition of a parallelogram given in Chapter 1.

2. If the length of *BC* is 7 and the vertical distance from *BC* to *D* is 4, what is the area of triangle *BCD*? What is the area of triangle *ABD*? What is the area of the parallelogram *ABCD*? How do you know?

MATH *Connections*: A Secondary Mathematics Core Curriculum

3. This can be computed using the 7 inch side and the altitude found in part (b):

$$\frac{1}{2} \cdot 7 \cdot 2.8 = 9.8 \text{ sq. in. (approx.)}$$

4. Once you know the altitude from part (b), the angles can be computed. Doing this provides a review of the Pythagorean Theorem, square roots, the TAN^{-1} function, and the angle sum of a triangle. Try to guide students to see that they can use TAN^{-1} to find the size of the two base angles if they know the lengths of the two parts of the base on either side of the altitude. These lengths can be computed by the Pythagorean Theorem.

$$2.8^2 + x^2 = 5^2, \text{ so } x = \sqrt{17.16} = 4.1 \text{ (approx.)}$$

Thus, the 7 inch side is divided into 4.1 inches and 2.9 inches by subtraction. Now the two base angles can be found, using a calculator.

$$\text{TAN}^{-1}\left(\frac{2.8}{4.1}\right) = 34° \text{ and } \tan^{-1}\left(\frac{2.8}{2.9}\right) = 44°$$

rounded to the nearest degree. The third angle must then be

$$180° - (34° + 44°) = 102°$$

2.47

These questions establish a formula that will be used in the chapter on the basic trigonometric functions.

1. In Chapter 1, a parallelogram is defined as a quadrilateral with congruent pairs of opposite sides. Thus, BC is congruent to AD and CD is congruent to AB. Since the diagonal BD is congruent to itself, $\triangle ABD$ and $\triangle BCD$ are congruent, by SSS.

2. The area of a triangle is $\frac{1}{2} bh$, where b is the base and h is the altitude (the height). In this case, $b = 7$ and $h = 4$, so the area of triangle BCD is 14. The area of $\triangle ABD$ is also 14. Since $\triangle ABD$ and $\triangle BCD$ are congruent, they have the same area. The area of the parallelogram is 28, the sum of the two triangular areas.

NOTES

2.6 Parallelograms and Congruent Triangles

3. If the length of *BC* is *b* and the vertical distance from *BC* to *D* is *h*, what is the area of triangle *BCD*? What is the area of triangle *ABD*? What is the area of the parallelogram *ABCD*? How do you know?

4. Write a general formula for the area of a parallelogram. Be sure to say what the letters in your formula represent.

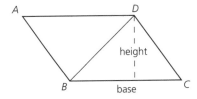

Display 2.36

Thinking Tip

Visualize. A mental picture often can lead you through an example more reliably than memorized steps or formulas.

Sometimes other combinations of three, or even two, pieces of information are enough to determine a triangle. Here are some examples to help you see which combinations work that way. As you work through them, try to visualize the given pieces of the triangle in your mind's eye.

2.48

In each of the following cases,

- If you think the given facts determine a particular triangle, draw it.

- If you think the given facts can be true for more than one triangle, draw two different (noncongruent) triangles that fit those facts.

- If you think that no triangle fits the given facts, explain why.

1. Two of the sides are 6 cm and 8 cm long, the included angle (the angle between them) is 40°.

2. Two of the sides are 6 cm and 8 cm long; an angle not between them is 40°.

3. Two of the angles are 30° and 45°; the included side (the side between them) is 5 cm long.

Published by IT'S ABOUT TIME, Inc. © 2000 MATHconx, LLC

3. Using the same reasoning as in the previous part, the area of △BCD is $\frac{1}{2}bh$, which is the same as the area of △ACD. Thus, the area of the parallelogram is twice the sum of the triangular area.

$$2 \cdot \frac{1}{2}bh = bh$$

4. If one side of a parallelogram has length b and the vertical distance from that side to its opposite side is h, then the area of the parallelogram is bh.

2.48

This is a *preliminary* drawing and visualizing exercise about *many* important ideas. It is intended to be exploratory, not definitive. The only issue that needs to be resolved by this discussion is what it means to say that a shape is determined by some information.

A good way for students to proceed here is by representing the given information with a picture, seeing if there is more than one way to do that. This will dictate whether or not there is exactly one triangle that fits. The experimental drawing can be done with Geometer's Sketchpad, if your students have access to it. Alternatively, after they have experimented with pencil, paper, ruler and protractor, you can show them some of these with a Sketchpad demonstration.

1. This triangle is determined. See Display 2.13T(a).

2. Two different triangles fit this description. See Display 2.13T(b).

3. This triangle is determined. See Display 2.13T(c).

Chapter 2

Additional Support Materials:

Assessments	Qty
Form (A)	1
Form (B)	1

Blackline Masters	Qty

Extensions	Qty

Supplements	Qty
Parallelograms and Congruent Triangles	4

4. Two of the angles are 30° and 45°; a side not between them is 5 cm long.

5. The three angles are 50°, 60°, and 70°.

6. The three angles are 60°, 70°, and 80°.

7. It is equilateral and has perimeter 21 cm.

Here's an example of how a situation like question 1 above might turn up in real life.

Smalltown owns part of Puddle Lake, including a shallow, sandy cove. The Recreation Department wants to put a float line across the cove to mark off a wading area for children, as is shown in Display 2.37. How long must the float line be?

We can't answer this question yet, of course, because we don't have any measurements. The cove could be only a few feet wide (unlikely) or several miles wide (also unlikely) or any size in between (far more likely). How can you attack the problem?

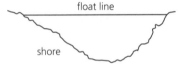

Display 2.37

One way is to get wet. Wade across the cove, stretching a long string from one shore point to the other. But today the water is much too cold. Another way is to think of the float line as part of a triangle that has two dry sides. Call the float line *AB* and pick a point *C* on shore so that the straight paths from *C* to both *A* and *B* are completely on dry land, as in Display 2.38. Now we can measure directly *AC*, *BC*, and the included angle, ∠*ACB*.

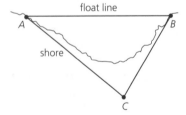

Display 2.38

Published by IT'S ABOUT TIME, Inc. © 2000 MATHconx, LLC

171

4. Two different triangles fit this description. An easy way to draw these is to recognize first that the third angle is determined (105°) because the angle sum must be 180°. The two cases, then, come from whether the given side is between 30° and 105° angles, or between 45° and 105° angles. See Display 2.13T(d_1 and d_2).

5. Infinitely many triangles fit this description. All of them are similar, but that's a story for later.

6. No triangles fit this description; the angle sum is 210°.

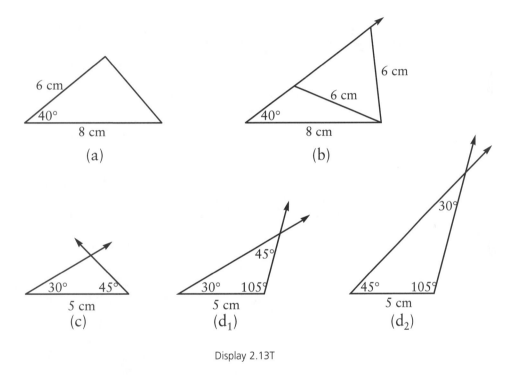

Display 2.13T

7. This triangle is determined. Since it is equilateral, each side must be $\frac{1}{3}$ of 21 cm long and all the angles must be equal, by symmetry.

NOTES

_____

_____

_____

_____

_____

Chapter 2

Once you know two sides and the included angle, a triangle is determined (up to congruence). Only one triangular shape and size will fit that description because the positions of the "free" ends of the two sides are fixed exactly by their distances from the vertex of the included angle. The line segment between those two fixed points is the third side of the triangle. In this case, the measurements for the dry sides of the float line triangle are: AC is 135 feet long, BC is 93 feet long, and $\angle ACB$ is 72°. Now what?

2.49

1. How long is the float line? Explain how you got your answer.

2. Is your answer *exactly* accurate? Do you think it is within a foot of being exact? Is it accurate enough for making the float line? Explain.

3. Which do you think is easier to measure in this situation—the lengths of the sides or the included angle? Why?

Here is a way to find the length of the float line without actually having to measure the angle between AC and BC.

- Extend AC through C along a straight line to a point A' such that $A'C$ is equal in length to AC. Do the same thing with BC, making $B'C$ equal to BC, as shown in Display 2.39.

- Notice that $\angle A'CB' = \angle ACB$. Why? This means that two sides of triangle ABC and the angle between them have the same measures as two sides of triangle $A'B'C$ and the angle between them.

- Since two sides and the included angle determine a triangle up to congruence, triangles ABC and $A'B'C$ must be congruent. This means that the float-line side, AB, must have the same length as the dry side $A'B'$. So, to find the length of the float line, you just have to measure the distance between A' and B'.

Published by IT'S ABOUT TIME, Inc. © 2000 MATHconx, LLC

2.49

This calls for students to make a careful scale drawing and measure it. There are more precise ways to get this answer, but they involve trigonometry. Moreover, the degree of accuracy required here will be satisfied by a careful drawing. A scale of 1 mm to the foot will allow for a drawing on a standard 8.5 × 11 inch sheet of paper. The answer is about 140 feet.

The third question is a setup for the next paragraph. It is expected (hoped) that most students will agree that, without precision instruments, angles are harder to measure than lengths.

NOTES

Chapter 2

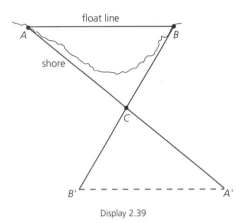

Display 2.39

The example we have just done illustrates a basic principle determining triangles: The measures of two sides of a triangle and the included angle are enough to determine the size and shape of the triangle. This principle is abbreviated as SAS—which stands for side-angle-side.

A Fact to Know: (SAS) If two sides and the included angle of one triangle have the same measures as two sides and the included angle of another triangle, then the triangles are congruent.

In Display 2.40, point E is the midpoint of AC, point F is the midpoint of AB, and DE is exactly half as long as AB and parallel to it. The exact size and shape of $\triangle ABC$ are not known.

1. Use SAS to explain why all four of the following triangles must be congruent.

$\triangle AFE \quad \triangle EDC \quad \triangle DEF \quad \triangle FBD$

2.50

2. Explain why D must be the midpoint of BC.

3. If the area of $\triangle ABC$ is 150 sq. in., what is the area of $\triangle DEF$?

2.50

This is a reinforcement exercise for SAS, as well as a review of some properties of angles of parallel lines cut by a transversal. It is good for small group work in class, where students can help each other and you can guide them, too, as needed. Questions 3 and 5 probe for student understanding of the implications of congruent. Question 4 emphasizes the fact that properties derived in this way apply to *all* triangles with the given properties. In mathematicians' terms, we are pointing out that the explanations, if done properly, are proofs of theorems.

1. A good way to approach is to take these triangles in order.

   (a) $\triangle AFE$ and $\triangle EDC$: $AE = EC$ because E is the midpoint of AC. $AF = DE$ because F is the midpoint of AB and DE is exactly half as long as AB. Finally, $\angle FAE = \angle DEC$ because they are corresponding angles of parallel lines (AB and DE) cut by a transversal (AC). Thus, $\triangle AFE \cong \triangle EDC$ by SAS.

   (b) $\triangle EDC$ and $\triangle DEF$: By previous congruence, $EF = CD$. Clearly, ED equals itself. Now, $\angle AFE = \angle FED$ because they are alternate interior angles of parallel lines (AB and DE) cut by a transversal (EF). But $\angle AFE = \angle EDC$, so $\angle FED$ must also equal $\angle EDC$. Thus, $\triangle EDC \cong \triangle DEF$ by SAS.

   (c) $\triangle DEF$ and $\triangle FBD$: As in part (a), $DE = FB$ because F is the midpoint of AB. Clearly, DF equals itself. Finally, $\angle BFD = \angle EDF$ because they are alternate interior angles of parallel lines (AB and DE) cut by a transversal (DF). Thus, $\triangle DEF \cong \triangle FBD$ by SAS.

2. Since all four triangles are congruent, CD and DB are corresponding parts of congruent triangles, so they must be equal in length. That is, D must be the midpoint of BC.

3. Congruence means that the triangles are identical in shape and size. Hence, all four triangles must have the same area. Since they tile $\triangle ABC$, each of the four must be $\frac{1}{4}$ of the total area. The area of $\triangle DEF$ is 37.5 sq. in.

NOTES

....

....

....

....

4. Do the answers to questions 1, 2, and 3 depend on knowing the exact size of the individual sides or individual angles of ABC? Justify your answer.

5. If you also know that the perimeter of △ ABC is 60 in., can you find the perimeter of △ DEF? If so, do it. Explain.

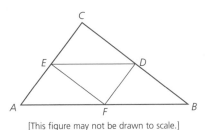

[This figure may not be drawn to scale.]

Display 2.40

Problem Set: 2.6

1. (a) Find the areas of these two parallelograms.
      (i) base = 13 ft., height = 5.2 ft.
      (ii) base = 19.7 m, height = 6.5 m

   (b) Find the areas of a parallelogram with sides of 12 ft. and 8 ft. and one angle of 45°. (*Hints:* Make a sketch. Apply the Pythagorean Theorem to find the height.)

2. In downtown Metropolis, land is expensive and taxes are high. When the new highway went through, the surveyors took a narrow triangular piece of land from *The Daily Planet*'s property. The sides of this triangular piece are 110 ft., 300 ft., and 400 ft. Since taxes are based on the square footage of the land, *The Daily Planet*'s management needs to know exactly how many square feet of land they lost, so that they can appeal to the City Assessor's Office for a reduction in their taxes. How much land did they lose? (*Hint:* Use some algebra and your calculator.)

4. No; the answers are independent of the precise dimensions of $\triangle ABC$. None of the arguments given here used the measure of a particular side or angle of $\triangle ABC$. Of course, the specific area measurement in question 3 puts some limitations on the overall size of $\triangle ABC$, but many different triangles can have the same area.

5. Yes. Because all four triangles are identical in shape and size, each side of $\triangle DEF$ is equal in length to half of one side of $\triangle ABC$. Thus, its perimeter is 30 inches, half of the perimeter of $\triangle ABC$.

Problem Set: 2.6

1. Part (a) of this problem requires only simple computation. Part (b) involves ideas from earlier sections.

   (a)

       (i) 67.6 sq. ft.

       (ii) 128.05 sq. m

   (b) The 45° angle is carefully chosen to make these computations easier. To find the height, drop a perpendicular from one corner to the line of the opposite 12 ft. side. That will form an *isosceles* triangle with base angles of 45° and a hypotenuse of 8 ft. The Pythagorean Theorem, then, says that

   $$h^2 + h^2 = 8^2$$

   This yields $h = \sqrt{32}$ (= approx. 5.66). The area is 12 times this, or about 67.9 sq. ft.

2. The triangle in this problem is too narrow for a convenient, accurate scale drawing. The numbers invite calculator use. Here is an outline of the solution, following the approach in the text.

   $$a^2 = 110^2 - x^2 = 300^2 - (400 - x)^2$$

   $$110^2 = 300^2 - 400^2 + 800x$$

   $$82{,}100 = 800x$$

   $$102.625 = x$$

   Substituting into an early equation and using a calculator, we have

   $$a^2 = 110^2 - 102.625^2 = 1568.109375$$

   so $a = 39.6$ ft. (approximately). By the area formula, the area of the triangle rounded to the nearest square foot is 7920 sq. ft.

3. Ripoff Realty Co. is selling riverfront lots along a straight stretch of the Rocky River. They are priced at $250 per front foot (measured along the riverbank), and the company says that they extend 250 feet back from the river along their other boundary lines. They advertise the land at "only $1 per square foot." Display 2.41 is a tracing from the town tax map, showing some of the lots. As you can see, the boundary line does not go back from the shore at right angles.

(a) Is the price of the land $1 per square foot, more than that, or less than that? Explain.

(b) By measuring the diagram carefully, find the height of Lot 1. Use the riverfront as the base. Then find the area of this lot.

(c) What is the price of Lot 1? How much is its cost per square foot?

(d) Find the area of Lot 2. What is its price? What is its cost per square foot?

(e) Write a function that gives you the area of a lot with x feet of riverfront.

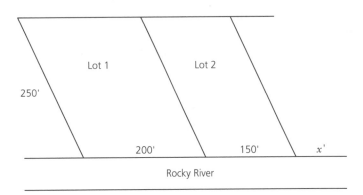

Display 2.41

4. Scientists want to know if the universe is expanding, contracting, or staying the same size. To do this, they need to know where each of the stars are. If the distances between stars get smaller, then the universe is contracting and will someday collapse. If the distances stay the same, then the universe is not getting larger or smaller. If the distances are increasing, then our universe is expanding.

175

3. (a) More. It would be exactly $1 per square foot if the lot were rectangular. The height of each 1' by 1' nonrectangular parallelogram in a 1 ft. strip back from the shore is less than 1 ft., making the area less than 1 sq. ft. This will come out of the later computations, but students should see the intuitive picture now.

   (b) The height is about $\frac{9}{8}$ of the 200' line, or about 225 ft. The area is approximately $200 \cdot 225 = 45{,}000$ sq. ft.

   (c) Its price is $200 \cdot \$250 = \$50{,}000$. It costs about $1.11 per square foot.

   (d) The height of this parallelogram is approximately 225 ft. (the same as for Lot 1), so the area is $150 \cdot 225 = 33{,}750$ sq. ft. Its price is $150 \cdot \$250 = \$37{,}500$, which is also about $1.11 per sq. ft.

   At this point, you might ask the class why the price per square foot doesn't seem to change with the lot size. Some students might actually see that this cost rate is tied to the scaling factor used to get the height of the parallelograms. The source of the numerical ratio may not be obvious, however. It's actually the ratio of the diagonal distance back from the shore—the height if the lot were rectangular—to the actual height of the parallelogram $\frac{250}{225} = 1.11\ldots$.

   (e) Area for x feet of shoreline $= 225x$.

4. This is a long story for a short problem. It describes an important, interesting, simple application of SAS to science. The underlying geometric principle here is that SAS guarantees that this triangle is determined. Hence, the given data is enough to determine the distance between the stars. However, the computational techniques learned so far are not enough to find this distance with any efficiency. Some elementary trigonometry makes this job much easier. It is a problem to which you might return after the trigonometry chapter, if students are interested in it.

Chapter 2

NOTES

How do you find the distance between two stars? You can't measure it directly. No one has ever been to another star; no one knows how to build a machine to get there. (But that may be only a matter of time.) So we have to do it from here. First, you need to know the distance from Earth to each of the stars. (A problem in the next section shows you how to do that.) Then you need to know the angle between them when you view them from Earth. For instance, if we want to know the distance between Zuben Eljanubi (pronounced "zoo bin ell juh *noo* bee") and Aldebaran (pronounced "all *deh* buh rahn"), you need to observe each star, get their distances from Earth, and measure the angle between the two sighting lines. (See Display 2.42.) In this case, the angle of separation is 122°, the distance to Zuben Eljanubi is 61 light-years, and the distance to Aldebaran is 60 light-years.

Explain why these measurements are enough information to determine the distance between Zuben Eljanubi and Aldebaran. What geometric principle in this section guarantees that these measurements are enough? Outline as clearly as you can the process of finding this distance. If you can find the distance, do it. If you can't, describe what part(s) of the process you don't yet know how to do.

2.6 Parallelograms and Congruent Triangles

NOTES

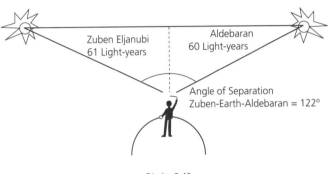

Zuben Eljanubi
61 Light-years

Aldebaran
60 Light-years

Angle of Separation
Zuben-Earth-Aldebaran = 122°

Display 2.42

5. In Chapter 1, you saw that the diagonals of a rhombus are perpendicular bisectors of each other. What about the converse of this statement: If the diagonals of a quadrilateral are perpendicular bisectors of each other, must that quadrilateral be a rhombus? Justify your answer either by giving a counterexample or by proving it (giving a logical argument that works in every case).

(*Hints:* Start by making sure you recall what *rhombus* and *perpendicular bisector* mean. Then sketch what you know about the diagonals. Does that determine the rest of the figure? Can you turn what you see into a logical argument?)

6. Suppose that the perpendicular distance from one of two lines to the other is the same in two different places. Must the lines be parallel? Give a logical argument to justify your answer.

(*Hint:* Draw a diagram of what it would look like if the lines were not parallel. Then label your diagram with letters to help you clarify your thinking and writing.)

Published by IT'S ABOUT TIME, Inc. © 2000 MATHconx, LLC

177

5. This converse is true. Suppose *ABCD* is a quadrilateral with diagonals *AC* and *BD* that meet at a point *E*. If the diagonals are perpendicular bisectors of each other, then all four angles at *E* are right angles, *AE* = *EC,* and *BE* = *ED*. This information determines four right triangles with corresponding legs of equal length. Draw and label a sketch to see this. Thus, all four triangles must be congruent, implying all four hypotenuses (the sides of the quadrilateral) must be congruent. Therefore, the quadrilateral is a rhombus.

6. This is an important application of the angle sum of a triangle. Yes, they must be parallel. Here is an outline of the argument.

   If not, they would meet at some point *P*, as shown in Display 2.14T. Suppose *AB* and *CD* represent the two places where there are equal perpendicular distances; that is, *AB* and *CD* are equally long, and ∠*BAC* and ∠*ACD* are right angles. Draw *BC*. Then

   $$\angle ACB + \angle ABC = 90° = \angle ACB + \angle BCD$$

   so, subtracting ∠*ACB* from both sides, we get ∠*ABC* = ∠*BCD*. Then, by SAS, triangles *ABC* and *DCB* are congruent because *BC* equals itself, so the angles at *D* are right angles. That's the critical idea! Now, if the angles at both *C* and *D* are right angles, then the hypothetical triangle *PCD* would contain two right angles, which is impossible. Hence, the intersection point, *P,* of the two lines can't exist.

   This result provides a theoretical test of whether or not two lines are parallel.

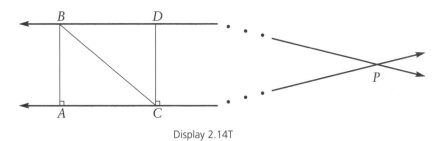

Display 2.14T

2.7 Other Tests for Congruent Triangles

Learning Outcomes

After studying this section, you will be able to:

Find the measures of all sides and all angles of a triangle if you know two angles and one side;

Give examples to show that knowing two sides and an angle *not* between them does not determine a triangle;

Give examples to show that three angles do not determine a triangle;

Describe the relationships between the sides and the angles of an isosceles triangle.

In the previous section you saw that a triangle is determined by any two of its sides and the angle between them. But sometimes only one side of a triangle can be measured. If the angles at either end of it can be measured, too, that's enough to determine the triangle, as you can see from Display 2.43. Because the measures of the angles are known, the other two sides of the triangle must lie along the dotted lines. But two lines that are not parallel must cross at one (and only at one) point; that point is the third vertex of the triangle.

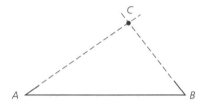

Display 2.43

Here is an example of how this fact can be used.

Two land developers are standing in a flat field at the base of a small mountain. They plan to put a ski lift on the side of the mountain, that is too rugged for a ski trail. To estimate the length of the main cable, they want to know the approximate straight-line distance from the mountaintop to the spot at which they are standing. How can they find out?

2.51

Can you describe a strategy for this problem based on the idea that two angles and the included side determine a triangle? How would you start to attack this problem? Does Display 2.44 help?

178

2.7 Other Tests for Congruent Triangles

This section continues the main theme of the previous one. It establishes the ASA and AAS conditions for determining a triangle (up to congruence), and then asks the students to examine two sets of conditions that do *not* determine a triangle: SSA and AAA.

2.51

This class discussion question should be done before moving on; it does not take long. Its main purpose is to get students focused on the problem and the principle at the same time. Once they look at Display 2.44, the idea should be pretty clear. Even if it's not, don't spend too much time discussing this. The solution is described in detail immediately after this question.

Chapter 2

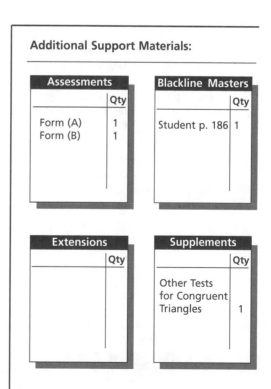

Additional Support Materials:

Assessments	Qty
Form (A)	1
Form (B)	1

Blackline Masters	Qty
Student p. 186	1

Extensions	Qty

Supplements	Qty
Other Tests for Congruent Triangles	1

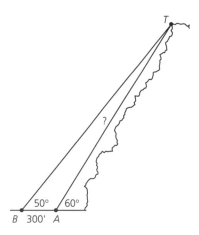

Display 2.44

Does Display 2.44 suggest a strategy to you? Here is the approach we were thinking of when we drew the picture.

- The developers are standing on flat ground at point *A*. Using a surveyor's tool, they can find the angle between the ground and a sight line from *A* to the mountaintop, *T*. That angle measures 60°. They want to know the length of *AT*.

- They move away from the mountain another 300 feet (to point *B*) and measure the angle between the ground and this sight line to the mountaintop; this angle measures 50°.

- Now they know two angles and the included side of a triangle, *ABT*: Side *AB* is 300 feet long, ∠*ABT* measures 50°, and they know the measure of ∠*BAT*, too. What is it? This means that the triangle is determined; they can easily find the approximate length of *AT* just by making a scale drawing and measuring that side.

Finish the developers' problem for them. Find the approximate distance from point *A* to the mountaintop. How close do you think your measured approximation is to the actual distance?

2.52

Published by IT'S ABOUT TIME, Inc. © 2000 MATHconx, LLC

2.52

Students should recognize that ∠*BAT* is 120° because it is the supplement of the 60° angle. This question asks them to do what the preceding description says — make a scale drawing and measure it. It is probably not a good idea to trust the picture in the text; the various sizing steps in the printing process might have distorted it out of scale. Besides, making a drawing from scratch is good practice in scaling. A reasonable scale for measuring is about $\frac{1}{2}$ inch per 100 feet. A fairly careful drawing should produce answers in the range of about 1300 to 1350 feet. The actual length is 1323 feet.

NOTES

Chapter 2

2.7 Other Tests for Congruent Triangles

The ski lift example illustrates that the measures of two angles of a triangle and the included side are enough to determine the size and shape of the triangle. This principle is abbreviated as ASA— which stands for angle-side-angle.

A Fact to Know: (ASA) If two angles and the included side of one triangle have the same measures as two angles and the included side of another triangle, then the triangles are congruent.

....

The ASA principle is the basis for **triangulation**, a location finding process used by surveyors, navigators, search and rescue teams, and others. The following problem shows you how it works for fire wardens in the north woods.

2.53

The lookout towers on Mt. Abraham and Snow Mountain are 29 miles apart. A fire warden in each tower watches for forest fires. When smoke rises above the trees, each warden measures the angle between the direction of the smoke and the line between the two towers. From the two angles and the distance between the towers, the wardens know exactly where to send the firefighters.

1. One day the wardens spot a column of smoke. From Mt. Abraham, the angle to the smoke is 44°. From Snow Mountain, the angle to the smoke is 37°. (See Display 2.45.) Make a scale drawing of the resulting triangle, and measure the approximate straight-line distance from each fire tower to the smoke.

Of course, the wardens don't draw and measure the triangle to find the location of the smoke. They use tools from trigonometry that you haven't learned yet. You can use your graphing calculator and linear equations to find the other vertex of the triangle (the smoke). Start by imagining that Mt. Abraham is at the origin of a coordinate system and Snow Mountain is on the *x*-axis at (29, 0). Refer to Display 2.46 for this setup and the following questions.

2. What is the slope of line L_1? What is its equation?

About Words

The literal meaning of *trigonometry* is measurement of triangles.

180

2.53

In case your students are curious, here's a little more detail about how the sighting is done quickly. In the middle of each tower is a circular map table, marked around the outside in degrees, just like a double protractor. A pointer arm pivots around the center of the table. The warden just points the arm at the smoke and reads the angle at the edge of the table.

1. Drawing and measuring gives students a kinesthetic way to see how ASA determines the other vertex (and hence the other sides and angle) of a triangle. They get to choose and use a measurement scale in a setting where reasonable accuracy makes a difference. They should find that the smoke is about $17\frac{1}{2}$ miles from Mt. Abraham and about $20\frac{1}{4}$ miles from Snow Mountain.

Parts 2–5 relate this material to linear equations and coordinate geometry. They are not critical to a basic understanding of ASA, but they provide a unifying link to **MATH** *Connections* Year 1.

2. The slope of L_1 is TAN (44°). The equation is $y = $ TAN $(44°) \cdot x$, or approximately $y = 0.97x$.

NOTES

Chapter 2

3. What is the slope of line L_2? What is its equation? Be careful; use some common sense here.

4. Graph lines L_1 and L_2 on your calculator. Then use TRACE to find their approximate intersection point.

5. Calculate the distances between this intersection point and the points for the two mountain towers. Do these answers agree (approximately) with your answers to part 1? If not, what explains the difference?

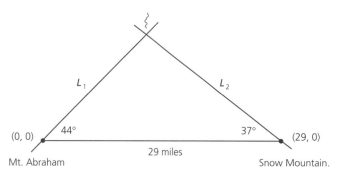

Display 2.45

Display 2.46

3. This slope is TAN (37°) in the negative direction; that is, –TAN (37°), approximately -0.75. To find the equation, plug in (29, 0) and solve for the *y*-intercept.

$$0 = -0.75 \cdot 29 + b$$

This yields *b* = 21.75, so the equation is *y* = -0.75*x* + 21.75.

4. The graph window limits will need to be set to accommodate the picture. You can let your students discover this for themselves, or you can remind them to reset the boundaries. Setting **X** between 0 and 30 and **Y** between 0 and 20 works fine. Graphing *y* = 0.97*x* and *y* = -0.75*x* + 21.75 yields an approximate intersection point of (12.6, 12.2).

5. This is an exercise for the distance formula and the calculator. To one decimal place, the distance between (12.6, 12.2) and (0, 0) is 17.5 (miles) and the distance between (12.6, 12.2) and (29, 0) is 20.4 (miles). Within reasonable limits of roundoff and approximation, these distances should agree with the measured answers for question 1.

NOTES

Chapter 2

If you know the measures of *any* two angles of a triangle, you also know the measure of the third angle, by subtraction. The angle sum of a triangle is 180°, so the measure of the third angle is 180° minus the measures of the other two angles. So, if you know one side and *any* two angles of a triangle, you actually know the angles at each end of the known side. This allows us to extend the ASA principle to a closely related case— often called angle-angle-side.

A Fact to Know: (AAS) If two angles and a side not between them in one triangle have the same measures as the corresponding two angles and a corresponding side in another triangle, then the triangles are congruent.

1. In Display 2.46, what is the measure of the angle at the smoke? How do you know?

2.54

2. A long distance hiker with a cellular phone falls in the woods and badly sprains her ankle. She can see the fire towers at Mt. Abraham and Snow Mountain, but neither warden in either tower can see her. She calls the warden at Snow Mountain and tells him that by using her compass she determined that the angle between her lines of sight to these two towers is about 105° and that she is directly between the Snow Mountain tower and a third fire tower that both she and the warden can see.

   (a) The Snow Mountain warden knows that the Mt. Abraham tower is 29 miles away. How can the warden figure out where to send the paramedics?

   (b) The angle between the sight lines from Snow Mountain to the Mt. Abraham tower and to the tower beyond the hiker is 60°. By making a scale drawing, locate the hiker by finding how far she is from each tower.

State a congruence principle that you think would be abbreviated as SSA. Look at Display 2.47; then explain how this figure shows that SSA is *not* a valid principle for determining a triangle. How close can you come to determining a triangle using SSA?

2.55

Published by IT'S ABOUT TIME, Inc. © 2000 MATHconx, LLC

2.54

The first question just illustrates the subtraction process. The second question shows how the AAS information for a triangle easily converts to an ASA determination of the triangle.

1. $180° - (44° + 37°) = 99°$

2. (a) The Snow Mountain warden needs to measure the angle between his sight lines to Mt. Abraham and to the third tower (which is directly in line with the hiker). Then, by subtracting that angle and the hiker's 105° angle from 180°, he will have the angle from Mt. Abraham to the hiker. Now the problem is an ASA problem, just like 2.53.

    (b) $180° - (105° + 60°) = 15°$. Choose a convenient scale and draw a base line to represent the 29 miles between the Snow Mountain and Mt. Abraham towers. Draw lines at 60° and 15° angles, respectively, from the two towers. Then measure the distances to their intersection point. Your students should find that the hiker is approximately 26 miles from Mt. Abraham and 8 miles from Snow Mountain. Note that it doesn't matter which side of the base line you use for this drawing; the distances come out the same on either side. In real life, the appropriate side would be obvious from the relative positions of the fire towers.

Problem 2 at the end of this section extends this example by asking students to compute these distances using their calculators and linear equations, as was done for 2.53.

2.55

The SSA principle would be something like this.

> If two sides and an angle not between them in one triangle have the same measures as the corresponding two sides and angle in another triangle, then the triangles are congruent.

Display 2.47 shows that it is not valid. If you treat $\angle A$, side AB (of length 10, for example), and another side BC (of length 7, for example) as given, then the figure shows that BC could be in either of two positions to form a triangle. *But that's all!* That is, if you know side side angle, then the triangle must be one or the other of only two possible sizes and shapes (up to congruence).

You know the SSS principle, that the lengths of all three sides determine exactly one triangular shape and size. What about AAA? Does knowing the three angles determine the size and shape of a triangle?

2.56

Choose three angle sizes that add to 180°. Then, using a protractor and a ruler, draw four triangles that have these angle sizes. Make the triangles as different as you can. Then do it again—pick three other angle sizes that add to 180° and draw four more triangles.

Write a paragraph describing what you observe, and propose a general principle for AAA. Explain how your principle relates to the triangles you drew.

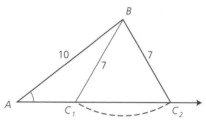

Display 2.47

In Chapter 1 you examined isosceles and equilateral triangles, using symmetry. You also worked with a straightedge (an unmarked ruler) and a compass to make accurate drawings. We're going to take another look at these things, but from a different point of view. We'll use just a ruler and a compass to construct these figures and explore their properties.

Why just a ruler and a compass? Because they're *simple.* Often, the simpler the tools you use, the clearer the underlying ideas become. In fact, we won't even use the markings on the ruler, just the straightness of its edge. We don't need to bother with measuring lengths or angles. All we really need are tools for making straight lines and circles. (If you're stuck on a desert island with just a board and a piece of string, you can still scratch these figures in the sand!) Using these tools, you'll be able to see clearly how the angle properties of isosceles and equilateral triangles relate to the principles of this section.

Thinking Tip

Take a simple approach.
Using simple, basic tools to attack a question sometimes reveals its connections to other ideas. Even when they don't work, seeing why not can be helpful.

183

2.56

This can be made into a discussion question if you don't want to assign it as writing. One way or another, it is important as a precursor to later work in this chapter for the students to see that the angles determine shape, but not size. That is, they should come to see that a reasonable statement of AAA is.

If the three angles of one triangle have the same measures as the three angles of another triangle, then the triangles are similar.

The observation of this exercise is not as trivial as it may appear. In fact, this property is characteristic of Euclidean geometry, *but not of the non-Euclidean geometries*, which are described in **MATH** *Connections* Year 3. In the non-Euclidean geometries, AAA *is* a valid congruence test!

NOTES

Chapter 2

Let's begin with isosceles triangles. Recall that a triangle is **isosceles** if two of its sides have the same length. Often an isosceles triangle is drawn with the third side at the bottom, and that side is called the **base**. Display 2.48 shows an isosceles triangle. The base is *RS*; the sides *RT* and *ST* are equal in length. The dashes form the line of symmetry. If you fold the triangle along the line of symmetry, the equal sides will match, and vertices *R* and *S* will match.

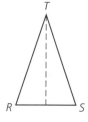

Display 2.48

2.57

Use a straightedge and a compass to draw an isosceles triangle without measuring, like this.

- Use your straightedge to make two line segments that meet at a point. Call that point *A*.
- Put the point of your compass at *A*, and draw a circular arc that intersects both line segments. Call these intersection points *B* and *C*.
- Connect *B* and *C* by a line segment.
1. Which two sides of △*ABC* are the same length? How do you know?

Now construct the line of symmetry, like this.

- Put your compass pivot point at *B*, make the compass opening span more than halfway to *C*, and draw a circle.
- Without changing the compass opening, move the pivot point to *C*, and draw a circle.
- Pick one of the two intersection points of the two circles and call it *D*. (The point farther from *A* will probably be easier to work with, but it doesn't really matter.)
- Draw the line *AD*.
2. Is *AD* *really* the line of symmetry? How can you be sure?

In the previous question, we said that *AD* is the line of symmetry for your isosceles triangle, △*ABC*. That is, *AD* divides △*ABC* into two congruent halves. How can we be so sure? After all, different people in your class started by drawing

184

2.57

This discussion of isosceles triangles is important for two reasons. First, it establishes by a logical argument the basic result that isosceles triangles have congruent base angles, and vice versa. This revisits a fact described by symmetry in Chapter 1. Second, the combination of the text presentation and the questions for the students encompasses applications of SSS, SAS, and AAS, all within a single context.

The triangle construction is straightforward and easy. It prepares the way for the construction of an angle bisector, the line of symmetry *AD*. This diagram will be used to derive the equal base angles result for isosceles triangles. The first important (obvious?) construction principle here is that the arc intersects the segments at points that are equidistant from *A*. *AB* and *AC* are radii of the same circle; the compass opening doesn't change; etc. The same idea justifies the important statement in the text right after this construction that *BD* and *CD* have the same length.

The final questions, "Is *AD really* the line of symmetry? How can you be sure?" are intended to focus students on the need to provide some justification for the claim. If they suggest folding their papers along that line to see if the triangle is symmetric, that's fine. It indicates that they understand what a line of symmetry is. Nevertheless, it might be well to suggest that a more accurate verification would be welcome. That's the point of the next material.

Chapter 2

NOTES

different angles, and this was written long before any of you drew your diagrams. We couldn't know in advance exactly what your triangle would look like, yet we predicted that *AD* would work for you. Here's how we knew.

In your diagram, draw segments *BD* and *CD*. Then label as *E* the crossing point of *AD* and *BC*. Now your diagram should look like Display 2.49. It might be turned differently, and it might be fatter or thinner than our diagram, but the letters show you how your diagram should match up with ours.

Do you remember how point *D* was constructed? What guarantees that *BD* and *CD* have the same length? Now look at the other sides of $\triangle ABD$ and $\triangle ACD$. Sides *AB* and *AC* have the same length because the original triangle was made that way, and side *AD* is common to both triangles. Therefore, by SSS, $\triangle ABD$ and $\triangle ACD$ are congruent. This means that

$$\angle BAD = \angle CAD$$

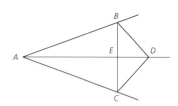

Display 2.49

That is, *AD* divides $\angle A$ exactly in half. That's why *AD* is called the **angle bisector** of $\angle A$.

Now look again at how *AD* divides the original isosceles triangle, $\triangle ABC$, into $\triangle ABE$ and $\triangle ACE$. Sides *AB* and *AC* are equal in length (why?), and side *AE* is common to both triangles. We know that $\angle BAD$ and $\angle CAD$ have the same measure (see above), so $\triangle ABE$ and $\triangle ACE$ must be congruent (by what principle from this section?). In other words, *AD* is the line of symmetry for the original isosceles triangle, $\triangle ABC$.

2.58 *AB* and *AC* are equal in length because they were constructed as the equal sides of an isosceles triangle. The congruence of $\triangle ABE$ and $\triangle ACE$ follows from SAS.

NOTES

We didn't do all that work just to convince you that we had the right line of symmetry all along. An important result follows from what we just did. In an isosceles triangle, the angles opposite the two equal sides are called the **base angles** of the triangle. In Display 2.49, the base angles of $\triangle ABC$ are $\angle ABE$ and $\angle ACE$. Because the two triangles formed by the angle bisector are congruent, we know that

The base angles of an isosceles triangle are equal.

The converse of this statement is also true. That is,

A triangle that has two equal angles *must* be isosceles.

Problem 5 at the end of this section asks you to prove that this is true. Think about it.

These facts about isosceles triangles apply easily to the special case of equilateral triangles. Since all three sides of an equilateral triangle have the same measure, we can apply the equal base angles idea to the angles opposite any two sides. Doing this twice (with different pairs of sides) tells us that all three angles must have the same measure. You can also see this from the triangle's three axes of symmetry. Since the angle sum of any triangle is 180°, each angle of an equilateral triangle must be 60°.

2.59

Write a detailed explanation of why all three angles of an equilateral triangle must be equal. Start with an equilateral triangle, $\triangle ABC$, and lead your reader step by step to the conclusion that $\angle A = \angle B = \angle C$.

A review of congruence tests for triangles.

• **SSS.** If the three sides of one triangle have the same lengths as the three sides of another triangle, then the triangles are congruent.

• **SAS.** If two sides and the included angle of one triangle have the same measures as two sides and the included angle of another triangle, then the triangles are congruent.

• **ASA.** If two angles and the included side of one triangle have the same measures as two angles and the included side of another triangle, then the triangles are congruent.

• **AAS.** If two angles and a side not between them in one triangle have the same measures as the corresponding two angles and a corresponding side in another triangle, then the triangles are congruent.

Published by IT'S ABOUT TIME, Inc. © 2000 MATHconx, LLC

2.59

This can be done either by a symmetry argument or by expanding on the isosceles triangle approach outlined in the previous paragraph. In the latter case, something like this, accompanied by an appropriate diagram, would be desirable.

△ABC is equilateral, so AB and AC have the same length. By the result for isosceles triangles, ∠B = ∠C. But AC and BC also have the same length, so ∠A = ∠B. Putting these two equalities together, we have

$$\angle A = \angle B = \angle C$$

A GAME (an in class, reinforcement, small group activity)

Here is a game, which can be set up as a team competition, for reviewing and reinforcing the basic principles for determining triangles. It involves some preparation on your part the first time you plan to use it, and a little in class scorekeeping. You will need to make up several triangle data sets, at least one set for each team. A triangle data set consists of 12 cards, containing these facts about a specific triangle, ABC.

- the 3 side measures
- the 3 angle measures
- the 3 altitudes
- perimeter
- area
- triangle type: isosceles, equilateral, or scalene (which you may have to define in class)

We have supplied two 8.5 × 11 inch sample sheets of data-set templates that can be photocopied onto heavy paper or card stock and cut apart.

Notes
- The element of chance in this game allows you to use data sets more than once for different teams. You could even play the game a number of times on different days, so that each team gets to use each data set.

- The term **scalene triangle** is not in the text, but it has been used on the data cards as a triangle type. It denotes a triangle with all sides of different length.

- For classes that show some interest in probability, some interesting questions arise here about the likelihood that the first two (or three or four) cards drawn will be enough to determine a particular triangle.

Rules
1. Each team starts with 700 points.
2. Each team is assigned a triangle data set controlled by you, the teacher.
3. The object of the game is to determine the triangle of the data set by spending as few points as possible. Determine means specify all sides and all angles, at least to within 0.1 of the measure units.

Problem Set: 2.7

1. For each part,
   - If you think the given facts determine a triangle, draw it.
   - If you think the given facts can be true for more than one triangle, draw at least two non-congruent triangles that fit these facts.
   - If you think that no triangle fits the given facts, explain why.

   (a) A triangle with sides 4, 7, and 5 cm.

   (b) A triangle with sides 3, 4, and 7 cm.

   (c) A triangle with sides 5 cm and 7 cm, and a 30° angle.

   (d) A right triangle with two 5 inch legs.

   (e) A right triangle; two of its sides are 8 cm and 10 cm.

   (f) An isosceles right triangle with hypotenuse 13 cm and a 50° angle.

   (g) An isosceles triangle containing angles of 50° and 80° and a 12 cm side.

   (h) An isosceles triangle containing angles of 50° and 60° and a 10 cm side.

   (i) An isosceles right triangle with a hypotenuse of 15 cm.

2. Earlier in this section you were asked to find the distance of an injured hiker from the Mt. Abraham and Snow Mountain lookout towers by making a scale drawing. Check the results of your drawing by using a coordinate system, writing two linear equations to describe the sight lines from the hiker to the towers, and using the TRACE function of your graphing calculator to find where the graph lines cross.

3. How far away is the star you saw last night? We can't travel there and measure the distance, so we have to be able to measure it from here. We *can* measure the angle made with the Earth's surface when we sight the star and the angle made again six months later, when the Earth is on the opposite side of its orbit. These two Earth orbit points and the star form an isosceles triangle (approximately). (Display 2.50) The base of this large triangle measures about 186,000,000 miles across. Orbits are nearly ellipses, so their bisector length changes with time, but we can choose sighting times for which this is approximately true. Then, using ASA, we can derive the distance between our solar system and the star, like this.

Published by IT'S ABOUT TIME, Inc. © 2000 MATHconx, LLC

187

4. The game proceeds in rounds. In the first round, each team chooses, at random, two cards from its data set. In each successive round, each team draws, at random, a card from its data set. After each draw, the team then gets some time (amount set in advance by you) to see if they have enough information to determine the triangle.

5. The first two cards drawn are free. Each subsequent card drawn by a team costs it points, as follows.

   3rd–10 pts,   4th–20 pts,   5th–30 pts,   etc.

6. A proposed wrong answer—an inaccurate determination of its triangle—costs the team 50 points.

7. The game is over when each team has determined its triangle. The team with the most points left wins.

Problem Set: 2.7

1. (a) Yes (SSS)
   (b) No triangle; 3 + 4 = 7
   (c) Two triangles: (1) 30°, 14°, 136°; sides 5, 2.4, 7;
       or (2) 30°, 116°, 44°; sides 5, 9, 7
   (d) Yes (SAS)
   (e) Two triangles: sides 6, 8, 10 or 8, 10, 12.8
   (f) No; you can't have a triangle with angles 50°, 50°, and 90°.
   (g) Two triangles; the 12 cm side could be the base or one of the congruent sides
   (h) No triangle; 50 + 50 + 60 ≠ 180 and 60 + 60 + 50 ≠ 180
   (i) Yes (ASA)

2. This refers to 2.54. The equations are $y = (\tan 15°)x$ and $y = -(\tan 60°)x + 50.23$. The equations can be used in this form or with a decimal approximation of the TAN values. Either way, the distances are 26.0 mi. from Mt. Abraham and 7.8 mi. from Snow Mountain.

3. This is a real world application of ASA. It also gives students practice in dealing with very large numbers and situations in which roundoff must be done with care and common sense.

Chapter 2

- For a particular star, suppose that the angle in June is 89.9999°. The angle measured in December is 89.9999°. (Notice that rounding off these measurements is *not* appropriate here.)

- The distance between the measurements (across the Earth's orbit around the Sun) is 186,000,000 miles. Half of this (93,000,000 miles) is the distance from either base angle to the perpendicular bisector of the base. This distance times TAN of the angle (89.9999° in this case) is the perpendicular distance from the center of the base to the opposite vertex. That perpendicular distance is the distance between our Sun and that star.

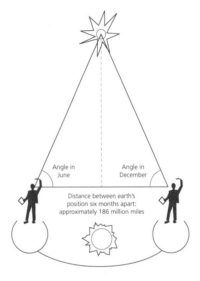

Display 2.50

(a) What is the approximate distance, in miles, between our Sun and this star?

(b) Light can travel 5,865,696,000,000 miles in a year; this length is called a **light-year**. How many light-years away from our Sun is this star?

(c) In June or December, approximately how many miles away from Earth is this star? How many light-years?

(d) Similar sightings are taken for another star, at different months (a half-year apart). Each angle is 89.99995°, and the Earth-orbit diameter for these months is

188

(a) In this case, tan(89.9999) = 572,957.8. Rounded off, we get

$$572{,}958 \cdot 93{,}000{,}000 = 53{,}285{,}094{,}000{,}000 \text{ miles}$$

(b) To find out how many light-years away the star is, just divide.

$$\frac{53{,}285{,}094{,}000{,}000}{5{,}865{,}696{,}000{,}000} = 9.08$$

That is, the star is 9.08 light-years away from our Sun.

(c) The answers are the same as the distance from the Sun, within roundoff error. The Pythagorean Theorem can be used to check the figures. The length of one leg of the right triangle is the distance from the Sun to the star; the length of the other leg is half the diameter of the Earth's orbit. This second length is so much shorter than the first that the difference it makes in the Pythagorean Theorem computation is swallowed up by the roundoff error.

(d) 105,424,234,300,000 miles; 17.97 light-years

(e) 655,320,478,200,000 miles; 111.72 light-years

Chapter 2

NOTES

184,000,000 miles. In miles and light-years, how far away is the star?

(e) Similar sightings are taken for a third star, at different months (a half-year apart). This time each angle is 89.999992°, and the Earth-orbit diameter for these months is 183,000,000 miles. In miles and light-years, how far away is the star?

4. One night in 1798, Captain Hardtack was sailing his American privateer northward, parallel to the east coast of Spanish Florida. To avoid the risk of capture by the Spanish, he had to stay out of their territorial waters, which extended 3 miles from shore. To check his location, Captain Hardtack sighted the beacon at Lighthouse Point at a 30° angle to the west of his course. (Display 2.51.) One mile further on, he sighted the same beacon at a 36° angle west of his course. Was he in Spanish waters or in international waters? How far offshore was he?

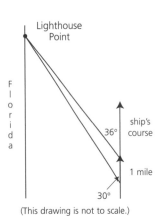

Lighthouse Point

Florida

36°

ship's course

1 mile

30°

(This drawing is not to scale.)

Display 2.51

5. Suppose you have a triangle, $\triangle ABC$, in which $\angle A = \angle B$. Justify the claim that $\triangle ABC$ must be isosceles. (*Hint:* Draw an angle bisector and think about the AAS principle.)

4. The person and event in this problem are fictitious. Hardtack is a hard, flour and water biscuit that was used on old sailing ships. However, the historical and geographical details are accurate. Eastern Florida was Spanish (again) in 1798, there is a place called Lighthouse Point between Boca Raton and Fort Lauderdale where the east coast runs almost directly north-south, and the internationally recognized territorial water limit at that time was 3 miles, the outer limit of a cannon shot.

This problem can be solved approximately by drawing a diagram to scale, but the results probably will not be very satisfying. Even a very careful drawing probably will not show conclusively whether or not the ship is within 3 miles of the shore. That distance is measured perpendicular to the shoreline. A definitive answer requires some computation. A calculator assisted approach like that used for 2.53 and for problem 2 will work.

Perhaps the most creative part of finding such a solution is the first step, choosing a convenient coordinate system. The choice most like what was done for 2.53 is to make the ship's course the x-axis, with $(0, 0)$ the point of the first sighting, as shown in Display 2.15T. Then the equations for the two sight lines are $y = (\tan 30°)x$ and $y = (\tan 36°)x - \tan 36°$. Your students can use two place decimal approximations, if they prefer: $y = 0.58x$ and $y = 0.73x – 0.73$) GRAPH and TRACE on the calculator to find the approximate crossing point $(4.8, 2.8$. These are the coordinates of Lighthouse Point in Display 2.15T. This y-coordinate is the perpendicular distance from the ship to the Florida coast, as the diagram illustrates. Thus, Captain Hardtack's ship is only 2.8 miles off the coast; it is within Spanish territorial waters.

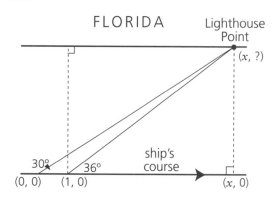

This diagram is not to scale.

Display 2.15T

5. Draw the bisector of $\angle C$, and let D be the point where it crosses side AB. Then

$$\angle ACD = \angle BCD$$

Since by hypothesis $\angle A = \angle B$, and CD is a side common to both triangular halves, the AAS principle applies to triangles CAD and CBD. The congruence of these triangles guarantees that $CA = CB$, so triangle ABC is isosceles.

2.8 Other Polygons

Learning Outcomes

After studying this section, you will be able to:

Describe the size and shape of a polygon by using triangulation;

Find the sum of the interior angles and the sum of the exterior angles of any polygon;

Compute the measures of the interior and exterior angles of regular polygons.

There are lots of different types and shapes of polygons. The simplest ones are triangles. Yet we have spent two sections studying them. Did you wonder why? The answer is back in Chapter 1. Do you remember what triangulation was about? Its key idea is,

Any polygonal region can be divided into nonoverlapping triangular regions by adding nonintersecting line segments between vertices of the polygon.

2.60

1. Draw a 2 inch by 3 inch rectangle. Triangulate it in as many different ways as you can. How many ways are there? How many triangles do you get each time?

2. Draw a pentagon that looks like home plate on a baseball diamond. Triangulate it. How many triangles do you get? How many different triangulations of this pentagon are there?

Home Plate

To keep things simple, we'll look mainly at polygons with no reflex angles (polygons in which every angle measures less than 180°). Such polygons are called **convex**. We will eventually get to formulas that apply to *all* polygons. Generalizing our approach to include non-convex polygons will be left as a discussion question for you later.

A polygon with more than three sides can be triangulated in different ways. But, no matter how you do it, the size and shape of the polygon is determined by the size and shape of its triangular pieces. (If you attach to any polygonal frame enough diagonal cross-pieces to triangulate it, the frame will be rigid.) In short, knowing about triangles tells you a lot about other types of polygons.

Here's an example of how this works. Recall the "SSS" test for congruence: When you know the lengths of all three

190

2.8 Other Polygons

The main purpose of this section is to show how triangulation allows shape and size features of polygons to be derived from triangle congruence facts. We establish the formula for computing the sum of the interior angles of a polygon, along with the fact that the sum of the exterior angles is always 360°. These two facts are used to derive formulas for computing the measure of the interior and exterior angles of regular polygons. These ideas will be used in the development of properties of circles in a later chapter.

2.60

1. There are only two ways to triangulate the rectangle, one for each diagonal. In each way the result is two triangles.

2. There are five different triangulations of a (convex) pentagon. There are five different ways to draw a first triangle, and two different triangulations of the remaining quadrilateral. However, these ten different processes only result in five different triangulations, each one obtained from two different starting triangles.

Chapter 2

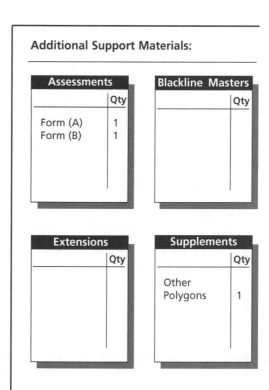

Additional Support Materials:

Assessments	Qty
Form (A)	1
Form (B)	1

Blackline Masters	Qty

Extensions	Qty

Supplements	Qty
Other Polygons	1

sides of a triangle, you know its shape. Do you think that there is an SSSS test for congruence of quadrilaterals?

> **What would it mean to say that a quadrilateral is determined by SSSS? Explain how Display 2.52 shows that the "SSSS test" doesn't work.**

2.61

Display 2.52

As you see, knowing the lengths of four sides does not determine a convex quadrilateral. You can make many different shapes by changing the angles between the sides. But what if *one* of the angles is also fixed? Is that enough information to determine the quadrilateral? The answer is yes, as you'll see from the following description.

Suppose you know the lengths of all the sides of a convex quadrilateral *ABCD*, the order in which they occur, and the measure of one angle, say ∠*A*, as in Display 2.53(a). Then triangulation shows that the measures of *all* the other angles are determined!

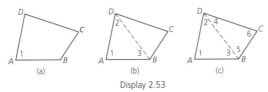

Display 2.53

Here's how.

- Triangulate *ABCD* by drawing segment *BD*.

- You know the lengths of sides *AB* and *AD* and the measure of the angle between them, so △*ABD* is determined by SAS. Therefore the length of *BD* is determined, along with the measures of ∠*ABD* and ∠*ADB*. These are marked as ∠2 and ∠3 in Display 2.53(b).

- Now, since you know the lengths of *BD*, *BC*, and *CD*, △*BCD* is determined by SSS. This means that the measures of ∠*BDC*, ∠*CBD*, and ∠*BCD* are determined. These are marked as ∠4, ∠5, and ∠6 in Display 2.53(c).

- One of the other three angles of the quadrilateral is ∠6. The measures of the other two come from adding ∠2 + ∠4 and ∠3 + ∠5. This means that the quadrilateral is determined (up to congruence).

Published by IT'S ABOUT TIME, Inc. © 2000 MATHconx, LLC

191

2.61

Saying that a quadrilateral is determined by SSSS would mean that lengths of the four sides of a quadrilateral determine its shape. Display 2.52 provides a counterexample. It shows that a rectangle can be squeezed into thinner and thinner parallelograms without changing the lengths of its sides.

NOTES

Chapter 2

a
2.62

Explain why a strong diagonal brace across one corner of a screen door will make the entire door rigid.

2.63

1. Suppose you know the lengths of all the sides of a pentagon and the order in which they occur. How many angles do you have to know to determine the pentagon? One? Two? More? Explain.

2. There is a pattern here, starting with triangles, then quadrilaterals, then pentagons. State the next step in the pattern as precisely as you can. Then try to justify your statement.

Triangulation leads to another interesting, useful property of polygons. We know that the angle sum of any triangle is 180°. We can use this fact and triangulation to show that the angle sum of a polygon is determined by the number of its vertices, according to a simple formula.

b
2.64

1. Draw a convex pentagon (any way you want). Call its vertices *A*, *B*, *C*, *D*, and *E*. Then triangulate your pentagon by drawing diagonals from *A*. How many triangles do you get?

2. What is the sum of the angles in *all* the triangles? Is each angle of each triangle at a vertex of the pentagon? What is the angle sum of the pentagon?

3. Draw a convex hexagon (any way you want). Call its vertices *A*, *B*, *C*, *D*, *E*, and *F*. Then triangulate your hexagon by drawing diagonals from *A*. How many triangles do you get?

4. What is the sum of the angles in *all* the triangles? Is each angle of each triangle at a vertex of the hexagon? What is the angle sum of the hexagon?

Published by IT'S ABOUT TIME, Inc. © 2000 MATHconx, LLC

2.62

A screen door is a quadrilateral (a rectangle) with fixed side lengths. A diagonal brace across one corner will fix the angle at that corner. By the triangulation argument above, this specifies the other three angles, thereby making the quadrilateral rigid.

2.63

Triangulation is the key to these questions.

1. One angle is not enough (try it), but two will determine a pentagon. There are two slightly different cases to consider, depending on whether or not the two known angles occur at adjacent vertices.

   (a) If not, then draw the diagonal across one angle to make a triangle. This triangle is determined by SAS, so the length of its third side (the diagonal you drew) is fixed. That side and the remaining three sides of the pentagon form a quadrilateral with one known angle, which is determined by the result in the text.

   (b) If the angles are adjacent, the same argument applies, except that the known angle of the remaining quadrilateral is obtained by subtracting one of the angles of the triangle from the second of the original known angles.

2. If you know the lengths of all the sides of a hexagon and three of its angles, then the hexagon is determined. As in question 1, draw a diagonal to form a triangle that includes one of the known angles. That triangle is determined, so the length of the diagonal is fixed. The diagonal and the remaining four sides form a pentagon with two known angles (one of them by subtraction, perhaps), and that pentagon is determined, by question 1.

2.64

Take some time to work through these questions with your students. The general pattern should emerge easily from the pentagon and hexagon examples. Display 2.16T exemplifies the kind of diagrams the students should be drawing for these examples, but the polygons they draw need not be so symmetric. In fact, it's good for them to see from the variety of their own drawings that the argument does not depend on how nice the polygon is.

The dodecagon question is intended to get students to recognize and use the numerical pattern *without* drawing anything; that's why the number of sides is so annoyingly large!

1. See Display 2.16T. Three triangles.

2. The sum of all the angles is $3 \cdot 180° = 540°$, which is the angle sum of the pentagon because the vertex of each angle of each triangle is also a vertex of the pentagon.

3. See Display 2.16T. Four triangles.

4. The sum of all the angles is $4 \cdot 180° = 720°$, which is the angle sum of the hexagon because the vertex of each angle of each triangle is also a vertex of the hexagon.

Chapter 2

5. Suppose you were to triangulate a convex dodecagon (a twelve-sided polygon) by drawing diagonals from one vertex. How many triangles would you get? What would be the angle sum of the dodecagon?

6. Can you see a general formula for the angle sum of an *n*-sided polygon? Try to write one down, as precisely as you can. Check your formula to see if it holds for triangles ($n = 3$) and quadrilaterals ($n = 4$).

Let's look carefully at the key ideas behind the questions you just worked through:

- When you triangulate a polygon, every angle of each triangle is part of some angle of the polygon, and there is no overlap. Thus, the angle sum of the polygon is the same as the sum of the angles of *all* the triangles—the number of triangles times 180°.

- If a convex polygon is triangulated with diagonals from a single vertex, the number of triangles depends only on the number of vertices, not on the shape of the polygon.

- From a single vertex, *A*, you can draw diagonals to every other vertex except the two vertices immediately on either side of *A*. Thus, if the polygon has *n* vertices, you can draw $n - 3$ diagonals. (Did you draw 2 diagonals in your pentagon and 3 diagonals in your hexagon?)

- As you draw the diagonals from *A* to successive vertices around the polygon, each one cuts out a single triangle. The last diagonal drawn cuts out its triangle from a quadrilateral, making one extra triangle. In other words, you get $n - 3$ triangles (one for each diagonal) plus one more a total of $n - 2$ triangles. Putting all these ideas together, we get:

A Fact to Know: The angle sum of an *n*-sided polygon is
$$(n - 2) \cdot 180°$$

5. You would get ten triangles. The angle sum of the dodecagon is
   $10 \cdot 180° = 1800°$, the angle sum of the ten triangles.

6. The angle sum of a convex *n*-gon is $(n - 2) \cdot 180°$.

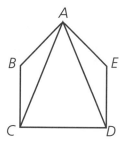 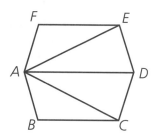

Display 2.16T

NOTES

2.65 The angle-sum formula is true for all *n*-sided polygons, but our explanation only works for convex polygons. How can the justification be extended to include nonconvex polygons?

Hint: Try drawing an example of a simple case. Can you use a diagonal to cut a nonconvex polygon into convex polygons? How do the angle sums of the pieces relate to the angle sum of the whole thing?

The angles we have been talking about are the ones that open to the inside of the polygon, of course. These are called the **interior angles** of the polygon. When we talk about the angle sum of a polygon, we mean the sum of the interior angles. Sometimes it is useful to look at the angle formed by one side of a polygon and the extension of a side next to it. This is called an **exterior angle**. (Display 2.54.)

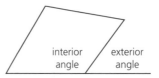

interior angle   exterior angle

Display 2.54

Imagine yourself walking around the perimeter of a convex polygon. The measure of an exterior angle is the amount you have to turn when you turn the corner at a vertex. For instance, if you're walking along side *AB* of the pentagon in Display 2.55 (from *A* to *B*), ∠1 is the amount you have to turn at *B* to get onto side *BC*.

2.66 Suppose you are walking along a convex polygon. As you go around it, how much do you have to turn to get back onto the side you started from? That is, what is your total number of degrees of turning? Does the number of vertices matter? (Display 2.55 might help you to visualize this.)

Published by IT'S ABOUT TIME, Inc. © 2000 MATHconx, LLC

2.65

This question can be omitted, if you wish. A rigorous, general argument is quite difficult at this level, but getting a general idea of how it works isn't too bad. The basic principle is to (1) cut the nonconvex polygon into convex pieces and use the formula on the convex pieces, and then (2) show that, when the pieces are reassembled, the arithmetic works just right.

For instance, suppose a hexagon *ABCDEF* has a reflex angle, $\angle A$, and that the diagonal *AD* cuts the hexagon into two convex quadrilaterals, *ABCD* and *ADEF*. Notice that the sum of the angles of these two quadrilaterals equals the angle sum of the original hexagon. Notice also that the side *AD* is counted twice, once in each quadrilateral. That is, the diagonal that separates the original polygon into two pieces actually adds 2 when the sides of the pieces are counted separately. Using the formula on the two convex quadrilaterals, we get the angle sum

$$(4 - 2) \cdot 180° + (4 - 2) \cdot 180° = 4 \cdot 180°$$

which equals $(6 - 2) \cdot 180°$, the result of applying the formula to the hexagon.

In general, you can think of such a polygon as having $m + n$ sides before it is subdivided, and then the insertion of the diagonal from the reflex angle adds one side to each piece, so that you have two convex polygons of size $m + 1$ and $n + 1$, respectively. Applying the formula to these two convex polygons, you get

$$(m + 1 - 2) \cdot 180° + (n + 1 - 2) \cdot 180°$$

which simplifies to $(m + n - 2) \cdot 180°$, as required.

The reasoning illustrated by this example can be extended to a proof of the general case, but that is well beyond the scope of this book.

2.66

The sum of the exterior angles of a polygon should become obvious as the students answer this question. To go around the polygon once and get back facing in the direction you started from, you need to make a full circle turn, 360°. The number of vertices (the number of corners you turn) doesn't matter. It's that simple. You might have students draw a polygon of their choice and then move a ruler around its sides, following the idea illustrated by Display 2.55.

Chapter 2

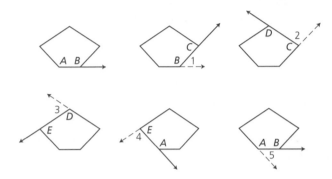

Display 2.55

If you walk around a typical city block, you make four 90° turns to get back to your original direction, a total of 360°. If you walk a convex polygonal path around a statue, it takes you the same total amount of turning to get back to your original direction, no matter how many corners you turn. This should make the following fact easy to remember.

A Fact to Know: The sum of the exterior angles of any convex polygon is 360°.

Here's a slightly more formal explanation of the exterior angle sum—one that doesn't depend on imagining that you're walking around a diagram. The interior and exterior angles at a vertex are supplementary (see Display 2.54). That is, their sum is 180°. So if we sum the interior-exterior pairs for all the vertices of an n-sided polygon, the total is $n \cdot 180°$. But the interior angles add to $(n-2) \cdot 180°$, so the exterior angles must add to the rest. That's 360°, no matter what n is.

If all the sides of a polygon have the same length and all its angles have the same measure, we call that polygon *regular*. An equilateral triangle is an example of a regular polygon.

2.67

1. What is the measure of an interior angle of an equilateral triangle? What is the measure of one of its exterior angles? How do you know?

2. What is the measure of an interior angle of a square? What is the measure of one of its exterior angles? How do you know?

195

2.67

This leads to the final two formulas of the section, which the students should be able to discover on their own. They are stated in the text to summarize the patterns suggested by these questions.

1. This is a reminder that the measure of an angle in an equilateral triangle is found by dividing 180° by 3. This same reasoning extends to exterior angles: Dividing 360° by 3 tells us that the measure of each exterior angle is 120°. Another way to derive the same exterior angle measure is to recall that each exterior angle is the supplement of an interior angle and subtract 60° from 180°.

2. All interior angles of a square measure 90°. Students probably already know this without doing any computation. Relating this answer to the fact that it is $\frac{1}{4}$ of $(4 - 2) \cdot 180°$ might serve to reinforce the formula, but it is not essential at this point. They should see that each exterior angle is also 90°.

Chapter 2

NOTES

2.8 Other Polygons

3. What is the measure of an interior angle of a regular pentagon? What is the measure of one of its exterior angles? How do you know?

4. What is the measure of an interior angle of a regular polygon with 100 sides? What is the measure of one of its exterior angles? How do you know?

5. What patterns do you see here?

Since all n interior angles of a regular n-sided polygon must be equal, the measure of any one of them can be found by dividing the sum of the interior angles by n. That is,

The measure of an interior angle of a regular

$$n\text{-gon} = \frac{(n-2) \cdot 180°}{n}$$

Since all n exterior angles of a regular n-sided polygon must be equal, the measure of any one of them can be found by dividing the sum of the exterior angles by n. That is:

The measure of an exterior angle of a regular n-gon $= \frac{360°}{n}$.

 2.68 Display 2.56 is an illustration from a woodworking book. How are the angle cuts shown there related to their corresponding geometric shapes? How are they related to interior or exterior angles?

Miter box settings, left and right, for making various geometric constructions *(Stanley Tools)*

→ 60°   60° ←   3 Sides

→ 30°   30° ←   6 Sides

→ 45°   45° ←   4 Sides

→ 22.5°   22.5° ←   8 Sides

→ 36°   36° ←   5 Sides

→ 15°   15° ←   12 Sides

From page 203 of *Complete Book of Woodworking*, by Rosario Capotosto (New York: Harper & Row, 1975).

Display 2.56

196

3. This case probably will require students to use either the formula for the interior angle sum or the exterior angle sum. In the former case, the measure of an interior angle of a regular pentagon is $\frac{1}{5}$ of $(5 - 2) \cdot 180°$, which is 108°. The measure of an exterior angle is the supplement of that, 72°, which can also be found as $\frac{1}{5}$ of 360°.

4. This part forces formula use. The measure of an interior angle is

$$\frac{(100 - 2) \cdot 180°}{100} = 176.4°$$

The measure of an exterior angle is the supplement of that, 3.6°. Alternatively, students might compute the exterior angle measure first, as $\frac{360}{100}$, then take its supplement to find the interior angle measure.

5. Encourage your students to express the patterns they see as formally as they can. The general formulas appear right after these questions. The students' discussion of this part should prepare them to understand and remember these formulas.

2.68

The cuts marked in the strip to the left of each polygonal shape show the wedge that must be cut out to make the resulting strip join at the proper angle to frame the shape. That is, if the marked double angle is cut out and the strip is bent down to join the edges of the cut, the angle made will be an interior angle of the regular polygon shown. The amount cut out is the measure of an exterior angle of the polygon (the supplement of the required interior angle).

If you have the time, it might be instructive to have students actually make a (paper) frame of one or two of these shapes by measuring and cutting out the angles shown. The hands-on experience reinforces the angle relationship much more emphatically than just reading about them.

NOTES

A review of important facts

The sum of the interior angles of an n-sided polygon is

$$(n-2) \cdot 180°$$

The measure of an interior angle of a regular n-gon is

$$\frac{(n-2) \cdot 180°}{n}$$

The sum of the exterior angles of any convex polygon is 360°.

The measure of an exterior angle of a regular n-gon is $\frac{360°}{n}$.

Problem Set: 2.8

1. Display 2.57 shows the lengths of the four sides of a quadrilateral $ABCD$. For each of the following sizes for $\angle B$, draw the quadrilateral $ABCD$.

   (a) 45°   (b) 90°   (c) 120°   (d) 30°   (e) 60°   (f) 10°

Side	Length
AB	7 cm
BC	10 cm
CD	8 cm
AD	5 cm

Display 2.57

2. Display 2.58 is a table of angle measures for regular polygons. Copy it and fill it in.

Number of Sides n	Sum of Interior Angles	Sum of Exterior Angles	Measure of 1 Interior Angle	Measure of 1 Exterior Angle
6				
7				
8				
10				
12				
16				
17				
24				

Display 2.58

Problem Set: 2.8

1. Perhaps the easiest way to do these is to draw the given angle with a protractor, measure off the 7 cm and 10 cm sides, and then use a compass to find the fourth vertex. Parts (a), (b), and (e) work fine; (c) is not possible. For (d) and (f), only a concave quadrilateral is possible.

2. See Display 2.17T. The exterior angle sum column was included to reinforce the fact that it is *always* 360°. Decimal answers are rounded to two places.

NOTES

....

....

....

....

....

....

....

....

....

....

....

....

....

Chapter 2

3. A common pattern on soccer balls is a black regular pentagon surrounded by five white regular hexagons.

   (a) Draw this pattern.

   (b) What is the ratio of hexagons to pentagons in this pattern?

   (c) Get a soccer ball to examine. How many black pentagons are on the ball? How many white hexagons are on the ball?

   (d) What is the ratio of white hexagons to black pentagons on the ball? Why isn't this answer the same as your answer for part (b)?

   (e) What is the sum of all the interior angles of all the black pentagons on the ball?

   (f) What is the sum of all the interior angles of all the white hexagons on the ball? What is the ratio of this number to your answer for part (e)?

   (g) When you divide the ratio in part (d) by the ratio in part (f), what number do you get? How does this relate to the angle sums of a pentagon and a hexagon? Is this a coincidence? Explain.

4. Polygons that are not convex are called concave. Write a direct definition of *concave polygon* in terms of angle measure.

5. Fenway Park, home of the Boston Red Sox, is a unique ballpark built in 1912. Unlike many modern ballparks, it is not symmetrical in the layout of its playing field, shown in Display 2.59. Using strong, but expensive, lightweight plastic, it might be possible to cover the entire playing field (both infield and outfield) when it rains. To estimate the cost of such a cover, the head groundskeeper needs a close approximation of the area of the playing field.

   (a) Explain how the head groundskeeper could use what you have learned about polygons to compute the area of the Fenway Park playing field.

   (b) Do the measurements shown in Display 2.59 give you enough information to determine the area of the playing field? If so, do it. If not, describe what other measurements you need.

Published by IT'S ABOUT TIME, Inc. © 2000 MATHconx, LLC

3. For this problem, you or someone in your class will need to bring in a soccer ball of standard design for students to examine.

(b) 5 to 1

(c) 12; 20

(d) 20 to 12 $\left(= \frac{5}{3}\right)$ Because the hexagons are used in more than one pattern; that is, they share edges with more than one pentagon. In fact, each hexagon borders on three pentagons, so there are only $\frac{1}{3}$ as many hexagons on the ball as there would be if all the patterns were counted separately (without overlap).

(e) $12 \cdot 540° = 6480°$

Number of Sides n	Sum of Interior Angles	Sum of Exterior Angles	Measure of 1 Interior Angle	Measure of 1 Exterior Angle
6	720°	360°	120°	60°
7	900°	360°	128.57°	51.43°
8	1080°	360°	135°	45°
10	1440°	360°	144°	36°
12	1800°	360°	150°	30°
16	2520°	360°	157.5°	22.5°
17	2700°	360°	158.25°	21.18°
24	3960°	360°	165°	15°

Display 2.17T

(f) $20 \cdot 720° = 14,400° \cdot \frac{14,4000}{6480} = \frac{20}{9}$ $(= 2.2222222)$

(g) The relationship underlying this part is a bit more difficult to see and express than the ideas in the rest of this problem. You might want to bypass it with some groups of students. The ratio is $\frac{3}{4}$. It's the same ratio: $\frac{540}{720} = \frac{3}{4}$. If you want to get the ratio of angle sums directly from the ratio of hexagons to polygons, you must multiply the numerator by 4 and the denominator by 3. Hence, to go back the other way, you multiply the angle sum of ratio by $\frac{3}{4}$.

If your students are intrigued by this, you might ask them to make their own geometric designs to put on a soccer ball, using some of the shapes they have studied. Then they might report on which figures were easier or more difficult to fit together with which others, which ones gave more interesting patterns, etc. This is an open-ended project that students can enjoy as they work with geometric ideas. Feel free to let the ideas lead wherever they will.

4. The point here is to emphasize that *convex* and *concave* are logical opposites. If a convex polygon must have the measure *every* angle less than 180°, then a concave polygon must have the measure of *some*

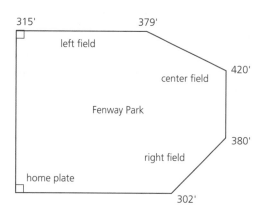

315'   379'

left field

center field   420'

Fenway Park

380'

right field

home plate

302'

(All measurements shown are direct distances from home plate.)

Display 2.59

6. Why do you think we limited our explanation of exterior angles to convex polygons? How can you change the explanation to make the exterior angle sum of *any* polygon equal 360°? Write one or two paragraphs explaining your thoughts about this.

(at least one) angle greater than 180°. The equal to 180° case does not usually arise because we normally do not consider a polygon to have a vertex in the middle of a straight side. If you want to extend the definition of polygon to include such things, then the equal to 180° case should be included in the definition of *convex*.

5. (a) Triangulate this hexagon into 4 triangles and then find the area of each triangle. This would not be quite exact because some small parts of the field, not shown explicitly in the figure, are difficult to measure.

   (b) No, there is not enough information. The only linear measurements are the five distances from home plate, which includes the lengths of the diagonals in a triangulation. Even assuming that the two angles on the left side are right angles, this is not enough information to determine the hexagon (make it rigid). You would either need almost all the side measurements, or several of the outfield angle measurements to complete the job.

6. This fairly sophisticated question can be used either for in class discussion or as a writing exercise. It illustrates a use for negative angle measure. The description of how to form an exterior angle gives you a strange picture at the vertex of a reflex angle; the extension of one side lies *inside* the polygon. Thus, the turn from that side to the next goes in the opposite direction (from the turns taken around nonreflex angles). For instance, if you are proceeding counterclockwise around the polygon, a turn at a reflex angle will be right, rather than left. You will have to undo that turn with an equal amount of left turning somewhere else. If you treat the exterior angles at reflex angles as having negative measure, the exterior angle sum comes out exactly right!

Chapter 2

NOTES

2.9 Stretching and Shrinking Angles and Areas

Learning Outcomes

After studying this section, you will be able to:

Use the fact that scaling preserves angle size and explain why it is true;

Use the fact that two triangles with all corresponding angles congruent must be similar;

Compute the area of a scaled figure from its original area and the scaling factor;

Find the scaling factor for a scaled figure from its original area and its scaled area.

In this chapter we have been talking about scaling and about angles. Do you think that scaling changes angle size?

2.69

In Display 2.60, △ A and △ B are similar.

1. What is the scaling factor? Do some measuring.

2. What are the slope measures of ∠1 and ∠2? How are they related?

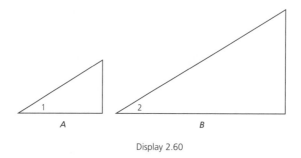

Display 2.60

Scaling always preserves angle size. To see why this must be true, think in terms of slope measure. Whenever two figures are similar, there is a scaling factor, k, such that each length in one figure is k times the corresponding length in the other. Now, the slope measure of an angle is the ratio of two lengths, say $\frac{a}{b}$. Then the slope measure of the corresponding angle in the similar figure is $\frac{ka}{kb}$ as in Display 2.61. But $\frac{ka}{kb} = \frac{a}{b}$, so the angle size must be the same in both figures.

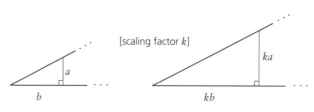

[scaling factor k]

Display 2.61

2.9 Stretching and Shrinking Angles and Areas

This section relates similarity to angle measure and to area. The fundamental mathematical ideas are these.

- Scaling does not change angle size at all.

- Congruence of corresponding angles is a sufficient test for similarity of triangles, but not for other polygons.

- If a similarity transformation changes length by a scaling factor k, then it changes area by k^2. We derive this by looking at the changes in squares and rectangles, the building blocks for measuring area.

2.69

These questions remind students of the connection between similarity and scaling. It provides a prototype example of why scaling preserves angle size.

1. The scaling factor is 2.

2. The exact measurements here will depend on the final printing size of this diagram, but the answers to these questions will not. In the original draft of this diagram, the horizontal and vertical sides of $\triangle A$ were 30 mm and 18 mm, respectively, so the slope measure of $\angle 1$ was $\frac{18}{30}$, which reduces to $\frac{3}{5}$. Your students' measurements of these side lengths should give them the same slope measure for $\angle 1$. Since the scaling factor is 2 , the lengths of the horizontal and vertical sides of $\triangle B$ are twice those of $\triangle A$, so the slope measure of $\angle 2$ is $\frac{2 \cdot 18}{2 \cdot 30}$, which also reduces to $\frac{3}{5}$. That is, $\angle 1$ and $\angle 2$ are equal. The important point for students to notice here is that the scaling factor cancels out of the slope ratio!

Chapter 2

Assessments   Blackline Masters   Extensions   Supplements
For Additional Support Materials see page T-411

A Fact to Know: Corresponding angles of similar polygons are congruent.

....

The previous fact can be stated in this form.

If two polygons are similar, then their corresponding angles must be congruent.

What is the converse of this statement? Give an example to show that the converse is *not* true.

2.70

In general, two polygons with congruent angles may or may not be similar. For triangles, however, the situation is more predictable.

A Fact to Know: (AAA) If the three angles of one triangle are congruent to the three angles of another triangle, then the triangles are similar.

....

Often the AAA statement is combined with its converse (which is true for all polygons) in this form.

Two triangles are similar if and only if their corresponding angles are congruent.

Do two angles determine the shape of a triangle? In particular, are all triangles that contain angles of 50° and 75° similar? Why or why not? Does one angle determine the shape of a triangle? Why or why not?

2.71

The previous facts about angles depend on knowing that if k is the scaling factor relating some figure A to a similar figure B, then every length in B is k times the corresponding length in A. For instance, if a side of A is 3 units long, then the corresponding side of B is $3k$ units long. But what about area? The area of a figure is measured in *square* units, not linear ones. Does the scaling factor affect areas in a predictable way? If so, how? The following example should help you see the answers to these questions.

2.70

The converse is: "If the corresponding angles of two polygons are congruent, then the polygons must be similar." A square and nonsquare rectangle provide an obvious counterexample. There are many others, of course.

This relates to Write this 2.56 in Section 2.7, in which the students were asked to investigate AAA, describe their observations, and propose a general principle. The principle is this converse, restricted to triangles.

2.71

This is not a deep question; it's just a way to reinforce the meaning of what was just said. Once two angles of a triangle are known, the third one is determined because the angle sum must be 180°. In particular, any triangle with angles of 50° and 75° must have a third angle of 55°. Hence, by AAA, all such triangles are similar.

Clearly, a single angle does not determine the shape of a triangle. This question is mostly a check to see if the students have understood the meaning of "determine the shape." A counterexample—of two right triangles with different shapes, for instance—disposes of this.

Chapter 2

Additional Support Materials:

Assessments	Qty
Form (A)	1
Form (B)	1

Blackline Masters	Qty

Extensions	Qty

Supplements	Qty
Stretching and Shrinking Angles and Areas	3

2.72

Movie star Monica Rich has tiled the 8 by 12 foot patio by her swimming pool with the pattern shown in Display 2.62. She used two kinds of custom made tiles. The plain ones are solid gold in color, and the others have a green dollar sign inlay. Each tile is one foot square and costs $100, with or without the inlay.

1. How much did the tiles for Monica's patio cost? How many tiles were used?

Monica's next door rival, Glenda Greenback, decides to build a much larger patio. Because she thinks that she is three times as rich as Monica, she plans to build a patio three times as long and three times as wide, using exactly the same kinds of tiles and the same pattern to cover it.

2. What are the dimensions of Glenda's patio?

3. The two rectangular patios are similar. What is the scaling factor?

4. How much will the tiles for Glenda's patio cost? How many tiles will be used?

5. Will Glenda spend three times as much as Monica for her patio tiles? Explain.

Tiles

   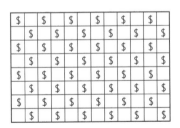

Display 2.62

The story of Monica's and Glenda's patios illustrates a simple, but *very* important, principle of scaling.

If a region is scaled by a factor of k, its area changes by k^2.

Published by IT'S ABOUT TIME, Inc. © 2000 MATHconx, LLC

2.72

This can be used for an in class discussion, but it should be done before more of the text is covered. The final question in this list captures the point of the story, which is to illustrate in a commonsense way that scaling by a factor of k changes area by a factor of k^2. The other parts of the problem are solved by routine arithmetic and should take very little time, *provided* that students visualize the scaling correctly.

1. There are 96 tiles (8×12), so the cost is $9,600.

2. 24 feet by 36 feet.

3. The scaling factor is 3.

4. There are 864 tiles (24×36), so the cost will be $86,400.

5. *This is the key idea. Make sure that students see the reason from the picture. The arithmetic formulation is not as important at this point.* Glenda will spend far more than 3 times as much. She will spend 9 times as much. Since the rectangle is expanded by a factor of 3 in each dimension (l and w), its area ($l \cdot w$) is expanded by a factor of 3^2 ($3l \cdot 3w = 3 \cdot 3 \cdot l \cdot w = 9lw$).

Chapter 2

NOTES

That is, if all the linear distances of some figure A are scaled by a factor of k to get a similar figure B, then any area enclosed by B is k^2 times the corresponding area enclosed by A. Let's see why this must always be true.

Area is measured in square units. Once you have chosen a unit length, you can think of the area of any region as made up of little 1 by 1 square tiles (and parts of tiles). You can find the approximate area of the region just by counting the squares. You can make your approximation better by choosing a smaller unit size. Now, what happens to the size of a square if you scale it by a factor of k?

Each side of square A in Display 2.63 is 1 pica long. A pica is a unit length used by printers. All the squares in this figure are similar to A. Why?

2.73

1. List the four scaling factors used to get squares B, C, D, and E from A.

2. List the areas of squares B, C, D, and E, in square picas.

3. How are the numbers you listed in part 2 related to the numbers listed in part 1?

4. If you had to add on another square, F, following the pattern of Display 2.63, what would its side length be? What would its area be?

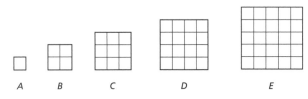

Display 2.63

Display 2.63 shows how the area of a square is affected by scaling. Algebra lets us express this principle in a way that is easily extended to rectangles and triangles. The area of a square with side length s is s^2. If that square is scaled by a factor k, then the new square has side length ks, so it has area $(ks)^2$. But $(ks)^2 = k^2 s^2$, which is just k^2 times the area of the original square.

Published by IT'S ABOUT TIME, Inc. © 2000 MATHconx, LLC

203

2.73

The pica was chosen as the unit here because of its relative obscurity. Since it is probably unfamiliar to most students, they will be more likely to focus on the meaning of "square" in square pica and not be lulled into inattention by the familiar sound of square inch or square foot, etc.

1. 2, 3, 4, 5

2. 4, 9, 16, 25

3. Each number in the second list is the square of the corresponding number in the first list.

4. Square *F* would have side length 6 picas and area 36 square picas.

Chapter 2

NOTES

The same reasoning holds for rectangles. If a rectangle has length l and width w, then the area inside it is lw. Now, if that rectangle is scaled by a factor k, then the new length and width are kl and kw, respectively. Thus, the area inside the scaled rectangle is

$$(kl)(kw) = k^2 \cdot lw$$

which is k^2 times the area of the original rectangle.

2.74

1. Write a formula for the area of a triangle with base b and height h.

2. Adapt the reasoning for rectangles to explain,

> If a triangle is scaled by a factor k, then the area of the scaled triangle is k^2 times the area of the original one.

What about regions that are not as nicely shaped as rectangles or triangles? How do we know that the same principle holds? For polygonal regions, there are two ways to answer this. The first uses triangulation. Since any polygon can be triangulated, and since the area of any scaled triangle is changed by the square of the scaling factor, then the area of any scaled triangulated region must also change by the square of the scaling factor.

2.75

Write a clear, detailed explanation of how triangulation makes the area scaling principle true for any pentagonal region. Somewhere in your explanation you should need to use a form of the Distributive Law; be sure to state clearly where and how you are using it.

The second approach applies to any planar region, whether or not it is bounded by a polygon. Recall (from Chapter 1) that we can approximate the area of any planar region by a grid of squares. Now, if we scale the region by a factor k, then the sides of each square are scaled by k, so the area of each square changes by k^2. This means that the area of the entire approximation changes by the factor k^2.

For instance, the area inside the irregular hexagon on the left side of Display 2.64 is approximated by 16 squares. The similar hexagon on the right has been scaled by a factor of 2. This means that the area of each of the original squares has become 4 times its original size, so the right hexagon encloses 4 times as much area as the left one does.

2.74

1. The area of the triangular region is $\frac{1}{2}bh$.

2. If the triangle is scaled by a factor k, then the new base and height are kb and kh, respectively. Thus, the area inside the scaled triangle is

$$\frac{1}{2}(kb)(kh) = k^2 \cdot \frac{1}{2}bh$$

which is k^2 times the area inside the original triangle.

2.75

You will have to decide how much clarity and precision to expect, based on your knowledge of your own students. For some students, you might want to turn this into a group discussion question, or simply explain the main idea by using an example with specific measurements. The main ingredients for the area scaling principle include,

Any pentagon can be triangulated into three triangles, T_1, T_2, and T_3. The area of the pentagonal region, A, is the sum of the areas inside the three triangles. Each of these triangles has a base and a height, which we mark with the same subscripts. Then

$$A = \frac{1}{2}b_1h_1 + \frac{1}{2}b_2h_2 + \frac{1}{2}b_3h_3$$

If the pentagonal region is scaled by a factor k, then so is each triangular region. This means that each triangular area changes by a factor k^2, so

$$\text{scaled } A = k^2 \cdot \frac{1}{2}b_1h_1 + k^2 \cdot \frac{1}{2}b_2h_2 + k^2 \cdot \frac{1}{2}b_3h_3$$

By the Distributive Law (for multiplication over addition), the k^2 term can be factored out of the right side of the equation, so

$$\text{scaled } A = k^2 \cdot (\frac{1}{2}b_1h_1 + \frac{1}{2}b_2h_2 + \frac{1}{2}b_3h_3) = k^2 \cdot A$$

Chapter 2

NOTES

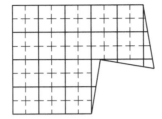

Display 2.64

If we make better and better approximations by choosing smaller and smaller squares, the k^2 factor applies each time, so the area of the region must change by the factor k^2.

A Fact to Know: If a planar region is scaled by a factor k, then the area of the scaled region is k^2 times the area of the original region.

If you know how the area of a figure should be changed by scaling, can you find the scaling factor needed? Yes, you can. Would you ever need to do that? You might. Here's an example of such a situation.

The sailmakers at Easylife Watercraft Corp. have designed a sail in the shape of a right triangle with one leg $1\frac{1}{2}$ times as long as the other. They can make this sail in a variety of different sizes. The sizes are based on area (because the area of a sail determines its wind resistance). Their prototype (model) is 4 ft. by 6 ft., with an area of 12 sq. ft. The boat designer in the next office needs sails of this shape with areas of 75 sq. ft., 84 sq. ft., and 93 sq. ft., for three different styles of a new boat. What are the required dimensions for these sails? How can you help the sailmakers figure this out?

Published by IT'S ABOUT TIME, Inc. © 2000 MATHconx, LLC

205

NOTES

Trying out a lot of different lengths to see if they fit all the conditions might work, if you're lucky, but it could take a long time. There's a faster, easier way, if you use a little algebra. The sailmakers need a scaling factor to use in each case. Now, for any scaling factor k, we know that the original area, A_o, is related to the scaled area, A_s, like this,

$$A_s = k^2 \cdot A_o$$

In this case, the original area is 12 sq. ft. The scaled area is what the designer wants; in the first case, it is 75 sq. ft. Thus, we have

$$75 = k^2 \cdot 12$$

so

$$\frac{75}{12} = k^2$$

That is,

$$k = \sqrt{\frac{75}{12}} = \sqrt{\frac{25}{4}} = \frac{5}{2} = 2.5$$

Actually, there are two square roots of $\frac{25}{4}$, one positive and one negative. We want the positive one here because the scaling factor must be positive.

These questions refer to the sailmakers' problem.

2.76

1. What are the dimensions of the sail with area 75 sq. ft.? How did you find them?

2. Find the dimensions of the sails with areas of 84 sq. ft. and 93 sq. ft. Use your calculator, and round your answers to two decimal places.

3. Write the formula for finding the scaling factor as a function of the area needed. Enter it into your calculator. What does X stand for? What does Y stand for?

4. Use your function from part 3 to help you find the dimensions of a sail with 100 sq. ft. of area.

A review of important facts.

• Corresponding angles of similar polygons are congruent.

• (**AAA**) If the three angles of one triangle are congruent to the three angles of another triangle, then the triangles are similar.

• If a planar region is scaled by a factor k, then the area of the scaled region is k^2 times the area of the original region.

2.76

The first two parts simply check on and reinforce the students' understanding of square roots and of the algebraic process described in the text. The other parts relate that understanding to functions. Writing the function in such a way that the calculator can handle it clarifies the roles of the dependent and independent variables in this situation.

1. The scaling factor is $\frac{5}{2}$ (= 2.5), so the dimensions of this sail can be found by multiplying the dimensions of the prototype sail by 2.5.
    $$2.5 \cdot 4 \text{ ft.} = 10 \text{ ft.}; \quad 2.5 \cdot 6 \text{ ft.} = 15 \text{ ft.}$$

2. Mimicking the algebra of the text, substituting 84 and then 93 for 75, we get

    $$84 = k^2 \cdot 12 \qquad 93 = k^2 \cdot 12$$

    $$\frac{84}{12} = k^2 \qquad \frac{93}{12} = k^2$$

    $$\sqrt{7} = k \qquad \sqrt{\frac{31}{4}} = k$$

    In the first case, the calculator value for $\sqrt{7}$, rounded to 2.65, is the scaling factor. The dimensions of this sail are $2.65 \cdot 4$ ft. = 10.6 ft. and $2.65 \cdot 6$ ft. = 15.9 ft. In the second case, the calculator value for $\sqrt{\frac{31}{4}}$, rounded to 2.78, is the scaling factor. The dimensions of this sail are $2.78 \cdot 4$ ft. = 11.12 ft. and $2.78 \cdot 6$ ft. = 16.68 ft.

3. $Y = \sqrt{\frac{X}{12}}$. The X stands for the sail area wanted; the Y stands for the scaling factor needed to get that area. You might want to emphasize here that this is a function because we can ignore the negative square root. The calculator will give you only the positive root.

4. The scaling factor, rounded to two places, is 2.89. The dimensions of the sail are 11.56 ft. and 17.34 ft.

Chapter 2

NOTES

Published by IT'S ABOUT TIME, Inc. © 2000 MATHconx, LLC

Problem Set: 2.9

1. Mathland is having a contest to pick a design for a triangular stamp in honor of Pythagoras. All designs must be enclosed in right triangles with sides of length 24 cm, 32 cm, and 40 cm. When the stamp is issued, the actual side lengths of the triangle will be $\frac{1}{8}$ of the design lengths. Copy and complete the table in Display 2.65. Then answer the following questions.

   (a) How does the perimeter of the design compare to the perimeter of the actual stamp?

   (b) How does the area of the design compare to the area of the actual stamp?

   (c) Why do you think Mathland chose a right triangle with side lengths 24 cm, 32 cm, and 40 cm?

   (d) Has the United States ever issued a triangular stamp? If so, when? Have any other countries issued triangular stamps? If so, can you name any?

	Design	Actual
Side lengths	24 cm, 32 cm, 40 cm	
Perimeter		
Area		

Display 2.65

2. This problem refers to the two pool patios described in this section. When Glenda Greenback designed her patio 3 times as long and 3 times as wide as the one Monica Rich had, she found that the tiles would cost her 9 times as much as Monica's did. Why? How can Glenda change her design so that the tiles only cost her (about) 3 times as much and her patio is still proportional to Monica's? What practical tiling difficulties are caused by your solution?

Problem Set: 2.9

1. See Display 2.18T for the completed table.

   (a) The perimeter of the design is 8 times as long as the actual perimeter.

   (b) The area of the design is 64 (= 8^2) times the size of the actual area.

   (c) This provides a good opportunity to discuss Pythagoras and this theorem. This triple of design numbers is a multiple of the basic Pythagorean triple 3–4–5.

   (d) The U.S. issued a triangular stamp in 1997 to commemorate Pacific 97, the international stamp exhibition in San Francisco. Its shape is an isosceles right triangle. A number of other countries have issued triangular stamps. If any of your students are stamp collectors, you might ask them to bring in examples to show. It would be particularly interesting if any of these stamps are not isosceles right triangles, or not right triangles at all. Isosceles right triangles make the printing and perforation patterns particularly simple.

	Design	Actual
Side Lengths	24 cm, 32 cm, 40cm	3 cm, 4 cm, 5cm
Perimeter	96 cm	12 cm
Area	384 sq. cm	6 sq. cm

Display 2.18T

2. This problem is about square roots. Since both dimensions of the rectangle changed by a factor of 3, the area changed by 3^2. In order to get the area 3 times as large and still proportional, Glenda needs to use a scaling factor k such that $k^2 = 3$. That is, she needs $k = \sqrt{3} = 1.732$ (approx.). The practical difficulty is that the tiles don't come out even; the tiles would have to be cut and pieced, making the cost slightly more than exactly 3 times Monica's to account for the wasted pieces of edge tile.

3. Kites come in all shapes and sizes, but any good kite design makes use of this important principle of aerodynamics:

For a given wind speed, the lift (force of air to lift up the kite) is directly proportional to the area of the kite. If the area of a kite is doubled, then its lift is doubled.

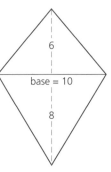

Display 2.66

A typical kite design has the form of two isosceles triangles, one pointed up and one pointed down, with a common base line, as in Display 2.66. In this case, the base is 10 in., the height of the upper triangle is 6 in., and the height of the lower triangle is 8 in. Make a copy of the table in Display 2.67 to use as you answer parts (a) − (d).

	Upper Triangle			Lower Triangle			Total Area
	Base	Height	Area	Base	Height	Area	
(a)	10	6		10	8		
(b)							
(c)						490	857.5
(d)			541.875				

Display 2.67

(a) Fill in all blanks in row (a) to find the total area of the kite.

(b) What happens to the total area of the kite when you double all dimensions? fill in row (b) to answer this question.

(c) Given the area of the bottom portion of the kite and the total area, as shown in row (c), fill in row (c).

(d) Given the area of the top portion of the kite, calculate the area of the bottom portion and the total area. Fill in row (d).

3. See Display 2.19T for the completed table containing the answers to parts (a)–(d).

   (e) The kite in (c) has $\frac{857.5}{280} = 3.06$ pounds of lifting force.

   The kite in (d) has $\frac{1264.375}{280} = 4.52$ pounds of lifting force.

   (f) To pick up 100 pounds, the total surface area of the kite must be $100 \cdot 280 = 28{,}000$ sq. in. The dimensions of a proportional kite can be found as follows.

   top triangle area + bottom triangle area = total kite area
   $$\frac{1}{2}bh_1 + \frac{1}{2}bh_2 = 28{,}000$$

   But $h_1 = 0.6b$ and $h_2 = 0.8b$, so

   $$\frac{1}{2}b(.6b) + \frac{1}{2}b(.8b) = 28{,}000$$
   $$0.3b^2 + 0.4b^2 = 28{,}000$$
   $$0.7b^2 = 28{,}000$$
   $$b^2 = 40{,}000$$

   Thus, the base, b, is 200 in., the upper height is 120 in. $(0.6b)$, and the lower height is 160 in. $(0.8b)$.

	Upper Triangle			Lower Triangle			Total Area
	Base	Height	Area	Base	Height	Area	
(a)	10	6	30	10	8	40	70
(b)	20	12	120	20	16	160	280
(c)	35	21	367.5	35	28	490	857.5
(d)	42.5	25.5	541.875	42.5	34	722.5	1264.375

Display 2.19T

As an example of how this information can be used, let's say for a given wind speed the lifting force for the kite described by row (a) is $\frac{1}{4}$ pound. Because the kite dimensions in (b) give us four times the area, the lifting force is four times that of (a). In other words, kite (b) will lift one pound with the same wind speed.

(e) Calculate the lift, in pounds, of the kites described by rows (c) and (d).

(f) Design a kite of the same proportions that could lift a human body weighing 100 pounds for this same wind speed. (Find the base length and the two heights.)

4. You are helping to design a large, outdoor concert theater, TriangleWood, in Massachusetts. Its floor plan is a large equilateral triangle, as shown in Display 2.68. The lengths in the figure are in yards. The triangle at the bottom is the stage and lighting area. Seating is in three sections, proceeding away from the stage so that each section and the stage and any sections before it form a triangle similar to the stage triangle. The sections of seats are priced according to their distance from the stage, with highest priced tickets for section 1, next highest for section 2, and least expensive tickets for section 3.

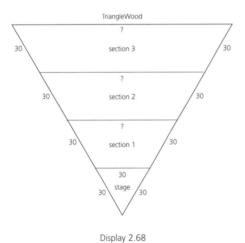

Display 2.68

Published by IT'S ABOUT TIME, Inc. © 2000 MATHconx, LLC

209

2.9 Stretching and Shrinking Angles and Areas

4. This problem reviews a variety of ideas from the chapter. Some parts are easier than others. The completed table appears in Display 2.21T.
   (a) The missing dimensions are found using the definition of an equilateral triangle. They are 60, 90, 120 yds.
   (b) This part asks students to recall how to use the slope measure of an angle (the calculator TAN function) to find the altitude of the triangle. Since this triangle is equilateral, half the base (15 yds.) multiplied by tan 60° is the altitude. Thus, the area is 389.71 sq. yds. (rounded to two places).
   (c) The shape of the theater is similar to that of the stage; it is an equilateral triangle with sides 4 times as long as the sides of the stage triangle. Since the linear scaling factor is 4, the scaling factor for the area is $4^2 = 16$. Thus, the area of the theater is

$$16 \cdot 389.71 = 6235.36 \text{ sq. yd.}$$

There is a simple, powerful visual verification of this result, which can also apply to the next part. If you fold up the stage into section 1, you will see that section 1 contains three copies of the stage triangle. Now fold that section into section 2 and observe that section 2 contains those three copies of the stage triangle plus two more. Finally, fold section 3 into section 4 and observe that section 4 contains those five copies of the stage triangle plus two more, and

$$1 + 3 + 5 + 7 = 16$$

Display 2.20T illustrates this visual argument, from which the answers to part (d) flow almost immediately.
   (d) The equilateral triangle formed by section 1 and the stage is similar to the stage with a scaling factor of 2, so its area is 2^2 times as large. Subtracting the stage area itself (one copy of the stage area), you have

$$3 \cdot 389.71 = 1169.13 \text{ sq. yd.}$$

The equilateral triangle formed by sections 1 and 2 and the stage is similar to the stage with a scaling factor of 3, so its area is 3^2 times as large. Subtracting the 2^2 copies of the stage area formed by section 1 and the stage, you have

$$5 \cdot 389.71 = 1948.55 \text{ sq. yd.05}$$

TriangleWood

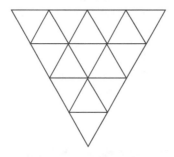

Display 2.20T

(a) Three of the lengths in Display 2.68 are marked "?". What are they? Remember: Each of the following triangles is equilateral:

section 1 + stage,
section 2 + section 1 + stage,
section 3 + section 2 + section l + stage

To complete the design of this theater, start by copying the table in Display 2.69. Then fill it in step by step as you work through parts (b)–(h).

	Area (sq. yds.)	No. of Seats	$ per Seat	Total $
stage		0	0	0
section 1		1350	$14	
section 2				
section 3				
Total:				

Display 2.69

(b) Find the area of the stage. Round your answer to two decimal places.

(c) Calculate the total area of the theater by scaling your answer to part (b).

(d) Use scaling and the answer to part (b) to find the area of each seating section. (*Hint*: The area of section 1 is the area of the equilateral triangle made up of section 1 and the stage, minus the area of the stage.) Check your results by comparing the sum of your areas with your answer to part (c).

(e) If section 1 has 1350 seats, calculate the numbers of seats in section 2 and section 3, using proportionality and assuming that each seat requires the same area (How should you round off your answers?)

(f) Find the total number of seats in this theater.

(g) The manager wants a full theater to bring in the same amount of money from the ticket sales for each section. If she prices section 1 at $14 a seat, how much does she charge for a seat in section 2? How much does she charge for a seat in section 3?

(h) If a concert is sold out, what is the total amount of money that the theater collects?

Published by IT'S ABOUT TIME, Inc. © 2000 MATHconx, LLC

210

Subtract the area of the equilateral triangle formed by the 9 copies of the stage from the total area of the theater (16 copies) to get the area of section 3

$$7 \cdot 389.71 = 2727.97 \text{ sq. yd.}$$

An interesting sidelight: The computations represented visually by Display 2.20T are the first four steps of the pattern for the sum of consecutive odd numbers.

$$1 = 1^2 \qquad 1 + 3 = 2^2 \qquad 1 + 3 + 5 = 3^2 \qquad 1 + 3 + 5 + 7 = 4^2$$

(e) Answers should be rounded (down) to the nearest whole seat; fractions of a seat make no sense in this context. Each seat takes up an area of $\frac{1169.13}{1350} = 0.866$ sq. yds. (approximately). Thus, there are

$\frac{1948.55}{0.866} \approx 2250$ seats in section 2 and $\frac{2727.97}{0.866} \approx 3150$ seats in section 3.

(f) This is simple addition: $1350 + 2250 + 3150 = 6750$ seats in all.

(g) At \$14.00 a seat, a sold out section 1 would bring in

$1350 \cdot \$14.00 = \$18,900$. To get the same revenue from section 2, she must charge $\frac{\$18,900}{2250} = \$8.40$ a seat. To get the same revenue from section 3, she must charge $\frac{\$18,900}{3150} = \$6.00$ a seat.

(h) A sold out concert brings in $3 \cdot \$18,900 = \$56,700$.

	Area (sq. yd.)	No. of Seats	$ per Seat	Total $
Stage:	389.71	0	0	0
Section 1:	1169.13	1350	$14.00	$18,900
Section 2:	1948.55	2250	$8.40	$18,900
Section 3:	2727.97	3150	$6.00	$18,900
Total:	6235.36	6750	—	$56,700

Display 2.21T

Chapter 2

2.10 Stretching and Shrinking Volumes

Just as area is measured in square units, so volume is measured in cubic units. For any unit length, you can think of the volume of something as if it were filled with small 1 by 1 by 1 cubes (and partial cubes). You can find the approximate volume of an object by counting the cubes. You make the approximation better by choosing a smaller cube size. Here's an exercise to help you develop your spatial imagination.

Look at the four boxes in Display 2.70.

1. One of the three taller boxes—A, B, C—is proportional to Box X. Which one do you think it is? Why? What do you think the scaling factor is?

2.77

2. If Box X holds a quart of applesauce, how much applesauce do you think Box A holds? What about Box B? Box C? Explain your answers.

3. If Box X measures 4 by 3 by 5 inches, what would be the measurements of a similar box with a scaling factor of 10? What is the volume of Box X in this case? What is the volume of the scaled box?

Learning Outcomes

After studying this section, you will be able to:

Compute the volume of a scaled figure from its original volume and the scaling factor;

Find the scaling factor for a scaled figure from its original volume and its scaled volume.

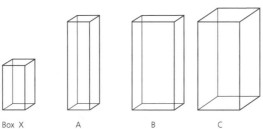

Box X   A   B   C

Display 2.70

2.10 Stretching and Shrinking Volumes

This section relates similarity to volume. The fundamental mathematical idea is,

> If a similarity transformation changes length by a scaling factor k, then it changes volume by k^3.

We derive this by looking at the changes in cubes and rectangular boxes, the building blocks for measuring volume.

2.77

This discussion question should be handled right away, so that students have the opportunity to extend the reasoning of the two dimensional case on their own. It also gives you a chance to observe which students have difficulty visualizing drawings of three dimensional shapes and which ones have good spatial imagination. At this stage, getting the right answer to these questions is not as important as starting to think in three dimensions. The relevant principles for three dimensional scaling will be developed in the next page or two.

1. The perspective drawing does not lend itself to exact, unambiguous measurement, but, since the problem states that one of the three boxes is proportional to X, only C looks about right. All three of the taller boxes are the same height, which is twice the height of Box X. Thus, the scaling factor should be 2, and the length and width of the base should also be doubled. Only Box C fits this description.

2. Again, these answers depend on visual approximation, rather than on precise measurement. The face dimensions can be measured exactly, but the depth depends on the perspective. Box A has the same base as Box X and is twice as high, so it holds twice as much applesauce (2 quarts). Box B is twice as wide as Box A, so it holds 4 quarts of applesauce. Box C looks to be twice as deep as Box B, so it holds 8 quarts of applesauce.

3. 40 by 30 by 50 inches. In this case the volume of Box X is $4 \cdot 3 \cdot 5 = 60$ cu. in. The volume of the larger box is $40 \cdot 30 \cdot 50 = 60,000$ cu. in.

Chapter 2

Assessments   Blackline Masters   Extensions   Supplements

For Additional Support Materials see page T-433

Published by IT'S ABOUT TIME, Inc. © 2000 MATHconx, LLC

Thinking Tip

Use appropriate notation. Sometimes describing a process with an algebraic formula will help you see how and why it works.

The ideas behind Display 2.70 lead to the principle of how volume is affected by scaling. As you know, the volume of a rectangular box is the product of its length, width, and height. If we write this statement algebraically, the formula tells us exactly how the volume of such a box is changed by scaling. Suppose a box has length l, width w, height h, and volume V. Then

$$V = l \cdot w \cdot h$$

If the box is scaled by a factor k, then each of its linear measurements–length l, width w, height h, and volume V is multiplied by k. Thus, the scaled volume, which we'll call V_k, is

$$V = kl \cdot kw \cdot kh$$
$$= k \cdot k \cdot k \cdot l \cdot w \cdot h$$
$$= k^3 \cdot l \cdot w \cdot h$$
$$= k^3 \cdot V$$

That is, the scaled volume is k^3 times the original volume.

Volumes of other figures are affected by scaling in the same way as volumes of boxes. In particular, the volume of a cube of edge length s is s^3, and if the cube is scaled by a factor k, the volume of the scaled cube is

$$(ks)^3 = k^3 s^3$$

That is, the scaled volume is k^3 times the original volume. Now, recall (from Chapter 1) that we can approximate the volume of any three dimensional shape by cubes. If we scale the shape by a factor k, then the volume of each cube changes by the factor k^3. This means that the volume of the entire approximation changes by k^3.

A Fact to Know: If a three dimensional figure is scaled by a factor k, then the volume it encloses is k^3 times the volume enclosed by the original figure.

2.78

1. A 2.5 by 8 by 10 foot rectangular bin holds plastic packing peanuts. What volume of peanuts will it hold? If a second bin is built, enlarging the dimensions of the first one by a factor of 3, what volume of peanuts will it hold? What will be the dimensions of the new bin?

Published by IT'S ABOUT TIME, Inc. © 2000 MATHconx, LLC

2.78

This is a routine reinforcement exercise.

1. 200 cu. ft.; 5400 cu. ft.; 7.5 by 24 by 30 feet

Chapter 2

Additional Support Materials:

Assessments	Qty
Form (A)	1
Form (B)	1
Chapter Test (A)	1
Chapter Test (B)	1

Blackline Masters	Qty

Extensions	Qty
Following 2.10 Build It Up & Tear It Down: A Problem Solving Strategy	1

Supplements	Qty
Stretching and Shrinking Volumes	1

2. A company is experimenting with juice cartons of various sizes. Their giant institutional size is 56 cm high and holds 68,600 cc of juice. They want to make a proportionally-sized container only 16 cm high. What scaling factor should they use? What volume will the smaller container hold?

If you know how the volume of a figure should be changed by scaling, can you find the scaling factor needed? Yes, you can. The following problem is an example of such a situation.

Market research tells the Crunchy Cereal Co. that consumers really like the shape of their regular size cornflakes box. The box is 11 inches by 8 inches by 2.5 inches. The company wants to keep this shape for its super-size and its single-serving size boxes.

2.79

1. The super-size box must have a volume of 400 cu. in. Rounded to two decimal places, what scaling factor should be used to make a box of the same shape as the regular box? What should the dimensions of the super-size box be?

2. The single-serving box must have a volume of 20 cu. in. Rounded to two decimal places, what scaling factor should be used to make a box of the same shape as the regular box? What should the dimensions of the single-serving box be?

Here is a famous story from ancient history.

2.80

In 430 B.C., there was a terrible plague in Athens. The desperate Athenians, seeking a way to stop the plague, appealed to the oracle of Apollo. The oracle told them to double the size of Apollo's cubical altar. They constructed a new altar, a cube with *each edge* twice as long as the edge of the old altar. Of course, this made the new altar eight times the size of the old one. Instead of stopping, the plague got even worse. Realizing their error, the Athenians appealed to Plato for help. After telling them that the oracle had given them this problem "to reproach the Greeks for their neglect of mathematics and their contempt of geometry,"[1] Plato set about finding the proper side length for a new altar whose volume was exactly twice that of the old one.

---

[1]David M. Burton, *The History of Mathematics* (Boston: Allyn and Bacon, Inc., 1985). P.134.

Published by IT'S ABOUT TIME, Inc. © 2000 MATHconx, LLC

213

2. The scaling factor is $\frac{2}{7}$. The smaller container holds
$68,600 \cdot \left(\frac{2}{7}\right)^3 = 1600$ cc.

2.79

This reverses the process of going from a linear scaling factor to a change in volume. It pushes students to recognize that the linear scaling factor can be derived from the ratio of change in volume by taking the cube root.

1. Call the column of regular box V_R, the volume of the super box V_S, and the unknown linear scaling factor k. We know from the work in this section that

$$V_S = k^3 \cdot V_R$$

Thus, the first step is to find the volume of the regular box.
$11 \cdot 8 \cdot 2.5 = 220$ cu. in. Substitute and solve for k.

$$400 = k^3 \cdot 220$$

so $k = \sqrt[3]{\frac{400}{220}} = 1.22$ (rounded). Use this scaling factor on the dimensions of the regular box to get the dimensions of the super box.
13.42 in. by 9.76 in. by 3.05 in.

2. This is an exactly analogous problem: $20 = k^3 \cdot 220$, so $k = \sqrt[3]{\frac{1}{11}} = 0.45$ (rounded). Thus, the dimensions of the single size box should be
4.95 in. by 3.6 in. by 1.125 in.

2.80

This story describes a scaling problem in which both the original volume and the scaled volume are known and the scaling factor is needed to construct the cube of the correct edge size. This can be done like the problems just before it, by solving the equation

$$\text{scaled volume} = k^3 \cdot \text{original volume}$$

for k. In this case, we can think of the original volume as 1 (using an edge of the original cube as the unit of measure) and the scaled volume as 2. Thus, the equation becomes

$$2 = k^3 \cdot 1$$

so $k = \sqrt[3]{2}$. Unfortunately, the calculator can only give a decimal approximation of this number (1.25992105), which probably wouldn't have been good enough for the picky oracle. In fact, a segment of length exactly $\sqrt[3]{2}$ cannot be constructed using only a compass and a straightedge, the classical construction tools. However, this fact was not proved until the 19th century—and then it was done using the sophisticated methods of abstract algebra.

Chapter 2

Explain how this story is related to the material of this section and how to solve the Athenians' problem. If you and your calculator were back in Athens in 430 B.C., do you think you could have solved the problem well enough to satisfy the oracle of Apollo? If so, do it. If not, explain why not.

REFLECT

In this chapter you learned many different facts, all related to similarity, scaling, and angle size.

- You learned about scaling factors for making different-size copies of the same shape.

- You saw two different ways to measure angles, by slope and by degrees, and you learned about the calculator functions that convert from one to the other.

- You saw relationships among the angles formed by parallel lines cut by a transversal, which led to the very important fact that the sum of the angles of *any* triangle is 180°.

- You learned about sets of measurements that determine a triangle up to congruence: **SAS**, **SSS**, **ASA**, and **AAS**.

- You saw how facts about triangles can be used to get information about other polygons.

- Finally, you saw how scaling affects areas and volumes of two and three dimensional shapes.

These facts are among the most important building blocks in all of geometry, as you will see in the chapters to come.

In the next chapter we take a much closer look at right triangles. Building on things such as slope measure, it develops and explains some very useful tools for dealing with angles. These tools turn into powerful, important functions that play important roles in many areas of mathematics and science. These ideas are the basis of the subject called *trigonometry*.

214

NOTES

Problem Set: 2.10

1. Elka wants to make beanbag chairs for her twins when they go away to college. She has a pattern for a shape like an 18 by 18 by 20-inch rectangular box. Her friend Liz used this pattern to make a chair for her daughter. Elka likes that chair, but doesn't think it is nearly big enough to be comfortable. She is thinking of enlarging the pattern by a factor of 2.

   (a) The amount of filling needed for the chair Liz made was 3.75 cu. ft. How much filling will Elka need for her chair design?

   (b) The beanbag filling comes in packages of 2 cubic feet, for $8.99 a package. How much did it cost Liz to fill the chair she made? How much would it cost Elka to fill the two enlarged chairs for her twins?

   (c) Elka thinks that it will cost too much to make the chairs she had planned. She decides to enlarge the pattern only by a factor of 1.5, instead. How much will the filling cost for these two chairs?

2. SugarSweet Company is making a new, larger sugar cube. They advertise that it contains three times the sugar of the cube that measures 1 by 1 by 1 cm. Calculate the dimensions of the larger sugar cube.

Published by IT'S ABOUT TIME, Inc. © 2000 MATHconx, LLC

Problem Set: 2.10

1. (a) $2^3 \cdot 3.75 = 30$ cu. ft. per chair.
   (b) It cost Liz $17.98 because she needed to buy two packages. It would cost Elka $269.70 because she would need 30 packages (15 for each chair).
   (c) The volume of an enlarged chair would be $1.5^3 \cdot 3.75 = 12.7$ cu. ft. (approximately). The total volume of the two chairs is approximately 25.4 cu. ft. This requires 13 packages at $8.99 each, for a total cost of $116.87.

2. This short problem echoes the story about the oracle of Apollo. The original volume is $1 \cdot 1 \cdot 1 = 1$ cc. If k is the scaling factor that triples the volume, then $k^3 \cdot 1 = 3$. Thus, $k = \sqrt[3]{3} = 1.44$ (approx.) Since each original side is 1 cm long, each new side is about 1.44 cm long.

NOTES

Chapter 2

3. Alan Arf, the famous pet sculptor, has been commissioned to carve a large marble dog biscuit for display outside the home office of the Postman's Friend Dogfood Co. To make a preliminary model of his work, Alan started with a 1 by 1 by 2.5 foot wooden block. That turned out to be just the right starting shape, so he wants to start the real sculpture with a block of marble that is proportional to the wooden block. He wants the marble block to be as large as possible. However, it has to be shipped by truck, and the maximum allowable shipping weight is 60,000 pounds. Assuming that the marble weighs 200 lb. per cubic foot, what are the dimensions of the largest marble block he can get?

4. In this section you read this argument.

    The volume of a cube of edge length s is s^3, and if the cube is scaled by *a* factor k, the volume of the scaled cube is

    $$(ks)^3 = k^3 s^3$$

    That is, the scaled volume is k^3 times the original volume.

    Rewrite this argument without *using any algebraic symbols or letters that stand for quantities*. Then write a paragraph explaining why letters and other symbols are used in mathematics.

Published by IT'S ABOUT TIME, Inc. © 2000 MATHconx, LLC

3. At 200 lbs. per cu. ft., the maximum volume he can have is 300 cubic feet. Let s be the smaller side length of the block. Then, keeping the same proportions,

$$\text{Volume} = l \cdot w \cdot h = s \cdot s \cdot 2.5s$$

so

$$300 = 2.5s^3$$

That is, $s = \sqrt[3]{120} = 4.93$ ft., rounded to two decimal places. The largest block he can get is approximately 4.93 by 4.93 by 12.33 feet.

4. This writing exercise has a dual purpose. It reinforces a key fact of the section by having the students read it again and write it out under somewhat trying conditions. It also illustrates the power and efficiency of algebraic notation, a theme introduced early in the **MATH** *Connections* Year 1 and worthy of periodic reminders.

Restating this short argument clearly without using algebraic notation is an annoyingly fussy task. The result might be something like this.

> The volume of a cube is the cube of its edge length—that is, its edge length multiplied by itself and by itself again. If the cube is scaled by a certain scaling factor, the volume of the scaled cube is the cube of the quantity obtained by multiplying the edge length by the scaling factor. This is the same as the cube of the scaling factor times the cube of the edge length. That is, the scaled volume is the cube of the scaling factor times the original volume. Whew!

Chapter 2

NOTES

MATH *Connections*: A Secondary Mathematics Core Curriculum

NOTES

2a

Chapter 3

Chapter 3 Planning Guide

Chapter 3 Introduction to Trigonometry: Tangles With Angles

Chapter 3 introduces the three basic functions of right angle trigonometry — sine, cosine, and tangent — and discusses the inverses of these functions in relation to the calculator. The Law of Sines and the Law of Cosines are explained and applied, and the graphs of the sine and cosine functions are connected with circular motion via the unit circle, setting the stage for parametric representation of circles in Chapter 4.

Assessments Form A (A)	Assessments Form B (B)	Blackline Masters
Quiz 3.1-3.2(A) Quiz 3.3(A) Quiz 3.4-3.6(A) Chapter Test(A)	Quiz 3.1-3.2(B) Quiz 3.3(B) Quiz 3.4-3.6(B) Chapter Test(B)	No Blackline Masters for this chapter

Extensions	Supplements for Chapter Sections	Test Banks

3.4   Vectors in a Plane
       "Favorite" Triangles
	3.1 The Sine of an Acute Angle — 4 Supplements
	 3.2 The Cosine of an Acute Angle — 2 Supplements
	 3.3 The Tangent of an Acute Angle — 3 Supplements
	 3.4 What Do These SIN $^{-1}$, COS $^{-1}$, and TAN $^{-1}$ Keys Do?
	       — 3 Supplements
	 3.5 The Law of Sines - The Law of Cosines —
	       2 Supplements
	 3.6 Sine and Cosine Curves: Going Around in Circles —
	       1 Supplement
		To be released

Pacing Range 3-5 weeks including Assessments
Teachers will need to adjust this guide to suit the needs of their own students. Not all classes will complete each chapter at the same pace. Flexibility — which accommodates different teaching styles, school schedules and school standards — is built into the curriculum.

Teacher Commentary is indexed to the student text by the numbers in the margins (under the icons or in circles). The first digit indicates the chapter — the numbers after the decimal indicate the sequential numbering of the comments within that unit. Example:

3.9

3.37

3.9

3.37

Student Pages in Teacher Edition　　　　**Teacher Commentary Page**

Observations

Helen Crowley
Southington High School, CT

"Chapter 3 is a very straightforward approach to triangle trigonometry. It's important because it lays the groundwork for some of the material students will do later with circles. Also, in the third year of the program an entire chapter is devoted to the trigonometric functions; so students' ability to learn and speak the vocabulary here in Year 2 is very helpful for their later work and understanding.

"We used to teach this type of trigonometry only to our best and brightest. But what I've found since teaching this chapter to all levels of students is that most of them really like this material — basically because of its very hands-on and meaningful applications."

Chapter 3

Farah Brown, M.D., Radiologist
Getting the Inside Story

Farah Brown wanted to be a doctor from high school days. "I always enjoyed science and math," she explains. "Also, my aunt was a nurse. I was very close to her and I admired her greatly. She helped me decide to become a doctor." Today, Farah is the vice chair of Radiology at Southwest Hospital and Medical Center in Atlanta, Georgia.

Farah majored in biology at Bishop College in Dallas, Texas. "At first, I thought I wanted to work in pediatrics, but I also found radiology fascinating." A few years later while attending medical school at Howard University she took an elective in radiology and that set her course. "For me, it's the perfect balance of research, academics and patient care," she explains.

Radiologists need to know how to read and interpret all the various types of imaging media, such as CAT scans, MRIs, as well as X rays. "The calculation of angles is often used to determine the positioning of bones from these images," Farah explains. "For example, with scoliosis, which is when a person's spine is bent in an 'S', the scope of the curvature is determined by a series of X rays that are taken from different angles while the patient is standing up. This is called a scoliosis series. Lines are drawn along the end point of the upper-most vertebra at the top of the curve and also at the end point of the lower-most vertebra at the bottom of the curve.

Second lines are then drawn that are perpendicular to the lines of the upper-most and lower-most vertebrae. The angle between the perpendiculars is the measured angle of scoliosis. These measurements," she continues, "help us to determine if the patient will outgrow the problem or if they will need surgery.

"I think it's important to decide what you want to do in life, and then go for it," declares Dr. Brown. "Be determined, be disciplined and stick to your goal. I hope I stand as a role model for young people in my community."

218

Published by IT'S ABOUT TIME, Inc. © 2000 MATHconx, LLC

Chapter 3 Introduction to Trigonometry: Tangles With Angles

The purpose of this chapter is to introduce students to trigonometry based on right triangles. The basic trigonometric functions sine, cosine, and tangent are introduced as ratios from similar triangles. It is important for students to understand that to find the sine of an acute angle, for example, one can use *any* convenient copy of that angle. It is also important for students to become aware of the power of trigonometry in making indirect measurements. Although each of the basic trigonometric functions is introduced in a separate section, students should not *compartmentalize* these ratios. It is suggested that teachers, after completing a section, make later references to problems from that section.

Since students are aware of the $\sin^{-1}$, $\cos^{-1}$, and $\tan^{-1}$ keys on a calculator, a section is devoted to explaining the use of these keys. Also, since students are able to graph $y = \sin x$, $y = \cos x$, etc., a final section is devoted to making a *connection* between the ratios they have been studying and circular motion.

All of the material in this chapter, with the exception of the Law of Sines and the Law of Cosines, is a prerequisite for later chapters in **MATH** *Connections*.

Chapter 3

Introduction to Trigonometry: Tangles With Angles

CHAPTER 3

3.1 The Sine of an Acute Angle

Have you ever flown a kite? If so, did you ever wonder how high the kite was above the ground?

Betty and Jake are on the beach flying kites.

Betty had 200 feet of string and none is left. Jake had 150 feet of string and none is left. A friend estimated the angles that the string made with the ground for each person (Display 3.1).

Published by IT'S ABOUT TIME, Inc. © 2000 MATHconx, LLC

219

3.1 The Sine of an Acute Angle

This section introduces students to the sine ratio based on similar right triangles. From the examples used, students should become aware of the power in historical as well as present day applications of this ratio in making indirect measurements.

Additional Support Materials:

Assessments	Qty
Form (A)	1
Form (B)	1

Blackline Masters	Qty

Extensions	Qty

Supplements	Qty
The Sine of an Acute Angle	4

Chapter 3

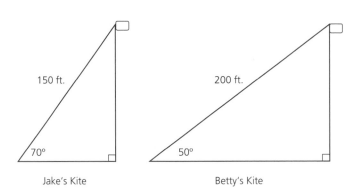

150 ft.

70°

Jake's Kite

200 ft.

50°

Betty's Kite

Display 3.1
Some displays in this chapter might not be to scale.

Which kite do you think is higher Jake's or Betty's? Why?

3.1

Determining the height of a kite can be a serious business, as the following example illustrates.

Humans have successfully harnessed the power of the wind for many purposes over the years. Recently, wind power is again being utilized as a source of renewable energy. In the Tehachapi Mountains of California, the wind is being captured by windmills and used to create electricity. One problem that scientists have in making good use of the wind is finding how high they should install the windmills. One easy way to find out at what height the wind is strongest is to fly a kite and measure how much force is on the string. But, how does one determine the height of the kite? Measuring the angle that the string makes with the ground allows them to calculate the height of the kite. The bigger the pull on the string, the stronger the wind.

Here is a typical problem that a "wind prospector" would need to solve: An engineer is flying a kite to measure the wind strength and lets out 39 feet of string. Assuming that the string is in a straight line, and that it makes an angle of 40° with the ground, calculate the height of the kite.

Two students, Rashad and Rolena remember that they studied *scaling* in **MATH** *Connections* and they decide to solve this problem using a scale diagram. Rashad decides to use a scale of 1 inch to each 10 feet and draws a diagram like the one in

220

Published by IT'S ABOUT TIME, Inc. © 2000 MATHconx, LLC

3.1 The Sine of an Acute Angle

3.1

Jake's kite is approximately 140.95 ft. high and Betty's is 153.21 ft. high. The diagrams are not to scale. Expect an assortment of answers.

NOTES

Display 3.2(a). He determines that the length of AC should be

$$\frac{39}{10} = 3.9 = 3\frac{15}{16} \text{ inches}$$

Then he draws CB perpendicular to the ground (AB) and measures the length of BC.

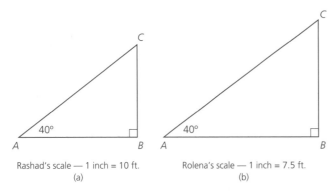

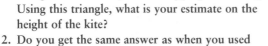
Rashad's scale — 1 inch = 10 ft.
(a)

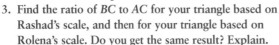
Rolena's scale — 1 inch = 7.5 ft.
(b)

Display 3.2

1. Draw a right triangle like that in Display 3.2(a) with an angle of 40° and a hypotenuse of $3\frac{15}{16}$ inches. What is the length of BC in inches?
2. Using Rashad's scale, what is your estimate for the height of the kite?

a
3.2

Rolena uses a similar method, but she chooses a scale of 1 inch to each 7.5 feet (Display 3.2(b)).

1. Using Rolena's scale, draw an appropriate triangle. Using this triangle, what is your estimate on the height of the kite?
2. Do you get the same answer as when you used Rashad's scale? Explain.
3. Find the ratio of BC to AC for your triangle based on Rashad's scale, and then for your triangle based on Rolena's scale. Do you get the same result? Explain.

b
3.3

The key idea here is that the triangles you have drawn are similar, and consequently the ratios of corresponding sides will always be equal. What this means is that for *any* right triangle with an angle measuring 40° the ratio of its sides will be the same.

Published by IT'S ABOUT TIME, Inc. © 2000 MATHconx, LLC

3.2

1. Lead students through this process. The measure of BC is about $2\frac{1}{2}$ inches.

2. About 25 ft.

3.3

1. Students again should estimate the height at 25 ft.

2. Answers should be the same because the triangles are similar.

3. Student answers will vary but the ratio should be about 0.64.

NOTES

Chapter 3

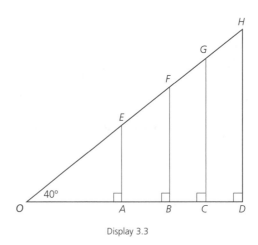

Display 3.3

As you see in Display 3.3, all of the right triangles involved are also similar, so the following ratios of lengths are equal.

$$\frac{AE}{OE} = \frac{BF}{OF} = \frac{CG}{OG} = \frac{DH}{OH}$$

For a 40° angle, mathematicians have found this ratio to be 0.643 (to three decimal places). Does this number agree with (or come close to) your ratios from Rashad's and Rolena's triangles? This ratio is called the sine of 40° and written sin 40°.

You will find a SIN key on your calculator and you will see how this key can help solve many problems without using any scale diagrams. For example, the problem of the wind prospector could be solved by simply noting in Display 3.4 that

$$\frac{opposite}{hypotenuse} = \sin 40° = 0.643$$

$$\frac{BC}{39} = \sin 40° = 0.643$$

or by cross multiplying

$$BC = 39(0.643) = 25.077$$

so the kite is about 25 feet high.

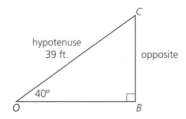

Display 3.4

Published by IT'S ABOUT TIME, Inc. © 2000 MATHconx, LLC

NOTES

The same procedure applies to any acute angle θ in a right triangle (Display 3.5). The **sine** of an acute angle θ in a right triangle is the ratio of the length of the side opposite θ to the length of the hypotenuse. That is,

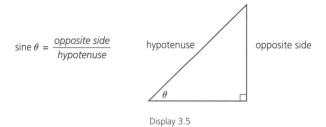

$$\text{sine } \theta = \frac{opposite\ side}{hypotenuse}$$

Display 3.5

About Symbols

The Greek letter θ, read theta, is frequently used in mathematics books to denote angles. Other Greek letters that are used include α, read alpha, and β, read beta.

The purpose of this section is to make you aware of how this ratio sine θ can be used to solve many measurement problems.

Everybody knows what a ball looks like. The word *ball* might bring to mind a baseball, basketball, or a bowling ball.

When viewed from a spaceship far above the Earth, the Earth looks like a ball.

You've probably seen pictures from a spaceship on TV or in magazines. A ball is also called a *sphere*, and the edge of one's view of a sphere or a ball looks like a circle.

This circle has a radius r which is also the radius of the sphere to which it is related.

Published by IT'S ABOUT TIME, Inc. © 2000 MATHconx, LLC

NOTES

3.4

1. How would you measure the radius of a baseball?

2. How would you measure the radius of the Earth?

It is interesting to know that a very good estimate of the radius of the Earth was made over 2000 years ago by a Greek astronomer named Hipparchus. He used the following ideas to estimate the radius of the Earth: Climb a mountain, say five miles high, to point *A* and look toward the horizon at point *B*, as in Display 3.6. He knew that triangle *ABC* was a right triangle. (You can learn why this is a right triangle in the Problem Set.)

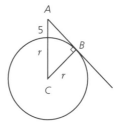

Display 3.6

Let's look at triangle *ABC* after it has been flipped, enlarged, and put into the position shown in Display 3.7.

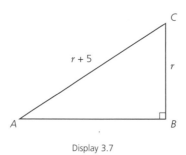

Display 3.7

Using instruments, the angle *CAB* was measured to be (about) 87.15°. Based on the ideas of our previous example, you should see that

$$\sin 87.15° = \frac{r}{r + 5}$$

or, using a calculator to five decimal places,

$$0.99876 = \frac{r}{r + 5}$$

Published by IT'S ABOUT TIME, Inc. © 2000 MATHconx, LLC

3.4

The approximate radius of a baseball is 1.45 in.

1. Let students explore this question.

2. Let students brainstorm, discussing what information is needed, and how it could be collected. They should consider how to calculate without tools. The approximate radius of the Earth is 4000 miles.

Note that in Display 3.6, line *AB* is tangent to the surface of the Earth and the radius is perpendicular at the point of tangency. This will be developed in Display 3.61 and in Chapter 5.

NOTES

Chapter 3

As a result of cross-multiplying, one obtains

$$0.99876 (r + 5) = r$$

or

$$0.99876\, r + 4.99380 = r$$

or

$$0.00124\, r = 4.99380$$

thus

$$r = 4027.258065 \text{ miles}$$

That is, the radius of the Earth is approximately 4027 miles.

Assuming a radius of 4027 miles, what is the circumference of Earth at the equator, assuming also that the Earth is round?

3.5

Jules Verne wrote the book *Around the World in Eighty Days* in 1873. The travelers in that book did not travel around the equator. However, suppose they did travel around the equator. What average speed, in miles per hour, would they have to maintain in order to go around the world in eighty days? What were the fastest ways to travel in 1873? It is not uncommon for jet planes to maintain an average speed of 550 miles per hour, even with refueling. How long would it take such a plane to go around the Earth? Does it matter that the plane is flying about 6 miles above the Earth?

3.6

Published by IT'S ABOUT TIME, Inc. © 2000 MATHconx, LLC

225

3.5

Remind students that the circumference may be found using the formula $C = \pi * \text{diameter}$. $C = \pi * 8054 = 25{,}302$ miles.

3.6

Using the formula $d = rt$; $25{,}302 = r(24 * 80)$ gives 13.18 mi. per hour. Students should have good ideas about means of travel in 1873—balloon, train, horse. It would take a jet plane 46.28 hours to circumnavigate the globe; at 6 miles above the Earth the plane will take 46.35 hours.

NOTES

Chapter 3

Problem Set: 3.1

Problems 1–7 will help you become familiar with computing the sine of an angle using your calculator. For each figure, find the value of x to two decimal places.

1.

60' x 30°

2.

5.4' x 83°

3.

6' x 25°

4.

x 8" 19°

5.

x 18' 32°

6.

17' x 40°

7.

x 179' 5.4°

Published by IT'S ABOUT TIME, Inc. © 2000 MATHconx, LLC

Problem Set: 3.1

1. 30' 2. 5.36' 3. 2.54' 4. 24.57" 5. 33.97' 6. 10.93' 7. 16.85'

NOTES

8. John, a student at Bates School, says that the figure in problem 7 represents the leaning tower of Pisa. Is John correct?

9. On your calculator, press SIN 0 ENTER. Can you explain the answer? What happens when you take the sine of angles that are greater than, but close to 0°?

10. On your calculator, press SIN 90 ENTER. Can you explain the answer? What happens when you take the sine of angles that are less than, but close to 90°?

11. Find the value of r in Display 3.8.

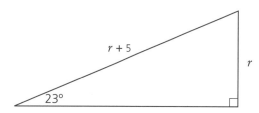

Display 3.8

12. In order to estimate the radius of the Earth, a person climbed a mountain 4 miles high and found that the angle $\angle CAB$ in the diagram below measures 87.4°.

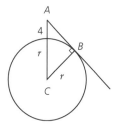

Display 3.9

What estimate of the radius of the Earth did this person get? Is there a mountain somewhere in the world which has a height of 4 miles above the Earth (sea level)?

Published by IT'S ABOUT TIME, Inc. © 2000 MATHconx, LLC

227

8. Of course this is the Leaning Tower of Pisa. Students should recognize the improper spelling of Pisa. The Leaning Tower of Pisa was constructed in 1174 in Tuscany, Italy. The Bell Tower was added in 1350. During construction, the uneven settling of the ground caused the building (which had a foundation too shallow to support the weight) to lean to the south. Engineers have advanced many proposals to halt further tilting, such as injecting thin cement into the foundation and surrounding subsoil, putting extra weight on the higher side, or pumping water away from the surrounding ground, but none of the proposals have been accepted. The tower is 179' on the north side and deviated 17' from the vertical. The angle of lean is approximately 5.4°.

9. If the angle is 0 degrees, then there is zero measure for the side opposite the angle. Suggest that students choose different small angles and compare the results in class. Some responses would be that the sine increases, that the measure is between 0 and 1, etc.

10. A calculator will indicate that sin 90° = 1. Suggest that students choose different angles close to, but less than, 90° and see that the sine is close to, but less than, 1. Also, have students draw right triangles with one angle close to 90°. They should see that the opposite side and the hypotenuse have approximately the same length so that the ratio is close to 1.

11. $0.3907 = \dfrac{r}{(r+5)}$; $0.3907(r+5) = r$; $r = 3.2061$

12. $\sin 87.4 = \dfrac{r}{(r+4)}$; $0.9990(r+4) = r$; $r = 3996$. Mount McKinley is approximately 4 miles high.

Chapter 3

13. (a) What is the area of the parallelogram in Display 3.10(a)?

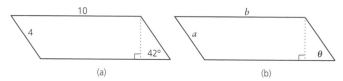

Display 3.10

(b) Generalize your solution to find a formula for the area of the parallelogram in Display 3.10(b).

14. (a) What is the area of the parallelogram in Display 3.11(a)?

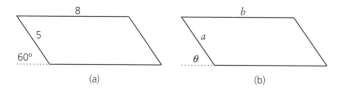

Display 3.11

(b) Generalize your solution to find a formula for the area of the parallelogram in Display 3.11(b).

15. Given a right triangle (Display 3.12)

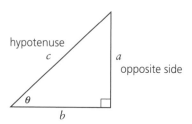

Display 3.12

it is customary to define the **cosecant of** θ, written csc θ, as

$$\csc \theta = \frac{hypotenuse}{opposite\ side} = \frac{c}{a}$$

(a) What is the relation between the sin θ and csc θ?

(b) Explain why there is no need for a **csc** key on a calculator.

16. Explain why one can consider

$$f(\theta) = \sin \theta, \text{ for } 0° < \theta < 90°$$

to be a function.

228

13. (a) Remind students that the area of a parallelogram is base * height. Height is 4 * sin 42° or 2.68 units. Area = 2.68 * 10 = 26.8 units. A discussion of the height relative to the sine of the angle should occur here.

    (b) Students should determine generally that Area = a(sin A)base.

14. (a) 5 * sin 60° * 8 = 34.64 sq. units

    (b) a(sin A) * b or ab(sin A) is the general form.

15. (a) These are reciprocal functions.

    (b) Students need to be aware of the x^{-1} key, which is the reciprocal key.

16. For every θ there is exactly one value for the sine of the angle.

NOTES

Chapter 3

17. When Hipparchus calculated the approximate radius of the Earth, he used an important fact about tangents to circles.

> The angle made by a tangent line and the radius at the point of tangency is a right angle.

How could he be sure? You actually know the answer, but you may not know that you know. We'll lead you through the reasoning which proves that this is always the case. We'll supply the questions; you supply the answers.

To help keep the notation clear, we have drawn and labeled the diagram in Display 3.13. It shows a line, t, tangent at P to a circle with center C. Now, either the angles made by t and PC are right angles or they're not, right? You will show that "they're not" is impossible. That is, the assumption that they are not right angles leads to a conclusion that can't possibly be true.

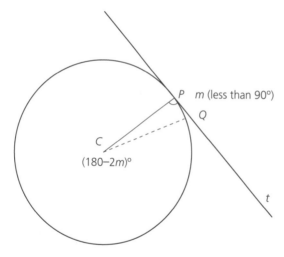

Display 3.13

(a) If the two angles formed by t and PC are not right angles, one of them must measure less than 90°. Why?

(b) If we call the measure of this smaller angle m, then $2m < 180°$. Why?

On the side of the smaller-than-right angle, we've drawn a line segment from C that makes a $(180 - 2m)°$ angle with PC, and extended it until it intersects at some point, Q.

(c) PCQ is a triangle. What is the measure of $\angle CQP$? How do you know?

17. This is a good example of an *indirect logical argument*. Something is proven true by proving its only logical alternative (its negation) false. All these questions can be answered from the material in Chapter 2, along with the definition of tangent.

(a) Together they form a straight angle (180°), so they can't both be greater than 90°.

(b) If $m < 90°$, then $2m < 2 * 90° = 180°$.

(c) *This is the key observation.* Its measure is m because the sum of the angles of any triangle must be 180°, so in this case

$$m + (180° - 2m) + ? = 180°$$
$$m - 2m + ? = 0$$
$$? = m$$

(d) Isosceles. $\angle QPC = \angle PQC$

(e) The same length. If two angles of a triangle are equal in measure, so are the sides opposite them.

(f) On the circle. Since QC is the same length as PC, which is a radius, then QC is also a radius.

(g) It can't happen because Q and P are different points on both the circle and on the tangent line t, but a tangent line only touches the circle in one point.

(h) ... PC and t must form right angles.

NOTES

Chapter 3

(d) What kind of triangle is *PCQ*? How do you know?

(e) Is *QC* longer, shorter, or the same length as *PC* ? How do you know?

(f) Is *Q* inside, outside, or on the circle? How do you know?

(g) Why can't this happen? *Hint:* What does it mean to say that a line is tangent to a circle?

(h) Since it is impossible for *PC* and *t* **NOT** to form right angles, . . . (Finish this sentence.)

18. When Jake was in school, students did not have calculators.

In order to find the sine of an angle, students had to use tables. Part of such a table is given in Display 3.14 where θ is measured in degrees.

θ	$sin\ \theta$	θ	$sin\ \theta$	θ	$sin\ \theta$	θ	$sin\ \theta$	θ	$sin\ \theta$
1	.0175	11	.1908	21	.3584	31	.5150	41	.6561
2	.0349	12	.2079	22	.3746	32	.5299	42	.6691
3	.0523	13	.2250	23	.3907	33	.5446	43	.6820
4	.0698	14	.2419	24	.4067	34	.5592	44	.6947
5	.0872	15	.2588	25	.4226	35	.5736	45	.7071
6	.1045	16	.2756	26	.4384	36	.5878	46	.7193
7	.1219	17	.2924	27	.4540	37	.6018	47	.7314
8	.1392	18	.3090	28	.4695	38	.6157	48	.7431
9	.1564	19	.3256	29	.4848	39	.6293	49	.7547
10	.1736	20	.3420	30	.5000	40	.6428	50	.7660

Display 3.14

(a) Are there any ideas you get about the sine from this table that you did not get before, when computing these numbers on your calculator?

(b) You have previously studied the idea of *linear interpolation*. Remember? Use the above table and linear interpolation to estimate sin 27.4°. Now compute sin 27.4° on your calculator. Do you think the two answers are close together?

230

Published by IT'S ABOUT TIME, Inc. © 2000 MATHconx, LLC

18. (a) Bring out the fact that as θ goes from 0 to 50, the value of $\sin(\theta)$ is increasing.
    (b) $\sin 27.4° = 0.4602$ (to four decimal places)

NOTES

Published by IT'S ABOUT TIME, Inc. © 2000 MATHconx, LLC

19. A baseball has a radius of 1.45 inches. The Earth has a radius of (about) 4000 miles.

(a) If a piece of string is put around a great circle on this baseball, how many inches of string are needed?

(b) If a piece of string is put around a great circle on this baseball, but then moved one inch "out" from the surface, how many inches of string must be added to the amount in part (a) to make a complete circle?

(c) How many inches of string are needed to go around the equator of the Earth?

(d) If a string is put around the equator of the Earth, but then moved one inch "out" from the surface, how many inches of string must be added to the amount in part (c) to make a complete circle?

(e) Do the answers to parts (b) and (d) make sense to you? Explain!

20. A new ski lodge is being built in Vermont, and the builder wants to allow for a skylight. Display 3.15 shows a cross-sectional plan for the roof. Calculate the height w, in meters, allowing for the skylight.

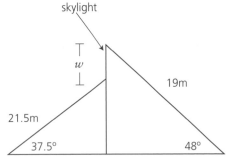

Display 3.15

Published by IT'S ABOUT TIME, Inc. © 2000 MATHconx, LLC

19. A reminder that the circumference of a circle is $2 * \pi *$ radius.
    (a) A great circle is on a plane that passes through the center of the baseball. (9.11 inches)
    (b) 15.93" with string tight, need approximately 6.28" more string.
    (c) $2 * \pi * 4000 * 5280 * 12 = 1,592,410,484$ inches of string.
    (d) 1,592,410,491 with approximately 6.28" more string.
    (e) A discussion here would be interesting, as the answers to (b) and (d) should surprise most students.

20. Look at the diagram below.

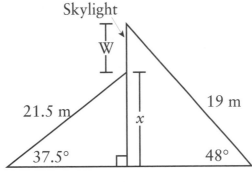

Display 3.1T

$\sin 37.5° = \dfrac{x}{21.5}$, so $x = 13.09$. Also $\sin 48° = \dfrac{y}{19}$, so $y = 14.12$.
Since $w = y - x$, it follows that $w = 1.03$ m.

NOTES

Chapter 3

3.2 The Cosine of an Acute Angle

Learning Outcomes

After studying this section, you will be able to:

Write the definition of the cosine of an acute angle in a right triangle as a ratio;

Use a calculator to find the cosine of an acute angle;

Use the cosine of an acute angle as a problem solving tool;

Explain how to estimate the distance from the Earth to the Moon.

Betty watched and enjoyed the Winter Olympics on TV. She thought that skiing looked easy and seemed to be a lot of fun, so she bought a pair of skis and went up to the mountains in Colorado to a ski jump. She was warned that learning to ski jump took a lot of time and practice, but Betty was sure there would be no problem. Just like the Olympic skiers, she went down, then up, and then down.

Boy, did she go down! Nobody really knows how many bones were broken, but she was in the hospital for several weeks. When Betty was first taken to the hospital, the doctors wanted X rays taken so that they could see where the bones were broken.

One of the problems faced by medical people is that X rays don't usually show exactly where a bone is broken. This happens because the bone is not always parallel to the X ray film. For example, suppose that we look at a side view. The horizontal line segment is supposed to be the film and the darkened line is a bone. The X mark on the bone indicates where a break is located (Display 3.16).

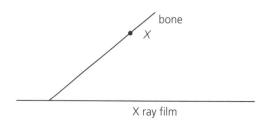

bone
X

X ray film

Display 3.16

3.2 The Cosine of an Acute Angle

This section introduces students to the cosine ratio based on similar right triangles. The example from medical science is a real life problem although it is usually a three dimensional problem rather than two dimensional. The historical example on the distance between the Earth and the Moon should be exploited to make students aware of the power of the cosine ratio in determining distances where direct measurements are difficult or impractical to make. It is suggested that you occasionally refer back to problems involving the sine ratio so that students do not lose sight of the fact that different ratios use different information.

Chapter 3

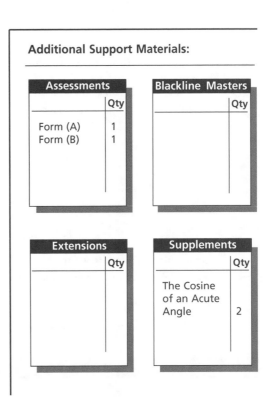

Additional Support Materials:

Assessments	Qty
Form (A)	1
Form (B)	1

Blackline Masters	Qty

Extensions	Qty

Supplements	Qty
The Cosine of an Acute Angle	2

Doctors would like to know the location of the break. It would help, for example, to know the distance L from A to X (Display 3.17).

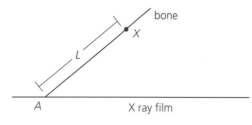

Display 3.17

What doctors can measure from the X ray film, however, is the distance AB indicated in Display 3.18.

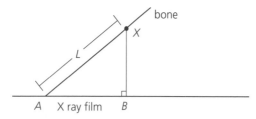

Display 3.18

Doctors frequently know (or can estimate) the angle XAB. They want to use this to find L. Suppose angle XAB is 30° (and the distance AB on the X ray film is 9 inches (Display 3.19).

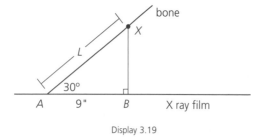

Display 3.19

Using a scale diagram, draw a triangle ABX similar to that in Display 3.19 and estimate the length L.

3.7

3.7

Students should discover that *L* is about 10.4 inches.

NOTES
_____

Chapter 3

Look closely at the right triangle *XAB* (Display 3.20).

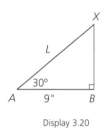

Display 3.20

From our study of similar triangles, we know that all of the right triangles shown in Display 3.21 are similar,

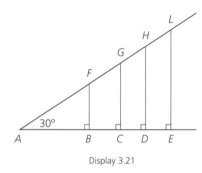

Display 3.21

so the following ratios of lengths are equal.

$$\frac{AB}{AF} = \frac{AC}{AG} = \frac{AD}{AH} = \frac{AE}{AL}$$

Indeed, for any right triangle with an acute angle of 30°, the ratio of lengths

$$\frac{adjacent\ side}{hypotenuse}$$

is going to be the same number (Display 3.22).

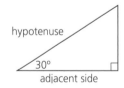

Display 3.22

234

NOTES

Mathematicians have found that this ratio, known as *cosine 30°*, is 0.8660 to four decimal places. Show how this ratio can be used to estimate the length *L* in Display 3.20 without using a scale diagram. Does this estimate agree with (or come close to) that obtained when you used a scale diagram?

a
3.8

One can follow the same procedure with any acute angle θ in a right triangle. The **cosine** of an acute angle in a right triangle is the ratio of the length of the adjacent side to the length of the hypotenuse (Display 3.23). That is,

$$\cos \theta = \frac{adjacent\ side}{hypotenuse}$$

hypotenuse

θ

adjacent side

Display 3.23

The purpose of this section is to make you aware of how this ratio cos θ can be used to solve many measurement problems.

As another example, consider the following situation.

b
3.9

1. The distance from the surface of the Earth to the surface of the Moon is about 240,000 miles. Olympic runners have been able to run about 14 miles per hour. What if an Olympic runner were able to keep on running at this speed along a road from the Earth to the Moon. How long would it take?

Published by IT'S ABOUT TIME, Inc. © 2000 MATHconx, LLC

235

$\cos 30° = \dfrac{9}{L}$, so $L = \dfrac{9}{\cos 30°} = 10.39$

3.8

3.9

1. Running problem: 17,142.86 hours at 14 mph; at this rate it would take 714.29 days.

2. Racing cars: 1411.76 hours at 170 mph or 58.82 days.

NOTES

Chapter 3

2. Racing cars have been known to travel more than 170 miles per hour. What if a race car were able to travel at 170 mph on a road 240,000 miles long from the Earth to the Moon. How long would it take?

How long did it take Apollo 11 to travel from the Earth to the Moon?

3.10

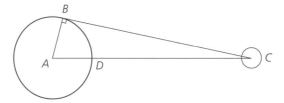

How did anyone come up with the estimate that the distance from the surface of the Earth to the surface of the Moon is about 240,000 miles? Remember Hipparchus, the Greek astronomer, who over 2000 years ago estimated the radius of the Earth to be about 4000 miles? Well, he also estimated the distance from the center of the Earth to the center of the Moon. Hipparchus used a diagram similar to that in Display 3.24.

Display 3.24

3.10 The answer is three days. If students are not familiar with Apollo 11 or do not know the answer, we suggest having them go to the library to check on this.

NOTES

He knew that the lengths of *AB* and *AD* were each about 4000 miles. He was also able to use instruments to measure angle *BAC* as 89.05°. Let's rotate triangle *ABC* and put it into the position shown in Display 3.25:

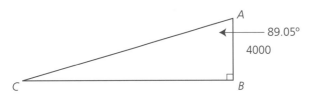

Display 3.25

From this display one observes

$$\cos 89.05° = \frac{4000}{AC}$$

or, using a calculator,

$$0.01658 = \frac{4000}{AC}$$

or

$$AC = \frac{4000}{0.01658} \approx 241,255 \text{ miles}$$

What a genius!

You have now seen two important ratios related to acute angles—the *sine* and the *cosine*. There is a useful relation between these ratios which will be needed for later material. The following activities should help you discover this relation.

1. In the table of Display 3.26, we have computed $(\sin 25°)^2 + (\cos 25°)^2$ for the first line. Using measures for angle *A* (other than 25°) copy and complete the table using a calculator.

3.11

Angle *A*	$(\sin A)^2 + (\cos A)^2$
25°	1

Display 3.26

Published by IT'S ABOUT TIME, Inc. © 2000 MATHconx, LLC

3.11

1. Students should fill in their table and then conjecture that the equation $\sin^2\theta + \cos^2\theta = 1$ is universally true. Remember to use ( ) and press keys as shown in the text. Suggest that students record the values before computing the sum. For example,
$$(\sin 25°)^2 = 0.1786; \quad (\cos 25°)^2 = 0.8214; \quad \text{sum} = 1$$

2. From the diagram,
$$\sin^2\theta + \cos^2\theta = \left(\frac{3}{5}\right)^2 + \left(\frac{4}{5}\right)^2 = \frac{9}{25} + \frac{16}{15} = \frac{25}{25} = 1$$

3. Lead students through this calculator activity.

4. (a) $\frac{b}{c}$ (b) $\frac{b^2}{c^2}$ (c) $\frac{a}{c}$ (d) $\frac{a^2}{c^2}$

   These lead to $\frac{b^2}{c^2} + \frac{a^2}{c^2} = \frac{(b^2 + a^2)}{c^2} = 1$

NOTES

Chapter 3

2. Look at the right triangle in Display 3.27.

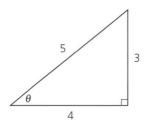

Display 3.27

What is $(\sin \theta)^2 + (\cos \theta)^2$?

3. What conjecture would you make about $(\sin q)^2 + (\cos q)^2$ for any angle? Let's examine additional examples of our conjecture, but let's use the table feature of the TI-82 (TI-83) to save time. Enter in the Y= list: $y_1 = (\sin x)^2$, $y_2 = (\cos x)^2$, and $y_3 = (\sin x)^2 + (\cos x)^2$. Make sure you are in Degree mode. Press 2nd WINDOW (The display shows TABLE SETUP.) and set the TblStart to 1, and △ Tbl to 1. Select AUTO for both variable choices. Press 2nd GRAPH (for Table). Use the right arrow key to access the column for y_3. What do you see? Now use your down arrow to scroll through 89 degrees. What results are you seeing in the y_3 column? Do you think the results will change if you work in increments of 0.5 degrees instead of 1 degree? Reset your TABLE SETUP menu and check the table columns.

4. Now look at the triangle in Display 3.28.

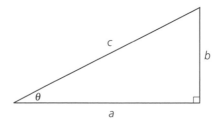

Display 3.28

NOTES

Write each of the following in terms of *a*, *b*, and *c*.

(a) $\sin \theta =$ (b) $(\sin \theta)^2 =$

(c) $\cos \theta =$ (d) $(\cos \theta)^2 =$

What do you notice about $(\sin \theta)^2 + (\cos \theta)^2$?
It is standard to write
$$(\sin \theta)^2 \text{ as } \sin^2 \theta$$
and
$$(\cos \theta)^2 \text{ as } \cos^2 \theta$$
The relation noted above can now be written as
$$\sin^2 \theta + \cos^2 \theta = ?$$

Problem Set: 3.2

Problems 1–5 will help you become familiar with computing
the cosine of an angle, using a calculator. For each figure, find
the value of *x* to two decimal places.

1.

2.

239

Problem Set: 3.2

1. $\cos 20° = \frac{3}{x}$

   $x = \frac{3}{0.9397}$

   $x = 3.19"$

2. $\cos 31° = \frac{5}{x}$

   $5.83" = x$

NOTES

3.

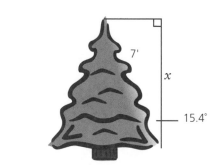

4.

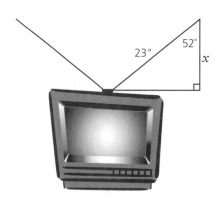

5.

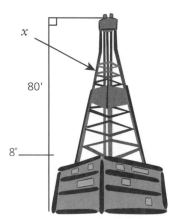

3. $\cos 15.4° = \dfrac{x}{7}$

$6.75' = x$

4. $\cos 52° = \dfrac{x}{23}$, so $x = 14.16"$ 5. $\cos 8° = \dfrac{80}{x}$, so $x = 80.79'$

NOTES

6. For an acute angle θ in a right triangle (Display 3.29), it is customary to define the **secant of** θ, written sec θ, as the ratio of the length of the hypotenuse to the length of the adjacent side. That is,

$$\sec \theta = \frac{hypotenuse}{adjacent\ side}$$

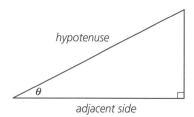

Display 3.29

(a) What is the relation between the sec θ and cos θ?

(b) Why there is no need for a **sec** key on a calculator?

(c) What is sec 31.7°?

7. For an acute angle θ, explain why neither sin θ nor cos θ can be greater than 1.

8. You want to put an antenna on a flat roof. The antenna tower is 17 feet high. A wire making an angle of 35° with the vertical side of the tower is to be used to help support the tower (Display 3.30). How long is the wire?

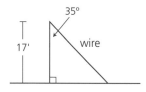

Display 3.30

9. Remember Jake who had to use tables to compute the sine of an angle? Well, believe it or not, he had to use other tables to compute the cosine of an angle. Part of such a table is given in Display 3.31 where θ is measured in degrees.

241

6. (a) They are reciprocals.
    (b) One can use the cos key and then the reciprocal key.
    (c) sec 31.7° = 1.18

7. Since the hypotenuse of a right triangle is the longest side, the denominator in the sine or cosine ratio will always be greater than the numerator, hence neither ratio can exceed 1.

8. If x denotes the length of the wire in feet, then $\cos 35° = \dfrac{17}{x}$, so $x = 20.75'$

NOTES

Chapter 3

3.2 The Cosine of an Acute Angle

θ	$\cos \theta$	θ	$\cos \theta$	θ	$\cos \theta$	θ	$\cos \theta$	θ	$\cos \theta$
1	.9998	11	.9816	21	.9336	31	.8572	41	.7547
2	.9994	12	.9781	22	.9272	32	.8480	42	.7431
3	.9986	13	.9744	23	.9205	33	.8387	43	.7314
4	.9976	14	.9703	24	.9135	34	.8290	44	.7193
5	.9962	15	.9659	25	.9063	35	.8192	45	.7071
6	.9945	16	.9613	26	.8988	36	.8090	46	.6947
7	.9925	17	.9563	27	.8910	37	.7986	47	.6820
8	.9903	18	.9511	28	.8829	38	.7880	48	.6691
9	.9877	19	.9455	29	.8746	39	.7771	49	.6561
10	.9848	20	.9397	30	.8660	40	.7660	50	.6428

Display 3.31

a) Are there any ideas you get about the cos θ from this table that you did not get before, when computing these numbers on your calculator?

b) Use the above table and linear interpolation to estimate cos 27.4°. Now compute cos 27.4° on your calculator. Do you think the two answers are close together?

c) How would you compare the table of sine values in Display 3.14 with the table of cosine values in Display 3.31?

10. If you position yourself at point P in the middle of one end of a board used for table tennis and look at the end of the table tennis net, the angle formed is 33.7°. The distance between a point Q at the end of the net and P is 5.4 feet. Find the length of the table tennis net and the length of the table shown in Display 3.32.

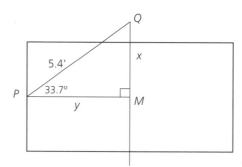

Display 3.32

9. (a) Ask students for their ideas. For example, they should observe that the cosine decreases in value as θ increases from 1° to 50°.

(b) Cosine 27.4° = 0.8878.

(c) Ask students to compare specific angles (e.g., sin 40° to cos 50°).

Also, the sine increases as the angle increases while the cosine decreases in value as the size of the angle decreases. Values between 1 and zero, all positive, and other comparisons may be entertained at this time.

10. Using the diagram in Display 3.2T,

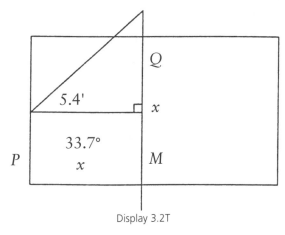

Display 3.2T

observe that (sin 33.7°) (5.4) = x, so x = 3 and the length of the net is 6 ft. From (cos 33.7°) (5.4) = y one obtains y = 4.5, so the length of the table is 9 feet. Numbers are rounded.

NOTES

3.3 The Tangent of an Acute Angle

Airports have used what are called *ceilometers* to find out how high the clouds are in order to see whether or not planes should be allowed to take off or land. A ceilometer consists of three pieces. The first item is a light projector (like a movie or slide projector, but bigger). This projector throws a bright beam of light vertically (straight up) into the clouds (Display 3.33).

Projector

Display 3.33

The light from the projector makes a spot of light on the clouds.

Another instrument, some distance away from the projector, detects the light spot (Display 3.34).

Published by IT'S ABOUT TIME, Inc. © 2000 MATHconx, LLC

Learning Outcomes

After studying this section, you will be able to:

Write the definition of the tangent of an acute angle in a right triangle as a ratio;

Use a calculator to find the tangent of an acute angle;

Use the tangent of an acute angle as a problem solving tool.

243

3.3 The Tangent of an Acute Angle

This section introduces students to the tangent ratio based on similar right triangles. *All* of the problems in this section are important. For example, one problem relates the tan θ to sin θ and cos θ. Another problem relates the idea of the tangent of an angle to the concept of *slope*. Again, it is suggested that you occasionally review problems involving the sine and cosine ratios.

Additional Support Materials:

Assessments	Qty
Form (A)	1
Form (B)	1

Blackline Masters	Qty

Extensions	Qty

Supplements	Qty
The Tangent of an Acute Angle	3

Chapter 3

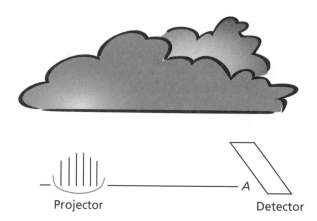

Display 3.34

At the location of the detector there is also an instrument that measures the angle at *A*. The distance from the projector to the detector is known. We now have a right triangle (Display 3.35) where the distance *CA* is known and the measure of angle *A* is known. Suppose *CA* has a length of 1500 feet and angle *A* measures 78° (Display 3.36).

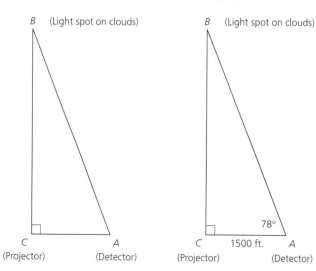

Display 3.35

Display 3.36

3.12

1. Using the cosine of an angle, find the length of *AB* in feet.
2. Using the answer from part 1 above and the Pythagorean Theorem, find the distance *CB* in feet. That is, find how high the clouds are.

244

3.12

1. $\cos 78° = \dfrac{1500}{AB}$

   $AB = 7214.60$ (to two decimal places)

2. $CB \approx 7057$ feet

NOTES

There is an easier way to solve this problem. From our study of similar triangles, we know that all of the right triangles in Display 3.37 are similar:

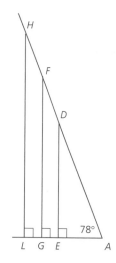

Display 3.37

so that the following ratios of lengths are equal:

$$\frac{HL}{AL} = \frac{FG}{AG} = \frac{DE}{AE}$$

Any one of these equivalent ratios is called the **tangent of 78°**, which is written **tan 78°**. In general, the **tangent** of an angle θ in a right triangle, written **tan** θ, is the ratio of the length of the opposite side to the length of the adjacent side (Display 3.38). That is,

$$\tan \theta = \frac{opposite\ side}{adjacent\ side}$$

245

NOTES

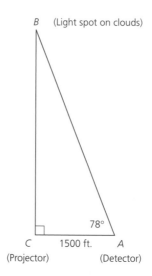

Opposite side

Adjacent side

θ

Display 3.38

Let's return to our problem of finding the cloud height (Display 3.39).

B (Light spot on clouds)

78°

C 1500 ft. *A*
(Projector) (Detector)

Display 3.39

3.13

1. Using a calculator, find tan 78°. (Make sure your calculator is in Degree mode.)
2. Using the result of the first problem, estimate the height of the clouds in Display 3.39. Does this result agree with your previous estimate?

Published by IT'S ABOUT TIME, Inc. © 2000 MATHconx, LLC

3.3 The Tangent of an Acute Angle

3.13

1. $\tan 78° = 4.7046$

2. If x denotes the height of the clouds, then $x = 1500 \tan 78° \approx 7057$ ft. which agrees with our previous estimate.

NOTES

For another example involving the tangent of an angle, consider the following: Wires and metal tubes are part of many different types of instruments and machines, including automobiles, walkmen, cameras, TV sets, etc.

During construction of such items one sometimes needs to know the diameter of the wires or tubes being used. One device that has been used for measuring diameters is the V-gauge. A side view of a V-gauge is given in Display 3.40.

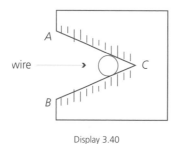

Display 3.40

For this particular V-gauge, the angle *ACB* measures 40°.

NOTES

a
3.14

1. How do you think a V-gauge is used to measure the diameter of the wire in Display 3.40?

2. Other than a V-gauge, do you know of other methods or other tools for measuring the diameter of a wire or a tube?

Let's magnify part of the side view of the V-gauge and insert the radius lines (Display 3.41).

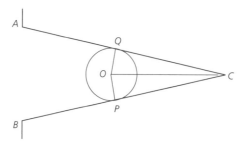

Display 3.41

In this diagram, *O* is the center of the circle representing the wire (or tube), while *P* and *Q* are the points where the wire touches the segments *CB* and *CA*, respectively.

b
3.15

1. What is the measure of angle *OPC*? Explain.

2. What is the measure of angle *OQC*? Explain.

3. What is the measure of angle *OCP* and of angle *OCQ*? Explain.

Our job is to find the length of the radius *OP*. By doubling this number we can compute the diameter of the wire.

c
3.16

If you know that the length of *CP* is 7mm, do you have enough information to find the length of *OP*?

248

Published by IT'S ABOUT TIME, Inc. © 2000 MATHconx, LLC

3.14

1. This deserves a light touch, but ask students for their ideas. Students should understand that the diameter must be calculated.

2. Other tools are calipers and anything else students can think of.

3.15

1. angle $OPC = 90°$ (radius perpendicular to tangent is intuitive)

2. angle $OQC = 90°$

3. angle OCQ and angle OCP are each $20°$

3.16

See what ideas students have. They should come up with $\tan 20° = \frac{OP}{7}$.
$OP = 2.55$ mm. Rounded to two decimal places.

NOTES

Chapter 3

Return to our V-gauge (Display 3.42).

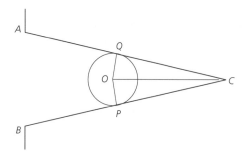

Display 3.42

We know that the measure of angle OCP is 20°. Thus the ratio $\frac{OP}{CP}$ is nothing but the tangent of 20°. That is,

$$\tan 20° = \frac{OP}{CP}$$

The tangent of 20° can be found on your calculator. First make sure you are in the degree mode. Then push the TAN 20 ENTER keys. You will find

$$\tan 20° = .3639702343$$

We now have

$.3640 = \frac{OP}{CP}$ (using four decimal places for tan 20°).

If, for example, we know that CP is 9 millimeters in length, then

$$.3640 = \frac{OP}{9}$$

so $OP = 3.2760$ mm, and it follows that the diameter of the wire is 6.5520 mm.

In this chapter we have been looking at ratios of lengths with names like sine, cosine, tangent, etc. The study of such ratios is known as *trigonometry*.

A Word to Know: Trigonometry is a branch of mathematics which deals with the connections between sides and angles of triangles and related geometric figures.

About Words

The word *trigonometry* comes from the Greek words *trigonon*, meaning triangle, and *metron*, meaning to measure.

249

NOTES

Problem Set: 3.3

Problems 1–7 will give you practice using your calculator to find the tangent of an angle. In each case, find *x*.

1.

4"
45°
x

2.

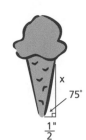

x
75°
$\frac{1}{2}$"

3.

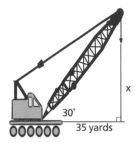

x
30°
35 yards

4.

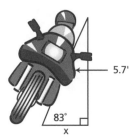

5.7'
83°
x

5

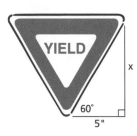

YIELD
x
60°
5"

6.

x
6' 3"
15.4°

7.

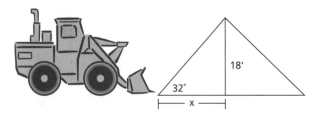

18'
32°
x

Published by IT'S ABOUT TIME, Inc. © 2000 MATHconx, LLC

Problem Set: 3.3

1. $x = 4"$ 2. $x = 1.87"$ 3. $x = 20.21$ yds.   4. $x = 0.7'$ 5. $x = 8.66"$

6. $x = 1.72'$ 7. $x = 28.81'$

NOTES

Chapter 3

8. In the Display 3.43, two tracking stations are located at points *A* and *B*. Points *A* and *B* are 40 miles apart. At the tracking stations, people are measuring the angles of a weather balloon located at point *C*.
   The measurements of the angles are given in the diagram. What is the height *h* of the weather balloon?

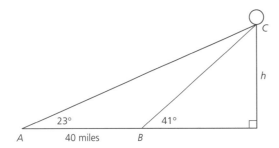

Display 3.43

9. The tangent of an angle can be written in terms of the sin θ and cos θ Explain how

$$\tan \theta = \frac{\sin \theta}{\cos \theta}$$

Recall that $\sin^2 \theta + \cos^2 \theta = 1$. By dividing both sides of this equation by $\cos^2 \theta$, show that

$$\tan^2 \theta + 1 = \sec^2 \theta$$

10. In a right triangle (Display 3.44), with an acute angle it is customary to define the **cotangent of** θ, written cot θ, to be the ratio

$$\cot \theta = \frac{adjacent\ side}{opposite\ side}$$

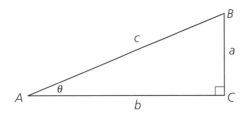

Display 3.44

(a) How is the cotangent of an angle related to the tangent of an angle?

(b) Why is there no need for a **cot** key on a calculator?

(c) What is cot 43.5°?

Published by IT'S ABOUT TIME, Inc. © 2000 MATHconx, LLC

251

8. Use $\tan 41° = \dfrac{h}{x}$ and $\tan 23° = \dfrac{h}{(x + 40)}$ giving $h = 33.18$ mi.

9. In Display 3.3T,

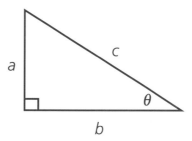

Display 3.3T

note that $\tan \theta = \dfrac{a}{b} = \dfrac{\left(\dfrac{a}{c}\right)}{\left(\dfrac{b}{c}\right)} = \dfrac{\sin \theta}{\cos \theta}$. Taking $\sin^2 \theta + \cos^2 \theta = 1$

and dividing both sides by $\cos^2 \theta$ gives

$$\left(\frac{\sin \theta}{\cos \theta}\right)^2 + 1 = \left(\frac{1}{\cos \theta}\right)^2$$

and since $\tan \theta = \dfrac{(\sin \theta)}{(\cos \theta)}$ and $\sec \theta = \dfrac{1}{(\cos \theta)}$, we get

$$\tan^2 \theta + 1 = \sec^2 \theta$$

10.   (a) The cotangent of an angle is the reciprocal of the tangent of that angle.
     (b) Just find $\tan \theta$ and press x^{-1} to find $\cot \theta$.
     (c) $\cot 43.5 = 1.0538$ to four decimal places.

Chapter 3

11. Using Display 3.45, explain the following identities:

$$\sin (90° - \theta) = \cos \theta \qquad \cos (90° - \theta) = \sin \theta$$

$$\tan (90° - \theta) = \cot \theta \qquad \cot (90° - \theta) = \tan \theta$$

$$\sec (90 - \theta) = \csc \theta \qquad \csc (90° - \theta) = \sec \theta$$

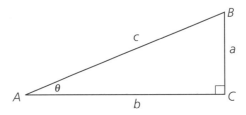

Display 3.45

12. A surveyor wants to find the height of the mountain in Display 3.46. The measurements indicated in the diagram are made. What is the height of the mountain?

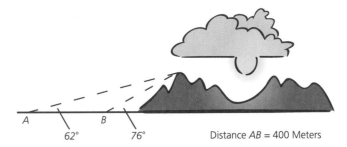

Distance $AB = 400$ Meters

Display 3.46

13. From two tracking stations A and B which are 400 miles apart, the elevation angles of a satellite are determined to be *32°* and *63°*, as illustrated in Display 3.47:

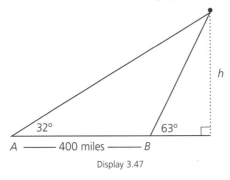

Display 3.47

11. Students should **not** assume sin(90° − θ) = sin 90° − sin θ. Emphasize the relationship between θ and 90° − θ. Remind students that complementary angles sum to 90°. Example if θ = 40°, sin(90° − 40°) = sin 50° = cos 40°.

12. Using the diagram in Display 3.4T,

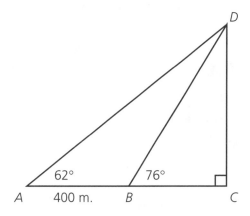

Display 3.4T

one has BC tan 76° = (BC + 400) tan 62°, which gives BC = 353.1715 m. Thus, DC = 353.1715 tan 76° or approximately 1416 meters.

13. Using the diagram in Display 3.5T,

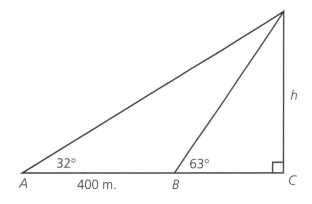

Display 3.5T

one has BC tan 63° = (BC + 400) tan 32°, which gives BC = 186.84 mi. Thus, h = 186.85 tan 63° or approximately 366.7 miles.

What is the height *h* of the satellite?

14. In forestry, trigonometry is sometimes used to determine the height of a tree. How do you think trigonometry is used to determine the height *h* of a tree (Display 3.48)? What measurements are made? Make up an example to show your ideas.

Display 3.48

15. (a) Using a calculator, compute tan 0°. How would you explain this answer to a friend?

    (b) What happens when you try to compute tan 90° on a calculator?

16. Explain why

$$f(\theta) = \tan \theta, \text{ for } 0° < \theta < 90°$$

can be considered a function.

17. In a coordinate plane, draw a straight line which has a positive slope. Explain how the slope of this line is related to the tangent of an angle.

Published by IT'S ABOUT TIME, Inc. © 2000 MATHconx, LLC

253

3.3 The Tangent of an Acute Angle

14. Look at the angle of elevation from the horizontal to the top of the tree and measure distance to the tree. Then use the tangent.

15. (a) Tan 0° = 0. An angle of 0° means the vertical distance is 0 for any horizontal distance traveled.

    (b) There may be an uproar when your students cannot find an answer for tan 90°. Show them $\tan \theta = \dfrac{\sin \theta}{\cos \theta}$, and cos 90° = 0. Therefore, tan 90° is undefined.

16. For every angle measure from 0° to 90°, there is one and only one value for tan θ. Students can test some values. Notice how the value of tan θ increases as θ increases.

17. This problem should not be omitted since it reinforces material previously studied. Tangent is rise-over-run. The slope is the tangent of the angle the line makes with the horizontal axis.

NOTES

Chapter 3

3.4 What Do These SIN⁻¹, COS⁻¹, and TAN⁻¹ Keys Do?

Learning Outcomes

After studying this section, you will be able to:

Use SIN⁻¹, COS⁻¹, and TAN⁻¹ keys on a calculator to solve inverse problems;

Explain how $\sin^{-1}x$, $\cos^{-1}x$, and $\tan^{-1}x$ can be viewed as inverse functions;

Identify the domains of the functions $\sin^{-1}x$, $\cos^{-1}x$, and $\tan^{-1}x$.

In the previous three sections you have become aware of uses for the SIN, COS, and TAN keys on a calculator. You will notice that there are second level keys marked SIN⁻¹, COS⁻¹, and TAN⁻¹. The purpose of this section is to introduce these keys by having you demonstrate their role in solving measurement problems.

3.17

1. Using your ruler and protractor, draw a 3-4-5 right triangle.

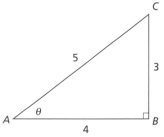

Display 3.49

Your job is to find the angle θ. Using your protractor, measure your angle θ as carefully as possible. What is your answer? Compare your answer with other students in the class.

2. We know from Display 3.49 that

$$\tan \theta = \frac{3}{4} = 0.75$$

$$\sin \theta = \frac{3}{5} = 0.60$$

$$\cos \theta = \frac{4}{5} = 0.80$$

But what is the angle θ? A problem like this is called an *inverse problem*. Take the angle you obtained in problem 1. Using your calculator, compute the tangent of your angle. Is it 0.75 or close to 0.75? Compute the sine of your angle. Is it 0.60 or close to 0.60? Compute the cosine of your angle. Is it 0.80 close to 0.80?

254

3.4 What Do These SIN⁻¹, COS⁻¹, and TAN⁻¹ Keys Do?

The purpose of this section is to introduce students to the *practical* use of the inverse trigonometric keys on a calculator. Although a *soft* reference is made to inverse functions, teachers should not get bogged down in the precise formulation of such references. Students should see the doing and undoing behavior that results from using the trigonometric keys and the inverse trigonometric keys.

3.17

1. Have students compare answers.

2. Student answers should be close.

Note that it would be appropriate to discuss with students the difference between $\text{TAN}^{-1}\,x$ (the angle whose tan is x) and x^{-1} (the reciprocal of x, which is $\frac{1}{x}$).

Chapter 3

Additional Support Materials:

Assessments	Qty
Form (A)	1
Form (B)	1

Blackline Masters	Qty

Extensions	Qty
3.4 Vectors in a Plane	1
"Favorite" Triangles	1

Supplements	Qty
What Do These SIN⁻¹, COS⁻¹, and TAN⁻¹ Keys Do?	3

3. In Display 3.50 we see that $\sin \alpha = \frac{5}{7} = 0.7143$ (to four decimal places). Using whatever method you want, try to find or estimate the angle or α (read *alpha*) in Display 3.50.

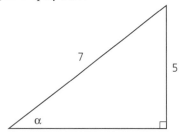

Display 3.50

The problems we are trying to solve, which we have called *inverse problems*, are just the type of problems for which the SIN⁻¹, COS⁻¹, and TAN⁻¹ on a calculator can be used. For example, what if you wanted to find the angle θ in Display 3.51:

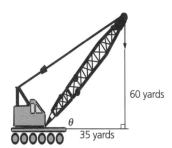

Display 3.51

You can see that

$$\tan \theta = \frac{60}{35} = 1.7143 \text{ (using four decimal places)}$$

We want to find an angle θ such that

$$\tan \theta = 1.7143$$

It is standard to write

$$\theta = \tan^{-1}(1.7143)$$

which is read "θ is an angle whose tangent is 1.7143." You can find such an angle θ on your calculator. Just press 2nd TAN (for TAN⁻¹) followed by 1.7143. You should get

$$\tan^{-1}(1.7143) = 59.74° \text{ (using two decimal places)}.$$

Published by IT'S ABOUT TIME, Inc. © 2000 MATHconx, LLC

255

3.   About 46°

NOTES

3.18

1. Using the **SIN**⁻¹ (2nd **SIN**) on your TI-83, find the angle β (read *beta*) in Display 3.52:

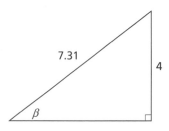

Display 3.52

2. Using the **COS**⁻¹ (2nd **COS**) on your TI-83, find the angle α in Display 3.53:

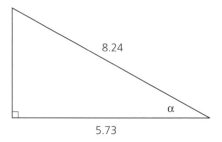

Display 3.53

One may regard sin θ, cos θ, and tan θ as functions with domain $0° < \theta < 90°$. In a similar way, $\sin^{-1}x$, $\cos^{-1}x$, and $\tan^{-1}x$, may be regarded as functions which behave as **inverse functions**. What do we mean by this? In the previous sections we have been entering angle measures, represented by variables θ, x, α or β, into a calculator and computing the sin, cos, or tan of the angle. For example, to compute sin θ, we keyed in the angle measure. (Display 3.54.)

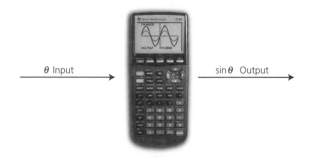

θ Input   sin θ Output

Display 3.54

256

3.18

1. $\beta = 33.17°$ 2. $\alpha = 45.94°$. Remind students that $0 < \alpha < 90$.

NOTES

Now we are reversing the process (Display 3.55).

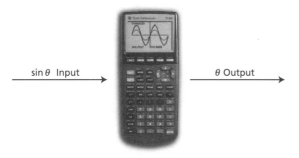

sin θ Input ————→ ————→ θ Output

Display 3.55

1. **As a numerical example, using your TI-83, find sin 24° (Display 3.56).**

3.19

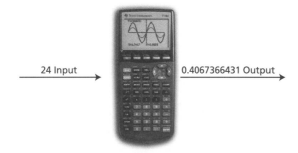

24 Input ————→ ————→ 0.4067366431 Output

Display 3.56

2. **Now, to find the angle measure that has a sin value of .4067366431, perform the following (Display 3.57).**

.4067366431 Input ————→ ————→ 24 Output

Display 3.57

Published by IT'S ABOUT TIME, Inc. © 2000 MATHconx, LLC

257

3.19

In 1. and 2., make sure students know how to use their calculators properly.

NOTES

Chapter 3

We can read $\sin^{-1}x$ as "the angle between 0 and 90 degrees whose sine is x."

3.20

1. Without using your calculator, what is $\tan^{-1}1$?

2. Without using your calculator, what is $\cos^{-1}(\cos 35°)$?

3. Without using your calculator, what is $\sin(\sin^{-1} 0.37542135)$?

4. From the work that we have done so far, what domains would you give to the functions $\sin^{-1}x$, $\cos^{-1}x$, $\tan^{-1}x$ respectively?

As an example of a situation in which these inverse functions can be useful, consider the following: The space station RIM is put in an equatorial orbit 500 miles above the Earth. We wish to locate tracking stations along the equator. Each tracking station has a scanning screen which covers 180° with the horizon as shown in Display 3.58.

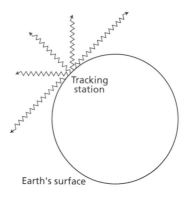

Tracking station

Earth's surface

Display 3.58

The problem is to locate tracking stations close enough to each other so that we do not have gaps where the space station is not being observed by at least one scanner, as in Display 3.59.

258

3.20

1. $TAN^{-1} 1 = 45°$ 2. 35° 3. 0.37542135 4. From previous work, students should see that the domain of $SIN^{-1}x$ or $COS^{-1}x$ is $0 < x < 1$ or $0 \leq x \leq 1$. The domain of $TAN^{-1}x$ is $0 < x$ or $0 \leq x$.

NOTES

Chapter 3

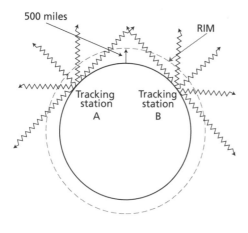

Display 3.59

Now, the furthest apart that stations A and B could be is illustrated in Display 3.60.

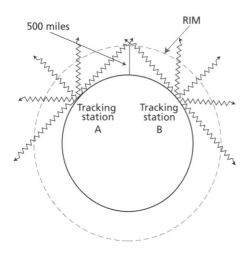

Display 3.60

Using 4000 miles as the radius of the Earth and observing the symmetry in the above figure, you should see that it is necessary to find the length of the arc (part of the circumference) *d* in Display 3.61.

Published by IT'S ABOUT TIME, Inc. © 2000 MATHconx, LLC

259

NOTES

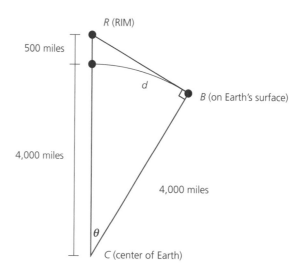

Display 3.61

3.21

1. Find the distance *d*. (*Hint*: Find the angle θ. Then use the fact that the length of an arc is proportional to its associated angle.) That is, in Display 3.62,

$$\frac{\theta}{360} = \frac{arc\ length\ d}{circumference}$$

2. How many stations are necessary to be sure there are no gaps along the equator?

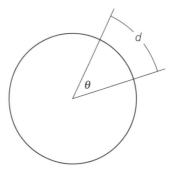

Display 3.62

3.21

1. Angle SBC is 90° and $\cos^{-1}\left(\frac{4000}{4500}\right) = 27.27° = \theta$.

   Thus, $d = 0.075739012 *$ circumference of Earth (25,132) = 1903.5 miles.

   Distance between stations is 3807 since the station can track incoming and outgoing.

2. The number of stations, $n = \frac{25,132 \text{ (circumference of Earth)}}{3807 \text{ (distance between stations)}} = 6.6$, so at least seven stations are needed.

NOTES

Chapter 3

Problem Set: 3.4

Problems 1–5 will help you become familiar with the "inverse" keys on your calculator. In each problem, find the measure of angle θ.

1.

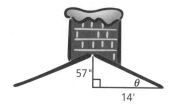

2.

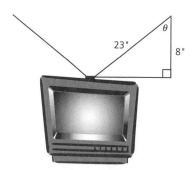

3.

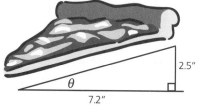

4.

Published by IT'S ABOUT TIME, Inc. © 2000 MATHconx, LLC

261

Problem Set: 3.4

1. 18.7°

2. 69.65°

3. 19.15°

4. 35.69°

NOTES

5.

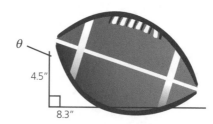

θ

4.5"

8.3"

6. A rectangle is 24 centimeters long and 10 centimeters wide. Find the angles that a diagonal makes with the sides.

7. A 40 foot ladder is used to reach the top of a 30 foot wall. If the ladder extends 4 feet past the top of the wall, what is the angle that the ladder forms with the horizontal ground?

8. A space station is put in an equatorial orbit 200 miles above the Earth. You want to locate tracking stations along the equator. Each tracking station has a scanning screen which covers 180° with the horizon. What is the longest distance allowed between two tracking stations so that there are no gaps?

5. 61.53°

6. 67.38°; 22.62°

7. 56.44°

8. Using the same procedure as in the example of this section, $1239 * 2 = 2478$ miles is the longest distance allowed between two tracking stations so that there are no gaps.

NOTES

Chapter 3

3.5 The Law of Sines– The Law of Cosines

There are two laws—one obeyed by sines, the other by cosines. In this section you will see how these laws expand a person's toolbox for solving measurement problems.

In the triangle *ABC* of Display 3.63, where all angles are acute, a perpendicular is dropped from *C* to the segment *AB*.

Learning Outcomes

After studying this section, you will be able to:

Explain the Law of Sines;

Use the Law of Sines in solving measurement problems;

Explain the Law of Cosines;

Use the Law of Cosines in solving measurement problems.

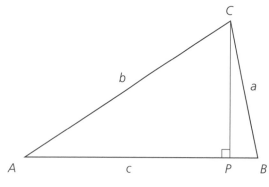

Display 3.63

The letter *P* is used to denote the point of intersection of this perpendicular and the segment *AB*. Observe that

$$\sin A = \frac{CP}{b}$$

and by cross multiplying you have

$$b \sin A = CP$$

1. Show that
$$a \sin B = CP$$

3.22

2. Explain why
$$b \sin A = a \sin B$$

3. Explain how one uses the result of problem 2 to obtain
$$\frac{\sin A}{a} = \frac{\sin B}{b}$$

263

3.5 The Law of Sines — The Law of Cosines

The title of this section gives an accurate account of the content. Although the Law of Sines and the Law of Cosines are powerful tools used in many applications, including engineering studies, some teachers regard this section as challenging material. It should be noted that this section is not a prerequisite for later chapters in **MATH** *Connections*.

3.22

1. From Display 4.63, $\sin B = \frac{CP}{a}$, so $a \sin B = CP$.

2. "Things equal to the same thing are equal to each other."

3. Divide both sides of the equation in question 2. by ab.

4. Drop a perpendicular from B to the side AC denoting the point of intersection by Q. Using the figure in Display 3.6T,

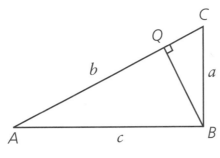

Display 3.6T

$\sin A = \frac{BQ}{C}$, so $c \sin A = BQ$. Also, $\sin C = \frac{BQ}{a}$, so $a \sin C = BQ$. It follows that $c \sin A = a \sin C$ or, dividing both sides by ac,

$$\frac{\sin A}{a} = \frac{\sin C}{c}$$

5. "Things equal to the same thing are equal to each other."

Chapter 3

Assessments   Blackline Masters   Extensions   Supplements

For Additional Support Materials see page T-541

4. Using a process similar to the above, show that

$$\frac{\sin A}{a} = \frac{\sin C}{c}$$

5. Explain why

$$\frac{\sin A}{a} = \frac{\sin C}{c} = \frac{\sin B}{b}$$

The equation in problem 5 above is known as the **Law of Sines.** This law can be a big help in obtaining measurements in triangles where some information is known. The following exercises will help to demonstrate this idea.

3.23

1. In the triangle of Display 3.64, find the length of *AC*, the length of *AB*, and the measure of angle *ACB*.

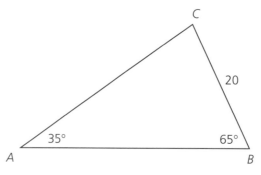

Display 3.64

2. In the triangle of Display 3.65, find the measures of the angles at *C* and at *A*.

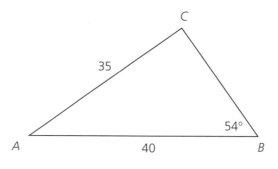

Display 3.65

Published by IT'S ABOUT TIME, Inc. © 2000 MATHconx, LLC

264

3.23

1. Using

$$\frac{\sin 35°}{20} = \frac{\sin 65°}{AC}$$

we obtain $AC = 31.60$. The measure of angle ACB must be $180° - 35° - 65° = 80°$. Using

$$\frac{\sin 35°}{20} = \frac{\sin 80°}{AC}$$

we obtain $AB = 34.34$.

2. Using

$$\frac{\sin 54°}{35} = \frac{\sin C}{40}$$

we obtain $\sin C = 0.9246$. Using $\sin^{-1}$, the angle $C = 67.61°$.

Since the sum of the angles of the triangle must be 180°, the angle at $A = 58.39°$.

Additional Support Materials:

Assessments	Qty
Form (A)	1
Form (B)	1

Blackline Masters	Qty

Extensions	Qty

Supplements	Qty
The Law of Sines — The Law of Cosines	2

Chapter 3

O.K. You have the idea of the Law of Sines. Now let's look at another law. This one involves cosines.

You are all familiar with the Pythagorean Theorem which states that for any right triangle, as illustrated in Display 3.66, $a^2 + b^2 = c^2$.

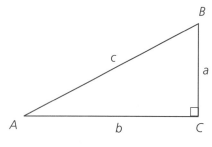

Display 3.66

Our object is to find out what happens if we keep the lengths a and b the same but change the right angle at C to an acute angle. Clearly the length c has changed, say to d (Display 3.67).

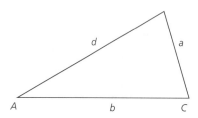

Display 3.67

Published by IT'S ABOUT TIME, Inc. © 2000 MATHconx, LLC

265

NOTES

3.24

Using a ruler and protractor, draw a 3–4–5 right triangle (Display 3.68(a)). Now, keeping the sides with lengths 3 and 4 the same length, draw another triangle with the right angle changed to one that is less than 90° (Display 3.68(b)). Measure the length d as carefully as you can. How does d^2 compare with $3^2 + 4^2$?

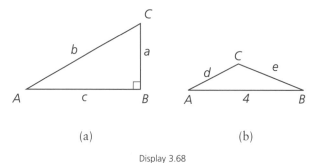

(a)   (b)

Display 3.68

In general, when one changes from

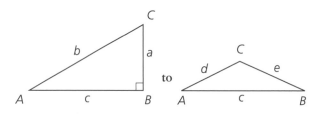

one would not expect $a^2 + b^2$ to equal d^2. Indeed, one should expect that

$$d^2 < a^2 + b^2$$

Mathematicians thought about this and said, "O.K., so d^2 is smaller than $a^2 + b^2$. But d^2 plus some number must equal $a^2 + b^2$. That is,

$$d^2 + (\text{some number}) = a^2 + b^2$$

As we change the angle at C, the 'some number' will change also, but maybe there is a pattern." Let's see if we can find such a pattern.

266

3.24

Students should find $d^2 < 3^2 + 4^2$.

NOTES

In Display 3.69, observe that a perpendicular was dropped from B to the side AC, the point of intersection marked as point P. The acute angle at C will be denoted θ.

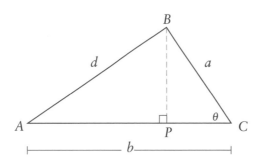

Display 3.69

1. Explain why $d^2 = (AP)^2 + (BP)^2$.

2. Explain why $BP = a \sin \theta$.

3. Explain why $PC = a \cos \theta$.

4. Show that $AP = b - a \cos \theta$.

5. Using the results in 1, 2, and 4 above, show that
   $d^2 = a^2 + b^2 - 2ab \cos \theta$.

   Hint: $\sin^2 \theta + \cos^2 \theta = 1$

   From the result in problem 5 above we have

$$d^2 = a^2 + b^2 - 2ab \cos \theta$$

or

$$d^2 + 2ab \cos \theta = a^2 + b^2$$

We found it! The missing number or the (some number) is no longer a mystery. That number is

$$2ab \cos \theta$$

Remember, we only got this number for an acute angle. Later, you will see that the same number works with *any* angle. This result is known as the **Law of Cosines** and is usually written in the form
$d^2 = a^2 + b^2 - 2ab \cos \theta$, where d is the side opposite θ.

Published by IT'S ABOUT TIME, Inc. © 2000 MATHconx, LLC

3.25

267

3.5 The Law of Sines — The Law of Cosines

3.25

1. This follows from the Pythagorean Theorem.

2. $\sin \theta = \frac{BP}{a}$, so $BP = a \sin \theta$.

3. $\cos \theta = \frac{PC}{a}$, so $PC = a \cos \theta$.

4. $AP = b - PC = b - a \cos \theta$.

5. Using the equation in problem 1,

$$d^2 = (b - a \cos \theta)^2 + (a \sin \theta)^2, \text{ or}$$

$$d^2 = b^2 - 2ab \cos \theta + a^2(\sin^2\theta + \cos^2\theta)$$

$$d^2 = a^2 + b^2 - 2ab \cos \theta$$

NOTES

Chapter 3

The following exercises are designed to help you become familiar with the Law of Cosines.

3.26

1. In the triangle of Display 3.70, find the length of the side *BC*.

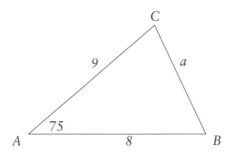

Display 3.70

2. In the triangle of Display 3.71, find the measure of the angle at *A*. *Hint:* Make use of cos⁻¹.

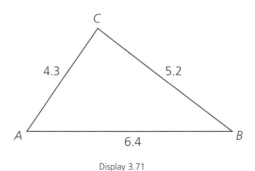

Display 3.71

It is hoped that you begin to see the power of the Law of Sines and the Law of Cosines. Obviously, you could solve measurement problems by literally going through the proof of these laws each time one was needed. However, the statements of these laws allow you to bypass that work and offer powerful tools for solving many measurement problems.

3.26

1. $(BC)^2 = 64 + 81 - 2(9)(8) \cos 75° = 107.73$, so $BC = 10.38$.

2. $(5.2)^2 = (6.4)^2 + (4.3)^2 - 2(4.3)(6.4) \cos A$, so $\cos A = .5888$.

   Using COS^{-1}, we find the angle at $A = 53.92°$.

NOTES

Chapter 3

Problem Set: 3.5

1. Two ships leave the harbor at Boston. The angle between their paths is 43°. One ship is traveling at a rate of 35 miles an hour, the other ship is traveling at a rate of 25 miles per hour. At the end of two hours, what is the distance between the two ships?

2. A Delta Airlines flight from Houston to Cincinnati, a distance of 1029 miles, encounters a violent thunderstorm immediately after takeoff and flies off course by 22.5°. After flying off course for 400 miles, how far is the plane from Cincinnati (Display 3.72)?

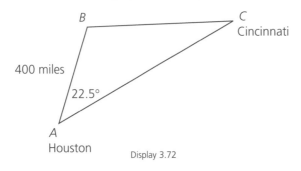

Display 3.72

3. In the triangle of Display 3.73, find the measure of the angle at *B*, the length of *AB*, and the length of *AC*.

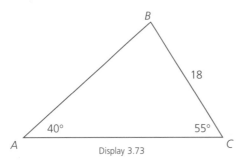

Display 3.73

4. There are three boats off the coast of Long Beach, California. The captain of boat *M* knows that boat *N* is 4.5 miles away and boat *P* is 5.3 miles away. The angle between the two sightings is 40° (Display 3.74).

    (a) How far apart are boats *N* and *P*?

    (b) The captain realized he made a mistake in calculating the angle between the two sightings. It should have been 32°. Using this angle, how far apart are boats *N* and *P*?

Published by IT'S ABOUT TIME, Inc. © 2000 MATHconx, LLC

269

Problem Set: 3.5

1. Using Display 3.7T, we have

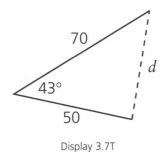

Display 3.7T

$$d^2 = 70^2 + 50^2 - 2(70)(50) \cos 43° \text{ or } d^2 = 2280.52, \text{ so}$$

$$d = 47.75 \text{ miles}$$

2. From Display 3.72, we have

$(BC)^2 = 400^2 + 1029^2 - 2(400)(1029) \cos 22.5° \text{ or } (BC)^2 = 458303.37,$
so $BC = 676.98$ miles

3. From Display 3.73, using the Law of Sines,

$$\frac{\sin 40°}{18} = \frac{\sin 55°}{AB}, \text{ so } AB = 22.94$$

Since the sum of the angles of the triangle is 180°, the angle at $B = 85°$.

Thus, $\frac{\sin 40°}{18} = \frac{\sin 85°}{AC}$ or $AC = 27.90$

4. (a) $(NP)^2 = (5.3)^2 + (4.5)^2 - 2(4.5)(5.3) \cos 40°$, which gives
      $NP = 3.44$ miles.
   (b) $(NP)^2 = (5.3)^2 + (4.5)^2 - 2(4.5)(5.3) \cos 32°$, which gives
      $NP = 2.81$ miles.

Chapter 3

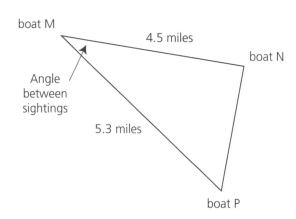

Display 3.74

5. (a) A Major League baseball diamond is a 90 foot square.
      The pitcher's mound is 60.5 feet from home plate.
      How far is it from the pitcher's mound to first base?

   (b) A Little League baseball diamond is a 60 foot square.
      The pitcher's mound is 46 feet from home plate.
      How far is it from the pitcher's mound to first base?

6. A large building has a roof which is slanted at an angle of
   15° from the horizontal. An antenna tower was previously
   installed in a vertical position on the roof. A person located
   100 feet from the base of the tower observes that the roof
   forms an angle of 24° with the top of the tower
   (Display 3.75). How high, in feet, is the tower?

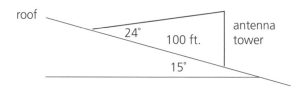

Display 3.75

7. Roland and Laura are 500 feet apart looking in the sky at a
   balloon that is between them and in the same vertical plane
   with them. Roland estimates that the sighting of the
   balloon makes an angle of 75° with the ground. From her
   viewpoint Laura estimates that the balloon makes an angle
   of 50° with the ground. Estimate the height of the balloon.

270

5. (a) From Display 3.8T,

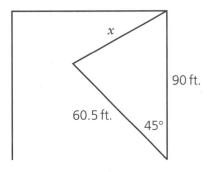

Display 3.8T

$x^2 = (60.5)^2 + (90)^2 - 2(60.5)(90) \cos 45°$, so $x = 63.72$ feet.
   (b) Using a procedure similar to that in part (a), we obtain a distance of 42.58 feet.

6. Using Display 3.9T, we have

$$\frac{\sin 24°}{x} = \frac{\sin 81°}{100 \text{ ft.}} \text{, so } x = 41.18 \text{ ft.}$$

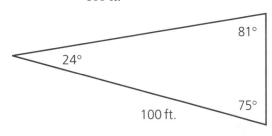

Display 3.9T

7. Ask students to conjecture whether or not AB is greater than, less than, or equal to 500 feet. Ask them to explain how they arrived at their conjecture. In Display 3.10T, angle $BAC = 55°$, so we have

$$\frac{\sin 55°}{500} = \frac{\sin 50°}{AB} \text{, so } AB = 467.58 \text{ feet}$$

Since $\sin 75° = \dfrac{h}{467.58 \text{ ft.}}$, it follows that $h = 451.65$ feet

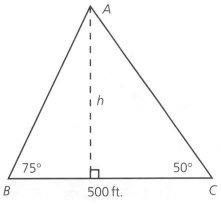

Display 3.10T

Published by IT'S ABOUT TIME, Inc. © 2000 MATHconx, LLC

Chapter 3

3.6 Sine and Cosine Curves: Going Around in Circles

On your TI-82 (TI-83), using the MODE key, make sure your calculator is in the Degree mode. Then, using the WINDOW key, insert the following numbers: Xmin = 0, Xmax = 720, Xscl = 10, Ymin = –2, Ymax = 2, and Yscl = 1.

Now, press the Y = key, then key Y₁ = sin X.

Press GRAPH, to obtain a graph of Y₁ = sin X.

1. How would you describe this curve to a friend?

2. Do you have ideas about where or when such a curve would occur in the real world?

3.27

   Using the same WINDOW settings as above, use the Y= key to set Y₂ = cos X,

   and using the GRAPH key, obtain a graph of Y₂ = cos X.

3. What ideas do you have about how these graphs are related to the sine and cosine of an acute angle that we have been studying in the previous sections?

3.28

   Write a paragraph on how the graph of Y₂ = cos X differs from the graph of Y₁ = sin X.
   Hint: You might want to graph Y₁ = sin X and Y₂ = cos X on the same screen.

3.29

Let's begin by looking at some situations where graphs that "look something like these" might occur.

In harbors off the ocean, the height of the water changes with the tides.

Learning Outcomes

After studying this section, you will be able to:

Identify real world situations where *wavy* or *repeating* curves arise;

Relate the coordinates of points on the circle $x^2 + y^2 = 1$ in the first quadrant to the sine and cosine of acute angles;

Extend the domains of the functions sin x, cos x, and tan x;

Explain how one arrives at the graphs of $y = \sin x$ and $y = \cos x$ that appear on a calculator screen.

Published by IT'S ABOUT TIME, Inc. © 2000 MATHconx, LLC

3.6 Sine and Cosines Curves: Going Around in Circles

This section will form a bridge between right triangle trigonometry and the circular functions. The latter topic appears in greater detail in Year 3 of **MATH** *Connections*. There is a need for this bridge since many students have seen the graphs of $y = \sin x$, $y = \cos x$, etc., on their calculators. The question posed by students is how these curves relate to the trigonometric functions previously discussed in this chapter. This section attempts to answer that question and to provide a foundation for extensions of the trigonometric functions which will be of value to students later.

1. Class discussion.

2. Nice area for discussions.
   Examples might include sound waves, daylight, biorhythm, etc.

3.27

3.28 Guide students to see that ordered pairs are in the form $(x, \sin x)$ or $(x, \cos x)$.

Some students may discuss the period of the function, but most should recognize they are the same curve but shifted, repetitive, etc.

3.29

Chapter 3

Additional Support Materials:

Assessments	Qty
Form (A)	1
Form (B)	1
Chapter Test (A)	1
Chapter Test (B)	1

Blackline Masters	Qty

Extensions	Qty

Supplements	Qty
Sine and Cosine Curves: Going Around in Circles	1

3.6 Sine and Cosine Curves: Going Around in Circles

In one harbor, the height of the water was measured as follows, where M denotes midnight on a certain day (Display 3.76).

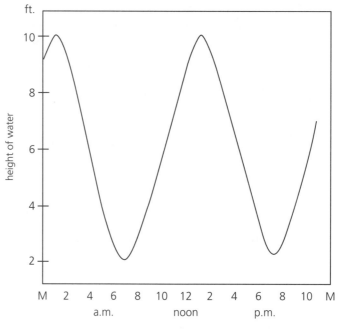

Display 3.76

3.30

1. Over what time periods does the water level appear to be getting lower (decreasing)?

2. Over what time periods does the water level appear to be getting higher (increasing)?

A monkey jumped onto a spoke of a windmill. You can see him on the left sides of Display 3.77. The wind is blowing and the windmill is turning clockwise at a steady rate. The monkey holds on tightly and doesn't fall off. As time goes by, the monkey's height above the ground changes.

272

Published by IT'S ABOUT TIME, Inc. © 2000 MATHconx, LLC

3.30

1. Approximately 1a.m.–7a.m. and approximately 1p.m.–7p.m. The cycle repeats about every 12 hours.

2. 7a.m.–1p.m., 7p.m.–1a.m.; about every 12 hours

NOTES

Chapter 3

Display 3.77

At the lowest point the monkey is 10 feet off the ground, and at his highest point he is 30 feet off the ground. What happens if we plot the monkey's height with time? A graph might look something like the following (Display 3.78).

a

3.31

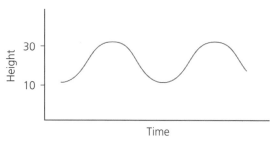

Display 3.78

How would you describe this graph to a friend?

The seasonal changes in the length of daylight may be represented by a graph. Atlanta, Georgia has its longest day with 14 hours of daylight on June 21 and its shortest day with about 9 hours, 20 minutes of daylight on December 21.

On a piece of graph paper, sketch the diagram in Display 3.79. Estimate the position of the two points, the longest day and the shortest day of the year. Estimate some other points and then draw a smooth curve through your points. How would you describe this curve to a friend?

b

3.32

Thinking Tip

Try to improve estimates. Any time you make an estimate, try to find some way to make a *better* one.

Published by IT'S ABOUT TIME, Inc. © 2000 MATHconx, LLC

3.6 Sine and Cosine Curves: Going Around in Circles

3.31

This question is meant to initiate class discussion.

3.32

Height will change over time.

NOTES

_____

_____

_____

_____

_____

_____

_____

_____

_____

_____

_____

_____

_____

_____

_____

Chapter 3

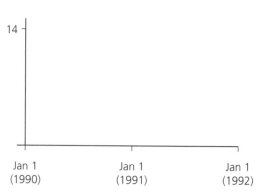

Hours of daylight in Atlanta, Georgia

Display 3.79

One might call the curves we've been looking at *wavy curves* or *repeating curves*. Such curves occur in many areas. For example, when a string is plucked on a guitar, the string vibrates (Display 3.80(a)), sending waves through the air. Let's look at how this occurs.

Think of the air around the string as consisting of many little balls of air (known as *molecules* of air).

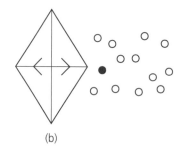

(a)   (b)

Display 3.80

Look at the ball of air that is darkened in Display 3.80(b). As the string vibrates, this ball of air moves back and forth just as the string does (Display 3.81).

Display 3.81

This ball of air hits other balls of air, which, in turn hit other balls of air—all the way to your ear, which you now hear

Published by IT'S ABOUT TIME, Inc. © 2000 MATHconx, LLC

274

NOTES

as music. The motion of the ball of air is looked at even closer in Display 3.82.

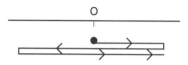

Display 3.82

We assume the ball of air is originally at **O**. The ball then moves back and forth as the string vibrates. Let's put a unit of measurement on the **O** line as follows (Display 3.83).

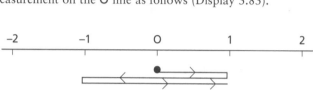

Display 3.83

As time goes by, the coordinate of the ball of air is going to change. On a piece of graph paper, sketch a graph of where the ball is located as time goes by (Display 3.84).

3.33

Coordinate of ball of air

Display 3.84

Does this graph look similar to the graph of $Y_1 = \sin X$ that you saw on your calculator? Explain!

3.34

We'll now help you see where the graph of $Y_1 = \sin X$ on your calculator comes from and how it is related to the sine of an angle.

Published by IT'S ABOUT TIME, Inc. © 2000 MATHconx, LLC

275

3.6 Sine and Cosine Curves: Going Around in Circles

3.33

Will start like a sine curve, but can be expected to have largest height get smaller as time goes by. Good discussion question.

3.34

You will want students to share their ideas.

NOTES

Chapter 3

To do this, we need points on a circle. Recall that a **circle** is the set of all points a fixed distance (called the *radius*) from a fixed point (called the *center*). When a circle is graphed in a Cartesian plane with center at (0, 0), its equation is surprisingly simple. To derive the equation, all you need to do is use the Pythagorean Theorem.

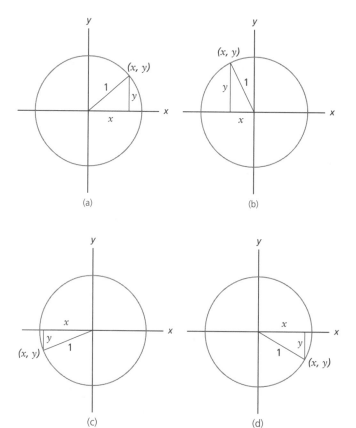

Display 3.85

The circles in Display 3.85 have radius 1, but you could use this procedure for a circle with any radius. Look at the triangles drawn in the circles. If x and y are the coordinates of a point on any one of the circles, applying the Pythagorean Theorem gives

$$x^2 + y^2 = 1$$

276

NOTES

In Display 3.85(a), let θ be the angle formed by the positive x axis and the line from the origin to the point (x, y). This information is shown in Display 3.86.

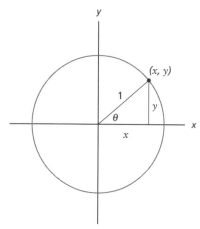

Display 3.86

Observe that

$$\sin \theta = \frac{y}{1} = y \text{ and } \cos \theta = \frac{x}{1} = x$$

That is, *the point (x, y) is the same point as $(\cos \theta, \sin \theta)$.* This fact allows us to extend our ideas about the sine, cosine, and tangent of an angle. Before doing this, however, we look at the point (x, y) above in a more precise way. We think of the angle as starting on the positive x-axis and ending with the line from the origin to the point (x, y), moving in a counterclockwise direction. Suppose we start with the positive x axis and end with the line from the origin to the point (c, d) in Display 3.87. The resulting angle is indicated in the figure.

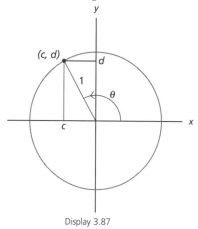

Display 3.87

Published by IT'S ABOUT TIME, Inc. © 2000 MATHconx, LLC

277

3.6 Sine and Cosine Curves: Going Around in Circles

NOTES

Chapter 3

Now we can see why people define

$$\cos \theta = c$$

and

$$\sin \theta = d$$

In this case, note that the cosine of θ is negative since c is negative. The sine of θ is positive, since d is positive.
Let's try an example! We want to find the coordinates of P in Display 3.88, where $\theta = 45°$.

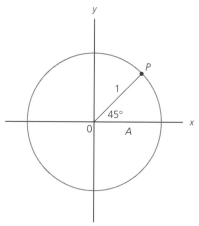

Display 3.88

Drop a perpendicular from P to the x-axis, intersecting the x-axis at point A (Display 3.89).

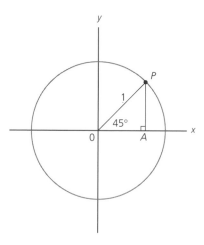

Display 3.89

NOTES

1. In Display 3.89, why is $OA = AP$?

2. From the diagram and the Pythagorean Theorem, we know that

$$(OA)^2 + (AP)^2 = 1$$

Show how this leads to

$$(OA)^2 = \tfrac{1}{2}$$

3.35

3. Using the result of problem 2, find the coordinates of the point P (to two decimal places).

4. Explain how the result of problem 3 shows that $\sin 45° = \cos 45° = 0.71$ (to two decimal places).

REFLECT

In this chapter you have been exposed to the basic ideas of *trigonometry*. This is a subject which is historically a significant and practical one. Historically, trigonometry played a role in the building of the Egyptian pyramids. Today, as well as yesteryear, trigonometry offers practical rules for surveying land, computing mountain heights, etc. The ideas in the final section of this chapter have been very useful in the study of electricity. In particular, alternating current (the kind used in households in the United States) involves back-and-forth surges of current representing a kind of "wavy" motion, similar to the motion depicted in sine and cosine curves. You will see more of this topic in a later book of **MATH** *Connections*.

Problem Set: 3.6

Problems 1–6 will help you become familiar with this new idea of sine and cosine. In each case, find the sine and the cosine of θ.

1.

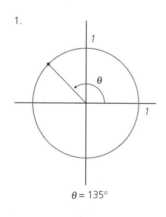

$\theta = 135°$

2.

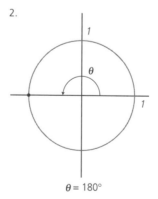

$\theta = 180°$

Published by IT'S ABOUT TIME, Inc. © 2000 MATHconx, LLC

3.35

1. Angle *OPA* must be 45°, so the triangle is isosceles. Thus $OA = AP$.
2. From 1. we can substitute OA for AP, getting

$$2(OA)^2 = 1 \quad \text{or} \quad (OA)^2 = \frac{1}{2}$$

3. The coordinates of *P* are (0.71, 0.71) rounded to two decimal places
4. The *y*-coordinate of *P* is sin 45°, while the *x*-coordinate of *P* is cos 45°. Thus,

   sin 45° = cos 45° = 0.71 rounded to two decimal places

Problem Set: 3.6

Note that in problems 1–9(b), decimals are rounded to two decimal places.

1. (−0.71, 0.71)   2. (−1, 0)

NOTES

Chapter 3

3.

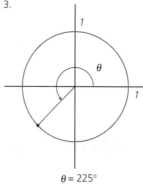

$\theta = 225°$

4.

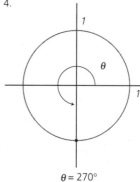

$\theta = 270°$

5.

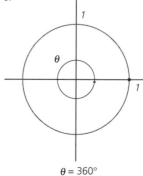

$\theta = 315°$

6.

$\theta = 360°$

7. Use a figure similar to the ones in problems 1–6, to determine in what quadrant are the sine and cosine of an angle both negative.

8. Use a figure similar to the ones in problems 1–6, to determine in what quadrant is the sine of an angle positive but the cosine of the angle is negative.

9. Using figures similar to the ones in problems 1–6, answer the following questions:

(a) What is sin 405°?
(b) What is cos 405°?
(c) How are sin 405° and sin 45° related? Explain.

(d) If sin A = 0.7843, where A is an angle measured in degrees, what will sin $(360° + A)$ be? Explain.

(e) If cos B = 0.3449, where B is an angle measured in degrees, what is cos $(720° + B)$? Explain.

Published by IT'S ABOUT TIME, Inc. © 2000 MATHconx, LLC

3. (-0.71, -0.71)   4. (0, -1) on the axis

5. (0.71, -0.71)   6. (1, 0) on the axis   7. 3rd quadrant

8. 2nd quadrant

9. (a) $\sin 405° = \sin 45° = 0.71$ (b) $\cos 405° = \cos 45° = 0.71$
   (c) They are equal. The point lands in the same position in both cases.
   (d) $\sin (360° + A) = \sin A = 0.7843$. The point lands in the same position in both cases.
   (e) $\cos (720° + B) = \cos B = 0.3449$. The point lands in the same position in both cases.

NOTES

Chapter 3

Appendix A: Using a TI-82 (TI-83) Graphing Calculator

A graphing calculator is a useful tool for doing many different mathematical things. Once you begin to use it, you'll find that it is powerful, fast, and friendly. In fact, your biggest difficulty may be just getting started for the first time! Because this machine can do a lot, it has lots of complicated looking buttons. But you don't have to know about *all* of them before you start to use *any* of them! The sooner you make friends with your electronic assistant, the more it will be able to help you. Let us introduce you to each other by trying a few simple things.

The Cover

The face of the calculator is protected from dirt and scratches by a cover that slides on and off from the top. When you're using the calculator, this cover slips on the back so that you won't lose it. Always put the cover back over the face of the calculator when you finish using it.

On, Off, 2nd , and Clear

To get the calculator's attention, just press ON (at the lower left corner of the calculator). What happens? Do you see a dark block blinking in the upper left corner of the screen? That's the **cursor**, which tells you where you are on the screen. The cursor is always at the spot that will be affected by the next button you push.

Notice that the word OFF is printed in color above the ON button, a little to the left of its center. Notice also that there is one key of the same color. It is the key marked 2nd at the left end of the second row.

When you push 2nd , it makes the next key that you push behave like what is marked above it on the left.

Try it. Push 2nd . What has happened to the cursor? Do you see an up arrow inside it as it blinks? That's to remind you that 2nd key has been pushed and will affect the next key

Published by IT'S ABOUT TIME, Inc. © 2000 MATHconx, LLC

Using a TI-82 (TI-83) Graphing Calculator

This appendix is *not* intended to replace the manual for the TI-82 (TI-83) graphing calculators. Rather, it has two purposes.

• It serves as a gentle introduction to the machine by way of some simple calculations, and

• It provides a convenient reference for some of the more commonly used elementary procedures.

Before using the graphing calculators with your class for the first time, **please check each one to see that it is reset to its factory settings and that it actually turns on and off.** It will be easier to answer your students' questions if all the calculators have working batteries and behave the same when they are first turned on.

NOTES

you choose. Now push [ON]. What happens? Did the cursor disappear? You should have a blank screen; the calculator should be off.

It's always a good idea to turn your calculator off when you finish using it. If you forget, the calculator will turn itself off after a few minutes to save its batteries. Sometimes when you are using it, you may put it aside and do something else for a little while. If it is off when you pick it up again, don't worry; just press [ON]. The screen will show what was there before it shut down.

Pressing [CLEAR] gives you a blank screen that is ready for new work. But the last thing you did is still stored. Press [2nd] then [ENTER] to bring it back.

Basic Arithmetic

Doing arithmetic on a graphing calculator is no harder than on a simpler calculator. In fact, it's easier. This calculator has a screen that lets you keep track of the problem as you enter it. Let's try a few simple exercises. Turn your calculator on.

- Pick two 3-digit numbers and add them. To do this, just key in the first number, press [+] and then key in the second number. Your addition problem will appear on the screen. Press [ENTER] to get the answer.

If you make a mistake when entering a number, you can go back and fix it. The [◁] key lets you move back (left) one space at a time. When you get to your mistake, just key in the correct number over the wrong one. Then move forward (right) to the end of the line by using the [▷] key.

For instance, to add 123 and 456, press 1 2 3 [+] 4 5 6 [ENTER]. The screen will show your question on the first line and the answer at the right side of the second line, as in Display A.1.

```
123+456
                  579
```

Display A.1

NOTES

- Now let's try the other three basic arithmetic operations. To clear the screen, press $\boxed{\text{CLEAR}}$. Then try subtracting, multiplying, and dividing your two 3-digit numbers. For instance, if your numbers are 123 and 456, press

$$1\ 2\ 3\ \boxed{-}\ 4\ 5\ 6\ \boxed{\text{ENTER}}$$

$$1\ 2\ 3\ \boxed{\times}\ 4\ 5\ 6\ \boxed{\text{ENTER}}$$

$$1\ 2\ 3\ \boxed{\div}\ 4\ 5\ 6\ \boxed{\text{ENTER}}$$

Your screen should look like Display A.2.

Notice that the display uses * for multiplication (so that it is not confused with the letter x) and / for division.

```
123−456
            -333
123*456
          56088
123/456
     .2697368421
```

Display A.2

- Here are two, button pushing shortcuts.

If you don't want to redo a problem with just a small change in it, you don't have to reenter the whole thing. $\boxed{\text{2nd}}$ $\boxed{\text{ENTER}}$ will bring back the last problem you entered. Just move to the place you want to change, key in the change, and press $\boxed{\text{ENTER}}$. For instance, add 54321 and 12345, as in Display A.3.

```
54321+12345
          66666
```

Display A.3

Published by IT'S ABOUT TIME, Inc. © 2000 MATHconx, LLC

NOTES

Now, to subtract 12345 from 54321, press [2nd] [ENTER];
the next line will show 54321 + 12345. Move your cursor
back to the + sign (using [◁]) and press [−]; then press
[ENTER]. Did you try it? Your screen should look like Display A.4.

```
54321+12345
              66666
54321−12345
              41976
```

Display A.4

Let's check to see that 41976 is the correct answer by adding
12345 to it and seeing if we get the first number back again.
Since you want to do something to the last answer, *you don't
have to reenter it.* Press [+]. Does your calculator show
Ans+ and the cursor? It should. If you press an operation key
right after doing a calculation, the machine assumes that you
want to perform this operation on the last answer. It shows
that last answer as Ans. Now key in 12345 and press [ENTER].
You should get back the first number, 54321.

A.1

1. Pick two 7-digit numbers and add them. What do
you get?

2. Now subtract the second number from the first.
Can you do it without rekeying the numbers? What
do you get?

3. Now multiply your two 7-digit numbers. What do
you get? What does the E mean?

4. Check the last answer by dividing the second of
your 7-digit numbers into it. Do it without rekeying
the last answer. Do you get your first number back
again?

Published by IT'S ABOUT TIME, Inc. © 2000 MATHconx, LLC

A-4

Basic Arithmetic

These questions are largely for routine practice. The use of seven-digit numbers helps to encourage the students to use the shortcuts, rather than just rekeying the entries. In parts 3 and 4, it serves the additional purpose of requiring them to deal with an answer displayed in scientific notation.

1. This is straightforward.

2. To do this without rekeying, use the entry key ⌷2nd⌷ ⌷ENTER⌷ to get back the addition line, move back to the + sign using the ⌷◁⌷ key, press ⌷−⌷ , then press ⌷ENTER⌋ .

3. The fact that the numbers chosen have seven digits guarantees that their product appears in scientific E notation. For example, the product of 1234567 and 2345678 appears as 2.895896651E12. This means that the product is actually

$$2.895896651 \times 10^{12} \quad \text{or} \quad 2{,}895{,}896{,}651{,}000$$

4. To check without rekeying the answer, just press ⌷÷⌷ , then key in the second seven-digit number. For our example, the display will show Ans/2345678. When you press ⌷ENTER⌋ the first seven-digit number will appear.

Multiply 98765432 by 123456. Now check the
product in two ways.

- Divide by pressing ⌈ ÷ ⌉ then entering 123456.
  Does it check?

a

A.2

- First reenter the product; then divide it by 123456.
  The product is in scientific notation. To enter it as
  a regular number, remember that the positive
  number after the E tells you to move the decimal
  that many places to the right. Does it check?

1. Divide 97533 by 525 and by 625. One of the
   answers you get will be exactly right, and the other
   one will be a very close approximation.

b

A.3

   - Which is which?

   - How can you tell?

   - If you hadn't been told that one of the answers
     is an approximation, how could you know?

2. When an answer is too long to be displayed with
   ten digits, the calculator shows a ten-digit
   approximation. Does it do this by just chopping off
   (truncating) the rest of the digits, or by rounding
   off? What test would you give your calculator to
   tell which way it does this?

1. Pick any three-digit number and note it down.

2. Repeat its digits in the same order to form a six
   digit number (like 123123, for example). Key this
   number into your calculator.

c

A.4

3. Divide your number by 7.

4. Divide your answer by 11. How do you do this
   without reentering the answer?

5. Divide the last number by 13. What do you notice
   about the result? Do you think that it is just a
   coincidence?

6. Pick another three-digit number and repeat steps 2–5.

7. Try to beat the system; see if you can pick a
   three-digit number that doesn't work this way.
   What might you try? Why?

8. Can you actually prove that the pattern you see
   works every time? How might you try to do this?

Published by IT'S ABOUT TIME, Inc. © 2000 MATHconx, LLC

This exercise illustrates the fact that some answers, particularly those expressed in scientific notation, are approximations. It also gives students a chance to deal with two other matters,

- rewriting a number from scientific notation to standard form; and
- experiencing the wraparound feature of the calculator's screen display.

To do the second check, students must convert the product 1.219318517E13 to the form 12,193,185,170,000 and key in

12193185170000 ÷ 123456 [ENTER]

This is too long to fit on a single line of the calculator display, so it is *automatically* wrapped around to the second line. There is no need to press any sort of "carriage return" key. In fact, trying to do so probably will result in an error. The screen should look like Display A.1T.

12193185170000/1
23456
        98765431.98

Display A.1T

These questions relate to the fact that answers are displayed with a maximum of 10 digits.

1. The easiest way to identify the exact answer is by observing that one of these answers has fewer than 10 digits; that one is exact. The next question actually tells the student this fact. The other is not, but you can't be *sure* just because it has 10 digits. The decimal form of the answer does not terminate because the divisor has prime factors other than 2 or 5.

   Multiplying back to check your answer by using Ans [×] will give exactly the original dividend *both* times; the calculator holds a more exact approximation than it shows. However, if you rekey each answer and multiply it by its divisor, you will get an inexact original dividend in one of these cases.

2. An easy test is to divide 2 by 3. The display .6666666667 clearly shows that the calculator rounds, rather than truncates.

This question illustrates how the efficiency of a calculator permits students to focus on emerging patterns without getting tangled in computation. Steps 2 – 5 result in the original three-digit number, regardless of what was chosen to begin with. Step 7 is intended to encourage students to think about finding exceptional cases. For instance, most students will choose three different digits for their first three-digit number, and very few will use 0. They might reasonably guess that a number with repeated digits or

The Two Minus Signs

The calculator has two minus signs. The one on the blue key looks like $\boxed{-}$ and the one on the gray key looks like $\boxed{(-)}$. The blue one, on the right, is for subtraction. It is grouped with the keys for the other arithmetic operations. To subtract 3764 from 8902, for example, you would key in

$$8\ 9\ 0\ 2\ \boxed{-}\ 3\ 7\ 6\ 4\ \boxed{ENTER}$$

Go ahead; do it. Do you get 5138?

The gray minus key, next to the $\boxed{ENTER}$ key at the bottom, is for making a number negative. It is grouped with the digit keys and the decimal point. To add the numbers -273, 5280, and -2116, for example, you would key in

$$\boxed{(-)}\ 2\ 7\ 3\ \boxed{+}\ 5\ 2\ 8\ 0\ \boxed{+}\ \boxed{(-)}\ 2\ 1\ 1\ 6\ \boxed{ENTER}$$

Try it. Notice that the display shows these negative signs without the parentheses, but they are smaller and raised a little. To see the difference between this negative sign and the subtraction sign, try subtracting the negative number -567 from 1234. Here are the keystrokes.

$$1234\ \boxed{-}\ \boxed{(-)}\ 567$$

The display should look like this:

$$1234 - {}^-567$$

Raising to a Power

To raise a number to a power, press $\boxed{\wedge}$ just before entering the exponent. Thus, to compute 738^5, press

$$7\ 3\ 8\ \boxed{\wedge}\ 5\ \boxed{ENTER}$$

The screen should look like Display A.5.

```
738^5
    2.1891817E14
```

Display A.5

with zeros in it would not work in the same way. Even though that turns out not to be the case, such conjectures are evidence that students are developing good thinking and exploration skills.

Proving that this "trick" works all the time is well within the reach of many students at this level. It rests on the fact that multiplication undoes what division does (and vice versa). Multiplying the three divisors, $7 \times 11 \times 13$, produces the number 1001, and multiplying a three-digit number by 1001 has the effect of repeating its digits. Thus, step 2 multiplied the original number by 1001, and steps 3, 4, and 5 divided by 1001 in three stages.

NOTES

The Menu Keys

Many keys bring a menu to the screen. A menu is a list of functions—things that the calculator is ready to do for you. For instance, press each of the keys across the row that starts with [MATH] . Don't worry about what all those lists say; just pick one out and look at it as you read the rest of this paragraph. Notice that it is actually a double menu. There are two cursors on it, shown as dark blocks. The one in the top left corner can be moved along the top line by using the [◁] and [▷] keys. Each time you move it to a new place on the top line, the menu below changes. The items in each lower menu are reached by using the other cursor, which can be moved up and down along the left side of the screen by using the [△] and [▽] keys.

Once you have put the cursor on the choice you want, you actually make the choice by pressing [ENTER] . This makes the calculator go back to its "home" screen and display your choice. To make the calculator do what you have chosen, press [ENTER] again.

1. **How many separate calculator functions can be reached through the menus of the [MATH] key?**

2. **How many separate calculator functions can be reached through the menus of the [MATRX] key?**

A.5

Entering Data in a List

The data handling tools are found through the statistics menu.

- Turn your calculator on and press [STAT] . You'll see a menu that looks like Display A.6.

EDIT CALC
1:Edit…
2:SortA(
3:SortD(
4:ClrList

TI-82

EDIT CALC TESTS
1:Edit…
2:SortA(
3:SortD(
4:ClrList
5:SetUpEditor

TI-83

Display A.6

Published by IT'S ABOUT TIME, Inc. © 2000 MATHconx, LLC

A.5

The Menu Keys

These questions serve the purpose of getting the students to focus on the dual nature of the menus. They also emphasize the wide ranging power of these machines. Finally, they provide a simple exercise in counting possibilities in a somewhat novel setting.

1. On the TI-82: 10 + 6 + 6 + 4 = 26; on the TI-83: 10 + 9 + 7 + 7 = 33.

2. On the TI-82:   5 + 11 + 5 = 21; on the TI-83: 10 + 16 + 10 = 36.

Entering Data in a List

This part is self explanatory. There are no differences between the TI-82 (TI-83) for this process.

Summaries of 1-Variable Data

This is another self explanatory part with no differences between the TI-82 (TI-83) calculators. You may need to remind students that the downward pointing arrow at the beginning of the last line of the display indicates that there are more lines of information below, which can be read by pressing ▽ .

- To enter data, make sure that the top cursor is on EDIT and the left cursor is on 1: . Then press $\boxed{\text{ENTER}}$. Your screen display should look like Display A.7, with the cursor right under L1.

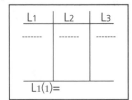

Display A.7

Note that if the display shows numbers in the L1 column, you'll have to clear the data memory. There are two ways to do this.

Get out of this display (by pressing $\boxed{\text{2nd}}$ $\boxed{\text{QUIT}}$) and go back to the $\boxed{\text{STAT}}$ menu. Press $\boxed{4}$. When ClrList appears, press $\boxed{\text{2nd}}$ $\boxed{1}$ then $\boxed{\text{ENTER}}$; Done will appear. Now go back to the $\boxed{\text{STAT}}$ screen and choose 1:Edit .

or

Without leaving this display, use the $\boxed{\triangle}$ and $\boxed{\triangleleft}$ keys to move your cursor to the top of the column and highlight L1. Press $\boxed{\text{CLEAR}}$ and then the $\boxed{\triangledown}$ key. List L1 should be cleared.

- Now it's time to enter the data. The calculator stores in its memory each data number you enter, along with an L1 label for that entry. The first number is called L1(1), and the second is called L1(2), and so on. We'll ignore the L2 and L3 labels for now. Key in the first data number, then press $\boxed{\text{ENTER}}$. Notice that L1(2) now appears at the bottom of the screen. Key in the second data number and press $\boxed{\text{ENTER}}$; and so on, until you have put in all the data. If you make a mistake, just use the arrow keys to move the cursor to your error, type over it correctly, then move back to where you were.

At this point, the calculator has all your data stored in a way that is easy to use, and the data will stay stored even after the calculator is turned off.

NOTES

Summaries of 1-Variable Data

It is easy to get summary information about data that is stored in a single list.

• Bring up the STAT menu.

• Move the top cursor to CALC. The side cursor should be on 1:1-Var Stats. Press ENTER.

• 1:1-Var Stats will appear on your screen. Enter the list you want the calculator to summarize. For instance, if you want a summary of the data in list L1, press 2nd 1 ; then press ENTER.

That's all there is to it! A screenful of information will appear. Sections 1.3–1.7 in Chapter 1 of Year 1 explain how to interpret that information.

Putting Data in Size Order

The TI-82 (TI-83) have built-in programs that will put your data in size order automatically. Do you have any data stored in L1? If not, enter ten or a dozen numbers at random, so that you can see how the following steps work.

1. Turn the calculator on and go to the STAT menu.

2. To see what is stored in L1, ENTER 1:Edit . Then move the cursor left to L1, if it's not there already. Make sure you have some data in this list.

3. Go back to the STAT menu and choose 2:Sort A(then press ENTER. Tell the calculator to sort the L1 list by pressing 2nd 1 , then ENTER. Your calculator screen should now say Done. To see what it has done, reopen List 1 (using STAT 1:Edit) . Your data should now be listed in ascending order — that is, from smallest to largest as you read down the list. The A in SortA(stands for ascending order.

Now go back to the STAT menu and choose 2:SortD(then press ENTER. Tell the calculator to sort the L1 list again. (Press 2nd 1 ENTER.)

A.6

1. When the screen says Done, what has your calculator done? Look at L1 again to help you answer this question.

2. What does the D in SortD(stand for?

A-9

Putting Data in Size Order

This should be a very quick exercise.

1. It sorts the numbers from largest to smallest as you read down the list.
2. The D stands for descending order.

If you haven't covered median yet, you can ignore the rest of this part until you get to Section 1.4 of Year 1.

NOTES

Once the data are in size order, it is easy to find the median. For example, if you have 21 data items in all, the median is just the 11th one in the sorted list. Scroll through the data (using the $\boxed{\triangle}$ key) until you find L1(11). Its value is the median. If you have 20 data items, the median is halfway between the 10th and 11th items in the sorted list. Scroll through the data until you find L1(10) and L1(11). Then calculate the number halfway between them.

Finding the mode is just as easy. Count repeated items in this list. The one that is repeated the most times is the mode.

The Graph Window

This kind of calculator is called a graphing calculator because it can *draw graphs*. The screen on a graphing calculator can show line drawings of mathematical relationships. It does this with two kinds of coordinate systems—*rectangular coordinates* or *polar coordinates*. In this part we shall use only rectangular coordinates; polar coordinates will appear much later. If you are not familiar with the idea of a rectangular coordinate system, you should review the first section of Chapter 3 in Year 1 now.

Your calculator leaves the factory with standard coordinate axes built in. To see what they look like, turn on your calculator and press $\boxed{\text{GRAPH}}$ (in the upper right corner). You should see a horizontal and a vertical axis crossing the middle of the screen. The horizontal axis is called the **x-axis**, and the vertical axis is called the **y-axis**. If your screen doesn't show this, press $\boxed{\text{ZOOM}}$ and choose 6:ZStandard . Examine this display carefully; then answer the following questions.

A.7

1. Assuming that the dots along each axis mark the integer points, what is the largest possible value on the *x*-axis? On the *y*-axis?

2. What is the smallest possible value on the *x*-axis? On the *y*-axis?

3. Does it look as if the same unit of measure is being used on both axes?

4. Why do you suppose the spacing between the units is not exactly the same everywhere on an axis? Do you think that this might cause a problem?

Published by IT'S ABOUT TIME, Inc. © 2000 MATHconx, LLC

The Graph Window

A.7

These questions are intended to get students to understand the purpose for some of the display adjustments that are available from various menus. These adjustment options will be described shortly.

1. 10 for both
2. -10 for both
3. No
4. Because the numbers of dots across and down are not multiples of 10. Both this and the apparent difference in unit length on the axes could be misleading later if not understood properly. The students probably can only guess at this now.

NOTES

The standard coordinate axis setting can be changed in several ways. This is done using the menu that appears when you press [WINDOW] . Try that now. You should get Display A.8.

```
WINDOW FORMAT          WINDOW
   Xmin = -10             Xmin = -10
   Xmax = 10              Xmax = 10
   Xscl = 1               Xscl = 1
   Ymin = -10             Ymin = -10
   Ymax = 10              Ymax = 10
   Yscl = 1               Yscl = 1
                          Xres = 1

      TI-82                  TI-83
```

Display A.8

Xmin and Xmax are the smallest and largest values on the *x*-axis (the horizontal axis); Ymin and Ymax are the smallest and largest values on the *y*-axis (the vertical axis).

Xscl and Yscl are the scales for marking off points on the axes. The setting 1 means that each single integer value on the axis is marked. To see how the scale value works, change Xscl to 2. Move the cursor down, using [▽], then just key in 2 in place of 1.) Now press [GRAPH] What change do you notice? Now go back to the WINDOW menu (press [WINDOW]) and change Yscl to 5. Return to the graph (press [GRAPH]). What has changed?

You can ignore the Xres = 1 line on the TI-83 for now. If you're really curious, see p. 3–11 of the TI-83 Guidebook.

Change the WINDOW **settings so that they look like Display A.9. Then look at the graph and answer these questions.**

A.8

1. **Where on the screen is the origin of the coordinate system?**

2. **Does it look as if the same unit of measure is being used on both axes?**

3. **Does it look as if the spacing between the units is the same everywhere on an axis?**

4. **What happens when you press [△] then [▽]?**

A-11

A.8

1. These settings provide a coordinate system with the origin in the lower left corner of the screen.
2. The integer points are marked on the axes, using the same distance as the unit of measure on both.
3. The units are uniformly spaced on each axis because the array of dots in the screen display is 95 by 63. The scale in this case is actually 10 dots to the unit in each coordinate direction.
4. When the two arrow keys are pressed, a cursor in the form of a cross appears exactly in the center of the screen, and the coordinates of its location are shown at the bottom: $x = 4.7$ and $y = 3.1$. This is discussed further in the next couple of paragraphs.

NOTES

```
WINDOW FORMAT
Xmin = 0
Xmax = 9.4
Xscl = 1
Ymin = 0
Ymax = 6.2
Yscl = 1
```
TI-82

```
WINDOW
Xmin = 0
Xmax = 9.4
Xscl = 1
Ymin = 0
Ymax = 6.2
Yscl = 1
Xres = 1
```
TI-83

Display A.9

If you have worked through the previous questions, you found that pressing △ , ▽ puts a cross exactly in the middle of your screen and two numbers at the bottom. The cross is the cursor for the graphing screen, and the numbers are the coordinates of the point at its center. In this case, the cursor is at (4.7, 3.1). It can be moved to any point on the graph by using the four arrow keys △ , ▽ , ◁ , ▷ at the upper right of the keypad.

A.9

Move the cursor to the point (4, 3). How far does the cursor move each time you press ◁ or ▷ ? How far does it move each time you press △ or ▽ ? Now move the cursor directly down to the bottom of the screen. What are the coordinates of the lowest point you can reach?

These new WINDOW settings are better than the standard one in some ways, and worse in others. Let's look again at the Standard coordinate system and compare it with the one we just saw. To get back to the standard settings, press ZOOM , then press 6 to choose ZStandard. The Standard coordinate axes should appear immediately.

A.10

These questions refer to the Standard coordinate axes.

1. Where is the cursor to begin with? How do you find it if you can't remember?

2. Try to move the cursor to the point (4,3). How close can you get to it?

3. How far does the cursor move each time you press ◁ or ▷ ?

4. How far does it move each time you press △ or ▽ ?

A-12

This is a simple exercise in understanding cursor movement. It also prepares the student for an investigation of scale changes. In this case, the cursor moves 0.1 unit each time you press any arrow key. This can be seen from the change in coordinates at the bottom of the screen. The lowest point directly beneath (4, 3) on this screen is (4, 0).

A.9

This is an important Exploration for understanding how the calculator deals with coordinate systems.

A.10

1. The cursor is at (0, 0) to begin with; it can be found by pressing △ ▽ or ◁ ▷ .

2. (4.0425532, 2.9032258)

3. 0.212766 of a unit, with some minor variations.

4. 0.3225807 of a unit, with some minor variations.

NOTES

5. Move the cursor directly down to the bottom of the screen. What are the coordinates of the lowest point you can reach?

6. In what ways is this coordinate system better than the one we set up for the previous set of questions? In what ways is it worse?

7. How might we fix the bad features of this system without losing the good ones?

Another useful WINDOW setting is 8:ZInteger in the ZOOM menu. When you press [8], coordinate axes appear, but they are still the standard ones. Press [ENTER] to get the Integer settings.

These questions refer to the Integer coordinate axes.

1. Try to move the cursor to the point (4, 3). How close can you get to it?

A.11

2. How far does the cursor move each time you press [◁] or [▷]?

3. How far does it move each time you press [△] or [▽]?

4. Why is this setting named Integer?

5. In what ways is this coordinate system better than the one we set up for the previous set of questions? In what ways is it worse?

6. How might we fix the bad features of this system without losing the good ones?

To plot a point (mark its location) on the graphing screen, go to the point-drawing part of the DRAW menu, like this.

Press [2nd] [PRGM] and move the top cursor to POINTS .

Choose 1 to make the [ENTER] key mark cursor locations. If you want to mark some points and erase others, choose 3. This lets the [ENTER] key change the state of any point the cursor is on; it will mark one that isn't already marked, and will unmark one that is. *Hint:* If you have plotted too many points and you want to start over, you can go to ZOOM menu and press [6]. This will wipe out everything you have plotted and return to the Standard coordinate settings. If you were using different coordinate settings, you will have to redo them in the WINDOW menu. If you want to erase some points, see Drawing Points on a graph section in the TI Guidebook.

Published by IT'S ABOUT TIME, Inc. © 2000 MATHconx, LLC

A-13

5. (4.0425532, -10)

6. There are many ways of answering these questions. A major advantage of the standard system is that it allows for negative coordinate values. It also has the same maximum and minimum values on each axis. The fact that the cursor does not move in "nice" increments is a nuisance, as is the fact that the horizontal single step amounts differ from the vertical ones. Students might also find it annoying that points with integer coordinates can't always be reached exactly.

7. This might be asking a lot of students who are unfamiliar with the calculator, but class discussion could be productive. To fix the drawbacks listed above while retaining the advantages, change the WINDOW settings so that the *x*-axis goes from −4.7 to 4.7 and the *y*-axis goes from −3.1 to 3.1. Remember to use $\boxed{(-)}$, instead of $\boxed{-}$, when entering the negative values. This will give you a coordinate system with (0, 0) in the middle of the screen, so that it will handle both positive and negative values. The cursor will move in increments of 0.1 in either direction, and hence all the points with integer coordinates can be reached exactly. The disadvantage to this system is its limited   range.   The exercises give students a chance to explore other options.

A.11

1. This Exploration should be easier than the previous one. The cursor can be moved exactly to (4, 3).

2. & 3. It moves exactly 1 unit each time any arrow key is pressed.

4. That is, all the points that can be plotted exactly must have integer coordinates; hence, it is called the Integer setting.

5. & 6. The last two parts are open-ended, as in the previous Exploration.

Problem Set: Appendix A

1. What WINDOW settings do you need in order to put the origin at the upper right corner of your screen? What can you say about the coordinates of the points that can be plotted on this screen?

2. What WINDOW settings do you need in order to put the origin at the upper left corner of your screen? What can you say about the coordinates of the points that can be plotted on this screen?

3. Choose the Integer setting for the coordinate axes and plot the points (30, 14), (-5, 20), (-26, -11), and (6, -30). Then write the coordinates of two points that lie within the area of the graph window but cannot be plotted exactly with this setting.

4. Find WINDOW settings to form a coordinate system such that the points (120, 80) and (-60, -40) are within the window frame.

   (a) How far does the cursor move each time you press ◁ or ▷ ?

   (b) How far does it move each time you press △ or ▽ ?

   (c) Can you put the cursor exactly on (120, 80)? If not, how close can you come? Plot this point as closely as you can.

   (d) Can you put the cursor exactly on (-60, -40)? If not, how close can you come? Plot this point as closely as you can.

   (e) Can you put the cursor exactly on (0, 0)? If not, how close can you come?

5. Find WINDOW settings to form a coordinate system such that the cursor can be put exactly on the points (20, 24.5) and (-17.3, -14).

   (a) What is the initial position of the cursor?

   (b) How far does it move each time you press ◁ or ▷ ?

   (c) How far does it move each time you press △ or ▽ ?

   (d) Can you put the cursor exactly on (0, 0)? If not, how close can you come?

Published by IT'S ABOUT TIME, Inc. © 2000 MATHconx, LLC

Problem Set: Appendix A

1. Set Xmax and Ymax to 0. All points that can be plotted must have both coordinates negative (or zero).

2. Set Xmin and Ymax to 0. All points that can be plotted must have a nonnegative x-coordinate and a nonpositive y-coordinate.

3. Any point within the axes ranges that does not have integers for both coordinates cannot be plotted exactly.

4. This can be done in many different ways. Answers to the specific questions depend on the choice of coordinate extremes.

5. Perhaps the easiest, but not the only way to do this is to set

    Xmin = -17.3, Xmax = 20, Ymin = -14, and Ymax = 20

    If these settings are used, then the rest of the answers are
    (a) (.95319149, 5.25)
    (b) approx. .3968 (with slight variations)
    (c) .6209677 (with minor variations in the last digit)
    (d) (.15957447, .28225806)

Drawing Histograms

Drawing a histogram is very easy. All you have to do is choose a few numbers to tell the calculator how wide and how tall to make the bars, as follows. Turn your calculator on and press WINDOW . The screen should look like Display A.10, maybe with different numbers.

```
WINDOW FORMAT
   Xmin = -10
   Xmax = 10
   Xscl = 1
   Ymin = -10
   Ymax = 10
   Yscl = 1

      TI-82
```

```
WINDOW
   Xmin = -10
   Xmax = 10
   Xscl = 1
   Ymin = -10
   Ymax = 10
   Yscl = 1
   Xres = 1

      TI-83
```

Display A.10

The numbers in this WINDOW list tell the calculator how to set the horizontal (X) and vertical (Y) scales.

- Xmin, an abbreviation of *X minimum*, is the smallest data value the picture will show. You should set it at some convenient value less than or equal to the smallest value in your data set.

- Xmax, an abbreviation of *X maximum*, is the largest data value the picture will show. Set it at some convenient value greater than or equal to the largest value in your data set.

- Xscl, an abbreviation of *X scale*, says how to group the data. It is the size of the base interval at the bottom of each bar of the histogram. For instance, Xscl = 10 will group the data by 10s, starting from the value of Xmin that you chose.

- Ymin is the smallest frequency of any data group. It is never less than 0, which usually is a good choice for it.

- Ymax represents the length of the longest bar. Choose a convenient number that is not less than the largest frequency of any data group, but not much larger.

- Yscl determines the size of the steps to be marked on the vertical (frequency) scale. For small data sets, set it to 1. If your setting for Ymax is much larger than 10, you might want to set Yscl larger than 1. A little experimenting will show you how to choose a helpful setting.

Published by IT'S ABOUT TIME, Inc. © 2000 MATHconx, LLC

A-15

Drawing Histograms

This is a self explanatory section. No exercises are included because there is ample opportunity to practice this process while working on problems in the text, particularly in Section 1.3 of Year 1.

NOTES

- If you have a TI-83, the last line at the bottom of this display is Xres = 1. It's a pixel resolution setting for graphing functions; ignore it for now.

Now your calculator is ready to draw a histogram.

- Press [STAT PLOT] (actually, [2nd] [Y=]), choose 1 and press [ENTER] .

- Choose these settings from each row by moving the cursor to them with the arrow keys and pressing [ENTER] each time.

  – Highlight On.

  – Highlight the histogram picture.

  – Set Xlist to the list containing your data (L1, L2, etc.).

  – Set Freq:1 .

Now press [GRAPH] — and there it is!

Drawing Boxplots

The TI-82 (TI-83) calculators can draw boxplots. All they need are the data and a few sizing instructions. Here's how to do it.

- Turn the calculator on, press [STAT] and choose 1:Edit... from the EDIT menu. Check which list contains the data you want to use. Let's assume it's in L1.

- Press [WINDOW] and set the horizontal (X) and vertical (Y) scales. If you have forgotten how to set your WINDOW, refer to "The Graph Window" section. Choose convenient numbers for the X range—Xmin less than your smallest data value and Xmax greater than your largest data value, but not too small or too large. You don't want the picture to get squeezed into something you can't see well! Also set Xscl to some convenient size.

- The Y settings don't matter as much. However, for the TI-82, if you set Ymin to –1 (Be sure to use the [(–)] key!) and Ymax to 4, the X scale will appear nicely in a readable

Published by IT'S ABOUT TIME, Inc. © 2000 MATHconx, LLC

Drawing Boxplots

This is another self explanatory section. No exercises are included because there is ample opportunity to practice this process while working on problems in the text, particularly in Section 1.5 of Year 1.

NOTES

location under the boxplot. For the TI-83, Ymin = -2 and Ymax = 2 work a little better.

- Press $\boxed{\text{STAT PLOT}}$ (actually, $\boxed{\text{2nd}}$ $\boxed{\text{Y=}}$), choose 1: and press $\boxed{\text{ENTER}}$. Select these settings from each row by moving the cursor to them with the arrow keys and pressing $\boxed{\text{ENTER}}$ each time.

   On; the boxplot picture; L1 from the Xlist; 1 from Freq

- Now press $\boxed{\text{GRAPH}}$ —and there it is!

- To read the five-number summary, press $\boxed{\text{TRACE}}$ and use the $\boxed{\triangleleft}$ and $\boxed{\triangleright}$ to display the five numbers one at a time.

Graphing and Tracing Lines

If you want the calculator to graph a line or a curve, you must first be able to describe the line or curve by an algebraic equation. Once you have the equation for what you want to draw, you must put it in the form

$$y = [\text{something}]$$

For a straight line, that's not a problem; we often put the equation in this form, anyway. For some other kinds of curves, putting them in this form can be a little messy. In this section we shall deal only with straight lines.

All graphing begins with the $\boxed{\text{Y=}}$ key. When you press this key for the first time, you get the screen in Display A.11.

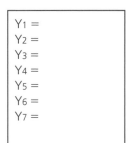

| Y₁ = |
| Y₂ = |
| Y₃ = |
| Y₄ = |
| Y₅ = |
| Y₆ = |
| Y₇ = |

Plot1   Plot2   Plot3
\Y₁ =
\Y₂ =
\Y₃ =
\Y₄ =
\Y₅ =
\Y₆ =
\Y₇ =

TI-82   TI-83

Display A.11

Graphing and Tracing Lines

This section should be helpful for students when they get to Chapter 3 of Year 1.

NOTES

These lines allow you to put in as many as ten different algebraic equations for things you want drawn. The subscript number gives you a way to keep track of which equation goes with which picture on the graph. To see how the process works, we'll make the first example simple—two straight lines through the origin.

Key in -.5X on the $Y_1=$ line, *using the* $\boxed{X,T,\theta}$ *key to make the* X; then press $\boxed{\text{ENTER}}$.

It is important to use $\boxed{X,T,\theta}$ for X because that's how the calculator knows that you are referring to the horizontal axis.

Key in -.25X on the $Y_2=$ line and $\boxed{\text{ENTER}}$ it.

Be sure to use the $\boxed{(-)}$ key for the negative sign. If you don't, you'll get an error message when you ask for the graph. If you want to wipe out one of these equations and redo it, just move the cursor back to the equation and press $\boxed{\text{CLEAR}}$.

Now your work is done. Press $\boxed{\text{GRAPH}}$ and just watch as the calculator draws the lines. If you forget which line goes with which equation, or if you want to see the coordinates of the points along your lines, press $\boxed{\text{TRACE}}$ and then move the cursor with the $\boxed{\triangleleft}$ and $\boxed{\triangleright}$ keys. When you do this, the coordinates of the cursor's position appear at the bottom of the screen. For the TI-82, a number appears in the upper right corner to tell you which equation you're tracing. For the TI-83, the equation appears in the upper left hand corner. In this example, when you press $\boxed{\text{TRACE}}$ you will be on $Y_1=$ -.5X, the first of the two lines we entered. Try it. Now move back and forth along this line.

To switch from one line to another, use the $\boxed{\triangle}$ and $\boxed{\triangledown}$ keys. Notice that, in this case, either of these keys gets you to the other line. That's because we are only graphing two equations. If we were graphing more than two, these keys would move up and down the *list of equations*, regardless of where the graphs appeared on the screen.

There is a way to remove the graph of an equation from the screen without erasing the equation from your list. For example, let us remove the line $Y_1=$ -.5X from the picture. Go back to the $\boxed{Y=}$ list. Notice that the $=$ sign of each equation appears in a dark block. This shows that the graph of

NOTES

this equation is turned <u>on.</u> To turn it off, move the cursor to the = sign and press ENTER . The dark block will disappear. To turn it back on, put the cursor back on = and press ENTER again.

Approximating Data by a Line

This section refers to a situation that commonly arises in the analysis of two variable data. Such data can be represented as points on a coordinate plane, and it is often useful to know if the pattern of points can be approximated by a straight line. A common way of doing this is called *least-squares approximation*. An explanation of this process and its use appears in Chapter 4 of Year 1. This calculator section provides a simple example of how to get the TI-82 (TI-83) to give you a least-squares approximation of a set of data.

Let's look at a very small, simple data set. The process is exactly the same for bigger, more complicated data sets. Here are four points of two variable data.

$$(1, 2) \quad (2, 3) \quad (3, 5) \quad (4, 6)$$

If you plot these points on a coordinate plane, you will see that they don't all lie on the same line. Don't just take our word for it; make a sketch! The calculator uses the least-squares method to find automatically the line of "best fit." Section 4.3 (in Chapter 4) describes how this method works and what best fit means. These are the instructions for getting the calculator to do all the tedious work for you.

First of all, you need to have the data entered in two *separate data storage lists. You get to* these lists by pressing STAT and choosing 1:EDIT... from the EDIT menu. When you press ENTER , you should get Display A.12.

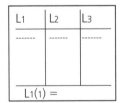

Display A.12

Approximating Data by a Line

This simple example relies on some of the calculator's default choices. For instance, the data are entered in lists L1 and L2, which are the default comparison lists for LinReg. To compare other data lists with this function, you must specify your list choices. See the calculator's instruction manual for details.

Note that when you go through the linear regression process described here, the correlation coefficient r shows up automatically on the TI-82, but not on the TI-83. To get it on the TI-83, go to the CATALOG menu, choose DiagnosticOn, and [ENTER] it. Then you will get both r^2 and r in the linear regression display.

NOTES

If the columns already contain data that you don't want, you can clear them out in either of two ways.

- Press [STAT] and choose 4:ClrList from the menu that appears. When the message ClrList appears, enter the name of the list you want to clear. (Press [2nd] [1] for L1, [2nd] [2] for L2, etc.) Then press [ENTER] ; the screen will say Done. Now press [STAT] to return to the process of entering data.

- Go to the MEM screen (press [2nd] [+]) and choose 2:Delete... (press [2]). Choose 3:List... from the menu that appears. The screen will show the name of each data storage list that contains data. Use the arrow keys to pick the ones that you want to clear out; press [ENTER] for each one. Now press [STAT] to return to the process of entering data.

Enter the first coordinate of each data point into list L1; put its second coordinate in list L2. The four data points of our example should appear as shown in Display A.13.

L1	L2	L3
1	2	-------
2	3	
3	5	
4	6	
-------	-------	

L2(5) =

Display A.13

Now we are almost done. Press [STAT] and go to the CALC menu. Choose LinReg(ax + b) . When you press [ENTER] , the screen will display an algebraic description of the line of best fit. For our example, it looks like Display A.14.

- The second line, y = ax + b, just tells you that the information is for slope-intercept form. Notice that the TI-82 (TI-83) use *a*, not *m*, for the slope here.

- The third line says that the slope is 1.4.

- The fourth line says that the y-intercept is .5.

Note that on the TI-82, the last line shows the **correlation coefficient**, a measure of how good the fit is. The correlation coefficient is not discussed in your textbook. A detailed explanation of how it works will have to wait until you study

NOTES

statistics in more depth. But, in case you are curious about it, here is a little more information. The correlation coefficient is always a number between –1 and 1, inclusive. 1 and –1 stand for a perfect fit, with all points exactly on the line. (1 is for lines with positive slope; –1 is for lines with negative slope.) The closer r is to 0, the worse the fit.

LinReg	LinReg
y = ax + b	y = ax + b
a = 1.4	a = 1.4
b = .5	b = .5
r = .9899494937	
TI-82	TI-83

Display A.14

Putting together this information about our example, we see that the least-squares line is described by the equation

$$y = 1.4x + .5$$

Graph the line $y = 1.4x + .5$. Are any of the four data points on it? How can you be sure?

A.12

Using Formulas to Make Lists

Sometimes it is useful to make a new list of data from an old one by doing the same thing to each data value. For instance, you might want to add a fixed number to each value, square each value, or find the distance of each value from some particular number. Instead of computing the new list one entry at a time, you can do it all at once if you can express your process as a formula.

Here's how the process works.

- Go to the STAT menu. Enter a list of data in L1, and then clear L2 and L3.

- To add 5 to each entry in L1, move the cursor over to the second column, then up to the heading, L2. The bottom line of your display should read L2= (without any number in parentheses).

A.12

There are two ways to check whether or not the points are exactly on the line. One is to substitute each one into the equation and see if the result is true. The other is to have the calculator plot the line with the Integer setting and move the [TRACE] cursor to the *x*-values 1, 2, 3, and 4. Either way, the students can see that none of the points are exactly on the line. By using the calculator, they will see the actual *y*-value of each point on the line with the same *x*-value as the data point they are checking, thus seeing how close the line comes to each data point.

Using Formulas to Make Lists

This section probably will be more useful to students after they have covered functions expressed as formulas. It is not essential to their basic understanding of the calculators. The process explained here is very much like that used in working with electronic spreadsheets. However, there is one crucial difference: The data must be in the "domain" list *before* the formula is entered at the top of the output column. Unlike spreadsheets, the TI-82 (TI-83) calculators do not store the formula. They simply use the formula to calculate the column entries, and then store only the entries. If you change a domain entry later, the corresponding entry in the output column will *not* change.

NOTES

- The trick here is to let the symbol L1 stand for each element of the list L1. That is, we make L1 *a variable*.
  Key in L1 + 5 ; the bottom of your screen should read
  L2 = L1 + 5 .

- Now press ENTER and watch the entire column for L2 fill out automatically!

- To list in L2, the square of each entry in L1, put the cursor on L2 (at the top of the column). Then enter L1^2
  (or L1 * L1).

- Now let us list in L3 the midpoint between the L1 entry and the L2 entry. Put the cursor back on L3 at the top of the column and press CLEAR . This removes the old formula. Now key in (L1 + L2)/2 and press ENTER .

A.13

1. List at least ten data values in L1.

2. Write a formula to list in L2 the distance between 17 and each entry in L1. Remember: Distances are never negative numbers. Then use it.

3. Write a formula to list in L3 the square of the difference (which may be negative) between each entry in L_1 and 17. Then use it.

4. Write a formula to list in L4 the square root of each entry in L3. Then use it.

5. How are columns L2 and L4 related? Explain.

Drawing Circles

To draw circles directly on a graph, use 9:Circle(in the DRAW menu. (The DRAW menu appears when you press
2nd DRAW .) 2:Line(can be used to draw segments, which lets you add radii, diameters, and other segments to your drawings of circles.

Before beginning, make sure that all the functions on your Y= screen are turned off. If they are not, their graphs will appear when you draw circles and segments. Also make sure that all STAT PLOTS are turned off.

Follow these instructions to draw a circle directly on a graph.

1. From the ZOOM menu, choose ZStandard (to clear any unusual WINDOW settings). Then choose ZSquare or ZInteger, which displays the graph window.

1. This is mostly routine practice, but it also illustrates how to get absolute value without using the abs function.

2. L2 = abs (17 − L1) or L2 = abs (L1− 17)

3. L3 = (L1 − 17)^2 or L3 = (L1 − 17) * (L1 − 17)

4. L4 = $\sqrt{L3}$

5. They are the same. Squaring makes a number positive and the calculator's value for square root is the positive root. The net effect of these two steps is to make positive whatever number you start with; that is, to give you its absolute value.

Drawing Circles

This material probably will be most useful for Year 2, particularly in Chapter 4.

NOTES

2. From the DRAW menu, choose 9:Circle(.

3. Choose a point for the center by moving the cursor to this point and pressing ENTER .

4. Choose the radius for your circle by moving the cursor this many units away from the center and pressing ENTER .

You can continue to draw circles by repeating the last two steps. To clear the screen before drawing a new circle, use :ClrDraw in the DRAW menu. If you want to stop drawing circles, press CLEAR .

Follow the steps above to draw each of these items.

1. a circle with center (0, 10) and radius 5

2. a circle with center (12, –7) and radius 15

3. four circles with center (0, 0)

a

A.14

You can also draw a circle from the Home Screen (the calculator's primary display WINDOW) by following these instructions. You can use this same method to draw circles from a program.

1. From the Home Screen, choose Circle(from the DRAW menu.

2. Input the coordinates of the center, followed by the radius; then press ENTER . For example, if you enter (0, 10, 5), the calculator will draw a circle with center at (0, 10) and radius 5, using whatever ZOOM WINDOW setting is current.

3. To return to the Home Screen, press CLEAR .

1. Draw a circle with center (3, 2) and radius 7 directly from the Home Screen. If your graph does not look like a circle, how can you adjust the graph WINDOW so that it does?

2. Draw four concentric circles around (0, 0) directly from the Home Screen. Earlier you were asked to draw this figure directly on a graph. Which method is easier for you? Why?

b

A.15

These questions are for practicing the calculator skill just described. (a) and (b) are straightforward. For (c), students can choose any radii for the four circles; they have to enter the center point in each case.

A.14

This is another skill reinforcement exercise.

A.15

1. Circles will look oval in Standard WINDOW setting and in any setting where the *x* and *y* axes are of equal length in calculator units. To get a circle that looks round, choose the ZSquare WINDOW setting in the ZOOM menu.

2. This is straightforward. Answers as to which method is easier are likely to vary, depending on the learning style preferences of the individual students.

NOTES

Appendix B:
Using a Spreadsheet

Computers give us many different tools for doing and using mathematics. One of these tools is called a **spreadsheet**. These days, a spreadsheet is an easy-to-use and very powerful computer program, but the idea of a spreadsheet is really much simpler and older than computers. Originally, a spreadsheet was just an oversized piece of paper, with lines and columns that made it easier for accountants and bookkeepers to keep their work in order.

You can make a spreadsheet on a lined piece of paper:

- Make a narrow border across the top and down the left side of the sheet.

- Divide the rest of the paper into columns from top to bottom. Six columns of about equal width will do for now.

- In the left margin, number the lines, beginning with 1, to the bottom of the page.

- Across the top margin, name each column with a letter from A to F in alphabetical order.

Your paper should look something like Display B.1.

	A	B	C	D	E	F
1						
2						
3						
4						
5						
6						
⋮						

Display B.1

Published by IT'S ABOUT TIME, Inc. © 2000 MATHconx, LLC

B-1

Using a Spreadsheet

This appendix is *not* intended to replace a manual for your electronic spreadsheet program. Rather, it has two purposes.

- It serves as a gentle introduction to electronic spreadsheets by way of some simple exercises.

- It provides a convenient reference for some of the more commonly used elementary procedures.

The instructions provided here are fairly generic. They have been crafted to apply equally well to Microsoft Excel and to Lotus 1-2-3, with appropriate comments about specific differences. You should be able to use this Appendix with virtually any electronic spreadsheet program. However, if you are using an older and/or less common spreadsheet, it probably would be a good idea to work through these instructions with it in some detail. In any event, your spreadsheet manual should be regarded as the definitive reference source.

NOTES

The Cell Names

Each box in this grid has its own address — the letter of its column followed by the number of its row. For instance, C4 refers to the box, third column (column C), on the fourth line (row). The electronic spreadsheets that computers handle look just like this, and each position in them is addressed in just the same way. Electronic spreadsheet manuals often call the boxes **cells**. We'll do the same thing, so that you become used to the term.

B.1

Here are a couple of questions to get you comfortable with the way cells are addressed:

- Make a copy of Display B.1 and shade in these cells: A2, B3, C4, D5, E6, A6, B5, D3, E2. What shape do you get?

- If you wanted Display B.1 to be shaded in a checkerboard pattern, with alternating cells filled in, which cells would you shade? Write out all their addresses. There's more than one way to do this.

The advantage of electronic spreadsheets over handmade ones is that the electronic ones do the computations for you, *IF* you ask them properly. If you know how to speak the language of your spreadsheet program, you can get it to do all the hard work very quickly. The main idea to remember is:

A spreadsheet is powerful because it can find and work with numbers that appear anywhere on it by using the cell names.

Therefore:

When working with a spreadsheet, always try to build what you want, step by step, from the first data you enter. The fewer numbers you have to enter, the easier it is for the spreadsheet to do your work.

Published by IT'S ABOUT TIME, Inc. © 2000 MATHconx, LLC

The Cell Names

B.1

The first question makes an X centered at C4. The second question can be done in two ways, depending on whether or not Cell A1 is to be shaded. If it is, then the cells to be shaded are

A1, C1, E1, B2, D2, F2, A3, C3, E3, B4, D4, F4, A5, C5, E5, B6, D6, F6

Otherwise, the shaded cells are

B1, D1, F2, A2, C2, E2, B3, D3, F3, A4, C4, E4, B5, D5, F5, A6, C6, E6

NOTES

The rest of this appendix shows you how to get an electronic spreadsheet to work for you. For practice, each new process will be introduced by using it to deal with this problem:

> You are sent to the local supermarket to buy at least 2 pounds of potato chips for a club picnic. The club treasurer tells you to spend as little money as possible.

Now, there are many different brands of potato chips, and each brand comes in several different size bags. How can you compare prices in a useful way? Well, the bag sizes are measured in ounces. If you divide the price of the bag by the number of ounces, you'll get the price per ounce (this approach is called *unit* pricing). We'll set up a spreadsheet to tell you the price per ounce of every kind of potato chip bag your market sells.

> *Don't just read the rest of this appendix*: **DO IT! Work along with the instructions using your own spreadsheet.**

Entering Numbers and Text

There are three different kinds of things you can put in a cell – numbers, text, and formulas. Most spreadsheets distinguish between numbers and text automatically:

1.   If you enter numerical symbols only, the entry is treated as a number.

2.   If you begin an entry with letters or other symbols not related to numbers (even if numbers are entered along with them), the entry is treated as text.

Note that if you want a number (such as a date or a year) or a number-related symbol (such as $) to be treated as a text entry, you have to tell the machine somehow. Check your user's manual for the way your spreadsheet program does it.

Display B.2 lists the prices of different brands and sizes of potato chips, including the special sale prices for the day. These are actual data from a supermarket. To enter these data in their

B-3

B.2 It is important to have the students actually work through this example, step by step, on a computer, if possible. If you have enough access to computers to allow for small group work, that probably would be best. If you only have access to one computer for demonstration purposes, have students take turns working through the steps. Either way, check their understanding at each stage and discuss difficulties as they arise.

Entering Numbers and Text

B.3 It is tempting not to repeat the brand names for different sizes of the same brand. However, it will cause serious problems when the rows are sorted because the brand name will not be carried along with the rest of the information for some rows. Discourage this particular economy of effort, or be prepared to have some students starting over again when they hit the sort step.

NOTES

Appendix B: Using a Spreadsheet

most useful form, you should use *three* columns—one for the brand, one for the weights (in ounces), and one for the prices. Put the information of Display B.2 into columns A, B, and C now.

Brand of Chip	No. of Ounces	$Cost of Bag
Cape Cod	11 oz.	2.49
Eagle Thins	9.5 oz.	1.99
Humpty Dumpty	6 oz.	1.19
Humpty Dumpty	10 oz.	1.68
Lay's	6 oz.	0.95
Lay's	14 oz.	2.79
O'Boisies	14.5 oz.	2.79
Ruffles	6 oz.	1.39
Ruffles	14 oz.	2.79
Tom's	6 oz.	1.39
Tom's	11 oz.	1.69
Wise	6 oz.	1.39
Wise	10 oz.	1.48

Display B.2

The standard column width of your spreadsheet probably is not big enough to handle some of the brand names. Find the Column Width command and adjust the width of column A to 15 spaces. While you're at it, you might as well adjust the width of column B (the ounces) and column C (the price) each seven spaces wide. This will make the display look a little neater.

NOTES

Entering Formulas

If you want the spreadsheet to calculate an entry from other data, you have to give it a formula to use. You also have to begin with a special symbol to let it know that a formula is about to be entered. The special symbol depends on the type of spreadsheet you have. Excel uses the symbol = ; Lotus 1-2-3 uses the symbol + ; your software might use something else.

Calculate the price per ounce of Cape Cod chips by entering the formula C1/B1 into cell D1. As soon as you enter it, the number 0.226363 should appear. This is correct, but more accurate than we need. Three decimal places should be enough. Find the spreadsheet command that fixes the number of decimal places and use it to set the column D display to 3 places.

Copying Formulas

To get the price per ounce of Eagle Thins, all you have to do is copy the formula from cell D1 to cell D2. Do that. Check the spreadsheet manual to see how to copy from one cell to another. As soon as you do it, the number 0.209 will appear. Now look at the formula itself. Notice that it says C2/B2; that is, when you copied the formula one cell below where it started, the spreadsheet automatically changed the cell addresses inside it by that amount. This automatic adjustment process is one of the most powerful features of the spreadsheet. Next we'll use it to get the price per ounce of *all* the other kinds of chips at once!

Repeated Copying

You can copy a cell entry over and over again, all at once, along as much of a row or column as you mark out. If the entry is a formula, the spreadsheet will automatically adjust the cell addresses in it at each step. In some spreadsheet programs (such as Excel), this is done by the Fill command. In others (such as Lotus 1-2-3), it is done as part of the Copy command, by highlighting the entire region of cells into which you want the formula copied.

Published by IT'S ABOUT TIME, Inc. © 2000 MATHconx, LLC

NOTES

Find out how this works for your spreadsheet. Then copy what's in D2 into cells D3 through D13 and watch all the per ounce prices appear immediately. At this point, your spreadsheet should look something like Display B.3.

	A	B	C	D
1	Cape Cod	11	2.49	0.226
2	Eagle Thins	9.5	1.99	0.209
3	Humpty Dumpty	6	1.19	0.198
4	Humpty Dumpty	10	1.68	0.168
5	Lay's	6	0.95	0.158
6	Lay's	14	2.79	0.199
7	O'Boisies	14.5	2.79	0.192
8	Ruffles	6	1.39	0.232
9	Ruffles	14	2.79	0.199
10	Tom's	6	1.39	0.232
11	Tom's	11	1.69	0.154
12	Wise	6	1.39	0.232
13	Wise	10	1.48	0.148

Display B.3

What *formula* is being used in cell D3? In D7? In D13?

B.4

Inserting Rows and Columns

Now let's put in column headings so that the spreadsheet is easier to understand. Move the cursor to the beginning of row 1 and use the Insert Row command of your spreadsheet to put in two rows at the very top. Cape Cod should now be in cell A3. We'll use the first row for headings and leave the second row blank. Enter Brand in A1, ounce in B1, price in C1 and enter $/oz. in D1. Change the width of column D to 7 spaces.

Because we've moved everything down, the row numbers no longer correspond to the number of brands listed. Make space to renumber the rows that list the brands, like this: Move the cursor to the top of the first column and use the Insert Column command to put two new columns at the far left. Cape Cod should now be in cell C3.

Repeated Copying

B.4   C3 /B3   C7 / D7   C13 /D13

NOTES

Numbering Rows

Now let's try a little experiment. We'll number the brands in two different ways. Make the two new columns, A and B, only 4 spaces wide. Now put the numbers 1 through 13 down these two columns, starting at the third row, in these two ways:

B.5

- In column A, enter each number by hand—the number 1 in A3, the number 2 in A4, and so on, down to the number 13 in A15.

- In column B, enter the formula B2+1 in cell B3. The number 1 will appear because the spreadsheet treats the empty cell B2 as if it had 0 in it. Now copy this formula into all the cells from B3 through B15.

Do columns A and B match? They should. If they don't, ask your teacher to help you find what went wrong. At this point, your display should look like Display B.4.

	A	B	C	D	E	F
1			Brand	oz.	$/bag	$/oz.
2						
3	1	1	Cape Cod	11	2.49	0.226
4	2	2	Eagle Thins	9.5	1.99	0.209
5	3	3	Humpty Dumpty	6	1.19	0.198
6	4	4	Humpty Dumpty	10	1.68	0.168
7	5	5	Lay's	6	0.95	0.158
8	6	6	Lay's	14	2.79	0.199
9	7	7	O'Boisies	14.5	2.79	0.192
10	8	8	Ruffles	6	1.39	0.232
11	9	9	Ruffles	14	2.79	0.199
12	10	10	Tom's	6	1.39	0.232
13	11	11	Tom's	11	1.69	0.154
14	12	12	Wise	6	1.39	0.232
15	13	13	Wise	10	1.48	0.148

Display B.4

Numbering Rows

B.5

The experiment actually takes place in the next step, when the rows are placed in order with respect to the per ounce price of the various bags of chips. The numbers entered by hand will go along with their original rows; however, the numbers entered by formula will remain as they are, numbering the rows from best deal to worst.

NOTES

Ordering Data

Another handy feature of an electronic spreadsheet is that it can put in order data that is listed in a column. It can put numbers in size order, either increasing or decreasing. Most spreadsheets can also put text entries in alphabetical order. To do this, you need to find the Sort command and tell it what list of data you want to rearrange. In Excel, Sort is in the Data menu; in Lotus 1–2–3, it's in the Select menu. The computer prompts you for a little more information, such as whether you want ascending or descending order, then does the sorting.

Note that some spreadsheets move entire rows when they sort; others can be told just to rearrange the data in a single column. Check your user's manual to see how your spreadsheet works. In this example, we assume that the spreadsheet moves entire rows when it sorts.

Let's rearrange the potato chip list according to the price per ounce, from most expensive to least expensive. Follow your spreadsheet's instructions to sort the per ounce prices in column F in ascending order. Which kind of potato chip is the best buy? Which is the worst buy?

Look at columns A and B.

B.6

1. Do they still match? What has happened? Explain.

2. What would have happened if you had entered the number 1 in B3, then entered the formula =B3+1 in B4? Explain.

Now that we have all this information, how do we find out how much it will cost the club for the 2 pounds of potato chips? Here's one plan:

• Compute the number of ounces in 2 pounds.

• Multiply the cost of 1 ounce by the total number of ounces needed.

Warning. There's something wrong with this approach; what is it?)

We'll do this on the spreadsheet because it provides an example of a different way to use cell addresses. To find the total number of ounces, we just multiply the number of pounds (2) by 16. Make these entries on the spreadsheet:

B.7

Published by IT'S ABOUT TIME, Inc. © 2000 MATHconx, LLC

Ordering Data

1. See B.5.

2. Because the B3 entry is not a variable, the 1 would stay with the Cape Cod row, causing the numbering in column B to start over at that point.

B.6

B.7

The problem with this approach is that the chip prices are not bulk prices. You can't buy the chips by the ounce; they're sold in bags of certain fixed sizes. We deal with this after discussing the use of constant cell addresses. Cell D18 will have the value 32.

NOTES

- In C17, enter number of lbs.; in D17, enter 2.

- In C18, enter number of oz.; in D18, put the formula that multiplies the entry in D17 by 16. (What is that value?)

Constant Cell Addresses

To find out how much 2 pounds of each kind of potato chip will cost, first set column G to display in currency format. Then move the cursor to cell G3. This should be the first blank cell at the end of row 3. We want this cell to show the number of ounces to be bought (in D18) multiplied by the price per ounce (in F3). Let's try it.

- Enter the formula D18*F3 in G3. The result should be $4.74.
  Is your first kind the Wise 10-oz. bag?

- So far, so good. Now copy this formula to the next line, in G4. What do you get? $0.00? How come?

- Look at the formula as it appears in G4. Does it say D19*F4? What happened?

Remember that when you shift a formula from one location to another, the spreadsheet automatically shifts every cell address in exactly the same way. We copied this formula to a location one row down from where it was, so the spreadsheet added the number 1 to the row number of each cell address in the formula. Now, we want that to happen to one of these addresses, but not to the other. That is, the cost of the kind of potato chip in row 4 should use the price per ounce in F4, but it should still use the total number of ounces from D18.

> To prevent the spreadsheet from automatically adjusting a cell address when a formula is moved, enter the cell address with a $ in front of its column letter and a $ in front of its row number.

B.8

This means that you should go back to cell G3 and enter the multiplication formula $D$18*F3. Now copy this to G4. Do you get $4.92? Good. If not, what went wrong? Ask your teacher if you need help figuring it out. Now copy this formula into cells G5 through G15. Column G now should show the cost for 2 pounds of each kind of potato chip in your list.

Published by IT'S ABOUT TIME, Inc. © 2000 MATHconx, LLC

Constant Cell Addresses

B.8

This is a fairly standard way of keeping a cell address fixed. However, some spreadsheets, particularly some older ones, use a different convention to distinguish between variable and constant cell addresses. Consult the user's manual; then advise your students accordingly.

NOTES

Go to G1, make this column 7 spaces wide and enter the word cost as the column heading.

B.9

1. According to column G, which kind of potato chip is the best buy?

2. Why is that *not* necessarily the best buy for your club?

3. What's wrong with letting this answer tell you what kind to buy? *Hint*: How many *bags* would you have to buy?

The INT Function

As the hint in the box above suggests, using the information in column G to guide your choice may not be a good idea because the supermarket sells potato chips by the bag. In order to know how much it will cost to get at least 2 pounds of chips, you first must know how many bags you'll need.

How do you do that? Easy, right? Just divide 32 oz. (2 lbs.) by the number of ounces in a single bag. If you get a mixed number, add 1 to the whole-number part.

For example, if you want at least 32 oz. in 10 oz. bags, divide 32 by 10. You get 3.2 as an answer, but, since you can't buy 0.2 of a bag of chips, you need 4 bags

There's a spreadsheet function—called INT—that makes this very easy to compute automatically. The INT function gives you the greatest integer less than or equal to the number you put into it. For instance:

$$INT\left(3\tfrac{1}{3}\right) = 3$$

$$INT(2.98) = 2$$

$$INT(5) =$$

Let's use this function to carry out the computation we just did, finding how many 10 oz. bags of Wise potato chips we need in order to have at least 2 pounds. But instead of entering the numbers in separately, we'll get them from other cells on the spreadsheet. Move to cell H3 and enter the formula

$$INT(\$D\$18/D3) + 1$$

Published by IT'S ABOUT TIME, Inc. © 2000 MATHconx, LLC

MATH *Connections*: A Secondary Mathematics Core Curriculum

B.9

1. Wise
2. and 3. See B.7 for explanations.

NOTES

Just to make sure you understand what we're doing, answer these questions before moving on:

1. What does $D$18 stand for?

2. Why are the $ symbols there?

3. What does D3 stand for?

4. What number is $D$18/D3?

5. What number is INT($D$18/D3)?

6. What number is INT($D$18/D3)+1?

7. If you copy this formula to cell H4, how will it read?

a

B.10

Now use the Fill command to copy this formula into cells H4 through H15. For each kind, the number you get says how many bags you need in order to have at least two pounds of chips. Put the heading "bags" at the top of this column H, and make the column 5 spaces wide.

Now we can finish the problem. To find the cost of at least 2 lbs. of each kind of chip, multiply the number of bags you need by the cost of a single bag. Enter a formula in I3 that does this; then copy it into I3 through I15. Finish your spreadsheet display by renaming column G cost 1 and naming column I cost 2 and changing the width of column I to 6 spaces.

1. If you *must* get at least 2 lbs. of chips and you want to spend as little as possible, which kind do you buy?

2. How many bags do you buy?

3. What does it cost you?

b

B.11

The next questions show off the power of spreadsheets for testing out different variations of a situation. Each part is exactly the same as above, except that the total number of pounds of chips is different. Answer each one by changing as little as possible on your spreadsheet.

1. If you *must* get at least 3 lbs. of chips and you want to spend as little as possible, which kind do you buy? How many bags do you buy? What does it cost you?

2. If you *must* get at least 4 lbs. of chips and you want to spend as little as possible, which kind do you buy? How many bags do you buy? What does it cost you?

c

B.12

The INT Function

B.10

1. 32 (the number of ounces in 2 pounds).
2. The $ symbols keep this cell address from changing when the formula is copied elsewhere.
3. 10 (the number of ounces in a single bag)
4. 3.2
5. 3
6. 4
7. INT($D$18/D4)+1

B.11

1. Tom's 11 oz. size
2. 3
3. $5.07. The finished spreadsheet should look like Display B.1T.

	A	B	C	D	E	F	G	H	I
1			Brand	oz.	$/bag	$/oz.	cost 1	bags	cost 2
2									
3	13	1	Wise	10	1.48	0.148	4.74	4	5.92
4	11	2	Tom's	11	1.69	0.154	4.92	3	5.07
5	5	3	Lay's	6	.95	0.158	5.07	6	5.70
6	4	4	Humpty Dumpty	10	1.68	0.168	5.38	4	6.72
7	7	5	O'Boisies	14.5	2.79	0.192	6.16	3	8.37
8	3	6	Humpty Dumpty	6	1.19	0.198	6.35	6	7.14
9	6	7	Lay's	14	2.79	0.199	6.38	3	8.37
10	9	8	Ruffles	14	2.79	0.199	6.38	3	8.37
11	2	9	Eagle Thins	9.5	1.99	0.209	6.70	4	7.96
12	1	10	Cape Cod	11	2.49	0.226	7.24	3	7.47
13	8	11	Ruffles	6	1.39	0.232	7.41	6	8.34
14	10	12	Tom's	6	1.39	0.232	7.41	6	8.34
15	12	13	Wise	6	1.39	0.232	7.41	6	8.34
16									
17			number of lbs.:	2					
18			number of oz.:	32					

Display B.1T

B.12

If the spreadsheet has been set up as described, each group of questions can be answered by changing only one entry on the spreadsheet, the total number of pounds shown in D17. Here are the answers.

1. 3 lbs.: 5 bags of Wise 10 oz. size, at a total cost of $7.40

3. If you *must* get at least 5 lbs. of chips and you want to spend as little as possible, which kind do you buy? How many bags do you buy? What does it cost you?

Problem Set: Appendix B

1. These two questions refer to the potato chip spreadsheet that you just made.

   (a) Add a column J that shows the total number of ounces of potato chips of each kind that you get when you buy enough bags to get at least two pounds of them. What formula will compute these numbers?

   (b) Add a column K that shows the number of *extra* ounces (more than 2 pounds) that you get when you buy enough bags to get at least two pounds of them. What formula will compute these numbers?

2. Make a spreadsheet like the one for the potato chips to deal with this problem:

   (a) Your favorite aunt runs a shelter for homeless cats. As a present for her birthday, you decide to give her 5 pounds of canned cat food. You want to spend as little money as possible. The brands, sizes, and prices for the canned cat food at the supermarket are shown in Display B.5. What brand and size is the buy, and how many cans of it should you get? What will it cost?

   (b) Your best friend thinks you have a great idea. She decides to buy your aunt 5 pounds of canned cat food, too. If you both chip in and buy a combined present of 10 pounds of canned cat food, what is the best buy of canned cat food for your combined present? Explain your answer?

Published by IT'S ABOUT TIME, Inc. © 2000 MATHconx, LLC

Appendix B: Using a Spreadsheet

2. 4 lbs.: 6 bags of Tom's 11 oz. size, at the total cost of $10.14
3. 5 lbs.: 14 bags of Lay's 6 oz. size, at the total cost of $13.30

Problem Set: Appendix B

1.   (a) Formula for column J (as it appears for J3): H3*D3
     (b) Formula for column K (as it appears for K3): J3—$D$18
         Note that the formula J3—32 also works for the original 2 lb. problem, but it doesn't adjust automatically for the 3, 4, and 5 lb. problems.

2. A spreadsheet solution for this problem is shown in Display B.2T. Much of it can be constructed by mimicking the potato chip spreadsheet setup. The only new wrinkle is the "*n* for *x*" pricing. This invites the insertion of two new columns, F for the number of cans that are bought for the price shown in column E; column G is for the price per can. The row order shown in Display B.2T results from sorting with respect to price per oz. (column H), from least to most.

   Here is how each column is constructed. Except for "number of oz.," each formula is shown as it would be in row 3; the data in its column is obtained by using Fill to copy the formula to the other cells in the column.

A   Number entered consecutively from 1 to 12.

B   Formula: B2+1

C   Brand entered individually, in alphabetical order (smaller size first within brands).

D   Ounces per can entered individually. Number of lbs. entered by hand in D16. Formula for number of oz.: D16*16

E   Prices entered individually; total price for group of cans, where applicable.

F   Number of cans bought for price in column E; entered individually.

G   Display set to 3 decimal places. Formula: E3/F3

H   Display set to 3 decimal places. Formula: G3/D3

I   Cost (if sold in bulk) for D16 pounds. Formula: $D$17*H3

J   Number of cans required for at least D16 pounds. Formula: INT($D$17/D3) +1

K   Cost for number of cans in column J. Formula: J3*G3
    (a)   The best deal for 5 lbs. is the 14 oz. size of Puss'n Boots; 6 cans are required
    (b)   However, the best deal for 10 lbs. is the 13 oz. size of 9 Lives; 13 cans are required, for a total cost of $6.37

Brand of Cat Food	No. of Ounces	Cost
Alpo	6 oz.	3 for $1.00
Alpo	13.75 oz.	$ .65
Figaro	5.5 oz.	$ .37
Figaro	12 oz.	$ .66
Friskies	6 oz.	$ .35
Friskies	13 oz.	$ .58
Kal Kan	5.5 oz.	4 for $1.00
Puss 'n Boots	14 oz.	$ .55
9 Lives	5.5 oz.	3 for $ .88
9 Lives	13 oz.	$ .48
Whiskas	5.5 oz.	3 for $1.00
Whiskas	12.3 oz.	$ .55

Display B.5

3. Here's a bonus question (It relates to problem 2.):

(a) Invent a problem about breakfast foods that is like the potato chip and cat food problems.

(b) Go to your local supermarket and gather the brand, size, and price information that you will need to solve your problem.

(c) Using the data you gather for part (b), set up a spreadsheet that solves the problem you invented in part (a).

Published by IT'S ABOUT TIME, Inc. © 2000 MATHconx, LLC

	A	B	C	D	E	F	G	H	I	J	K
1			Brand	oz.	price	#	$/can	$/oz.	cost 1	bags	cost 2
2											
3	10	1	9 Lives	13	0.49	1	0.490	0.038	3.02	7	3.43
4	8	2	Puss' n Boots	14	0.55	1	0.550	0.039	3.14	6	3.30
5	6	3	Friskies	13	0.58	1	0.580	0.045	3.57	7	4.06
6	12	4	Whiskas	12.30	0.55	1	0.550	0.045	3.58	7	3.85
7	7	5	Kal Kan	5.50	1.00	4	0.250	0.045	3.64	15	3.75
8	2	6	Alpo	13.75	0.65	1	0.650	0.047	3.78	6	3.90
9	9	7	9 Lives	5.50	0.88	3	0.293	0.053	4.27	15	4.40
10	4	8	Figaro	12	0.66	1	0.660	0.055	4.40	7	4.62
11	1	9	Alpo	6	1.00	3	0.333	0.056	4.44	14	4.67
12	5	10	Friskies	6	0.35	1	0.350	0.058	4.67	14	4.90
13	11	11	Whiskas	5.50	1.00	3	0.333	0.061	4.85	15	5.00
14	3	12	Figaro	5.50	0.37	1	0.370	0.067	5.38	15	5.55
15											
16			number of lbs.:	5							
17			number of oz.:	80							

Display B.2T

Note that there is an interesting detail here, if you want to take the time to pursue it. Notice that the 5th, 6th and 7th kinds of cat food show the same price per oz. in column H. But the bulk costs of D17 ounces in column I is different! How can that be? A brief discussion can lead to the fact that the computer stores the answers to its computations in a much more exact form than it usually shows.

3.   Students' answers to the bonus question will vary.

Appendix C: Programming the TI-82 (TI-83)

After you have been using the TI-82 (TI-83) for a while, you may notice that you are repeating certain tasks on your calculator over and over. Often you are repeating the same sequence of keystrokes, which can become very tiresome. Programs give you a way to carry out long sequences of keystrokes all at once, saving you a great deal of time and energy.

In this appendix we will show you some simple TI-82 (TI-83) programs and how to enter and use them. In the textbook, there are some other programs which you will find useful in solving problems.

Correcting Mistakes

When you enter a program you will almost surely make some keying mistakes. You can use the arrow keys to back up and key over any mistakes. To insert something new, rather than keying over what is already there, give the insert command (INS above the [DEL] key) by keying

[2nd]　[DEL]

Use the [DEL] key to delete the current character.

Entering Programs

To enter a program, give the [NEW] command under the [PRGM] menu by keying

[PRGM]　[◁]　[ENTER]

Your calculator should look like Display C.1. You are now in program writing mode. Whatever you key in will be stored in the program you are creating, rather than being executed directly. To get out of program writing mode, give the QUIT command.

(-)

APPENDIX C _____

Appendix C: Programming the TI-82 (TI-83)

Display C.1

Next you need to name your program so that you can use it. We will start with a very short and not very useful program just to test your ability to enter a program and run it. Give your program the name ADD. Normally, to enter the capital letters that are above and to the right of some of the keys you must press the ALPHA key first. When naming a program, however, the calculator goes into ALPHA mode automatically. This means you *don't* have to press the ALPHA key when entering the letters in the program name. Key in

Your calculator screen should now look like Display C.2

Display C.2

We now need to enter the actual program commands. Our test program will ask for two numbers and then add them. Each line of the program begins with a colon. At the end of each line of the program press ENTER . The first line of our program asks for the first of the two numbers it will add. The two numbers that we tell the calculator to add are called the *input* for the program. The Input command is the first item under the I/O section of the PRGM menu. We will store the input in memory A. Key in

C-2

The TI screen should now look like Display C.3.

```
PROGRAM: ADD
: Input A
: ■
```

Display C.3

The next line in the program asks for another number and stores it in memory location B. Enter the second line now, based on the way you entered the first line. Your screen should now look like Display C.4.

```
PROGRAM: ADD
: Input A
: Input B
```

Display C.4

The third line adds the numbers stored in memories A and B and stores the result in memory C. Key in

ALPHA   A   +   ALPHA   B   STO ▷   ALPHA   C   ENTER

The new screen is in Display C.5.

```
PROGRAM: ADD
: Input A
: Input B
: A + B→C
: ■
```

Display C.5

We finish our program with a statement which displays the result of adding the two numbers (now stored in memory C). The display command Disp is the third item under the I/O section of the PRGM menu.

Published by IT'S ABOUT TIME, Inc. © 2000 MATHconx, LLC

C-3

APPENDIX C _____

Key in

[PRGM]   [▷]   [3]   [ALPHA]   [C]

The resulting screen is in Display C.6

```
PROGRAM: ADD
: Input A
: Input B
:A + B→C
:Disp C
:■
```

Display C.6

We are done writing the program! To quit programming mode use the [QUIT] key (above the [MODE] key). The program is automatically saved. Key in

[2nd]   [QUIT]

You are now back to the Home Screen, where you started.

Running Programs

To run the program we just keyed in, we go to the EXEC section of the PRGM menu, key in the number of the program we want to run, and then press [ENTER] . We will assume that the program named ADD that we just entered is program number 1. Key in

[PRGM]   [1]   [ENTER]

If you entered the program correctly, a question mark appears asking for input. If there is an error, look at the next section on editing programs. This question mark is produced by the first line of your program. You are being requested to type in the first of two numbers, which will then be added by the program. Let's suppose that we want to add the numbers 4 and 5. Press [4] then press [ENTER] . A second question mark appears asking for the second number. Press [5] and press [ENTER] again. The result, 9, should appear. The screen now looks like Display C.7.

C-4

Published by IT'S ABOUT TIME, Inc. © 2000 MATHconx, LLC

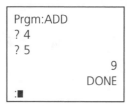

Display C.7

To run the program again, just press the ENTER key. You don't have to go through the PRGM menu to run the program the second time, as long as no other calculations have been performed in between. Try adding two other numbers to see how this works.

Quitting Programs

If you are in the middle of running a program and you want to stop the program, press ON key. To try this out, run the ADD program again, but this time when the first question mark appears, press ON . The screen should look like Display C.8.

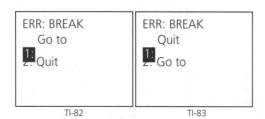

Display C.8

Press 2 to quit the program and return to the Home Screen. Pressing 1 puts you back in program writing mode at the point in the program where you stopped the program.

Editing Programs

If your program doesn't work, or if you just want to make changes to a program, you use the EDIT section of the PRGM menu. Key in

PRGM ▷ 1

C-5

APPENDIX C

This should put you back in the ADD program (assuming it is program 1). Your screen should look just as it did when you left the program writing mode (see Display C.6). Use the arrow keys and the insert [INS] and delete [DEL] keys as explained in the Correcting Mistakes section.

To open space for a new line, put the cursor at the beginning of a line, give the insert command [INS] and then press [ENTER] . To try this on your ADD program, use the arrow keys to put the cursor at the beginning of the second line of the program and key in

[2nd]   [DEL]   [ENTER]

Your screen should look like Display C.9.

```
PROGRAM: ADD
: Input A
:
: Input B
: A + B →C
: Disp C
:
```

Display C.9

The blank line we just created will not affect the program, so we can just give the QUIT command to leave the program writing mode.

A Useful Program

Now that you have some practice with writing, editing and running programs, let's take a look at a program that you might really find useful.

Graphing With Parameters

Suppose that we want to graph the equation of a straight line, say $y = ax + 5$, for several values of a. The constant a is called a *parameter*. First we can enter the expression AX + 5 as expression Y1 under the Y= menu. We can then store numbers in memory A and press [GRAPH] . The problem is that we only see the graph for one value of A at a time. The following program allows you to easily produce graphs for many values of A and keep all of the graphs on the screen together.

Published by IT'S ABOUT TIME, Inc. © 2000 MATHconx, LLC

C-6

Enter the program shown in Display C.10, using what you learned from the **Entering Programs** section. Name the program PARAMS. Note: DrawF is item 6 under the DRAW menu (above the [PRGM] key) for the TI-82. Y₁ is item number 1 of the Function sub menu under the **Y-vars** menu (above the [DRAW] [VARS] key). For the TI-83, Y₁ is found by keys

[VARS] [▷] [1] [1] [ENTER]

```
PROGRAM: PARAMS
: Input  A
: DrawF  Y₁
: ■
```

Display C.10

The program is simple, but saves quite a few keystrokes. You put in a value for A, and then the function is graphed using the DrawF command.

To use this program you must store your function in function memory Y₁ and then *turn off* Y₁ (put the cursor on the = and press ENTER). Your Y= WINDOW should look like Display C.11. Notice that the = is *not* highlighted, indicating the function is off.

```
Y₁ = AX + 5
Y₂ =
Y₃ =
Y₄ =
Y₅ =
Y₆ =
Y₇ =
Y₈ =
```

Display C.11

To set the graph WINDOW to the Standard setting, press the 6 under the ZOOM menu. Your WINDOW settings should appear as in Display C.12.

Published by IT'S ABOUT TIME, Inc. © 2000 MATHconx, LLC

APPENDIX C

WINDOW FORMAT
Xmin = –10
Xmax = 10
Xscl = 1
Ymin = –10
Ymax = 10
Yscl = 1

TI-82

WINDOW FORMAT
Xmin = –10
Xmax = 10
Xscl = 1
Ymin = –10
Ymax = 10
Yscl = 1
Xres = 1

TI-83

Display C.12

Now run the program. Try starting with an A value of 1. Press
[1] then [ENTER] in response to the question mark. You
should see a graph of the function $y = 1x + 5$. To run the
program again, first press the [CLEAR] key (to get back to the
Home Screen) then [ENTER] . Try an A with a value of –2 this
time. Now both the graphs of $Y = AX + B$ for A = 1 and for
A = –2 should be on the screen, as shown in Display C.13.

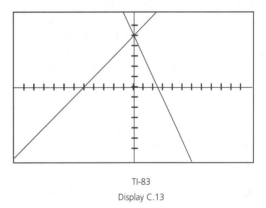

TI-83
Display C.13

If you want to clear the graph screen, use ClrDraw, which is
item 1 under the DRAW menu.

You only need to change the function stored in Y_1 to graph any
other function with one parameter. For instance, try graphing
the function $y = a^x$ for various a values.

Published by IT'S ABOUT TIME, Inc. © 2000 MATHconx, LLC

C-8

Appendix D: Linear Programming With Excel

The graphical method of solving Linear Programming problems is explained in the text. The limitation of this method is that it is applicable only to problems with two variables.

Linear Programming is one of the most used mathematical methods in real-world problem solving. Only rarely are two variables present in a realistic problem. Mathematicians have developed methods to solve Linear Programming problems with any number of variables; a computer program is then needed to carry out the computations. One commonly used computer program which solves Linear Programming problems is called **LINDO™**.

Several spreadsheet programs can solve Linear Programming problems. Microsoft Excel, Lotus 1-2-3, and Quattro Pro are such spreadsheet programs. We will look at how Excel 5.0 solves linear programming problems, but we will not explain the method Excel uses. This is known as treating the program as something mysterious—we can follow the instructions for using the program, but we don't know how the program gives a solution to the problem. Knowing how to solve simple problems graphically helps us to understand the output from the program, even if we don't understand the exact method the computer is using. Just imagine that Excel is using a method similar to the one you learned for two variable problems.

Our first example will be a very simple problem with only two variables. Then we can solve the problem graphically as in the textbook and check our answer against the answer from the computer. We will then extend the problem to three variables; here a graphical solution is not possible.

Problem

A new housing development is being built near Bart's house. Bart has noticed that the construction workers often leave the site to get lunch. Always on the lookout to earn money, Bart figures that he can make lunches for the workers and sell them at a

D-1

Appendix D: Linear Programming With Excel

profit. We will assume there are enough workers and Bart can sell all of the sandwiches that he can make.

Bart decides to make two types of lunches. The first lunch will have two sodas and one sandwich (the Thirsty Worker Lunch) and the second type of lunch will have two sandwiches and one soda (the Hungry Worker Lunch). Bart plans to buy the sandwiches and sodas from a local deli for $3.00 per sandwich and $0.50 per can of soda. He will sell the Thirsty Worker Lunches for $5.00 and the Hungry Worker Lunches for $8.00. This means that Bart's profit for each Thirsty Worker Lunch is $1.00 and his profit on each Hungry Worker Lunch is $1.50.

Bart has one problem. The deli doesn't open until 11:30 a.m., which is too late to make lunches and have them ready for the workers. He figures he needs to buy his supplies the night before, but that means he needs to keep the (24 cans) of soda in the family refrigerator. Bart finds a cooler in the basement that will hold 20 sandwiches.

How many Hungry Worker Lunches and how many Thirsty Worker Lunches should Bart prepare in order to make the most money? His constraints are that he can use only 20 sandwiches and 24 sodas as explained above.

Solution

SETUP

First we need to formulate the problem as a linear programming problem. Let x represent the number of Thirsty Worker Lunches and y the number of Hungry Worker Lunches that Bart prepares. Then Bart's profit P is

$$P = 1.00x + 1.50y$$

The soda constraint would be

$$2x + y \leq 24$$

and the sandwich constraint would be

$$x + 2y \leq 20$$

The other two constraints which we don't want to forget are

$$x \geq 0 \text{ and } y \geq 0$$

D-2

Computer Solution

Our goal is to set up the spreadsheet as shown in Displays D.1 and D.2 and to show the formulas that you actually key into each cell. Display D.2 shows what the result should look like on your spreadsheet. To get this result, follow the steps below.

1. Key in a title for the spreadsheet in cell A1; we used "Bart's Lunch Business." Don't key in any quotation marks. We dressed up the title a bit by making the font larger (12 point) and using the Outline style; just select cell A1 and choose Font from the Format menu.

2. Key in x in cell A3, y in cell B3 and P = $1.00x + 1.50y$ in cell C3.

3. Cells A4 and B4 will represent the initial guess for x and y. These guesses don't have to be good; they just have to make sense. The easiest guesses are 0 for both x and y, since they satisfy all the constraints. Therefore, key in 0 in A4 and 0 in B4.

4. Key in = $1.00 * A4 + 150 * B4$ in cell C4. This represents the profit for the x and y you chose. You should see 0 appear since x and y are now 0.

5. Key in the word constraints in cell A6. We will use row 7 to label the constraints, and row 8 to put in the constraints as formulas.

6. Key in $x + 2y < = 20$ into cell A7 and $2x + y < = 24$ into cell B7 as labels for the sandwich and soda constraints.

7. Key in the **left side only** of the sandwich constraint into cell A8. Therefore you key in = $A4 + 2 * B4$ into cell B7. Similarly key in = $2 * A4 + B4$ into cell B8. At this point zeros should appear in these cells since x and y are both 0.

	A	B	C
1	Bart's Lunch Business		
2			
3	x	y	P=1.00x+1.50y
4	0	0	=1*A4+1.5*B4
5			
6	constraints		
7	x+2y<=20	2x+y<=24	
8	=A4+2*B4	=2*A4+B4	

Display D.1

APPENDIX D

8. Select cells A3 through C8 and choose CELLS: Alignment from the Format menu. Choose center for horizontal alignment. Then choose CELLS: Number from the Format menu and select 0.00. Your spreadsheet should now look like Display D.2

	A	B	C
1	Bart's Lunch Business		
2			
3	x	y	P=1.00x+1.50y
4	0.00	0.00	0.00
5			
6	constraints		
7	x+2y<=20	2x+y<=24	
8	0.00	0.00	

Display D.2

We are now ready to tell the computer to find the solution to our linear programming problem. We use a capability of Excel called the Solver to get the solution. You may have noticed that we have not actually specified all of the information for the constraints. In particular, we need to tell Excel that cells A4 and B4 need to be positive (x and y should be positive), that cell A8 should be less than 20 and cell B8 should be less than 24 (the sandwich and soda constraints). We do this as shown below.

9. Choose Solver from the Tools menu. The goal is to get the Solver dialogue box to look like Display D.3.

10. Type C4 in the Set Target Cell box. You don't need to type the $s; they will be added by Excel automatically. This box tells the computer which cell to maximize; in our problem C4 is the cell that represents Bart's profit.

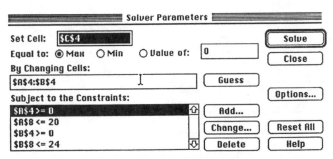

Display D.3

11. Type A4:B4 in the By Changing Cells box. This instructs the computer to adjust the cells in this range (the number of

Appendix D: Linear Programming With Excel

Thirsty Worker and Hungry Worker Lunches in our problem) until cell C4 is at a maximum.

12. Put the constraints into the Subject to the Constraints box. For each you must click the Add button, which brings up another dialogue box as shown in Display D.4. Key in the Cell Reference and the Constraint value (the right-hand side of the constraint inequality). Click on the < = drop-down menu to choose < = or > = (you can also choose = or int for integer).

Cell Reference:		Constraint:
$A$8	<= ⬇	=20

OK	Cancel	Help

Display D.4

13. Click the Max button in the Equal To line to indicate that this is a maximization problem (it is probably already chosen).

14. Click the Solve button, and Excel will attempt to solve the problem. Excel will then report whether it found a solution or not. If a solution was found, just click OK in the dialogue box that pops up, and the values of the variables which provide the solution will have replaced the initial guesses that you gave in step 3.

Bart's Lunch Business

x	y	P=1.00x+1.50y
9.33	5.33	17.33

Constraints:

x+2y<=20	2x+y<=24
20.00	24.00

Display D.5

15. Summarize your findings and explain the spreadsheet for someone who might not be familiar with the problem. Display D.5 shows the solution to our problem, as well as a short verbal description of the results. We also dressed up

our report with a little formatting (using Borders from the Format menu and turning off the gridlines with Display from the Option menu). Note that, in this problem, we needed to round our results since fractional parts of a lunch do not make sense.

Summary of Findings

Bart is going to sell two types of lunches. We let x represent the number of Thirsty Worker Lunches, which contain two sodas and one sandwich. We let y represent the number of Hungry Worker Lunches, which contain one soda and two sandwiches. Bart's constraints are that he can use at most twenty sandwiches and twenty-four sodas. His profit P is $1.00 on each Thirsty Worker Lunch and $1.50 on each Hungry Worker Lunch.

The tables in Display D.5 resulted from performing a linear programming analysis of the problem. What they show is that Bart should make 9 Thirsty Worker Lunches and 5 Hungry Worker Lunches. The values in the table need to be rounded since Bart can't make a fraction of a lunch. His profit will be less than the $17.33 shown in the table; his actual profit will be

$$1(9) + 1.5(5) = \$16.50$$

Extension to Three Variables

Suppose that Bart decided to make a third type of lunch with 2 sandwiches and 2 sodas (Super Lunches). Let z represent the number of Super Lunches. Bart will sell Super Lunches for $9.00; his profit on these lunches would be $2.00. Then the new profit formula would be

$$P = 1.00x + 1.50y + 2.00z$$

The new constraints would be

$$2x + y + 2z \leq 24 \text{ and } x + 2y + 2z \leq 20$$

for soda and sandwiches. Display D.6 shows what formulas you would type into the cells. Display D.7 shows how the spreadsheet would look before solving.

Published by IT'S ABOUT TIME, Inc. © 2000 MATHconx, LLC

	A	B	C	D
1	Bart's Lunch Business			
2				
3	x	y	z	P=1.00x+1.50y+2.00z
4	0	0	0	=1*A4+1.5*B4+2*C4
5				
6	constraints			
7	x+2y+2z<=20	2x+y+2z<=24		
8	=A4+2*B4+2*C4	=2*A4+B4+2*C4		

Display D.6

	A	B	C	D	E
1	Bart's Lunch Business				
2					
3	x	y	z	P=1.00x+1.50y+2.00z	
4	0.00	0.00	0.00	0.00	
5					
6	constraints				
7	x+2y+2z<=20	2x+y+2z<=24			
8	0.00	0.00			

Display D.7

When you now invoke the Solver, there are several changes you must make in the Solver dialogue box. You need to add the constraint C4 > = 0 ($z \geq 0$ in the problem) into the Subject to Constraints box, change the By Changing Cells box to A4:C4, and change the Set Target Cell box to D4. After these changes, click Solve; the spreadsheet displays the solution to the new problem as shown in Display D.8.

	A	B	C	D	E
1	Bart's Lunch Business				
2					
3	x	y	z	P=1.00x+1.50y+2.00z	
4	4.00	0.00	8.00	20.00	
5					
6	constraints				
7	x+2y+2z<=20	2x+y+2z<=24			
8	20.00	24.00			

Display D.8

We see by looking at Display D.8 that the addition of a new type of lunch has a significant effect on the solution to Bart's problem. Now Bart should make 4 Thirsty Worker Lunches and 8 Super Lunches and no Hungry Worker Lunches. His profit goes up from $16.50 to $20. We don't need to round this time since the values of the variables come out as whole numbers.

Published by IT'S ABOUT TIME, Inc. © 2000 MATHconx, LLC

Appendix D: Linear Programming With Excel

A big advantage to using the computer solution for this type of problem (besides being able to solve problems with more than two variables) is that we can easily change any part of the problem and get instant feedback on how the answer changes. For example, if Bart increases the amount he charges for the Hungry Worker Lunches, common sense tells us that at some number it would become profitable to make some of these lunches. What is that number?

To answer the previous question, you could try increasing the selling price of Hungry Worker Lunches to $8.60 to see if this changes the solution. This changes the profit on these lunches to $2.10. The only change in the problem is that the new profit formula is

$$P = 1.00x + 2.10y + 2.00z$$

Just change cells D3 and D4 to reflect the new information and run the Solver again. We find that, indeed, it is now profitable to provide some Hungry Worker Lunches (the result is interesting—check it out). With more guess and check we could pin down exactly the point where the y variable enters the problem.

Follow up Exercise

Carry out the process that was started. Keeping all other quantities in the problem constant, try different values for the price for the Hungry Worker Lunches until you find the number at which it just becomes profitable to make some of these lunches. Thus, it should be the case that if you lower the price of these lunches by any small amount, the solution to the Linear Programming problem has $y = 0$ in it, but if you increase the price by any small amount the solution for y is greater than 0. Discuss what happens to all variables and the total profit as you make these changes.

Published by IT'S ABOUT TIME, Inc. © 2000 MATHconx, LLC

GLOSSARY   2.a.

acute angle An angle of measure less than 90° (but more than 0°).

alternate interior angles Two nonadjacent interior angles on opposite sides of a transversal that intersect two lines.

altitude (of a triangle) A line segment drawn from one vertex to the opposite side, that is perpendicular to the side.

angle A figure formed by two line segments or rays with a common endpoint.

angle bisector A line or ray that divides an angle in half.

axis of symmetry A line that divides a figure in half so that each half is a mirror image of the other.

base unit In a system of measurement, a unit which is chosen (for convenience) and by which other units of measure are defined.

complementary angles Two angles whose measures have a sum of 90°.

congruent angles Two angles that have the same measure.

congruent figures Figures that have the same shape and size.

constant A number or symbol representing a value that doesn't change.

constant of proportionality The number that one variable is multiplied by in a direct proportion, or the number that is divided by one variable in an inverse proportion.

converse (of a universal statement) A statement which interchanges the subject and the predicate of the given universal statement.

convex polygon A polygon in which the measure of each angle is less than 180°.

corresponding angles The angles, one interior and one exterior, on the same side of the transversal that intersects two lines.

cosine (of an acute angle) In a right triangle, the cosine of an acute angle is the ratio of the length of the adjacent leg to the length of the hypotenuse.

counterexample An example that proves a universal statement to be false.

Published by IT'S ABOUT TIME, Inc. © 2000 MATHconx, LLC

cubic inch A cube with each edge one inch long.

cubic meter A cube with each edge one meter long.

direct variation A relationship between two variables such that one is a positive constant times the other.

directly proportional (variables) Two variables such that one is a positive constant times the other.

discrete Separate, distinct.

discrete mathematics The branch of mathematics that deals with processes related to counting separate, distinct objects.

domain (of an equation) The set of all numbers for which an equation makes sense (is either true or false).

equilateral polygon A polygon in which all sides have the same length.

exterior angle (of a polygon) An angle formed by one side of a polygon and the extension of an adjacent side.

geometric construction A procedure for creating a geometric object with a compass and an unmarked straightedge.

gnomon The upright, triangular component of a sundial.

hypotenuse The longest side of a right triangle; the side opposite the right angle.

identity (equation) An equation that is true for *all* numbers in its domain.

interior angles (of a polygon) The angles that open toward the inside of the polygon.

inverse cosine An acute angle whose cosine is a specified number between 0 and 1.

inverse sine An acute angle whose sine is a specified number between 0 and 1.

inverse tangent An acute angle whose tangent is a specified positive number.

inverse variation A relationship between two variables such that one is a positive constant divided by the other.

inversely proportional (variables) Two variables such that one is a positive constant divided by the other.

isosceles triangle A triangle with two sides of equal length.

leg (of a right triangle) One of the sides of a right triangle that is not the hypotenuse.

line segment A set of points on a line consisting of two endpoints and all the points between them.

Mercator map A flat map of the world that represents directions accurately.

model A representation of something physical or mathematical considered important for a particular purpose.

obtuse angle An angle of measure greater than 90° and less than 180°.

parallel lines Straight lines in a plane that never intersect, no matter how far they are extended.

parallelogram A quadrilateral with both pairs of opposite sides congruent; equivalently, a quadrilateral with both pairs of opposite sides parallel.

perimeter The distance around (the boundary of) a figure; its length as a path.

perpendicular bisector A line that intersects a given segment at right angles and divides it into two equal parts.

perpendicular lines Two lines that intersect at right angles; i.e., two lines that form congruent adjacent angles.

polygon A polygonal path that starts and ends at the same place and doesn't intersect itself anywhere in between.

polygonal path A sequence of line segments each connected to the next by a common endpoint.

proportion An equality between two ratios.

Pythagorean triple Three positive numbers a, b, and c such that $a^2 + b^2 = c^2$.

ratio One number divided by another; a common fraction.

ray Part of a line that starts at a particular point and extends infinitely far in one direction.

reflex angle An angle of measure greater than 180°, and less than 360°.

regular polygon A polygon with all sides the same length and all angles equal in measure.

rhombus A quadrilateral with all its sides congruent (the same length).

right angle An angle of measure 90°.

right triangle A triangle that has a right angle as one of its

Published by IT'S ABOUT TIME, Inc. © 2000 MATHconx, LLC

G-3

three angles.

scaling factor The constant that describes the size relationship between two similar objects.

side (of a polygon) Any one of the line segments that determines the polygon.

similar objects Two objects such that the distance between any two points of one object is a particular constant times the distance between the corresponding points of the other object. Objects that have the same shape.

sine (of an acute angle) In a right triangle, the sine of an acute angle is the ratio of the length of the side opposite the angle to the length of the hypotenuse.

slope measure (of an angle) The perpendicular distance from any chosen point on one ray of the angle to the other ray divided by the distance from the vertex to the foot of the perpendicular of the other ray.

straight angle An angle of measure 180°.

supplementary angles Two angles whose measures have a sum of 180°.

tangent (of an acute angle) In a right triangle, the tangent of an acute angle is the ratio of the length of the side opposite the angle to the length of the adjacent leg.

transversal A straight line that intersects two or more other coplanar straight lines at distinct points.

triangulation The process of dividing a polygon into nonoverlapping triangles.

unit cube A cube that measures one unit of length along each edge.

universal statement A statement of the form: "All [SOMETHING] are [SOMETHING ELSE]."

vertex A common endpoint of two sides of a polygon or an angle.

vertical angles Two angles such that the angles formed by two intersecting lines do not have a common side.

volume (of a three dimensional object) The number of unit cubes (of some unit length) needed to fill up the space it occupies.

Published by IT'S ABOUT TIME, Inc. © 2000 MATHconx, LLC

Index

2.a.

Published by IT'S ABOUT TIME, Inc. © 2000 MATHconx, LLC

I- I

Published by IT'S ABOUT TIME, Inc. © 2000 MATHconx, LLC

Published by IT'S ABOUT TIME, Inc. © 2000 MATHconx, LLC

NOTES

NOTES

NOTES

NOTES

NOTES

NOTES

MATH *Connections*: A Secondary Mathematics Core Curriculum